Dying, Death, and Bereavement 11/12

EDITORS

George E. Dickinson, PhD
College of Charleston

George E. Dickinson, Professor of Sociology at the College of Charleston, received his PhD in sociology from LSU in Baton Rouge and his MA in sociology and BA in biology from Baylor University. He came to the College of Charleston in 1985, having previously taught in Minnesota and Kentucky. The recipient of both NSF and NEH grants, Dickinson has presented more than 50 papers at professional meetings and has been the author/co-author of over 70 articles in peer-reviewed journals, primarily on end-of-life issues. In addition, he has co-authored/co-edited 21 books/anthologies (with Michael R. Leming), including *Understanding Dying, Death and Bereavement* 7th ed.,Wadsworth Publishers, 2011. His research and teaching interest in end-of-life issues goes back to 1974 when he taught a course on death and dying and in 1975 when he began research on medical schools and physicians. He is on the editorial boards of *Mortality* (UK) and the *American Journal of Hospice & Palliative Medicine* (US). He was the 2002 recipient of the Distinguished Teacher/Scholar Award and the 2008 Distinguished Research Award at the College of Charleston, a South Carolina Governor's Distinguished Professor Award in 2003 and 2008, and the Death Educator Award from the Association for Death Education and Counseling in 2009. In 1999 he was a Visiting Research Fellow in palliative medicine at the University of Sheffield's School of Medicine (UK) and in 2006 at Lancaster University's Institute for Health Research (UK). Earlier, Dickinson did postdoctoral studies at Pennsylvania State University (gerontology), at the University of Connecticut (medical sociology), and at the University of Kentucky's School of Medicine (thanatology).

Michael R. Leming, PhD
St. Olaf College

Michael R. Leming is Professor of Sociology and Anthropology at St. Olaf College. He holds degrees from Westmont College (BA), Marquette University (MA), and the University of Utah (PhD) and has done additional graduate study at the University of California in Santa Barbara. He is the co-author (with George E. Dickinson) of *Understanding Dying, Death and Bereavement* 6th ed.,Wadsworth Publishers, 2007, and *Annual Editions: Dying, Death and Bereavement* 10th ed., McGraw-Hill, 2008 and *Understanding Families: Diversity, Continuity, and Change,* Two Editions (Harcourt Brace, 1995). He is also the co-editor (with Raymond DeVries and Brendan Furnish) of *The Sociological Perspective: A Value-Committed Introduction* (Zondervan, 1989) and HYPERLINK "www.sagepub.com/book.aspx?pid=9608" *Handbook of Death and Dying,* 2 Edited Volumes (with Clifton D. Bryant, Charles K. Edgley, Michael R. Leming, Dennis L. Peck, Sage Publications, Inc. 2003).

Dr. Leming is the founder and former director of the St. Olaf College Social Research Center, former member of the board of directors of the Minnesota Coalition on Terminal Care and the Northfield AIDS Response, and has served as a hospice educator, volunteer, and grief counselor. For the past nine years he has directed the Spring Semester in Thailand program (HYPERLINK "www.AmazingThailand.org" www.AmazingThailand.org), affiliated with Chiang Mai University and open to American students. He and his wife are happy to live in Thailand during Minnesota's coldest months.

ANNUAL EDITIONS: DYING, DEATH, AND BEREAVEMENT, TWELFTH EDITION

Published by McGraw-Hill, a business unit of The McGraw-Hill Companies, Inc., 1221 Avenue of the Americas, New York, NY 10020. Copyright © 2011 by The McGraw-Hill Companies, Inc.

Some ancillaries, including electronic and print components, may not be available to customers outside the United States.

Annual Editions is published by the **Contemporary Learning Series** group within The McGraw-Hill Higher Education division.

1 2 3 4 5 6 7 8 9 0 QDB/QDB 1 0 9 8 7 6 5 4 3 2 1 0

ISBN 978–0–07–805078–7
MHID 0–07–805078–2
ISSN 1096–4223

Managing Editor: *Larry Loeppke*
Developmental Editor: *Dave Welsh*
Permissions Supervisor: *Lenny J. Behnke*
Senior Marketing Communications Specialist: *Mary Klein*
Project Manager: *Robin A. Reed*
Design Coordinator: *Margarite Reynolds*
Buyer: *Sandy Ludovissy*
Media Project Manager: *Sridevi Palani*

Compositor: Laserwords Private Limited
Cover Image: © Getty Images/Purestock (inset); Royalty-Free/CORBIS (background)

Library in Congress Cataloging-in-Publication Data
Main entry under title: Annual Editions: Dying, Death, and Bereavement. 2011/2012.
1. Dying, Death, and Bereavement—Periodicals. I. Dickinson, George E., and Leming, Michael R., *comp.* II. Title: Dying, Death, and Bereavement.
658'.05

Editors/Academic Advisory Board

Members of the Academic Advisory Board are instrumental in the final selection of articles for each edition of ANNUAL EDITIONS. Their review of articles for content, level, and appropriateness provides critical direction to the editors and staff. We think that you will find their careful consideration well reflected in this volume.

ANNUAL EDITIONS: Dying, Death, and Bereavement 11/12
12th Edition

EDITORS

George E. Dickinson
College of Charleston

Michael R. Leming
St. Olaf College

ACADEMIC ADVISORY BOARD MEMBERS

Preface

In publishing ANNUAL EDITIONS we recognize the enormous role played by the magazines, newspapers, and journals of the public press in providing current, first-rate educational information in a broad spectrum of interest areas. Many of these articles are appropriate for students, researchers, and professionals seeking accurate, current material to help bridge the gap between principles and theories and the real world. These articles, however, become more useful for study when those of lasting value are carefully collected, organized, indexed, and reproduced in a low-cost format, which provides easy and permanent access when the material is needed. That is the role played by ANNUAL EDITIONS.

Dying, death, and bereavement have been around for as long as humankind, yet as topics of discussion they have been "offstage" for decades in contemporary American public discourse. In the United States, dying currently takes place away from the arena of familiar surroundings of kin and friends, with approximately 80 percent of deaths occurring in institutional settings such as hospitals and nursing homes. Americans have developed a paradoxical relationship with death: We know more about the causes and conditions surrounding death but have not equipped ourselves emotionally to cope with dying, death, and bereavement. The purpose of this anthology is to provide an understanding of dying, death, and bereavement that will assist in better coping with and understanding our own deaths and the deaths of others.

Articles in this volume are taken from professional and semiprofessional journals and from popular publications written for both special populations and a general readership. The selections are carefully reviewed for their currency and accuracy. Over half of the articles have been changed from the previous edition through updating and responding to comments of reviewers. Most of the articles refer to situations in the United States, yet other cultures are represented. We strive to have current articles, though a few may be earlier than 2006, due to readers' requests to maintain them in this updated issue.

The reader will note the tremendous range of approaches and styles of the writers from personal, first-hand accounts to more scientific and philosophical writings. Some articles are more practical and applied, while others are more technical and research-oriented. If "variety is the very spice of life," this volume should be a spicy venture for the reader. Methodologies used in the more research-oriented articles range from quantitative (e.g., surveys/questionnaires) to qualitative (e.g., interviews/observation). Such a mix should especially be of interest to the student majoring or minoring in the social sciences. If a particular article seems too technical for your background, do not bog yourself down with the statistical analysis, rather look ahead to the discussion and conclusions.

These articles are drawn from many different periodicals, thus exposing the reader to a variety of publications in the library. With interest stimulated by a particular article, the student is encouraged to pursue other related articles in that particular journal.

This anthology is organized into eight units to cover many of the important aspects of dying, death, and bereavement. Though the units are arranged in a way that has some logical order, one can determine from the brief summaries in the table of contents and the cross-references in the topic guide whether another arrangement would better fit a particular teaching situation. The first unit is on issues in dying and death. Unit 2 takes a life-cycle approach and looks at the developmental aspects of dying and death at different age levels. The third unit concerns the process of dying. Unit 4 is on the topic of suicide. The fifth unit is about animals and death. The sixth unit is on ethical issues of dying and death, whereas Unit 7 contains articles which deal with death rituals and funerals. Finally, Unit 8 presents articles on bereavement.

Annual Editions: Dying, Death, and Bereavement 11/12 is intended for use as a supplement to augment selected areas or chapters of textbooks on dying and death. The articles in this volume can also serve as a basis for class discussion about various issues in dying, death, and bereavement.

Annual Editions: Dying, Death, and Bereavement is revised periodically to keep the materials timely as new social concerns about dying, death, and bereavement develop. Your assistance in the revision effort is always welcome. Please complete and return the postage-paid *article rating form* at the back of the book. We look forward to your input.

George E. Dickinson
Editor

Michael R. Leming
Editor

Contents

UNIT 1
Issues in Dying and Death

UNIT 2
Dying and Death across the Life Cycle

The concepts in bold italics are developed in the article. For further expansion, please refer to the Topic Guide.

UNIT 3
The Dying Process

UNIT 4
Suicide

The concepts in bold italics are developed in the article. For further expansion, please refer to the Topic Guide.

UNIT 5
Animals and Death

UNIT 6
Ethical Issues Regarding Dying and Death

The concepts in bold italics are developed in the article. For further expansion, please refer to the Topic Guide.

UNIT 7
Funerals

UNIT 8
Bereavement

The concepts in bold italics are developed in the article. For further expansion, please refer to the Topic Guide.

The concepts in bold italics are developed in the article. For further expansion, please refer to the Topic Guide.

Correlation Guide

The *Annual Editions* series provides students with convenient, inexpensive access to current, carefully selected articles from the public press. **Annual Editions: Dying, Death, and Bereavement 11/12** is an easy-to-use reader that presents articles on important topics such as *the dying process, funerals, bereavement,* and many more. For more information on *Annual Editions* and other *McGraw-Hill Contemporary Learning Series* titles, visit www.mhhe.com/cls.

This convenient guide matches the units in **Annual Editions: Dying, Death, and Bereavement 11/12** with the corresponding chapters in one of our best-selling McGraw-Hill Psychology textbooks by DeSpelder/Strickland.

Annual Editions: Dying, Death, and Bereavement 11/12	The Last Dance: Encountering Death and Dying, 9/e by DeSpelder/Strickland
Unit 1: Issues in Dying and Death	**Chapter 1:** Attitudes toward Death: A Climate of Change **Chapter 4:** Death Systems: Mortality and Society **Chapter 15:** The Path Ahead: Personal and Social Choices
Unit 2: Dying and Death across the Life Cycle	**Chapter 2:** Learning about Death: The Influence of Sociocultural Forces **Chapter 10:** Death in the Lives of Children and Adolescents **Chapter 11:** Death in the Lives of Adults **Chapter 13:** Risks, Perils, and Traumatic Death
Unit 3: The Dying Process	**Chapter 4:** Death Systems: Mortality and Society **Chapter 5:** Health Care Systems: Patients, Staff, and Institutions **Chapter 7:** Facing Death: Living with Life-Threatening Illness **Chapter 14:** Beyond Death/After Life
Unit 4: Suicide	**Chapter 12:** Suicide
Unit 5: Animals and Death	**Chapter 10:** Death in the Lives of Children and Adolescents
Unit 6: Ethical Issues Regarding Dying and Death	**Chapter 5:** Health Care Systems: Patients, Staff, and Institutions **Chapter 6:** End-of-Life Issues and Decisions
Unit 7: Funerals	**Chapter 3:** Perspectives on Death: Cultural and Historical **Chapter 8:** Last Rites: Funerals and Body Disposition
Unit 8: Bereavement	**Chapter 9:** Survivors: Understanding the Experience of Loss

Topic Guide

This topic guide suggests how the selections in this book relate to the subjects covered in your course. You may want to use the topics listed on these pages to search the Web more easily.

On the following pages a number of websites have been gathered specifically for this book. They are arranged to reflect the units of this Annual Editions reader. You can link to these sites by going to www.mhhe.com/cls

All the articles that relate to each topic are listed below the bold-faced term.

Advanced directive
25. What Living Wills Won't Do

AIDS
12. End-of-Life Care around the World: Achievements to Date and Challenges Remaining

Animals and death
6. Death in Disney Films: Implications for Children's Understanding of Death
21. Treat People Like Dogs
22. When a Cherished Pet Dies
23. Book Profiles Furry Angel of Death: Oscar the Cat
24. Veterinary Hospice: Ways to Nurture Our Pets at the End of Life

Assisting grievers
7. Saying Goodbye
8. Helping Military Kids Cope with Traumatic Death
15. When Death Strikes without Warning
22. When a Cherished Pet Dies

Attitudes toward death
2. Death, Dying, and the Dead in Popular Culture
6. Death in Disney Films: Implications for Children's Understanding of Death
13. Are They Hallucinations or Are They Real? The Spirituality of Deathbed and Near-Death Visions
27. Ethics and Life's Ending: An Exchange

Bereavement and grief
1. Grief in the Age of Facebook
6. Death in Disney Films: Implications for Children's Understanding of Death
8. Helping Military Kids Cope with Traumatic Death
15. When Death Strikes without Warning
22. When a Cherished Pet Dies
28. When Students Kill Themselves
33. The Grieving Process
34. Disenfranchised Grief
35. Enhancing the Concept of Disenfranchised Grief
36. The Increasing Prevalence of Complicated Mourning: The Onslaught Is Just Beginning
37. Counseling with Children in Contemporary Society
38. A Grim Fight for 'Proper Burial'
39. Parents and the Death of a Child
40. Coping with the Loss of Loved Ones

Brain death
4. Brain Death Guidelines Vary at Top US Neurological Hospitals

Caregivers
9. Needs of Elderly Patients in Palliative Care
12. End-of-Life Care around the World: Achievements to Date and Challenges Remaining
15. When Death Strikes without Warning
25. What Living Wills Won't Do

Children
6. Death in Disney Films: Implications for Children's Understanding of Death
7. Saying Goodbye
8. Helping Military Kids Cope with Traumatic Death
15. When Death Strikes without Warning

Communication
2. Death, Dying, and the Dead in Popular Culture
6. Death in Disney Films: Implications for Children's Understanding of Death
7. Saying Goodbye
8. Helping Military Kids Cope with Traumatic Death
27. Ethics and Life's Ending: An Exchange

Coping
7. Saying Goodbye
8. Helping Military Kids Cope with Traumatic Death
10. Altered States: What I've Learned about Death & Disability
15. When Death Strikes without Warning
22. When a Cherished Pet Dies
40. Coping with the Loss of Loved Ones

Counseling
37. Counseling with Children in Contemporary Society

Cultural situations
3. How Much Is More Life Worth?
9. Needs of Elderly Patients in Palliative Care
12. End-of-Life Care around the World: Achievements to Date and Challenges Remaining
13. Are They Hallucinations or Are They Real? The Spirituality of Deathbed and Near-Death Visions
15. When Death Strikes without Warning
16. Suicide Rates in the World: 1950–2004
18. Ethical, Legal, and Practical Issues in the Control and Regulation of Suicide Promotion and Assistance over the Internet

Dead human remains
3. How Much Is More Life Worth?
7. Saying Goodbye
22. When a Cherished Pet Dies

Death defined
7. Saying Goodbye
13. Are They Hallucinations or Are They Real? The Spirituality of Deathbed and Near-Death Visions
17. On "Intention" in the Definition of Suicide

Death fear/anxiety
2. Death, Dying, and the Dead in Popular Culture
6. Death in Disney Films: Implications for Children's Understanding of Death
7. Saying Goodbye
8. Helping Military Kids Cope with Traumatic Death

Internet References

The following Internet sites have been selected to support the articles found in this reader. These sites were available at the time of publication. However, because websites often change their structure and content, the information listed may no longer be available. We invite you to visit www.mhhe.com/cls for easy access to these sites.

Annual Editions: Dying, Death, and Bereavement 11/12

General Sources

An Introduction to Death and Dying
www.bereavement.org

This electronic book was created to help those who grieve and those who provide support for the bereaved. Sections include Grief Theories, Death Systems, Ritual, and Disenfranchised Grief.

Yahoo: Society and Culture: Death
http://dir.yahoo.com/Society_and_Culture/Death_and_Dying

This Yahoo site has a very complete index to issues of dying and a search option.

UNIT 1: Issues in Dying and Death

Agency for Health Care Policy and Research
www.ahcpr.gov

Information on the dying process in the context of U.S. health policy is provided here, along with a search mechanism. The agency is part of the Department of Health and Human Services.

Brain Injury and Brain Death Resources
www.changesurfer.com/BD/Brain.html

Visit this site to investigate the debate concerning brain death. When is someone dead? Go to the philosophy of life, consciousness, and personhood page to get specifics.

Growth House, Inc.
www.growthhouse.org

Growth House is a nonprofit organization working with grief, bereavement, hospice, and end-of-life issues, as well as pain, AIDS/HIV, suicide, and palliative care issues.

Mortality Rates
www.trinity.edu/~mkearl/b&w-ineq.jpg

This site contains a graphic representation of the U.S. death rates of different social groups to ascertain social inequities.

WWW Virtual Library: Demography and Population Studies
http://demography.anu.edu.au/VirtualLibrary

A definitive guide to demography and population studies, with a multitude of important links, can be found here.

UNIT 2: Dying and Death across the Life Cycle

CDC Wonder on the Web—Prevention Guidelines
http://wonder.cdc.gov

At this Centers for Disease Control site, there are a number of papers on suicide prevention, particularly relating to American youth.

Children with AIDS Project
www.aidskids.org

This organization's role is to develop fuller understanding of children with and at risk of AIDS, including medical, psychosocial, legal, and financial issues. The mission of the organization is to develop local and national adoptive, foster, and family-centered care programs that are effective and compassionate.

Light for Life Foundation
www.yellowribbon.org

The Yellow Ribbon Program of the Light for Life Foundation provides educational material for American youth aimed at preventing youth suicide through the provision of easy access to support services.

National SIDS Resource Center
www.sidscenter.org

The National Sudden Infant Death Syndrome Resource Center (NSRC) provides information services and technical assistance on SIDS and related topics.

Palliative Care for Children
www.aap.org/policy/re0007.html

The American Academy of Pediatrics maintains this page, which gives a model for providing palliative care for children living with a life-threatening disease or terminal condition.

UNIT 3: The Dying Process

American Academy of Hospice and Palliative Medicine
www.aahpm.org

This is the only organization in the United States for physicians that is dedicated to the advancement of hospice/palliative medicine, its practice, research, and education. There are also links to other websites.

Hospice Foundation of America
www.hospicefoundation.org

Everything you might need to know about hospice and specific information on the foundation is available at this website.

Hospice Hands
http://hospice-cares.com

An extensive collection of links to hospice resources can be found at this site. Try "What's New" to access the *ACP Home Care Guide,* a book whose goal is to support an orderly problem-solving approach in managing care of the dying at home.

National Prison Hospice Association
www.npha.org

This prison hospice association promotes care for terminally ill inmates and those facing the prospect of dying in prison.

The Zen Hospice Project
www.zenhospice.org

The Zen Hospice Project organizes programs dedicated to the care of people approaching death and to increasing the understanding of impermanence. The project also runs a small hospice in San Francisco. There are links here to related information on the Web.

UNIT 4: Suicide

Articles on Euthanasia: Ethics
http://ethics.acusd.edu/Applied/Euthanasia

This site covers biomedical ethics and issues of euthanasia in many ways, including recent articles, ancient concepts, legal and legislative information, selected philosophical literature, websites, and a search engine.

Euthanasia and Physician-Assisted Suicide
www.religioustolerance.org/euthanas.htm

This website covers euthanasia in the United States, as well as status of euthanasia elsewhere in the world and recent developments.

Kearl's Guide to the Sociology of Death: Moral Debates
www.trinity.edu/~mkearl/death-5.html#eu

An Internet resource on the ethics of biomedical issues that includes issues of dying and death, such as euthanasia, is found here.

Internet References

The Kevorkian Verdict
www.pbs.org/wgbh/pages/frontline/kevorkian

This website from PBS features two thought-provoking interviews that explore the future for assisted suicide in the United States. What are the dangers and needed safeguards if it is legalized? How should we view Dr. Kevorkian's role in spotlighting this issue?

Living Wills (Advance Directive)
www.mindspring.com/~scottr/will.html

The largest collection of links to living wills and other advance directive and living will information is available at this website.

Not Dead Yet
www.notdeadyet.org

The Americans with Disabilities organization uses this website to mobilize Americans against euthanasia and mercy killing. Information about the Hemlock Society is also available here.

Suicide Awareness: Voices of Education
www.save.org

This popular Internet suicide site provides information on suicide (both before and after), along with material from the organization's many education sessions.

UNOS: United Network for Organ Sharing
www.unos.org

This website of the United Network for Organ Sharing includes facts and statistics, resources, and policy proposals regarding organ transplants.

Youth Suicide League
www.unicef.org/pon96/insuicid.htm

International suicide rates of young adults in selected countries are available on this UNESCO website.

UNIT 5: Animals and Death

The Humane Society of the United States
www.humanesociety.org/about/departments/faith/francis_files/the_grief_over_a_pets_death_.html

This is the preeminent organization dealing with animal treatment issues.

Pet Loss Support Page
www.pet-loss.net/emotions.shtml

This site is dedicated to helping those who have experienced the personal loss of a loved pet.

UNIT 6: Ethical Issues Regarding Dying and Death

Articles on Euthanasia: Ethics
http://ethics.acusd.edu/Applied/Euthanasia

This site covers biomedical ethics and issues of euthanasia in many ways, including recent articles, ancient concepts, legal and legislative information, selected philosophical literature, websites, and a search engine.

Euthanasia and Physician-Assisted Suicide
www.religioustolerance.org/euthanas.htm

This website covers Euthanasia in theUnited States, as well as status of euthanasia elsewhere in the world and recent developments.

Kearl's Guide to the Sociology of Death: Moral Debates
www.Trinity.Edu/~mkearl/death-5.html#eu

An Internet resource on the ethics of biomedical issues that includes issues of dying and death, such as euthanasia, is found here.

The Kevorkian Verdict
www.pbs.org/wgbh/pages/frontline/kevorkian

This website from PBS features two thought-provoking interviews that explore the future for assisted suicide in the United States. What are the dangers and needed safeguards if it is legalized? How should we view Dr. Kevorkian's role in spotlighting this issue?

Living Wills (Advance Directive)
www.mindspring.com/~scottr/will.html

The largest collection of links to living wills and other advance directive and living will information is available at this website.

Not Dead Yet
www.notdeadyet.org

The Americans with Disabilities organization uses this website to mobilize Americans against euthanasia and mercy killing. Information about the Hemlock Society is also available here.

UNOS: United Network for Organ Sharing
www.unos.org

This website of the United Network for Organ Sharing includes facts and statistics, resources, and policy proposals regarding organ transplants.

UNIT 7: Funerals

Cryonics, Cryogenics, and the Alcor Foundation
www.alcor.org

This is the website of Alcor, the world's largest cryonics organization.

Funeral Consumers Alliance
www.funerals.org

The Funeral Consumers Alliance is the only group that monitors the funeral industry for consumers regarding funeral guides, planning, and issues of social concern.

Funerals and Ripoffs
www.funerals-ripoffs.org/-5dProf1.htm

Sponsored by the Interfaith Funeral Information Committee and Arizona Consumers Council, this website is very critical of the funeral industry and specializes in exposing funeral home financial fraud.

The Internet Cremation Society
www.cremation.org

The Internet Cremation Society provides statistics on cremations, links to funeral industry resources, and answers to frequently asked questions.

UNIT 8: Bereavement

Bereaved Families of Ontario Support Center
www.bereavedfamilies.net

The Self-Help Resources Guide at this site indexes resources of the Bereaved Families of Ontario Support Center along with more than 300 listings of other resources and information that are useful to the bereaved.

The Compassionate Friends
www.compassionatefriends.org

This self-help organization for bereaved parents and siblings has hundreds of chapters worldwide.

Practical Grief Resources
www.indiana.edu/~famlygrf/sitemap.html

Here are lists of Internet and print resources that are available for understanding and coping with grief.

Widow Net
www.widownet.org

Widow Net is an information and self-help resource for and by widows and widowers. The information is helpful to people of all ages, religious backgrounds, and sexual orientation who have experienced a loss of a spouse or life partner.

UNIT 1
Issues in Dying and Death

Unit Selections

Key Points to Consider

- Why do we fear death? What can one do to overcome such a fear?

- How is death defined medically? How is the brain death definition of death useful to hospitals?

- What is a good death to you? What is a good death to one diagnosed with a terminal illness? Would the two definitions differ? If you had your choice, how would you like to die? Do you feel that most individuals around the world die in a way they would wish to die?

- What procedures are followed in handling a dead body in the intensive care unit of a hospital? What is the role played by nurses in such a situation?

- How are dying and death portrayed in the media, music, recreation, and humor? Are you aware of how often dying and death are a part of a television program, a movie, music, or are included in a joke? Why do you think that jokes about death are popular? How has the Internet impacted how we relate to dying, death, and bereavement?

- How does the discipline of sociology view dying and death?

- Given the high cost of medications, how does one weigh the cost against the "worth" of life? Are a few more days/weeks of life really worth the high cost of such?

Student Website
www.mhhe.com/cls

Internet References

Agency for Health Care Policy and Research
www.ahcpr.gov
Brain Injury and Brain Death Resources
www.changesurfer.com/BD/Brain.html
Growth House, Inc.
www.growthhouse.org
Mortality Rates
www.trinity.edu/~mkearl/b&w-ineq.jpg
WWW Virtual Library: Demography and Population Studies
http://demography.anu.edu.au/VirtualLibrary

Death, like sex, is a rather taboo topic. British anthropologist Geoffrey Gorer's writing about the pornography of death in the mid-twentieth century seemed to open the door for publications on the subject of death. Gorer argued that death had replaced sex as contemporary society's major taboo topic. Because death was less common in the community, with individuals actually seeing fewer corpses and being with individuals less at the time of death, a relatively realistic view of death had been replaced by a voyeuristic, adolescent preoccupation with it. Our modern way of life has not prepared us to cope any better with dying and death. Sex and death have "come out of the closet" in recent decades, however, and now are issues discussed and presented in formal educational settings. Baby Boomers are aging and changing the ways we handle death. In fact, end-of-life issues are frequently discussed in the popular media, as evidenced by the recent popular television shows *Six Feet Under* and *Family Plots* and numerous documentaries and other drama series about hospitals and emergency rooms. Yet, we have a long way to go in educating the public about these historically taboo subjects.

We are beginning to recognize the importance of educating youth on the subject of dying and death. Like sex education, death education (thanatology, literally "the study of death") is an approved topic for presentation in elementary and secondary school curricula in many states, but the topics (especially death and dying) are optional and therefore rarely receive high priorities in the classroom or in educational funding. With the terrorist attacks on the United States, Spain, and England, the wars in Iraq and Afghanistan, and various natural disasters around the world, an increased interest in death and dying in the curricula could have a positive impact on helping to cope with these various megadeath-related situations.

Many (most?) individuals have a fear of death. Just what is a "good death"? These topics are addressed in the articles entitled "Death, Dying, and the Dead in Popular Culture" and "Criteria for

© McGraw-Hill Companies. Facebook entry courtesy of Stacy Faley Vize.

a Good Death." Different interpretations may occur for different social contexts as to what is a "good death."

What is the value of a human being? How do we measure this? Dan Brock's "How Much Is More Life Worth?" discusses the high cost of drugs in treating individuals with a terminal illness and asks if the financial cost of medications is really worth a few weeks or months of extended life.

When is a person dead? The "brain death" definition of death is one of the more definitive definitions of death, yet brain death guidelines vary in U.S. hospitals, as noted in "Brain Death Guidelines Vary at Top US Neurological Hospitals."

Other issues discussed in this section include the impact of technology, particularly the Internet and Facebook, on how death and grief are handled.

Grief in the Age of Facebook

Elizabeth Stone

On July 17 last year, one of my most promising students died. Her name was Casey Feldman, and she was crossing a street in a New Jersey resort town on her way to work when a van went barreling through a stop sign. Her death was a terrible loss for everyone who knew her. Smart and dogged, whimsical and kind, Casey was the news editor of the *The Observer,* the campus paper I advise, and she was going places. She was a finalist for a national college reporting award and had just been chosen for a prestigious television internship for the fall, a fact she conveyed to me in a midnight text message, entirely consistent with her all-news-all-the-time mindset. Two days later her life ended.

I found out about Casey's death the old-fashioned way: in a phone conversation with Kelsey, the layout editor and Casey's roommate. She'd left a neutral-sounding voice mail the night before, asking me to call when I got her message, adding, "It's OK if it's late." I didn't retrieve the message till midnight, so I called the next morning, realizing only later what an extraordinary effort she had made to keep her voice calm. But my students almost never make phone calls if they can help it, so Kelsey's message alone should have raised my antenna. She blogs, she tweets, she texts, and she pings. But voice mail? No.

Paradoxically it was Kelsey's understanding of the viral nature of her generation's communication preferences that sent her rushing to the phone, and not just to call boomers like me. She didn't want anyone to learn of Casey's death through Facebook. It was summer, and their friends were scattered, but Kelsey knew that if even one of Casey's 801 Facebook friends posted the news, it would immediately spread.

So as Kelsey and her roommates made calls through the night, they monitored Facebook. Within an hour of Casey's death, the first mourner posted her respects on Casey's Facebook wall, a post that any of Casey's friends could have seen. By the next morning, Kelsey, in New Jersey, had reached *The Observer*'s editor in chief in Virginia, and by that evening, the two had reached fellow editors in California, Missouri, Massachusetts, Texas, and elsewhere—and somehow none of them already knew.

In the months that followed, I've seen how markedly technology has influenced the conventions of grieving among my students, offering them solace but also uncertainty. The day after Casey's death, several editorial-board members changed their individual Facebook profile pictures. Where there had been photos of Brent, of Kelsey, of Kate, now there were photos of Casey and Brent, Casey and Kelsey, Casey and Kate.

Now that Casey was gone, she was virtually everywhere. I asked one of my students why she'd changed her profile photo. "It was spontaneous," she said. "Once one person did it, we all joined in." Another student, who had friends at Virginia Tech when, in 2007, a gunman killed 32 people, said that's when she first saw the practice of posting Facebook profile photos of oneself with the person being mourned.

Within several days of Casey's death, a Facebook group was created called "In Loving Memory of Casey Feldman," which ran parallel to the wake and funeral planned by Casey's family. Dozens wrote on that group's wall, but Casey's own wall was the more natural gathering place, where the comments were more colloquial and addressed to her: "casey im speechless for words right now," wrote one friend. "i cant believe that just yest i txted you and now your gone . . . i miss you soo much. rest in peace."

Though we all live atomized lives, memorial services let us know the dead with more dimension than we may have known them during their lifetimes. In the responses of her friends, I was struck by how much I hadn't known about Casey—her equestrian skill, her love of animals, her interest in photography, her acting talent, her penchant for creating her own slang ("Don't be a cow"), and her curiosity—so intense that her friends affectionately called her a "stalker."

This new, uncharted form of grieving raises new questions. Traditional mourning is governed by conventions. But in the age of Facebook, with selfhood publicly represented via comments and uploaded photos, was it OK for her friends to display joy or exuberance online? Some weren't sure. Six weeks after Casey's death, one student who had posted a shot of herself with Casey wondered aloud when it was all right to post a different photo. Was there a right time? There were no conventions to help her. And would she be judged if she removed her mourning photo before most others did?

As it turns out, Facebook has a "memorializing" policy in regard to the pages of those who have died. That policy came into being in 2005, when a good friend and co-worker of Max Kelly, a Facebook employee, was killed in a bicycle accident. As Kelly wrote in a Facebook blog post last October, "The question soon came up: What do we do about his Facebook profile? We had never really thought about this before in such a personal way. How do you deal with an interaction with someone who is no longer able to log on? When someone leaves us, they don't leave our memories or our social network. To reflect that reality, we created the idea of 'memorialized' profiles as a place where people can save and share their memories of those who've passed."

Casey's Facebook page is now memorialized. Her own postings and lists of interests have been removed, and the page is visible only to her Facebook friends. (I thank Kelsey Butler for making it possible for me to gain access to it.) Eight months after her death, her friends are still posting on her wall, not to "share their memories" but to write to her, acknowledging her absence but maintaining their ties to her—exactly the stance that contemporary grief theorists recommend. To me, that seems preferable to Freud's prescription, in "Mourning and Melancholia," that we should detach from the dead. Quite a few of Casey's friends wished her a merry Christmas, and on the 17th of every month so far, the postings spike. Some share dreams they've had about her, or post a detail of interest. "I had juice box wine recently," wrote one. "I thought of you the whole time:(Miss you girl!" From another: "i miss you. the new lady gaga cd came out, and if i had one wish in the world it would be that you could be singing (more like screaming) along with me in my passenger seat like old times."

It was against the natural order for Casey to die at 21, and her death still reverberates among her roommates and fellow editors. I was privileged to know Casey, and though I knew her deeply in certain ways, I wonder—I'm not sure, but I wonder—if I should have known her better. I do know, however, that she would have done a terrific trend piece on "Grief in the Age of Facebook."

ELIZABETH STONE is a professor of English, communication, and media studies at Fordham University. She is the author of the memoir *A Boy I Once Knew: What a Teacher Learned From Her Student* (Algonquin, 2002).

Death, Dying, and the Dead in Popular Culture

Keith F. Durkin

Fulton and Owen (1987) have observed that for members of the generation born after World War II, individuals who generally lack firsthand experience with death, the phenomenon of death and dying has become abstract and invisible. Americans, like members of many other societies, attach fearful meanings to death, dying, and the dead (Leming and Dickinson 2002). Moreover, it is has frequently been suggested that the United States has become a "death-denying" culture. A number of scholars have documented the various ways in which Americans attempt to deny death (e.g., DeSpelder and Strickland 2002; Leming and Dickinson 2002; Mannino 1997; Oaks and Ezell 1993; Umberson and Henderson 1992). For example, we have a societal taboo against frank discussions about death and dying. When we do refer to these topics, it is normative for us to use euphemisms, such as *passed away* or *expired*. Furthermore, in the United States death typically occurs in the segregated environments of hospitals and nursing homes, and we typically relegate the task of handling the dead to professionals, such as funeral directors.

Although the United States is a death-denying society, Americans may be said to have an obsessive fascination with death and death-related phenomena. As Bryant and Shoemaker (1977) observe, "Thanatological entertainment has been and remains a traditional pervasive cultural pattern both in the United States and elsewhere, and has become very much a prominent and integral part of contemporary popular culture" (p. 2). For instance, death, dying, and the dead "regularly appear in various informational and entertainment media" (Walter, Littlewood, and Pickering 1995:581). Accordingly, the mass media have become a primary source of information about death and dying for most Americans.

In this chapter, I explore the various manifestations of death, dying, and the dead in contemporary U.S. popular culture. This discussion is not intended as an exhaustive exposition of this topic; rather, I seek to address the more prominent examples of this phenomenon. These include portrayals of death, dying, and the dead on television, in cinema, in music, and in products of the print media, as well as in recreational attractions, games, and jokes. Additionally, I explore the social import of the presence of these thanatological themes in popular culture.

Television

Nearly every American household has at least one television set, and a large percentage have several. Death and dying are brought directly into homes via the medium of television. According to DeSpelder and Strickland (2002), in an average issue of *TV Guide,* approximately one-third of the listings "describe programs in which death and dying feature in some way" (p. 35). These topics appear in soap operas, crime dramas, mysteries, documentaries, and comedies. Many of the current top-rated shows, such as *ER* and *CSI,* prominently feature death and dying. The popular "reality" show *Survivor* deals with a type of symbolic death. In fact, death and dying are the most frequently appearing social topics even in religious television programming (Abelman 1987). Recently, the unique series *Six Feet Under,* the ongoing saga of a family that owns and operates a mortuary, has proven to be compelling for many viewers.

Many people have expressed tremendous concern about the amount of violent death featured on U.S. television. According to the National Institute of Mental Health, by the time the average American reaches age 16, he or she has seen 18,000 murders on television (Kearl 1995). It has been estimated that violent death "befalls five percent of all prime time characters each week" (Gerbner 1980:66). Violent death is not limited to prime-time programming, however. The cartoons that are featured on Saturday mornings contain an average of 20 to 25 violent acts per hour, and many of these acts result in the apparent deaths of characters (Wass 1995). However, unlike in reality, cartoon characters have their deaths "reversed with no serious consequences to their bodily functions" (Mannino 1997:29).

Death has also long been a mainstay of televised news programming, but with the advent of cable television and satellite broadcasting, death coverage has taken on a new dimension. The Gulf War of 1991 was a major news event, with live coverage of the battles as they occurred. An average of 2.3 million households tuned in daily to the O. J. Simpson trial, the so-called Trial of the Century (Durkin and Knox 2001). The funeral of Diana, Princess of Wales, was seen on television "by 31 million people in Britain and two billion worldwide" (Merrin 1999:53). The tragic terrorist attacks on the World Trade Center and the Pentagon on

September 11, 2001, were a media event that transpired on live television:

> Every major network, as well as many specialized cable networks (e.g., VH1 and MTV) featured live coverage of the events as they unfolded. According to Nielsen Media Research, 80 million Americans watched television news coverage on the evening of September 11th. . . . In the days following September 11th, there was around-the-clock coverage of the subsequent reaction to the attack, the rescue efforts, and the eventual military retaliation. (Durkin and Knox 2001:3–4)

Cinema

Thanatological themes have traditionally been, and continue to be, an extremely popular element of the cinematic enterprise. For instance, death and dying feature prominently in westerns and war movies. There have also been many successful film dramas about dying, including *Love Story, Dying Young, Stepmom, My Life,* and *Sweet November.* Death has even been the topic of comedies, such as *Weekend at Bernie's* and *Night Shift.* As Kearl (1995) notes, beginning in the 1970s, a popular motif "involved attacks on humanity by the natural order—frogs, bees, sharks, meteors, earthquakes, and tidal waves". A vast array of movies have featured "disastrous life-threatening phenomena such as diseases (e.g., AIDS, Ebola-like virus), massive accidents (e.g., airplane crashes, nuclear plant accidents) and natural disasters" (Bahk and Neuwirth 2000:64). Ghost movies (e.g., *Truly, Madly, Deeply* and *Ghost*) as well as thrillers such as *Flatliners* have used the near-death experience as a narrative focus (Walter et al. 1995).

Many movies have a decidedly morbid focus. Young people appear to be particularly fascinated by films that feature violent deaths (Leming and Dickinson 2002). Zombie films such as *Dawn of the Dead* and *Night of the Living Dead* not only feature the undead but have scenes containing gruesome acts of violence and murder. The notorious serial killer Jack the Ripper has been featured in a large number of films, including *Murder by Decree, A Study in Terror,* and *Man in the Attic* (Schecter and Everitt 1997). A number of recent films have portrayed the activities of murderers, including *Silence of the Lambs, Hannibal, American Gothic,* and *Natural Born Killers.* In the popular *Faces of Death* series, which appeared in video rental outlets in the mid-1980s, "actual death was displayed, with images of suicides, executions, and autopsies" (Kearl 1995:28).

One specific genre of horror film, the slasher movie, has become especially popular in recent years. According to Molitor and Sapolsky (1993):

> The genre can be characterized as commercially released, feature length films containing suspense evoking scenes in which an antagonist, who is usually a male acting alone, attacks one or more victims. The accentuation in these films is extreme graphic violence. Scenes that dwell on the victim's fear and explicitly portray the attack and its aftermath are the central focus of slasher films. (P. 235)

Slasher movies feature plenty of sex and large teenage body counts (Strinati 2000). Examples include *Halloween, Friday the 13th, Nightmare on Elm Street, Slumber Party Massacre,* and *Motel Hell.* In 1981, 25 slasher movies were ranked among the 50 top-grossing films of that year (Strinati 2000). The impact of slasher films has extended far beyond the cinema; for example, the mayor of Los Angeles proclaimed September 13, 1991, Freddy Krueger Day, in honor of the killer featured in the *Nightmare on Elm Street* film series (Lewis 1997).

Music

Historically, thanatological themes have been present in nearly all musical styles. For instance, folk songs about serial killers date back well into the 19th century (Schecter and Everitt 1997). Death-related themes are also present in many operas and classical musical pieces. These motifs have played a major role in the recording industry. Interestingly, one of the first recordings ever "produced for the Edison phonograph featured an actor reading the shocking confessions of H. H. Holmes, the notorious nineteenth-century "Torture Doctor" (Schecter and Everitt 1997:185). However, death became particularly prominent in the popular music of the so-called Baby Boom generation's teenage years (Kearl 1995). In the 1950s, a musical genre often referred to as "coffin songs"—songs featuring themes related to dying and grief (e.g., "Last Kiss")—became popular with young Americans (DeSpelder and Strickland 2002). The eminence of death-related motifs continues to this day. At times, this can assume remarkable configurations. For example, the funeral of Diana, Princess of Wales, produced pop artist Elton John's hit single "Candle in the Wind '97" (Merrin 1999), which is a lyrically rearranged version of an earlier John song about the dead movie icon Marilyn Monroe. Moreover, a large number of musicians have died in tragic and untimely fashion. Some examples include John Bonham, Kurt Cobain, Jimi Hendrix, Buddy Holly, Janis Joplin, John Lennon, Bob Marley, Keith Moon, Jim Morrison, Elvis Presley, Bon Scott, and Ritchie Valens.

The music that is popular with today's young people frequently has a morbid element that emphasizes death's destructive and catastrophic nature (Fulton and Owen 1987). Examples include songs about homicide, suicide, and extremely violent acts (Wass et al. 1988; Wass, Miller, and Redditt 1991). Many members of our society consider such topics to be particularly unsavory and antisocial, and, accordingly, a number of groups have been particularly vocal in their criticism of this music. For instance, as Wass et al. (1991) note, "A number of professionals, their representative organizations such as the American Academy of Pediatricians and the National Education Association, various child advocacy groups, including the Parent's Music Resource Center, and others have suggested that such lyrics promote destructive and suicidal behavior in adolescents" (p. 200).

The themes of death and destruction play an especially prominent role in two of the most popular styles of contemporary music: heavy metal and rap. Many heavy metal bands have names associated with death, such as Megadeath, Anthrax, Slayer, and Grim Reaper. Examples of heavy metal song titles include "Suicide Solution," "Highway to Hell," and "Psycho Killer." The band Guns N' Roses even recorded a cover version of the song

"Look at Your Game Girl," which was written by the infamous murderer Charles Manson (Schecter and Everitt 1997).

In rap music, the violent lyrics of artists such as Snoop Dogg, Dr. Dre, Eazy-E, and Puff Daddy have generated a great deal of controversy. In fact, one of the most successful rap recording companies is named Death Row Records. Examples of rap song titles include "Murder Was the Case," "Sex, Money, and Murder," and "Natural Born Killers." The song that rapper Eminem performed at the Grammy Awards in 2001, "Stan," describes a murder-suicide. Rap music came under national scrutiny after performer Ice-T released the song "Cop Killer." The murders of rap artists Tupac Shakur and Notorious B.I.G. in recent years have also served to enhance the deadly image of this style of music.

Print Media

Dying, death, and the dead are principal themes in much of American literature (Bryant and Shoemaker 1977). Westerns, war novels, mysteries, and true-crime books are exceptionally popular with readers. Violent death is a ubiquitous theme in popular fiction (Fulton and Owen 1987). Books about hospitals and doctors are also fairly successful (Bryant and Shoemaker 1977). Death and dying are even featured in children's stories (DeSpelder and Strickland 2002; Umberson and Henderson 1992). Newsmagazines frequently publish stories that deal with death and dying, often featuring these stories on their covers. Even comic books have featured the exploits of notorious serial killers (Schecter and Everitt 1997).

Reports of death and dying are common in daily newspapers. The deaths of ordinary people are usually reported only in brief obituaries, unless a person has died in some sensational fashion. Newspapers report the deaths of public figures such as politicians, celebrities, and musical artists in far greater detail (Walter et al. 1995). For instance, the *Seattle Times* ran a front-page feature on the death of rock star Kurt Cobain, complete with photos of the suicide scene (Martin and Koo 1997).

In general, newspapers tend to overemphasize catastrophic causes of death (Combs and Slovic 1979). As Walter et al. (1995) observe, those dramatic deaths that are "boldly headlined and portrayed in the news media are extraordinary deaths" (p. 594). The image of the burning World Trade Center towers was featured on the front pages of many newspapers on September 12, 2001.

Newspaper depictions of death and dying are not always so explicit, however. When Umberson and Henderson (1992) conducted a content analysis of stories about the Gulf War that appeared in the *New York Times,* they found a striking absence of explicit references to death. Instead, the stories frequently employed governmentally inspired euphemisms such as "collateral damage" when discussing death. Moreover, the stories repeatedly quoted State Department and military spokespersons who talked about efforts to keep casualties to a minimum.

One form of print media that scholars have traditionally overlooked is the supermarket tabloid. The weekly circulation of the six major tabloids (*Star, Sun, National Enquirer, National Examiner, Globe,* and *Weekly World News*) is about 10 million, with an estimated readership of about 50 million (Bird 1992). As Durkin and Bryant (1995) note, these publications are full of thanatological content. Articles about murders, accidents, celebrity

health scares, and dead celebrities are common, as are stories about paranormal phenomena such are reincarnation, ghosts, and near-death experiences. Health advice regarding the prevention of life-threatening medical problems can be found in some tabloids. In fact, Durkin and Bryant report that the *National Enquirer* has "received an award from the American Cancer Society for medical stories that the paper provided" (p. 10).

Recreation

Aside from their presence in the media, dying, death, and the dead play an important role in the recreational activities of many Americans. As Bryant and Shoemaker (1977) note, many people show an "interest in, and morbid fascination with, facsimiles of the dead, the pseudo dead as it were" (p. 12). An example of this common fascination is the ever-popular wax museum. Also, the traveling museum exhibit of objects from King Tut's tomb was a nationwide sensation. In fact, actual dead bodies have sometimes been used for sideshow exhibits. According to Bryant (1989):

> For many years carnival concessionaires have displayed various kinds of odd bodies and curious corpses . . . because the public was fascinated with such unusual exhibits. A particularly morbid type of display that was common to carnivals was the exhibition of deformed fetuses in jars of formaldehyde, euphemistically known in the trade as "pickled punks." (P. 10)

In a somewhat similar vein, Bunny Gibbons, a sideshow exhibitor, displayed the "Death Car" of serial killer Ed Gein at county fairs throughout the Midwest (Schecter and Everitt 1997).

Some scholars have adopted the term *dark tourism* to refer to "the presentation and consumption (by visitors) of real and commodified death and disaster sites" (Foley and Lennon 1996:198). For example, since 1994, one of the more popular tourist attractions in Los Angeles has been the Brentwood condominium where Nicole Brown Simpson and Ronald Goldman were murdered (Schecter and Everitt 1997). Battlefields such as Gettysburg have traditionally been successful tourist attractions, as has the site of the assassination of President John F. Kennedy (Foley and Lennon 1996). During times of disaster, public safety officials often experience major problems in controlling curiosity seekers motivated by the chance to experience novel situations firsthand (Cunningham, Dotter, and Bankston 1986). Authorities have labeled this phenomenon *convergent behavior* (Bryant 1989).

Cemeteries and burial sites are also popular tourist attractions. For instance, the Forest Lawn cemetery near Hollywood is internationally known as the "cemetery of the stars" (Morgan 1968). Arlington National Cemetery in Virginia has millions of visitors annually (Bryant and Shoemaker 1977). As Frow (1998) reports, Graceland, the former home and burial site of music legend Elvis Presley, "is the object of both everyday pilgrimage and especially intense commemoration during the vigils of Tribute Week, culminating in the candle-lit procession around Presley's grave on the anniversary of his death" (p. 199). Merrin (1999) notes that when a telephone hot line was first opened for members of the public to order tickets to visit the grave of Princess Diana, it was "reported that up to 10,000 calls a minute had been attempted at peak times" (p. 58).

Games, a popular form of recreation, frequently contain thanatological themes. War toys and board games featuring characters like Casper the Friendly Ghost are popular with children. Video games such as *Mortal Combat* and *Duke Nukem* feature vivid images of violent deaths (see Funk and Buchman 1996). Several million copies of the *Ouija Board*, which is touted as a means of communicating with the dead, have been sold (Bryant and Shoemaker 1977). As Schecter and Everitt (1997) report, the thanatological themes in games can assume morbid dimensions:

> Though it is unlikely to become the next *Trivial Pursuit,* a board game called *Serial Killer* set off a firestorm of outrage when it was put on the market a few years ago. . . . [It] consisted of a game board printed on a map of the United States, four serial killer game playing pieces, crime cards, outcome cards, and two dozen plastic victims (in the possibly ill-advised form of dead babies). (P. 31)

Jokes

Humor is a mechanism that allows for the violation of taboos regarding the discussion of death-related topics (Mannino 1997). A vast array of jokes deal with death, dying, and the dead. Thorson (1985) identifies two major varieties of death humor. The first is humor associated with the body. This includes jokes about cannibalism, funerals, undertakers, burials, and necrophilia. The second type, humor associated with the personality, includes jokes about suicide, homicide, memories of the departed, grief, executions, deathbed scenes, last words, and the personification of death.

Some jokes about death, dying, and the dead involve what has frequently been referred to as *gallows humor.* This term originated "from the genre of jokes about the condemned man or helpless victim, and is often generated by the victims themselves" (Moran and Massam 1997:5). An excellent example is Freud's classic anecdote about a man who joked on his way to the gallows. Currently, gallows humor is conceptualized as more of a philosophical posture than a specific repertoire of jokes (Van Wormer and Boes 1997). This type of humor is intentional (Thorson 1985) and tends to express "a cynical, morbid focus on death" (Sayre 2001:677).

An especially violent and cruel strain of death humor spread through American popular culture in the 1980s (Lewis 1997) and is still popular today. AIDS jokes are the classic example of this type of humor, in which the common tactic is to "specify an outgroup and make fun not only of death but also of dying people" (Thorson 1993:21). Moreover, many jokes are told about particular murderers and accused murderers (e.g., Jeffrey Dahmer and O. J. Simpson). Additionally, a variety of jokes circulate in relation to disasters such as the crash of ValuJet Flight 592 in Florida and the destruction of the space shuttle *Challenger* (see Blume 1986). Americans have also created macabre humor surrounding the Ethiopian famine, the Gulf War, and the mass suicide of the Branch Davidians. Such jokes "invite us to be amused by images of bodily mutilation, vulnerability, and victimization" (Lewis 1997:253). Controversial by its very nature, this insensitive type of humor is particularly offensive to many people (Thorson 1993); their responses ensure a dialectic, which increases the humor's entertainment value.

The Postself

Many of the manifestations of death and the dead in U.S. popular culture deal with what has been termed the *post-self*. This is especially true for deceased celebrities and other public figures. The postself is the reputation and influence that an individual has after his or her death. According to Shneidman (1995), this "relates to fame, reputation, impact, and holding on" (p. 455). The postself constitutes a form of symbolic immortality, whereby "the meaning of a person can continue after he or she has died" (Leming and Dickinson 2002:143). In essence, the deceased person continues to exist in the memories of the living (Shneidman 1995). On a cultural level, this functions symbolically to blur the bifurcation between the living and the dead (Durkin and Bryant 1995).

As Frow (1998) observes, the fame of dead celebrities sometimes assumes a pseudoreligious dimension in contemporary society: "A small handful of stars and public figures experience this adoration that raises them beyond the human plane . . . [such as] Elvis, Rudolph Valentino, Lenin, Stalin, Hitler, Mao, James Dean, Kurt Cobain, Bruce Lee, Che Guevara, and Evita Peron" (p. 199). Perhaps the most prominent example of this phenomenon in recent years is Princess Diana, whose tragic and untimely death has resulted in what has been characterized as the "Diana grief industry" (Merrin 1999:51). The devoted can buy Diana dolls, books, plates, videos, stuffed animals, key chains, ashtrays, T-shirts, towels, mugs, spoons, stamps, posters, and more. Although this phenomenon has certainly been highly profitable for a vast array of entrepreneurs, some people find it particularly distasteful. For instance, British Prime Minister Tony Blair has condemned the sale of Princess Diana collectibles as the tacky exploitation of Diana's memory (Merrin 1999).

Discussion

On the one hand, the contemporary United States is frequently described as a death-denying society. Numerous scholars have observed that recent generations of Americans lack the firsthand familiarity with death and dying that their ancestors had (e.g., Fulton and Owen 1987; DeSpelder and Strickland 2002; Leming and Dickinson 2002). Accordingly, many Americans express a great deal of death anxiety. On the other hand, many Americans also have an obsessive fascination with death, dying, and the dead (Oaks and Ezell 1993; Umberson and Henderson 1992). Nowhere is this paradox more apparent than in our popular culture. Television programming, movies, songs, the print media, games, jokes, and even recreational activities are fraught with thanatological content.

This seeming contradiction may be read at several levels, in that there are differential interpretations. The most obvious, albeit superficial, interpretation is that the United States is not as much of a death-denying society as many writers contend. A second explanation for the paradox is that our society is, indeed, a death-denying one, but our insulation from death causes us to crave some degree of information and insight concerning death, and we feed that craving through popular-culture depictions of death and dying. This situation would be not unlike the Victorian period in Great Britain and the United States, during which sexual Puritanism was an ideological mainstay of the value system, but nevertheless there was a significant demand for clandestine, salacious accounts of sex and sexual activity, such as smuggled "dirty" books from Europe.

Another interpretation of the contradiction between the death-denying nature of U.S. society and the saturation of death themes in the American mass media is that the treatment of death as entertainment and humor is simply an extension of, or another configuration of, death denial. By rendering death into humor and entertainment, we effectively neutralize it; it becomes innocuous, and thus less threatening, through its conversion and ephemerality in the media. This is, perhaps, the more compelling explanation.

Death is a disruptive event, not only for the individual who dies but for the larger social enterprise as well. Consequently, all societies must construct mechanisms to deal with death's problematic impacts (Blauner 1966). As Pine (1972) notes, the "beliefs and practices of the members of a society toward dying and death are largely dependent upon that society's social organization" (p. 149). Popular culture serves as a type of collective vision by which meanings are socially constructed, which in turn "greatly influences our norms, beliefs, and subsequent actions" (Couch 2000:25). It appears that the thanatological themes in U.S. popular culture function as a mechanism that helps Americans to deal with death. As Bryant (1989) notes, death, dying, and the dead "are traumatic and anxiety producing topics, and can be better confronted if they are socially neutralized" (p. 9).

Such social neutralization can help to assuage the disruptive impact of death and dying for the individual. This can occur in three related ways. First, in the context of popular culture, death, dying, and the dead are frequently reconceptualized into forms that stimulate something other than primordial terror. These phenomena may be considered fascinating, entertaining, and even humorous, depending on the social context. Bryant (1989) observes that when death is camouflaged in such a manner, "individuals can more comfortably indulge their curiosity about, and fascination with, such concerns" (p. 9). For instance, a visit to Elvis Presley's grave, to the site of the JFK assassination, to the spot where Nicole Brown Simpson and Ronald Goldman were murdered, or to the Forest Lawn cemetery near Hollywood might be considered part of a vacation. Moreover, many individuals find it thrilling to be frightened by horror and death at the movies (Leming and Dickinson 2002). Also, newspaper accounts of violent or accidental deaths may engender some voyeuristic, albeit convoluted, pleasure "or some macabre enjoyment in the misfortunes of others" (Walter et al. 1995:586). Similarly, many of the outrageous stories that appear in supermarket tabloids such as the Weekly World News and the Sun "appear to have no purpose other than catering to accident watchers" (Bird 1992:54).

Second, appreciation of many of the types of thanatological themes found in our popular culture requires some detachment on the part of the individual. Like spectators at professional wrestling matches, viewers of horror movies are required to suspend disbelief (Weaver 1991). Children or adolescents playing violent video games must detach themselves from the depictions of primal carnage occurring before their eyes. The quintessential example of this phenomenon is thanatological humor. Humor functions as a type of defense mechanism, allowing people to cope with the fear and anxiety associated with death and dying (Moran and Massam 1997; Oaks and Ezell 1993; Sayre 2001; Thorson 1993).

Enjoyment of this type of humor requires us to laugh at our own mortality (Thorson 1985). As Lewis (1997) notes, the appreciation of a so-called killing joke "calls for the adoption of a playful detachment from an act of violence or suffering" (p. 264).

Finally, some observers have argued that the tremendous amount of exposure to death, dying, and the dead that we receive through our popular culture may make us more accepting of these phenomena (Oaks and Ezell 1993). This saturated environment of thanatological concerns may function to inure individuals to death and dying, thus diluting or counteracting their anxiety about these phenomena (Bryant and Shoemaker 1977). Durkin and Bryant (1995) speculate that "the inordinate amount of attention afforded to thanatological themes in the tabloids may actually help to desensitize the reader" (p. 11). Similarly, Wass et al. (1991) suggest that the ubiquitous death-related themes in popular music might help adolescents confront their anxieties about these phenomena, given that death and dying are seldom discussed in the home or the classroom.

Conclusion

The United States is commonly characterized as a death-denying society. Americans frequently attach fearful meanings to thanatological concerns, have taboos against frank discussions about death and dying, and relegate the task of handling the dead to professionals. Nonetheless, death, dying, and the dead occupy a prominent place in our popular culture. Thanatological themes appear frequently in television programming, cinema, the print media, jokes, and recreational activities. Dead celebrities also play an important role in our popular culture. These thanatological elements of popular culture function as a mechanism to help individuals deal with the disruptive social impacts of death and dying. They help us to redefine death as something other than a terror, and enjoyment of these themes requires some detachment on the part of the individual. It has also been argued that we may be more accepting of death, dying, and the dead because of our frequent exposure to these phenomena through our popular culture.

References

Abelman, Robert. 1987. "Themes and Topics in Religious Television Programming." Review of Religious Research 29:152–69.

Bahk, C. Mo and Kurt Neuwirth. 2000. "Impact of Movie Depictions of Volcanic Disasters on Risk Perceptions and Judgements." International Journal of Mass Emergencies and Disasters 18:63–84.

Bird, S. Elizabeth. 1992. For Enquiring Minds: A Cultural Study of Supermarket Tabloids. Knoxville: University of Tennessee Press.

Blauner, Robert. 1966. "Death and Social Structure." Psychiatry 29:378–94.

Blume, Delorys. 1986. "Challenger 10 and Our School Children: Reflections on the Catastrophe." Death Studies 10:95–118.

Bryant, Clifton D. 1989. "Thanatological Crime: Some Conceptual Notes on Offenses Against the Dead as a Neglected Form of Deviant Behavior." Paper presented at the World Congress of Victimology, Acapulco.

Bryant, Clifton D. and Donald Shoemaker. 1977. "Death and the Dead for Fun (and Profit): Thanatological Entertainment as Popular Culture." Presented at the annual meeting of the Southern Sociological Society, Atlanta, GA.

Combs, Barbara and Paul Slovic. 1979. "Newspaper Coverage of the Causes of Death." *Journalism Quarterly* 56:837–43.

Couch, Stephen R. 2000. "The Cultural Scene of Disasters: Conceptualizing the Field of Disasters and Popular Culture." *International Journal of Mass Emergencies and Disasters* 18:21–37.

Cunningham, Orville R., Daniel L. Dotter, and William B. Bankston. 1986. "Natural Disasters, Convergence, and Four-Wheel Drive Machines: An Emergent Form of Deviant Behavior." *Deviant Behavior* 7:261–67.

DeSpelder, Lynne Ann and Albert Lee Strickland. 2002. *The Last Dance: Encountering Death and Dying,* 6th ed. New York: McGraw-Hill.

Durkin, Keith F. and Clifton D. Bryant. 1995. "Thanatological Themes in the Tabloids: A Content Analysis." Presented at the annual meeting of the Mid-South Sociological Association, Mobile, AL.

Durkin, Keith F. and Kristy Knox. 2001. "September 11th, Postmodernism, and the Collective Consciousness: Some Sociological Observations." Presented at the annual meeting of the Mid-South Sociological Association, Mobile, AL.

Foley, Malcolm and J. John Lennon. 1996. "JFK and Dark Tourism: A Fascination With Assassination." *International Journal of Heritage Studies* 2:198–211.

Frow, John. 1998. "Is Elvis a God? Cult, Culture, and Questions of Method." *International Journal of Cultural Studies* 1:197–210.

Fulton, Robert and Greg Owen. 1987. "Death and Society in Twentieth Century America." *Omega* 18:379–95.

Funk, Jeanne and Debra D. Buchman. 1996. "Playing Violent Video and Computer Games and Adolescent Self Concept." *Journal of Communication* 46:19–32.

Gerbner, George. 1980. "Death in Prime Time: Notes on the Symbolic Functions of Dying in the Mass Media." *Annals of the American Academy of Political and Social Science* 447:64–70.

Kearl, Michael C. 1995. "Death in Popular Culture." Pp. 23–30 in *Death: Current Perspectives,* 4th ed., edited by John B. Williamson and Edwin S. Shneidman. Mountain View, CA: Mayfield.

Leming, Michael R. and George E. Dickinson. 2002. *Understanding Death, Dying, and Bereavement,* 5th ed. New York: Harcourt College.

Lewis, Paul. 1997. "The Killing Jokes of the American Eighties." *Humor* 10:251–83.

Mannino, J. Davis. 1997. *Grieving Days, Healing Days.* Boston: Allyn & Bacon.

Martin, Graham and Lisa Koo. 1997. "Celebrity Suicide: Did the Death of Kurt Cobain Influence Young Suicides in Australia?" *Archives of Suicide Research* 3:187–98.

Merrin, William. 1999. "Crash, Bang, Wallop! What a Picture! The Death of Diana and the Media." *Mortality* 4:41–62.

Molitor, Fred and Barry S. Sapolsky. 1993. "Sex, Violence, and Victimization in Slasher Films." *Journal of Broadcasting and Electronic Media* 37:233–42.

Moran, Carmen and Margaret Massam. 1997. "An Evaluation of Humour in Emergency Work." *Australasian Journal of Disaster and Trauma Studies* 3:1–12.

Morgan, Al. 1968. "The Bier Barons." *Sociological Symposium* 1:28–35.

Oaks, Judy and Gene Ezell. 1993. *Death and Dying: Coping, Caring and Understanding,* 2d ed. Scottsdale, AZ: Gorsuch Scarisbrick.

Pine, Vanderlyn R. 1972. "Social Organization and Death." *Omega* 3:149–53.

Sayre, Joan. 2001. "The Use of Aberrant Medical Humor by Psychiatric Unit Staff." *Issues in Mental Health Nursing* 22:669–89.

Schecter, Harold and David Everitt. 1997. *The A-Z Encyclopedia of Serial Killers.* New York: Pocket Books.

Shneidman, Edwin S. 1995. "The Postself." Pp. 454–60 in *Death: Current Perspectives,* 4th ed. edited by John B. Williamson and Edwin S. Shneidman. Mountain View, CA: Mayfield.

Strinati, Dominic. 2000. *An Introduction to Studying Popular Culture.* London: Routledge.

Thorson, James A. 1985. "A Funny Thing Happened on the Way to the Morgue: Some Thoughts on Humor and Death, and a Taxonomy of Humor Associated With Death." *Death Studies* 9:201–16.

———. 1993. "Did You Ever See a Hearse Go By? Some Thoughts on Gallows Humor." *Journal of American Culture* 16:17–24.

Umberson, Debra and Kristin Henderson. 1992. "The Social Construction of Death in the Gulf War." *Omega* 25:1–15.

Van Wormer, Katherine and Mary Boes. 1997. "Humor in the Emergency Room: A Social Work Perspective." *Health and Social Work* 22:87–92.

Walter, Tony, Jane Littlewood, and Michael Pickering. 1995. "Death in the News: The Public Investigation of Private Emotion." *Sociology* 29:579–96.

Wass, Hannelore. 1995. "Death in the Lives of Children and Adolescents." Pp. 269–301 in *Dying: Facing the Facts,* 3d ed., edited by Hannelore Wass and Robert A. Neimeyer. Washington, DC: Taylor & Francis.

Wass, Hannelore, M. David Miller, and Carol Ann Redditt. 1991. "Adolescents and Destructive Themes in Rock Music: A Follow-Up." *Omega* 23:199–206.

Wass, Hannelore, Jana L. Raup, Karen Cerullo, Linda G. Martel, Laura A. Mingione, and Anna M. Sperring. 1988. "Adolescents' Interest in and Views of Destructive Themes in Rock Music." *Omega* 19:177–86.

Weaver, James B. 1991. "Are Slasher Horror Films Sexually Violent?" *Journal of Broadcasting and Electronic Media* 35:385–92.

How Much Is More Life Worth?

Dan W. Brock

vastin, Genentech's monoclonal antibody that it proposes to offer at twice the dose (and twice the price tag) to treat breast and lung cancer, has already made billions of dollars for the company through its original use—treating colon cancer. Now, with a potential pool of hundreds of thousands more patients, financial analysts predict its United States sales alone could grow nearly sevenfold to $7 billion by 2009.[1]

Extremely expensive drugs are hardly new. The pharmaceutical companies have long argued that these prices are justified by the extraordinarily high costs of getting new drugs to market. They typically estimate those costs at $800 million, which is said to reflect both the high costs of the large clinical trials required by the FDA to establish safety and efficacy, as well as the fact that only a small minority of potential new drugs ultimately makes it to market. The patent system for pharmaceuticals is designed to encourage research and development of new drugs by protecting the returns from successful drugs. Since the marginal costs of producing new drugs like Avastin are typically tiny in comparison to their patent protected prices, pharmaceutical companies could not justify the very large costs of research and development unless the patents prevented other companies from producing and selling them at those marginal costs.

Drug prices raise many controversial issues. Is the $800 million figure typically cited by the industry accurate, or are the real costs substantially less? Does the patent system primarily encourage the development of biologically new compounds, or does it instead promote so-called "me-too" drugs? Why do—and should—Americans pay substantially higher prices for drugs than citizens of other developed countries? Such economic, legal, and political issues are of great importance, but they apply across the industry broadly.

What is apparently new with Avastin is the justification that Genentech has offered for its extremely high price. Instead of relying on the traditional cost recovery argument, which would be hard to sustain if the estimates of a $7 billion market by 2009 are anything near accurate, the company is appealing to a new rationale—namely, the inherent value of life-sustaining therapies. It has priced Avastin based on "the value of innovation, and the value of new therapies," according to Susan Desmond-Hellman, the president of product development at Genentech.[2]

What should we make of this argument? How should the economic value of a life-extending intervention be determined? Is that value a justified basis for setting the price of the intervention? We have less experience addressing that first question in this country because most insurance plans do not explicitly and openly give weight to costs in making coverage decisions. The Centers for Medicare and Medicaid Services (CMS) is explicitly foreclosed by law from taking account of cost-effectiveness in decisions about coverage of new interventions.[3] While this rule has been criticized (correctly in my view), so long as it remains in place CMS's decisions look only at whether a drug "is reasonable and necessary in the diagnosis or treatment of illness or injury,"[4] without regard to costs. Since many private insurance plans tend to follow CMS in their coverage decisions, they too fail to explicitly consider cost-effectiveness or the economic values assigned to life extension.

Only the combination of patent protection together with purchasers' failure to consider cost-effectiveness and to bargain with Genentech will enable it to sell Avastin at the proposed price.

We can get some help if we look abroad. In the United Kingdom, the National Center for Clinical Excellence (NICE) is charged with evaluating new technologies (broadly construed to include new drugs) for coverage by the National Health Service. Cost-effectiveness is a principal criterion in their evaluations using quality-adjusted life years (QALYs) as the benefit measure. Although NICE denies using any strict cost per QALY threshold, an analysis of their decisions suggests a threshold of approximately $50,000 per QALY.[5] No simple inference that this is an appropriate threshold in the United States is possible, among other reasons because the United Kingdom spends less than half as much per capita on health care as does the United States. In this country the value of a statistical life typically used in evaluating safety and health regulations and programs is in the neighborhood of $6 million, and the cost per QALY threshold is around $100,000.[6]

How much does Avastin cost per QALY produced? In use for colon cancer it is taken on average for eleven months and adds five months to life. If we assume usage and benefits will be the same for lung and breast cancer, which of course they may not be, this comes to a bit over $230,000 per life year, before any quality of life adjustment. Since chemotherapy is usually continued along with Avastin and the unpleasant side effects of that treatment are substantial, any reasonable quality of life adjustment would certainly raise the cost per QALY of Avastin significantly above the cost per life year estimate of $230,000. All of these numbers and estimates are crude, but they are enough to suggest that the cost per life year or per QALY of Avastin in the treatment of breast and lung cancer will substantially exceed typical guidelines used in the evaluation of other medical and nonmedical programs that extend lives.

These rough guides for maximum costs per life year or per QALY are caps, barring special circumstances, on the justified costs of such programs. But that does not imply that it is always justified to charge these maximums. Suppose you see a stranger fall off a dock who calls for help because he can't swim. The fact that if you throw him a life ring and save him, he will experience thirty more QALYs than he would if he drowns now would not justify your charging him $100,000 per QALY, or $3 million to throw him the life ring. We have an ethical obligation to save others from loss of life when we can do so with little if any risk or cost to ourselves. Exploiting desperate circumstances to extract the full economic value of the benefit received would be wrong.

Genentech, however, is a for-profit corporation, not an individual moral agent. It might argue that it is entitled to charge whatever the market will bear for the products it develops; it has no specific obligations to patients to make its products available for less. Someone who owns a building or a piece of land has no obligation to sell for any less than the best price another is willing to pay. Likewise, if Genentech were to manufacture a drug not under patent, then it would be entitled to set the price for it, leaving the market to determine whether there were buyers and whether other producers can undercut its sales or drive down the price. In a competitive market, the price should settle at the costs of production plus a reasonable profit to the producer.

But of course the patent system for pharmaceuticals makes their market anything but competitive. As a matter of law, patents allow drug companies to charge whatever they can command, and in practice, the major purchasers of drugs in this country have limited or no ability to bargain for lower prices. That is not, however, an ethical justification for charging whatever the market will bear. Suppose we discover that Avastin combined with a very cheap older chemotherapeutic agent that is off patent is vastly more effective in the treatment of breast and lung cancer than previously thought—instead of extending life on average for five months, it extends life for five years, twelve times as long as originally thought. On Genentech's reasoning, they would now be justified in charging twelve times the $100,000 now proposed for the five months gain in life extension,

despite no increase in the costs of developing and producing the drug. But that surely is not ethically correct. Absent patent protection, Genentech would not be able to increase the price to reflect the increase in benefit. Other competitors would come into the market to sell it closer to the costs of production, which don't change when it is discovered to be far more beneficial than originally thought. Even with patent protection, insurers who could consider the drug's cost-effectiveness, either at the current proposed price or at the new higher price if it were found to be more effective, could reasonably deny coverage on grounds that it was not cost effective and exceeded their willingness to pay a limit of, say, $100,000 per QALY.

So there are two fundamental ethical problems with Genentech's defense of the price of Avastin. First, it greatly exceeds any of the usual standards for economic evaluation of life-extension. Even granting that it can justifiably be priced in terms of the economic value of extending life, it is very overpriced. Only the combination of patent protection together with purchasers' failure to consider cost-effectiveness and to bargain with Genentech will enable it to sell Avastin at the proposed price. Second, even the $100,000 standard should be understood as a cap on prices, not what is ethically justified regardless of the costs of development and production.

Drug companies' traditional justification for high drug prices—that they were needed to cover the very high costs of developing new drugs—is at least plausible in principle, even if controversies remain about what those costs really are. This new justification—that high prices reflect the value of extending life—does not stand up to even minimal scrutiny.

Notes

1. A. Berenson, "A Cancer Drug Shows Promise, at a Price That Many Can't Pay," *New York Times,* February 15, 2006.

2. Ibid.

3. S.R. Tunis, "Why Medicare Has Not Established Criteria for Coverage Decisions," *New England Journal of Medicine* 350 (2004): 2196–98.

4. M.R. Gillick, "Medicare Coverage for Technological Innovations—Time for New Criteria?" *New England Journal of Medicine* 350 (2004): 2199–203.

5. M.D. Rawlins and A.J. Culyer, "National Institute for Clinical Excellence and Its Value Judgments," *British Medical Journal* 329 (2004): 224–27.

6. W.K. Viscusi, "The Value of Risks to Life and Health," *Journal of Economic Literature* 31 (December 1993): 1912–46; W.C. Winkelmayer et al., "Health Economic Evaluations: The Special Case of End-Stage Renal Disease Treatment," *Medical Decision Making* 22 (September-October 2002): 417–30.

DAN W. BROCK, "How Much Is More Life Worth?" *Hastings Center Report* 36, no. 3 (2006): 17–19.

Brain Death Guidelines Vary at Top US Neurological Hospitals

SUSAN JEFFREY

A new survey shows wide variation in brain death guidelines among leading neurological institutions in the United States, differences that may have implications for the determination of death and initiation of transplant procedures, the researchers say.

Under the Uniform Determination of Death Act, guidelines for brain death determination can be developed at the institutional level, leading to potential variability in practice, David M. Greer, MD, from Massachusetts General Hospital, in Boston, and colleagues report. Although there are guidelines on brain death determination from the American Academy of Neurology (AAN), they are not binding at the local level.

Results of this survey, published in the January 22 issue of *Neurology*, now suggest that substantial variation is in fact present even among top US hospitals.

"It was very concerning that there was a huge mismatch between what is set forth in the practice parameters from the AAN and what is actually being stipulated at local hospitals," Dr. Greer told *Medscape Neurology & Neurosurgery* when their findings were first presented in October 2007 at the 132nd Annual Meeting of the American Neurological Association.

Although it is possible that actual performance at these hospitals is better than what is suggested by the protocols, he noted, "We have no evidence of that."

Top 50 Hospitals

For the study, the authors requested the guidelines for determination of death by brain criteria from the *US News and World Report* top 50 neurology/neurosurgery institutions in 2006. There was an 82% response rate to their request, from 41 institutions, but 3 did not have official guidelines, leaving protocols from 38 hospitals for evaluation.

The guidelines were evaluated for 5 categories of data: guideline performance, preclinical testing, clinical examination, apnea testing, and ancillary tests. They compared the guidelines directly with the AAN guidelines for consistencies and differences.

"Major differences were present among institutions for all 5 categories," the authors write. "Variability existed in the guidelines' requirements for performance of the evaluation, prerequisites before testing, specifics of the brain-stem examination and apnea testing, and what types of ancillary tests could be performed, including what pitfalls and limitations might exist."

For example, with regard to preclinical testing, it was surprising to find that the cause of brain death was not stipulated in a large number of guidelines, they note. "Of concern was the variability in the apnea testing, an area with the greatest possibility for inaccuracies, indeterminate testing, and potentially even danger to the patient," they note. "This included variability of temperature, drawing of an [arterial blood gas sample] ABG prior to testing, the proper baseline [partial pressure carbon dioxide] pCO_2, and technique for performing the test. Although a final pCO_2 level was commonly stated (most often 60 mm Hg), specific guidelines in a situation of chronic CO_2 retention, clinical instability, or inconclusive testing were commonly lacking. A surprising number (13%) of guidelines did not specify that spontaneous respirations be absent during the apnea test."

In the category of guideline performance, there was a "surprisingly low rate of involvement of neurologists or neurosurgeons in the determination." Further, the requirement that an attending physician be involved was "conspicuously uncommon."

"Given a technique with some complexity as well as potential medical-legal implications, we find it surprising that more institutions did not require a higher level or more specific area of expertise," they write.

Their findings suggest that stricter AAN guidelines may be in order, they conclude. "Given the fact that the guidelines put forth by the AAN are now 13 years old, perhaps now is the time that they be rewritten, with an emphasis on a higher degree of specific detail in areas where there is greater variability of practice. Furthermore, perhaps now there should be standards by which individual institutions are held more accountable for their closeness to, or variability from, national guidelines."

Coauthors on the study were Panayoitis Varelas, MD, PhD, and Shamael Haque, DO, from Henry Ford Hospital, in Detroit, Michigan, and Eelco Wijdicks, MD, PhD, from the Mayo Clinic, in Rochester, Minnesota.

A "Disturbing Pattern of Nonuniformity"

In an editorial accompanying the paper, James L. Bernat, MD, from Dartmouth-Hitchcock Medical Center, in Lebanon, New Hampshire, points out that Greer and colleagues have shown that "physicians declaring brain death in leading neurology departments in the United States practice with a disturbing pattern of nonuniformity."

Some of these variations are inconsequential, he notes, but some could make a serious difference in outcomes. "Practices that do not require demonstrating an anatomic lesion sufficient to explain the clinical findings, do not rigorously exclude potentially reversible metabolic and toxic factors, do not properly test brain-stem function, or do not require proper apnea testing are consequential because they could yield an incorrect determination of death," he writes.

Although brain death has to be determined correctly to maintain confidence in high-quality medical care and the organ-procurement enterprise, he writes, in addition to accuracy, "it is desirable to achieve a uniformity of practice using the optimal guidelines."

"I suggest that the AAN, the American Neurological Association, and Child Neurology Society jointly empanel a task force to draft evidence-based guidelines, including specific recommendations for conducting the clinical and confirmatory tests for brain death," Dr. Bernat continues. "Once these guidelines have been accepted and published, neurologists should act as envoys to ensure that they become incorporated into hospital policies throughout the country and help implement them locally."

This task force could also update the guidelines at intervals to accommodate emerging technologies as they are validated, such as noninvasive neuroimaging tests measuring the absence of intracranial blood flow, he writes. "The most daunting global problem of establishing worldwide uniformity of brain death guidelines is a task for the World Federation of Neurology."

Dr. Greer reports receiving speaker honoraria from Boehringer-Ingelheim Pharmaceuticals Inc. Disclosures for coauthors appear in the paper.

Criteria for a Good Death

This brief paper advances the concept of a "good death," outlines ten specific criteria for a good death, and proposes a simple golden rule for optimal dying.

EDWIN SHNEIDMAN, PhD

By almost universal common consent, death has a bad reputation. Words like awful and catastrophic are practically synonymous with death. Good and death seem oxymoronic, incompatible, mutually exclusive. Given all this, what then can it mean to speak of a good death? Are some deaths better than others? Can one plan to improve on one's death? My answer to these questions is yes, and that is what this brief paper is about.

In a previous article about a related topic (Shneidman, 1998), I discussed how *suicide*—the meaning and connotations of the A good death is one word—had palpably changed over the last 230 years. The entries on suicide traced in fifteen different editions of the *Encyclopedia Britannica* indicate that suicide has mutated from being a sin and a crime (involving the punishment of the corpse and the survivors) to being a mental health issue meriting the therapeutic and sympathetic response of others. Death is the over-arching topic of suicide and is more culturally gyroscopic, slower to change, yet subject to shifts in the cultural zeitgeist. If one begins, somewhat arbitrarily, in the Middle Ages with another related topic— courtly love, specifically courtship (DeRougemont, 1940)— one sees that there were elaborate rules for courtly love and for courtly deportment in general. The goal was to be able to do admittedly difficult tasks with seeming effortlessness and without complaint (Castiglione, 1528/1959); in other words, with grace.

The challenge for this paper is to propose some criteria for a good death—a sort of report card of death, a fantasied optimal dying scenario—and to provide a chance to debate what a good death ought to be.

There is no single best kind of death. A good death is one that is appropriate for that person. It is a death in which the hand of the way of dying slips easily into the glove of the act itself. It is in character, on camera, ego-syntonic. It, the death, fits the person. It is a death that one might choose if it were realistically possible for one to choose one's own death. Weisman (1972) has called this an appropriate death.

A decimal of criteria of a good death can be listed. The ten items include (see also Table 1):

1. *Natural.* There are four modes of death—natural, accident, suicide, and homicide (NASH). Any survivor would prefer a loved one's death to be natural. No suicide is a good death.

2. *Mature.* After age 70. Near the pinnacle of mental functioning but old enough to have experienced and savored life.

3. *Expected.* Neither sudden nor unexpected. Survivors-to-be do not like to be surprised. A good death should have about a week's lead time.

4. *Honorable.* Filled with honorifics but not dwelling on past failures. Death begins an ongoing obituary, a memory in the minds of the survivors. The Latin phrase is: *De mortuis nil nisi bonum* (Of the dead [speak] nothing but good).

5. *Prepared.* A living trust, prepaid funeral arrangements. That the decedent had given thought and made arrangements for the necessary legalities surrounding death.

6. *Accepted.* "Willing the obligatory," that is, accepting the immutables of chance and nature and fate; not raging into the night; acceding to nature's unnegotiable demands.

7. *Civilized.* To have some of your loved ones physically present. That the dying scene be enlivened by fresh flowers, beautiful pictures, and cherished music.

8. *Generative.* To pass down the wisdom of the tribe to younger generations; to write; to have shared memories and histories; to act like a beneficent sage.

9. *Rueful.* To cherish the emotional state which is a bittersweet admixture of sadness, yearning, nostalgia, regret, appreciation, and thoughtfulness. To avoid depression, surrender, or collapse; to die with some projects left to be done; by example, to teach the paradigm that no life is completely complete.

Table 1   Ten Criteria for a Good Death

Natural

A natural death, rather than accident, suicide, or homicide

Mature

After age 70; elderly yet lucid and experienced

Expected

Neither sudden nor unexpected; some decent warning

Honorable

Emphasis on the honorifics; a positive obituary

Prepared

A living trust; prearranged funeral; some unfinished tasks to be done

Accepted

Willing the obligator; gracefully accepting the inevitable

Civilized

Attended by loved ones; with flowers, pictures, and music for the dying scene

Generative

To have passed the wisdom of the tribe to younger generations

Rueful

To experience the contemplative emotions of sadness and regret without collapse

Peaceable

With amicability and love; freedom from physical pain

---

10. *Peaceable.* That the dying scene be filled with amicability and love, that physical pain be controlled as much as competent medical care can provide. Each death an ennobling icon of the human race.

I end with a sweeping question: Is it possible to formulate a Golden Rule for a good death, a maxim that has the survivors in mind? I would offer, as a beginning, the following Golden Rule for the dying scene: Do unto others *as little as possible.* By which I mean that the dying person consciously try to arrange that his or her death—given the inescapable sadness of the loss-to-be—be as little pain as humanly possible to the survivors. Along with this Golden Rule for dying there is the copperplated injunction: Die in a manner so that the reviews of your death speak to your better self (as a courtier distinguished by grace) rather than as a plebian marked by coarseness and complaint. Have your dying be a courtly death, among the best things that you ever did. It is your last chance to get your neuroses under partial control.

References

Castiglione, B. (1959). *The book of the courtier.*, trans. Charles S. Singleton. Garden City, NY: Anchor Books. Originally published in 1528.

DeRougemont, D. (1940). *Love in the western world.* Princeton, NJ: Princeton University Press.

Shneidman, E. S. (1980). *Voices of death.* New York: Harper & Row.

Shneidman, E. S. (1998). Suicide on my mind; Britannica on my table. *American Scholar,* 67(3), 93–104.

Weisman, A. (1972). *On dying and denying.* New York: Behavioral Publications.

EDWIN S. SHNEIDMAN is professor of Thanatology Emeritus, UCLA and founder of the American Association of Suicidology.

Address correspondence to Edwin S. Shneidman, 11431 Kingsland St., Los Angeles, CA 90066.

UNIT 2

Dying and Death across the Life Cycle

Unit Selections

Key Points to Consider

• With children experiencing death situations at an average age of eight years, what societal steps can be taken to help children better cope with the death of a person? What do you recall from your own childhood experiences with death? Were these experiences positive or negative?

• Coping with a dying family member or friend is certainly a challenging experience for anyone. What sources exist to aid with such a trauma in one's life? How can physicians help parents relieve misplaced guilt over the death of a newborn or a small child?

• What is the stress like for small children to have a mother or father fighting in the military overseas? How can these children be helped when that military family member dies?

• How is death depicted in Walt Disney films? Can these animated characters help children to learn about dying and death and put them in a better position to cope with these situations?

• How can caregivers to helped to lessen their "assignment" of dealing with a dying family member? What kinds of support are available for caregivers?

• What particular needs do elderly persons in a palliative care unit have?

Student Website

www.mhhe.com/cls

Internet References

CDC Wonder on the Web—Prevention Guidelines
http://wonder.cdc.gov
Children with AIDS Project
www.aidskids.org
Light for Life Foundation
www.yellowribbon.org
National SIDS Resource Center
www.sidscenter.org
Palliative Care for Children
www.aap.org/policy/re0007.html

Death is something that we must accept, though no one really understands it. We can talk about death, learn from each other, and by better understanding death conceptualization at various stages and in different relationships within the life cycle, we can help each other. It is not our intent to suggest that age should be viewed as the sole determinant of one's death concept. Many other factors influence this cognitive development, such as level of intelligence, physical and mental well-being, previous emotional reactions to various life experiences, religious background, other social and cultural forces, personal identity and self-worth appraisals, and exposure to, or threats of, death. Indeed, a child in a hospital for seriously ill children is likely more sophisticated regarding death, as she/he may be aware of dying and death, more so than an adult who has not had such experiences. Nonetheless, we discuss dying and death at various stages from the cradle to the grave or, as some say, the womb to the tomb.

Research on very young children's conceptions of death does not reveal an adequate understanding of their responses. Adults, many decades later, recall vivid details about their first death experiences, whether a pet or a person, and for many it was a traumatic event filled with fear, anger, and frustration. How might we help with such situations? "Death in Disney Films" might aid in working with children trying to understand dying and death. Additionally, "Saying Goodbye" and "Helping Military Kids Cope with Traumatic Death" are articles which address these issues. News anchor Katie Couric writes about talking to her children some ten years after the death of their father from colon cancer.

The death of a child and the death of a spouse are both in the top five list of 100 stressors that an individual has in life. The death of a child is so illogical, as the child has not lived through the life cycle. One can anticipate attending the funeral of a grandparent and then a parent. We do not, however, anticipate attending the funeral of a child, since the adult is "expected" to

© Photodisc/SuperStock

die before the child. Such is the rational sequence of the life cycle.

As individuals move into the "autumn" of their lives and are classified as "elderly," death surrounds them, and they are especially made aware that they are reaching the end of the tunnel. Though old age is often pictured as gloom and doom, it can be viewed as "the best is yet to be," as poet Robert Browning noted. The aging professional athlete Satchel Paige observed years ago that aging is really mind over matter—as long as you don't mind, it really doesn't matter. You are as old (or young) as you feel. Research suggests that the elderly are accepting of death, having lived a normal life span, and are grateful for the life they have had. Some of these issues are addressed in Wijk and Grimby's "Needs of Elderly Patients in Palliative Care." In this article the authors discuss the end-of-life needs of elderly patients in a Swedish geriatric palliative care unit.

Death in Disney Films: Implications for Children's Understanding of Death

MEREDITH COX, ERIN GARRETT, AND JAMES A. GRAHAM

Introduction

Death is an aspect of life that is not only inevitable but also painful, especially for children. Children do not have the knowledge or experience that adults have; thus, they are often unprepared to deal with the death of a loved one or even of a beloved cartoon character in a movie. Furthermore, it is not until about 10 years of age that healthy children achieve an understanding that death is irreversible, permanent, and inevitable (Brent, Speece, Lin, Dong, & Yang, 1996).

If death is a concept that many young children do not have a working understanding of, then why is it such a prominent theme in children's media, specifically in Disney movies? Do Disney's portrayals influence children's comprehension of death? The current content analysis describes and analyzes the portrayal of death in selected animated Disney films. In order to examine the possible affect that death scenes in Disney films might have for children, it is necessary to understand how children conceive of death.

Children's Understanding of Death

Many of the classic Disney movies target young audiences who do not have very developed or accurate concepts of death. For instance, many children younger than five years old do not understand that death is final, and inevitable (Grollman, 1990; Speece & Brent, 1984). Between the ages of five and nine, children who do acknowledge the permanence and inevitability of death see death as something that only applies to older adults (Grollman, 1990; Speece & Brent, 1984). Some children who do not have a complete understanding of death often will fill in gaps in understanding with fantasy elements (Baker, Sedney, & Gross, 1992), which may be taken from the media that children view, such as Disney movies. If the media, specifically some Disney films, convey unrealistic messages about death, then aspects of those portrayals are likely to be internalized by children. These less than desirable notions about death may have an impact on how children will view later instances of death.

In general, children's comprehension of death depends on two factors: experience and developmental level. First, children's experiences with death (i.e., actual experience and what they have been told about death) are critical to their understanding of death (Speece & Brent, 1984). Second, the developmental level of the child also must be taken into account when examining the comprehension of death (Brent et al., 1996; Willis, 2002). For example, Willis pinpointed four aspects of death that children and adults do not view in the same way: irreversibility, finality, inevitability, and causality. Children may not understand that death is permanent and that it cannot be "fixed" or reversed. They also do not have enough life experience to realize that death is inevitable for all living things. Furthermore, because they do not think abstractly, some young children do not understand the causality of death.

There is much support to the idea that children have a very limited understanding of death (e.g., Baker et al., 1992; Brent et al., 1996; Grollman, 1990; Speece & Brent, 1984; Willis, 2002), and the partial understanding they do have is often based on fuzzy logic (Brent et al., 1996). Brent et al. found that most children do not fully understand that death is a universal, irreversible, and nonfunctional state (meaning that dead beings cannot do the things that the living do) until the age of 10 years. Interestingly, it was also found that even after children reach this level of understanding they might continue to struggle with the idea that death is final, possibly because of certain religious beliefs. However, this may suggest a more mature understanding of death rather than a less mature one (Brent et al., 1996). Children with immature, binary concepts of death see people as either alive or dead, and do not consider the idea that there may be any other options based on religious values and ideas about afterlife.

According to Baker et al. (1992), the process of grieving after a loss and coming to understand death is a process that consists of psychological tasks that children progress through to eventually overcome their grief. The first stage involves *understanding what death is,* knowing its characteristics, and being able to recognize when it has happened. At this stage, it is important for children to feel self-protected, meaning that they need to know that just because someone or something has died does not mean the child or his or her family is in any immediate danger.

The middle phase involves *understanding that death is a reality and accepting the emotions that come along with that realization.* This may include reflecting on times spent with the deceased loved one and coming to terms with the fact that he or she is gone while still maintaining memories and an internal connection to that person. Thus, we should not give children the false hope that a loved one may "come back" after death, and we should not discourage them from remaining emotionally attached to the deceased individual (Baker et al., 1992). This phase shows a marked difference in the way that children and adults grieve. Many adults move through the process more quickly than children do because they may understand and have more actual experience with the concept of death. Thus, many adults do not have to spend as much time figuring out what has happened when a loved one is suddenly gone, as would a child.

The last phase of this process involves a *reorganization of a child's sense of identity and his or her relationships with others and with the environment.* The child will also be able to invest emotionally him- or herself in relationships with others without being overly afraid of losing that person to a death. At this stage, a well-adjusted child still remembers the loved one without fearing excessively that others will die and is able to cope with those memories and any sadness associated with them (Baker et al., 1992).

Parents' Role in Children's Comprehension of Death

There are other reasons why children may misunderstand death beyond the obvious cognitive limitations. Many children tend not to discuss death with their parents or friends because they think the subject is too unpleasant, frightening, or even unnecessary (Wass, Raup, & Sisler, 1989). The manner in which some parents communicate with their children about death may influence the child's comprehension of it. When it comes to talking about death, a lot of parents do so in a way that is very confusing and potentially harmful to children (Ryerson, 1977; Willis, 2002). It seems that some parents' main objective shifts from explaining and teaching to *protecting.* For instance, rather than telling children why and how people die they may focus on downplaying the emotionality, seriousness, and reality of death.

Though their intentions are good, many adults often hinder children's understanding of death by using confusing terms and abstract language to explain the concept to them. They may say that someone has "passed away," which does not convey a realistic portrayal of death to children (Willis, 2002). They may use euphemisms (such as "sleeping for a long time" or "taken a long trip") in an attempt to downplay the impact of death in order to protect children, which only serves to confuse them. These phrases convey to the young child that the loved one who has "passed away" may "wake up" from their long nap or "come home" from their voyage (Willis, 2002). Furthermore, describing death to children as a long "sleep" is not only confusing but may foster a fear of going to sleep among children (Grollman, 1990).

Ryerson (1977) points out that sometimes parents avoid the topic of death altogether and are very awkward about discussing it with children. Many parents' hesitation to talk to children about death in a straightforward way likely stems from their own fears of death, which may have origins in the way that their own parents spoke to them about it. The implication is that this matter-of-fact manner of explaining death is likely to perpetuate a cycle of faulty communication between parents and children. Ryerson describes the mourning process in children as well as ways to help children cope with death. The use of fairy tales may be a source of identification and interest for children, and they can be used to facilitate discussion between children and adults about death and grieving.

The fairy tale has served as the most honest and clear-cut managing of death available to children over the ages (Dobson, 1977). According to Dobson (1977), its main purpose is to stimulate children's intellect and help them tackle their "darkest and scariest thoughts about separation, rejection, abandonment, and death" (p. 175). Fairy tales often contain non-threatening references to death, which makes them appropriate for use with children. Fairy tales, many of which have inspired many Disney films, present interesting and somewhat controversial portrayals of death and grieving.

Popular Children's Films, Children's Grieving Processes, and Death Education

The present study is an exploratory analysis of death from animated Disney movies. In general, there is limited research that examines the relationship between popular children's films and children's comprehension of death. For instance, Sedney (1999) examined the portrayal of grief in young characters in children's films. The films all had hopeful messages showing the possibility for a happy life following the death of a loved one. However, the films showed differing degrees of grieving. Sedney points out that sometimes deaths are unacknowledged completely, which is an aspect that is common to children's films, especially among those with missing parents. In other cases, there is an acknowledgment of death, but it is not grieved, as in *Bambi.* In contrast, in *The Lion King,* death *is* acknowledged and the young character grieves and displays a gamut of typical grieving emotions ranging from self-blame and anger to profound sadness. Sedney describes the merits of *The Lion King's* grief portrayal because it offers a realistic view of grief as well as a resolution to sadness. For this reason, this particular film has the potential to be an effective teaching tool to serve as a basis of discussion on the topic of death with children.

In contrast with Sedney (1999, 2002) who found positive aspects of portrayals of death in children's films, Schultz and Huet (2001) examined the highest grossing American films and Academy Award nominees and concluded that the majority of portrayals of death are unrealistic and sensational, and are rarely accompanied by realistic and normal grief reactions. This was true about some children's films as well. Many of the films did not either acknowledge death or use "death terminology," lending further support to the idea that our culture has taboos about discussing death in a straightforward manner

(Schultz & Huet, 2001). Interestingly, Schultz and Huet point out that the Motion Picture Association of America (MPAA) does not distinguish between types of violence and death when considering ratings, which also affects audiences, and most notably children.

As previously emphasized, the amount of research done on the media's influence on children's understanding of death is very limited. Many death educators propose some form of death education for children (Wass et al., 1989). How is this education to be initiated? We propose that using popular animated Disney films may be one way to intervene and may provide a foundation for discussion between children and adults about death. Specifically, we examined the portrayal of death and grieving in Disney films geared toward children, focusing on five factors: character status, depiction of death, death status, emotional reaction, and causality.

Method
Film Selection
The analyzed content consists of 10 Disney Classic animated full-length feature films. The movies were selected only if a death occurred or was a theme in the plotline. The movies were chosen from various decades in order to sample the portrayal of death across time in Disney films. The first animated Disney full-length feature film was released approximately 60 years ago; thus, films were selected from both the first 30 years of production (pre-1970s) and from the last 30 years (post-1970s). Due to a lack of full-length films with death scenes released before the 1970s, only three movies were selected from that period, whereas seven were selected from more recent decades. This limited selection could also be attributed to the fact that full-length animated Disney movies were released on an average of three per decade in the past, whereas 14 were released in the 1980s and 1990s. The films were not chosen haphazardly; rather, the researchers went through the plot outlines of all animated Disney Classic films and chose from that list, being careful to select both older classics and more modern films that children are familiar with today. The movies examined for this study were: *Snow White and the Seven Dwarfs* (1937), *Bambi* (1942), *Sleeping Beauty,* (1959), *The Little Mermaid* (1989), *Beauty and the Beast* (1991), *The Lion King* (1994), *The Hunchback of Notre Dame* (1996), *Hercules* (1997), *Mulan* (1998), and *Tarzan* (1999).

Coding Categories
Two coders watched the movies together and coded the data individually. Each character's death was analyzed by the following five coding criteria.

Character Status
This category refers to the role the character that died played in the plot. We coded for two different types of characters. First, a *protagonist* is a character that is seen as the "good guy," hero/heroine of the movie, or the main character whom the story revolves around. An *antagonist* is a character who is seen as the "bad guy," villain, nemesis, or enemy of the protagonist.

Depiction of Death
Refers to how the character's death was shown in the film. In an *explicit death* the audience sees that the character is definitely dead because the body is shown being physically damaged/killed and/or the dead, motionless body is shown on screen. An *implicit death* refers to one in which the audience can only assume that the character is dead based on the fact that they do not appear again in the film and/or that they have encountered something that would presumably result in death. Examples include seeing a shadow of a dead body or a character falling off a cliff. *Sleep death* refers to an instance in which a character falls into a state of prolonged sleep. Generally, this is the result of a spell due to an original intent to kill.

Death Status
This category refers to if a death was a true end of life or if it was shown as something negotiable that does not necessarily represent the absolute end of life. A *permanent/final* death is one in which the character does not return in any form. A *reversible* death is one where a character returns in one of two ways. A *reversible-same form* death is one in which the character seemingly comes back from a dead or seemingly dead state in his or her original body. In a *reversible-altered form* death, the character returns either in a physically transformed state or in the form of a spirit.

Emotional Reaction
Refers to how the other characters in the movie responded to or dealt with death. *Positive emotion* refers to a character or characters being visibly happy (e.g., smiling, cheering) or showing signs of relief. *Negative emotion* refers to a character or characters reacting with frustration, remorse, anger, or with general signs of sadness (e.g., crying). *Lacking emotion* refers to characters reacting to death as if it is inconsequential or the death is not dealt with or acknowledged by all characters.

Causality
Causality refers to what led to or caused the death and whether the death was portrayed as being justified or unjustified. In a *purposeful* death, a character dies as the result of another character's intent to harm or kill him or her. An *accidental* death refers to one where the death was unintentional and was the result of an unplanned event. In addition to being either purposeful or accidental, death events were also coded as being either *justified* or *unjustified*. *Justified* deaths were ones in which the character who died had done something that warranted punishment; the general message conveyed was that they "deserved" to die. *Unjustified* deaths were ones in which the character did not do anything wrong; there was a sense that they did not deserve to die.

Intercoder Reliability
Two coders rated the selected films. Intercoder reliability was judged as acceptable if the raters achieved more than 70% agreement on all categories, using Cohen's Kappa. The reliability between coders was tested on a randomly selected subsample of

Table 1   Depiction of Death by Character Type

Depiction of Death	Protagonist	%	Antagonist	%	Total
Explicit death	7	63.64	4	36.36	11
Implicit death	3	30.0	7	70.0	10
Sleep death	2	100.0	0	0	2
Total	12	52.17	11	47.83	23

Note. Percentages are row percentages.

Table 2   Death Status by Character Types

Death Status	Protagonist	%	Antagonist	%	Total
Reversible/Same	4	100	0	0	4
Reversible/Altered	2	100	0	0	2
Permanent/Final	7	41.18	10	58.82	17
Total	13	56.52	10	43.48	23

Note. Percentages are row percentages.

four films (40% of the sample). Intercoder reliability was computed for each of the five categories of interest: character status ($K = 1.00$), depiction of death ($K = 0.92$), death status ($K = 1.00$), emotional reaction ($K = 1.00$), and causality ($K = 0.87$).

Results

Our study examined the portrayal of death and grieving in Disney films geared toward children, and focused on five factors.

Character Status

A total of 23 death scenes occurred in the 10 Disney films analyzed. Protagonists and antagonists were portrayed nearly equally in those scenes. Out of the 23 characters who died, 52% were protagonists ($n = 12$) and 48% ($n = 11$) were antagonists (see Table 1).

Depiction of Death

Implicit death accounted for 43% of total deaths ($n = 10$) and explicit death ($n = 11$) accounted for 48%. We found that 64% of explicit deaths occurred among protagonists ($n = 7$) while only 36% of explicit deaths were the deaths of antagonists ($n = 4$). In contrast, implicit deaths occurred more among antagonists: 70% of antagonists died in implicit death scenes ($n = 7$), whereas only 30% of protagonists did ($n = 3$). Sleep death was not nearly as common as "real" death portrayals, occurring in 9% of death instances ($n = 2$). Both sleep deaths occurred among protagonists (see Table 1).

Death Status

A large majority of deaths (74%) were portrayed as permanent, final, and irreversible ($n = 17$). Out of the permanent deaths, 59% were those of antagonists ($n = 10$) and 41% were

protagonists ($n = 7$). Reversible death occurred in 26% of death scenes ($n = 6$). Of the six reversible deaths, 67% ($n = 4$) of characters returned in their same form and 33% ($n = 2$) reappeared in altered forms. All of the reversible deaths were among protagonists (see Table 2).

Emotional Reaction

In terms of reactions to a character's death, the most prevalent type of emotion displayed by characters was negative emotion, which occurred in 48% of death scenes ($n = 11$). Negative emotions included typical grieving responses such as fear, crying, and expressing anger or frustration over a loss. Out of the negative emotional responses, 91% ($n = 10$) were for the deaths of protagonists, whereas only 9% ($n = 1$) resulted from the death of an antagonist. Positive emotion, indicated by happiness, relief, or celebration of a loss, occurred in only 13% of deaths ($n = 3$). Positive emotion resulted solely from the deaths of antagonists.

Interestingly, neutral or lacking emotion occurred in 39% of death scenes ($n = 9$), which is nearly as frequently as grieving/negative emotion did. The majority of instances of lacking emotion (78%) were associated with the deaths of antagonists ($n = 7$), whereas only 22% of protagonist deaths resulted in neutral or lacking emotion ($n = 2$) (see Table 3).

Causality

Purposeful deaths occurred most frequently, i.e., 70% ($n = 16$) of all deaths. Out of these purposeful deaths, 38% ($n = 6$) were justified and 62% ($n = 10$) were unjustified. Accidental deaths made up 30% of total deaths ($n = 7$). Out of accidental deaths, 71% ($n = 5$) were justified and 29% ($n = 2$) were seen as unjustified. When justification was considered, regardless of motivation or cause of death, it was found that the respective prevalences of justified and unjustified deaths were nearly

21

Table 3   Emotional Reactions by Character Type

Emotional Reaction	Protagonist	%	Antagonist	%	Total
Positive emotion	0	0	3	100	3
Negative emotion	10	90.9	1	9.1	11
Lacking emotion	2	22.22	7	77.78	9
Total	12	52.17	11	47.83	23

Note. Percentages are row percentages.

Table 4   Cause of Death by Character Type

Cause of Death	Protagoniste	%	Antagonist	%	Total
Accidental–justified	0	0	5	100	5
Accidental–unjustified	2	100	0	0	2
Purposeful–justified	0	0	6	100	6
Purposeful–unjustified	10	100	0	0	10
Total	12	52.17	11	47.83	23

Note. Percentages are row percentages.

equal: justified deaths accounted for 48% of all deaths ($n = 11$) and unjustified deaths accounted for 52% of deaths ($n = 12$).

When both aspects of the causality category were considered together (purposeful/accident and justified/unjustified), the following was found: all purposeful, justified deaths resulted in the death of an antagonist ($n = 6$), and all purposeful, unjustified deaths were those of the protagonists ($n = 10$). All of the accidental, justified deaths were to antagonists ($n = 5$) and the accidental, unjustified deaths were to all protagonists ($n = 2$) (see Table 4).

Discussion

The purpose of our content analysis was to examine the depiction of death in Disney movies. Based on the content analysis of 23 death scenes in 10 Disney films, several trends were observed. Each of the five aspects of death portrayals is discussed separately.

Character Status

The deaths shown in the films were comprised of almost equal numbers of protagonists and of antagonists. This demonstrates a fair distribution of the portrayal of "good" and "bad" characters, showing that both character types are susceptible to death. Many children viewing these scenes receive the message that even good characters that we care about may also die (Brent et al., 1996; Willis, 2002).

Depiction of Death

The depictions of explicit and implicit deaths were fairly equal. Explicit deaths were seen more in scenes where protagonists died. This can be viewed as a positive point because these scenes demonstrate real, explicit deaths of characters to whom the viewer has developed an attachment. However, this can be potentially traumatic for some children because they actually must witness a death. An example is seen in *The Lion King,* where a child must watch as Mufasa is thrown to his death.

The fact that implicit deaths occurred mostly among antagonists may send the message that their deaths are inconsequential in comparison to those of the protagonists. This can perhaps be seen as negative due to the fact that the antagonists' deaths are often merely implied (rather than being explicitly described).

Though sleep deaths only occurred twice out of 23 total deaths, it is important to discuss the implications of this type of portrayal. The sleep deaths occurred in two older films: *Sleeping Beauty* and *Snow White,* which is likely due to the fact that before the 1970s presenting death to audiences in animated films was not considered as big of an issue as it is today. Instead, the issue was dealt with through the use of the sleep deaths, in which spells meant to incur death were magically altered to produce only sleep in characters, rather than death. The fact that sleep deaths did not occur in Disney films released post-1970s may be an indication that children's exposure to death has increased and is now a somewhat less taboo issue in our society.

Death Status

The majority of deaths shown in the selected Disney films were permanent. This is a positive message because it enforces the idea that death is a permanent phenomenon, a concept that many young children do not fully grasp (Baker et al., 1992; Brent et al., 1996; Grollman, 1990; Willis, 2002). Seeing this in Disney films might help some children develop this understanding sooner. However, if they are left unaided in understanding these scenes, they may be upset at the permanence of death. Therefore, because many young children lack the cognitive abilities and experiences required to comprehend the concept of death fully, it is important for parents or teachers to guide them through the processes of learning about death.

Of the deaths that occurred, only six were shown as reversible. All of these reversible deaths occurred among protagonists, showing that antagonists or "bad guys" do not get a second chance at life, at least in some Disney films. Protagonists, on the other hand, fare much better. Half of the protagonists that had died in all 10 films "came back" in some way. An example of a scene that represents this concept is one in which Mufasa returns to communicate with Simba in *The Lion King*. This shows many children that loved ones can always be a part of them, even after death. However, young children may confuse this idea with the notion that the deceased may actually return (Worden & Silverman, 1996).

Emotional Reaction

In terms of emotion shown over death, almost all of the negative emotion was shown as a result of protagonist's deaths. This may provide some children who lack experience with death with a model of grieving (Baker et al., 1992). Presumably, when children see characters grieve and show sadness or frustration over the deaths of loved ones, they may learn that these are acceptable and normal behaviors.

Positive emotional reactions to death occurred solely for antagonists. However, this was not common; the deaths of only three "bad guys" resulted in positive emotion such as visible happiness and relief over their deaths. Most of the deaths that lacked any real emotional reactions were those of antagonists. This shows that the death of a character that is disliked may not warrant clapping and cheering but that it is not worth recognizing it at all. In addition, when one of these deaths *is* acknowledged, it is done in a positive and celebratory manner.

Causality

It was found that all of the justified deaths within the 10 Disney films were those of antagonists. This further demonstrates the trend in Disney films to vilify the antagonists to a point where they are seen as deserving their death. Along the same lines, all unjustified deaths were those of protagonists, showing that good characters never deserve to die.

The deaths of antagonists often result from accidents. However, we are made aware by the films that the antagonists deserve to die because they have done negative things, usually to a protagonist. The fact that they die accidentally allows them to "get what they deserve" while still allowing the protagonists to look good. In other words, protagonists are too good to kill others; thus, the antagonists must die accidentally. For example, in *Beauty and the Beast,* Gaston (the antagonist) stabs the Beast (the protagonist). The Beast, writhing in pain, "accidentally" causes Gaston to lose his balance on the castle tower, which results in Gaston falling to his implied death. When protagonists died, antagonists most often purposely killed them. This further demonstrates the evil of the antagonists.

Conclusions

The purpose of this content analysis was to examine how death is depicted in Disney films. This study is limited in scope, but it serves as a good starting point for the work of others in the area of animated film and children's understanding of death. We are not making conclusive statements about the effects of media on actual children; however, we are suggesting possibilities worth further examination. Our conclusions, based on the content analysis of 10 Disney films containing 23 death scenes, indicate that Disney's portrayal of death may be both good and bad; yet they can serve as effective learning tools for children. Some portrayals of death in Disney films send ambiguous messages about death and may be confusing to many young children. As stated earlier, some young children do not have the cognitive ability or experience to understand death fully (Brent et al., 1996; Speece & Brent, 1984; Willis, 2002). Furthermore, many animated Disney films contain moral implications. The results from this content analysis indicate that the antagonists ("bad guys") deserve to die. These aspects of death in the film may serve as discussion points for parents to talk about their own family's beliefs and morality.

These films may give children something to relate to when they are experiencing a loss. Watching films in which characters die may help children understand real death in a way that is less traumatic and threatening. Based on many of the movie scenes, children may better learn how to deal with death in terms of grieving and understanding what has happened when someone or something dies.

Depictions of death may also serve as springboards for discussion between children and adults about death. As previously mentioned, many parents try to downplay the severity and reality of death when discussing it with children (Grollman, 1990; Ryerson, 1977; Willis, 2002). However, using Disney movies may be a more comfortable way of discussing this difficult topic for both parents and children. Even films with unrealistic messages about death can be used as tools for pursuing discussion about death. Parents can watch Disney films with their children and verbally walk them through a death scene, deconstructing aspects that may be unrealistic and clarifying points that are exaggerated or confusing. This idea of using Disney films to discuss death can be extended to educational and counseling settings as well.

Though our content analysis provides interesting insight into the portrayal of death in Disney films, there are some limitations of this study that should be addressed. First, because the current study focused solely on Disney movies that were known to contain death, our sampling method was one of convenience. Future research may benefit from examining a wider variety of children's media. In addition, due to the small sample of films, the results may not generalize to other animated features. Continuing studies should be done on other types of animated films besides Disney movies.

Further studies may be done utilizing concrete hypotheses based on current findings. The findings from this and future studies can be used to implement new ways of educating children about death, both in home and counseling settings, possibly using Disney films as springboards for discussion. It may also be interesting to examine the next wave of Disney films, as they are released, to determine whether Disney's past and current trends in death portrayals remain the same. Although findings in this area may someday enlighten the creators of Disney movies to their potential to impact children's conceptions of death.

References

Baker, J. E., Sedney, M. A., & Gross, E. (1992). Psychological tasks for bereaved children. *American Journal of Orthopsychiatry, 62,* 105–116.

Brent, S. B., Speece, M. W., Lin, C., Dong, Q., & Yang, C. (1996). The development of the concept of death among Chinese and U.S. children 3–17 years of age: From binary to "fuzzy" concepts? *Omega: The Journal of Death and Dying, 33,* 67–83.

Dobson, J. (1977). Children, death, and the media. *Counseling and Values, 21*(3), 172–179.

Grollman, E. A. (1990). *Talking about death: A dialogue between parent and child* (3rd ed.). Boston: Beacon Press.

Ryerson, M. S. (1977). Death education and counseling for children. *Elementary School Guidance and Counseling, 11,* 165–174.

Schultz, N. W., & Huet, L. M. (2001). Sensational! Violent! Popular! Death in American movies. *Omega: The Journal of Death and Dying, 42,* 137–149.

Sedney, M. A. (1999). Children's grief narratives in popular films. *Omega: The Journal of Death and Dying, 39,* 315–325.

Sedney, M. A. (2002). Maintaining connections in children's grief narratives in popular film. *American Journal of Orthopsychiatry, 72,* 279–288.

Speece, M. W., & Brent, S. B. (1984). Children's understanding of death: A review of three components of a death concept. *Development, 55,* 1671–1686.

Wass, H., Raup, J. L., & Sisler, H. H. (1989). Adolescents and death on television: A follow-up study. *Death Studies, 13,* 161–173.

Willis, C. A. (2002). The grieving process in children: Strategies for understanding, educating, and reconciling children's perceptions of death. *Early Childhood Education Journal, 29,* 221–226.

Worden, J. W., & Silverman, P. R. (1996). Parental death and the adjustment of school-age children. *Omega: The Journal of Death and Dying, 33,* 91–102.

Saying Goodbye

Sooner or later, you'll have to explain the concept of death to your child. Our guide will make it easier to find the right words.

CHRISTINA FRANK

When her great-uncle died a couple of years ago, my daughter Lucy, then 4, took it pretty well. And she seemed to really grasp what death meant. Or so I thought. A few days after the memorial service, she began peppering me with questions: "When will Uncle Jerry be undead?" "Where did he go?" "Now that he died, will he be born again?"

I didn't know what to say. And I'm far from the only parent who has stammered her way through an awkward conversation on the topic. "Death is very difficult for young children to understand, and it can be tough to explain," says *Parents* advisor David Fassler, M.D., clinical professor of psychiatry at the University of Vermont College of Medicine, in Burlington. The best advice: Keep your answers as short and simple as possible, and use these responses as a model.

Q: My 4-year-old keeps asking me, "Mommy, why did Grandma die?" What should I say?

A: When a little kid asks such a big question, you may be tempted to soft-pedal the truth. Don't do it: Telling him that "Grandma went to sleep" or "We lost Grandma" will only backfire. "You might confuse your child or even make him afraid to go to sleep at night," says Dr. Fassler.

Instead, say something like, "Your grandma died because she was very old and sick. She doesn't talk or eat or breathe anymore, and we won't see her again. But the love we had for her will stay with us forever." If it helps, you can compare a person's life to a tree's leaves, which bloom in the spring, then change color and die in the fall.

When Donna Maria Johnson's father died, she told her kids, Vanessa, then 5, and Brooks, then 3, that when people get very old, their bodies stop working, just like when a toy's batteries run out. "But then I explained that you can't replace a person's batteries," says the mom from Charlotte, North Carolina. "That made sense to them."

Q: My father died recently, and my daughter wants to know where he is now. What should I say?

A: That depends upon your religious beliefs. "For many families, heaven is an important source of comfort," says Greg

---

Am I Going to Die, Mommy?

When a young child hears that someone died, it's natural for him to wonder whether he'll die too. When he asks, respond honestly but gently. You might say, "Everybody dies eventually, but most people live for a long, long time, and I'm sure you will too." Let him know that you'll do everything in your power to keep him safe and healthy. Your child may also start worrying about your well-being. If he does, say something like, "Honey, I plan to live a very long time—until you're a grown-up with kids of your own."

Adams, director of the Center for Good Mourning at Arkansas Children's Hospital, in Little Rock. But don't introduce it too early: The notion of a person being dead physically but alive in a spiritual place is too abstract for most kids under age 5. "Until they are ready, heaven can wait," Adams says.

You can also let your child decide for herself about the afterlife. Say something like, "No one knows for sure. Some people think you go to heaven when you die, while others believe people come back on earth as different creatures. What do you think?"

Q: My aunt is dying. Should I take my 5-year-old with me to visit her in the hospital?

A: Ask him if he'd like to go, suggests Donna Swain, a clinical bereavement counselor at the Center for Grief and Loss at Stella Maris Hospice, in Timonium, Maryland. Since seeing a sick person in the hospital can be scary—will she be hooked up to tubes and IVs? will she be able to talk?—prepare your child beforehand.

When Michael Zacharias's sister Lynne was diagnosed with non-Hodgkin's lymphoma, his two daughters, who were 5 and 3 at the time, visited her weekly. "They saw her decline gradually, so it wasn't such a shock," says the Glen Allen, Virginia, dad. "My wife, Melissa, and I explained that Aunt Lynne would lose her hair and later on that she might not be able to talk. But Lynne's eyes lit up every time we came, and I think seeing her disease progress made it easier for the girls to accept her death."

Q: Since my mother died, I've been crying a lot. Will it harm my kids to see me like this?

A: No. Watching Mommy break down might frighten your kids, but only for a moment. And it will also teach them an important lesson: Adults cry when they're very sad too. So if you can't leave the room to be by yourself, sob away. Just make sure they know you're okay and that you'll take care of them like you always do.

Clare Leschin-Hoar faced this situation when her father died of lung cancer when her children were 7 and 4. "I didn't try to hide my grief," says the Mansfield, Massachusetts, mom. "I wanted them to see how much I loved and missed my dad." To her surprise, the kids wound up comforting her, which eased her sadness.

Q: My brother is taking his kids to our uncle's funeral, but mine are only 5 and 2. What should I do?

A: Use your judgment. Although kids may bring comfort to grieving relatives, they can also be disruptive at funerals. It's unrealistic to expect children under 6 to sit quietly through a service. So if they go, take along a friend or a sitter who can watch them and focus on their needs and reactions. "This will make it easier for your kids," says Dr. Fassler.

You should also factor in the likely atmosphere of the ceremony. If it's for someone who died young or unexpectedly, the intense emotions may be difficult for your child to handle. But if the person lived a long, happy life, the mood will probably be a lot lighter. If you decide to let your child attend, give him a preview: "Everyone who loved Uncle Steve wants to remember all the great things about him. That's what a funeral is for."

Connor Shinberger went to her great-grandmother's funeral when she was almost 4. "We told her that she had to be quiet, just like in church, and that we would probably cry, because we're sad that Grandma Roxy isn't with us anymore," says her mom, Darcie, from Macomb, Illinois. "She asked if Grandma would know we were there, and I explained that we would only see her body, because her soul went to heaven to live with Grandpa and keep watch over us. She seemed to accept that pretty easily, and she behaved very well."

Q: My 7-year-old daughter is heartbroken over losing our beloved cat. How should we pay tribute?

A: For a child, losing a pet can be as emotional as saying good-bye to a close relative, if not more so. Holding a funeral or making a memorial book with pictures, drawings, and even the animal's collar can be a great way to help her gain closure, says Swain.

Lisa Waller's children were devastated when their dog, Rhett, had to be put to sleep. "We made Jack, who was 6, and Rachel, who was 3, a special album with photos of them together with Rhett," says the Marietta, Georgia, mom. "This helped them remember the wonderful times they had with him."

Although she was tempted to get a new pet right away, Waller felt it was important for her kids to face Rhett's loss rather than simply replacing him. "But Santa brought stuffed-animal boxer pups for both children for Christmas," she says. "Jack sleeps with his every night and calls him Rhett."

Helping Military Kids Cope with Traumatic Death

LINDA GOLDMAN, MS, LCPC, FT

Ordinary fears are a normal part of a child's developmental growth, and children create internal and external mechanisms to cope with these fears. But a child's ordinary fears can be transformed into very real survival fears in the face of severe trauma. After children experience the death of a parent, they often feel alone and different. Frightened because their once comfortable world now seems unpredictable and unsafe, they may react in ways that we as adults can truly not judge, understand, or anticipate. The impact of a dad's or mom's death in the military can be so traumatically disturbing that the terror involved with the death and the way the parent died may override a child's ability to grieve in a natural way, and share sadness and frustration.

Events can cause panic, stress, and extreme anxiety in kids' lives, and the feelings are heightened with each new instance reported in the media. The terror that grips our children in these circumstances emerges from situations that suddenly overwhelm them and leave them feeling helpless, hopeless, and unable to cope. Trauma is defined by the Encarta® World English Dictionary as "an extremely distressing experience that causes severe emotional shock and may have long-lasting psychological effects." This unexpected and shocking event destroys a child's ability to cope and function in a normal way.

Children can suffer from a state of trauma that can develop into Post-Traumatic Stress Disorder, in which present events trigger memories of trauma resulting in panic, anxiety, disorientation, fear, and all the psycho-physical feelings associated with the traumatic memory.

Signs of Traumatized Children

Seven-year-old Joey's dad was killed in Iraq. He constantly questioned Mom. "Tell me exactly what happened. Did my Dad suffer?" Joey had nightmares and regressed to bedwetting. Tyler's dad was killed by a stray bullet during military combat. His father would always tell him "Nothing can stop me from coming home." Tyler constantly worries about where the bullet hit him, did it hurt him, was he unprotected, and did he die instantly. He began having stomachaches and panic attacks, worrying his mom could get killed too. Jonathan's dad was killed in a firefight in Iraq. Instead of being honored as the son of a military hero, he was often victimized on the playground by a school bully. Jonathan kicked him and both boys were punished. His grades dropped from straight A's to F's after his dad died.

Many young people may experience physical, emotional, cognitive, and behavioral symptoms. These signals range from stomachaches and nightmares to poor grades, isolation, depression, regression, and hostility.

Caring adults need to recognize the signs of grieving and traumatized children, and they need to be aware of the techniques and resources available to help bring safety and protection back to the child's inner and outer world. For example, listening to children's thoughts and feelings, and providing a safe means of expression helps teachers, parents, and educators reinforce their ability to ensure a safe and protected environment.

Traumatized children tend to recreate their trauma, often experiencing bad dreams, waking fears, and recurring flashbacks. Young children have a very hard time putting these behaviors into any context of safety. Many withdraw and isolate themselves, regress and appear anxious, and develop sleeping and eating disorders as a mask for the deep interpretations of their trauma. Young children engage in post-traumatic play by compulsively repeating some aspect of the trauma.

The most common identifying factors that children are re-experiencing the event are play reenactment, nightmares, waking memories, and disturbing thoughts and feelings about the event. Sometimes kids avoid reminders of the traumatic event and show little conscious interest.

Many traumatized children exhibit hyper arousal by increased sleep problems, irritability, inability to concentrate, startle reactions, and regressive behaviors.

When caring adults can identify traumatized kids, they can normalize grief and trauma signs and develop ways kids can express their feelings and emotions. Parents, educators, and other caring professionals can model, present, and support comfortable ways to bring safety and protection back into kids' lives.

Young children developmentally live in an egocentric world filled with the notion that they have caused and are responsible for everything. George's dad was deployed to Iraq twice. Over and over George explained to his teacher. "It's my fault my dad died. I should have made him stay home from Iraq." Some kids may also feel survival guilt. They may think, "Why am I living when so many others have died?" Adults can reframe guilt and magical thinking from "What could I have done?" to "What can I do now?"

At-Risk Behaviors

Children may begin to exhibit at-risk behaviors after a traumatic event. The frequency, intensity, and duration of these behaviors are important factors to consider. Children may experience post-traumatic stress, revisiting the traumatic event through outside stimulus like photos, music, and the media, or by reliving the sights and sounds of the tragedy in their minds. Expect children to re-experience a degree of their original trauma on the anniversary of their parent's death.

The following behaviors may be indicators that a child may benefit from professional help:

- Sudden and pronounced change in behavior
- Threat of suicide or preoccupation with suicide, evidenced through artwork or writing
- Harmful acts to other children or animals
- Extreme confusion or incoherence
- Evidence of substance abuse—drugs, alcohol, etc.
- Sudden change of grades
- Avoidance or abandonment of friends
- Angry or tearful outbursts
- Self-destructive behavior
- Inability to eat or sleep
- Over-concern with own health or health of a loved one
- Giving away important possessions
- Sudden unexplained improvement in behavior or schoolwork
- Depression, isolation, or withdrawal

Activities That Help Kids Express Thoughts and Feelings

Helping children to establish a sense of order in an ever-changing and chaotic world is important. Not only do we want our kids to realize they are survivors of a difficult event, but they also need to know that their life still has continuity and meaning. Parents and educators working with traumatized children should keep to the daily routine as much as possible. This allows kids to feel a renewed sense of security.

Establishing family activities also has a reassuring effect on children. Preparing meals together, eating dinner as a family, reading stories aloud, or playing family games can help to reestablish a sense of normalcy to kids' lives. It is important to initiate safe places for kids to express their ideas. This can be done by finding quiet times at home, in the car, or on a peaceful walk. Being with children without distractions can produce a comfortable climate to begin dialogue. Bedtime should be a reassuring time, too. Often, this is the time children choose to talk about their worries. Parents can consider an increase in transition time, storytelling, and book reading to create a peaceful, uninterrupted nighttime environment.

Hope for the Future

The sudden death of a mom or dad in military service can shatter a child's emotional and physical equilibrium and stability. Too many boys and girls experience fear, isolation, and loneliness after a parent's traumatic death. Faced with a myriad of losses ranging from parental death, moving, change of school, reduced income level, and public mourning, many children are left in a world where they see no future and no protection.

One goal of trauma work with children is to restore safety and protection to children who have experienced the loss of a parent in combat. Another goal is to provide parents and youth workers with information, understanding, and skills related to the issues creating trauma. With these tools we can help our children become less fearful and more compassionate human beings, thereby increasing their chances of living in a future world of increased inner and outer peace.

LINDA GOLDMAN is the author of *Life and Loss, Children Also Grieve, Raising Our Children to Be Resilient,* and *Breaking the Silence: A Guide to Help Children with Complicated Grief.* She works with traumatized children in her practice near Washington, D.C. Email: Linda. goldman@verizon.net, Web: www.childrensgrief.net

Needs of Elderly Patients in Palliative Care

Helle Wijk, RN, PhD and Agneta Grimby, PhD

Europe's population is aging and more people are dying from chronic diseases. Still, the range and quality of palliative care services remain rather limited and inadequate. According to the World Health Organization, many Europeans who are terminally ill die in unnecessary pain and discomfort because their health systems lack skilled staff and do not widely offer palliative care services.

Even though evidence may be lacking and the empirical studies characterized by a high degree of heterogeneity, some important areas seem to stand out considering the elderly patient's views and needs in the terminal phase of life.[1] Assessments of quality of life have shown that the lowest scores are related to the physical domain, followed by the existential, supportive, and social domains.[2] A similar trend can be observed among people wishing to hasten death.[3] Actions to avoid nutritional and pain problems are also crucial at the end-of-life stage, as are avoiding inappropriate prolongation of dying and having a sense of control.[4]

To be able to provide high-quality palliative care, it is important for the health care staff to see and understand the special needs and wishes of the patients; however, knowledge, methods, and programs for this are sparse. The patients themselves seem not to be the one to blame.[5] On the contrary, studies have demonstrated that older people are willing to talk about death and dying in a rather spontaneous way.[6]

Existing empirical evidence on elderly patients' thoughts about death and dying has so far mostly been collected after cross-sectional, quantitative, or qualitative designs, mainly using personal interviews. Open conversations are considered the optimal way of learning about needs at the end-of-life stage. The method, however, is time consuming for daily practice, where somewhat more fixed estimates of needs may be preferred.

Identifying desires and needs of the palliative patient may provide increased quality of care. This pilot study about needs at the end of life aims at describing the individual reports from 30 elderly palliative patients on their needs and their ranking of these needs by degree of concern.

Method

Participants

Thirty consecutively chosen patients, admitted for palliative care at the Geriatric Department, Sahlgrenska University Hospital in Gothenburg, Sweden, were willing to join the study. Inclusion criteria were strength enough to perform an interview and Swedish mother tongue. Exclusion criteria were aphasia, dementia, or lack of strength. The respondents (15 men and 15 women) were an average age of 79 years (75 for men, 81 for women) and had a 50:50 background of manual labor and white-collar jobs.

The primary diagnosis was different types of cancer, with a variation of length of illness of 1 month to several years. All but 1 of the patients were admitted to the palliative unit from another health care institution. All patients signed an informed consent before they participated in the study. The study was approved by the Ethics Committee of the Faculty of Medicine, University of Gothenburg, Sweden.

Procedures

The survey included demographic data and information about reason for admittance and state of health at the time of admittance, reactions to the admittance, and awareness of illness. The information was retrieved partly through patients' files and partly through patient interviews.

Individual needs were identified by semistructured interviews by a research nurse (PhD student) at the palliative unit of the Geriatric Department at Sahlgrenska University Hospital. Most of the interviews were conducted, if possible, once a week and at daytime between 9:00 AM and 2 PM. Interview length was 20 to 30 minutes in 50%; 30% lasted 30 to 60 minutes, 2 interviews lasted for more than an hour, and 2 were very short due to the patient's fatigue.

The introductory question was "How do you feel today?" This was followed by questions about (1) the patient's ranking of important needs for the moment, (2) things in particular that the patient wanted help with at the moment, and

(3) things in particular that the patient wanted to speak about at the moment. The patient was asked to try to rank the different needs by the degree of concern. The answers were categorized according to physical, psychologic, social, and spiritual needs.

Statistical Analysis

For statistical trend tests, the Fisher exact test and permutation trend tests were used.[7] All results given refer to $P < .05$ unless otherwise stated.

Results

Most patients (61%) wanted to spend their last days in their own home, whereas the rest preferred to stay at an institution where "one would receive the best help." The most common symptoms before admission were pain, lack of appetite, anxiety, sleeplessness, fatigue, vomiting, cough, and shortness of breath (Table 1). At admission, more than 50% of the patients were not quite sure of their diagnosis; of the transition from curative to palliative care, 30% were completely sure, and 20% were completely unsure. The figures were very similar among the relatives. This was mostly due to incomplete former information, not to language or communication problems.

Before admission, 11% of the patients needed practical help with most daily services, but 20% had not been in need of any help at all. The helpers were next of kin (63%), a close friend (10%), and different people (11%). Most patients considered the help to be pretty good or good, but 5 of the patients were less satisfied. More than 50% of the patients considered it pleasant to receive professional care. A few patients felt it as a relief not being a burden to their family; 4 felt resigned or depressed.

Most interviews were experienced as less strenuous. All of the patients reported some type of need. If only 1 kind of need was reported, this was rated as a primary one. More patients ranked the physical needs as primary compared with the psychologic needs, which in turn were more important than the social needs (Table 2). Spiritual needs were only mentioned by 1 person. In the first interview, 14 patients ranked their physical needs as primary, 6 as secondary, and 2 as tertiary. Ten patients ranked their psychological needs as primary, 8 ranked them as secondary, and 1 as tertiary. Social needs were ranked as primary by 6 patients; just as many patients ranked them as secondary as well as tertiary. The rankings were equal in interviews II and III.

In the continued interviews, which comprised a reduced number of patients, the ranking changed in favor of the nonphysical dimensions of need. There was no significant trend related to the kind of need; they varied extensively from 1 interview to another. Correlation analysis on primary needs and symptoms/troubles resulted in no significant outcomes apart from nausea, which was related to physical need ($P < .025$). No significant correlations were found

Table 1 Reported/Registered Symptoms and Problems at the First Interview with 30 Patients

Symptom	Patients, n	Little	Some	Much	Missing Data
Pain	12	3	7	8	0
Shortness of breath	21	1	3	5	0
Cough	23	2	1	4	0
Vomiting	9	7	4	11	0
Loss of appetite	4	5	12	8	1
Diarrhea	20	4	4	2	0
Obstipation	15	3	7	5	0
Incontinence, fecal	25	2	3	—	0
Incontinence, urinary	21	—	2	4	3
Fever	27	—	2	1	0
Bleeding	28	1	1	—	0
Pressure sores	30	—	—	—	0
Bad smells	29	1	—	—	0
Lack of energy	16	2	4	8	0
Depression	21	6	3	—	0
Nervousness	10	10	8	2	0
Sleeplessness	17	7	3	3	0
Confined to bed	12	9	6	3	0
Caring need	4	15	7	4	0
Comatose	29	1	—	—	0
Other[a]	20	3	2	5	0

[a]unsteadiness, 5 patients; infection, cramps, swollen legs, personality change, 1 patient.

between the remaining primary needs (psychologic, social, and spiritual) and symptoms or troubles.

Physical Needs

Many of the physical needs ranked as primary were related to pain. Quotes from different patients reveal a fear of pain, which for many patients seemed to be equal to the experience of pain itself. Other types of needs of a physical character ranked as primary were often related to severe nausea or feebleness. Shortness of breath and a feeling of choking resulted in agony of death. Cough, phlegm, and oral hygiene problems were a recurrent source of irritation for some patients. The lack of opportunities for taking care of personal hygiene made some of the men and women feel in physical decay. Others complained about being cold, that they didn't get any better, or that they wanted to get well and be discharged. A few of the patients had more unusual requests of a physical character.

Table 2 Reported Primary, Secondary, and Tertiary[a] Needs of Patients at the Geriatric Palliative Ward

Interview	Respondents	Physical Needs	Psychologic Needs	Social Needs	Spiritual Needs
I	30	14-6-2	10-8-1	6-6-6	0-0-0
II	20	10-6-3	6-5-1	4-3-2	0-0-0
III	10	6-0-0	3-2-1	1-2-1	0-0-0
IV	4	2-0-1	1-2-0	1-1-0	0-0-0
V	2	2-0-0	0-1-0	0-0-0	0-0-0
VI	2	1-1-0	0-0-0	0-1-0	1-0-0
VII	1	0-0-0	1-0-0	0-1-0	0-0-0
VIII	1	0-1-0	1-0-0	0-0-1	0-0-0

[a]The combinations of figures refer to the number of patients reporting primary, secondary, and tertiary types of needs, respectively.

The physical needs of a secondary nature (ie, the second most important need) were often similar to the primary ones, which may or may not have been attended to.

Tertiary physical needs mainly concerned the feeling of feebleness. A few patients emphasized the importance of appearance and getting good food.

"I suffer from such perspirations, sometimes I'm soaking wet. To remain without any pain the rest of my days! Shortness of breath and pain make me scared. Spare me this feebleness, feels awful, may as well finish the old man."

"Don't want to be so tired [falls asleep several times during the conversation], that's the only thing!"

"I want to feel cleaner, don't even have the strength to care for my personal hygiene! My only wish is that I get to lie comfortably, but now I have been given a comfortable mattress."

"There is a draft from the fan. I get cold easily, at the same time I perspire a lot. I suffer a lot from it. The nausea is troublesome, but it comes and goes. I want my hair to grow back. The scalp is itchy from the wig and it is so hot. Some people say that the hair may turn blond and curly when it grows out, we'll have to wait and see [laughs]."

Psychologic Needs

Anxiety, uncertainty, and security were explicit and frequent primary psychologic needs among many of the patients. A feeling of longing was often directed towards their home environment, belongings, and "the ordinary" and "freedom." But at the same time, staying at home was associated with anxiety and worry. The wish for taking 1 day at a time and not having to contemplate the future occurred quite frequently.

There was a need for seclusion to get some peace and quiet, maybe to have the opportunity to see relatives, and to be freer to express emotions and reactions to the situation.

A common wish was to think back on their lives, maybe to recapitulate. Some of the patients pointed to psychosocial needs, for example, to restore broken relationships and becoming reconciled before it was too late.

Physical and psychologic fatigue often went hand-in-hand, and they often seemed to have a reciprocal effect. The power of initiative sometimes fell short, but if conquered, there was a feeling of great victory. For example, a patient who had been lying in a draft found the greatest triumph (primary need) when he succeeded at closing the vent. "I knew I could make it. One should never give up!" Worries could also be directed towards variations in psychologic functions such as memory and cognitive functioning.

The psychologic needs to find a meaning in life, feel security, or have opportunities to go out were ranked as second most important (secondary). So were also worries about the future for the spouse and other relatives. Pleasurable needs could include the opportunity to have a good meal. Moreover, there were also expressed needs for contemplating, thinking over their life and to summing up things, and finally, to having their life substantiated by telling others of what their life had been like.

Quite a few psychologic needs were given a tertiary ranking, for example, a mixed anxiety and expectation when awaiting a move to a nursing home or feeling the need to keep their private room.

"What is it going to be like? Where will I end up? What if I didn't have to worry about what the future is going to look like. Want to avoid the anxiety of feeling nauseous and vomiting all the time, don't dare to go anywhere, not even to the hairdresser."

"Want to avoid thinking ahead, just want to relax, take it easy, one day at a time."

"There is no point in wishing to see what the future holds; how my grandchildren will do in life or what is going to happen to the world. No use in worrying; better to live in the present and to take one day at a time."

"I only want to be left in peace."

"I lack the strength to both think and do things now. It's a shame."

"If only I didn't have to wait for answers about everything and being worried about people at home!"

Social Needs

The primary needs of a social nature were often associated with visits from family and close friends, reunions, and practical and economical tasks when moving back home or to a nursing home.

Social needs of a secondary nature often included, as did the primary ones, contact with or care for the family. For a few of the patients, that meant reunion or reconciliation. Practical tasks related to finances or accounting also came up as well as being given some privacy.

Social needs, which had been ranked as tertiary, were also similar to primary and secondary wishes; that is, they comprised troubles about family and finances, the longing for their relatives and privacy, but also retrieving parts of their former way of life.

"Mostly I wish to come home to friends and family. I do have to think about my wife, to help each other and to be together!"

". . . to see my brother, never told you that I have a brother, did I? I regret not staying in contact with him during all these years. But I do hear from my son now. It made me happy and moved me. But is it too late now?"

"I need to have someone to talk to about anything but illness all the time!"

"I want the caravan to be ready, cleaned and connected to the car. I need to sort my finances. I don't have a will, do I?"

"Mostly, I'm worried about the boy; what's going to happen when I'm gone. How will he do in school?"

"Want to be able to handle my bills and finances."

Spirituality

One person had a primary need of a spiritual nature. However, spiritual needs of secondary and tertiary rank did not occur.

"I've started to ponder. Ask myself if I'm religious. I've never thought about those things before, but I do now."

Discussion

During the 4 months of observation, the initial (at admission) general state seemed to be dominated by a rather extensive need for care, bad physical condition with nausea, emaciation, pain, anxiety, and feebleness. The palliative care, however, appeared to have had a rapid and intended effect on the physical troubles. Because the observations were made only at the ward, the state and needs of the patients were recorded most thoroughly during the first period after admission. A small portion of the patients could be interviewed for a longer period, a few of them until their deaths.

To have the opportunity to speak about one's fear of being in pain and to have it confirmed that pain relief could be guaranteed seemed to dominate the physical picture of need and was just as prominent as the need of pain relief itself. These findings may suggest that adequate pain relief was accomplished but that the memory of the pain itself was very dominating and strong. Perhaps it points to a need for assurance of relief of recurrent pain. However, the frequent wishes of reduced nausea and increased energy were more difficult to fulfil because of type and course of illness.

Successful pain relief and other types of palliative care may be behind the fact that a great number of psychologic needs were reported. The relief of physical needs may have facilitated the expression of needs of security when being cared for in the hospital. One patient did even admit of pleasurable aspects of life, for example, to allow oneself to long for something or somebody, or maybe to have that feeling of longing fulfilled. It could mean having satisfied the need to come back home to well-known things or being offered a good meal. Many of those who had been uneasy at the time of admission later seemed to have improved their abilities to better specify needs and wishes of psychologic nature, particularly if symptoms of the disease did not stand in the way.

Social needs bore a clear socioeconomic touch. Many patients wished to be with their life partner or children, as well as to look over and secure their future lives. To make sure there were enough pension benefits and savings for continuous care also seemed be important. Moreover, patients expressed a longing for having things taken care of. Issues that had been ignored for a lifetime were now of highest priority, maybe because the patient suspected that not much time was left.

Very few of the patients were interviewed when they were in the very final stage of their lives. Maybe that was one of the reasons why only 1 patient expressed a wish to talk about existential issues and their relation to divine powers (spiritual-existential needs). Great psychologic torment, remorse over the past, and a wish for forgiveness or understanding from significant individuals was also expressed.

Interpreting and describing a strict mapping or preference of needs in the terminal stage of life is risky, however. Depending on the state of illness, identifying and reporting needs can be difficult. Boundaries between categories of needs can become blurry, and the intensity of wishes can be hard to perceive. There may be rapid and wide variations in needs, and individual and unstable preference on wishes can vary under different circumstances.

Conclusion

Despite the limitations of the study, considering the small number of patients, certain tendencies could be noticed in the outcome. Physical pain overshadows everything, at least in the very last stage of life. Furthermore, pain seems to hinder the recognition of other psychologic, social, and spiritual needs. Merely the fear of physical pain, originating from prior experiences of pain, may be the most common feeling to be relieved from. Other important needs appear when pain and other health problems, for example, vomiting and shortness of breath, no longer generate fear of death. The feeling of security mediated by the presence of loved ones, as well as worries about their future, seems to occupy a severely ill person's mind even during the last days of his or her life.

The study was small, and the results may not be accurate for all types of palliative units; however, it did seem to confirm former, unrecorded observations of the priorities of needs among our patients. We intend to repeat the study including a larger number of patients to further investigate end-of-life needs.

Notes

1. Hallberg, RI. Death and dying from old people's point of view. A literature review. *Aging Clin Exp Res.* 2004;16:87–103.
2. Lo RS, Woo J, Zhoc KC, et al. Quality of life of palliative care patients in the last two weeks of life. *J Pain Symp Man.* 2002;24:388–397.
3. Kelly B, Burnett P, Pelusi D, Badger S, Varghese F, Robertson M. Terminally ill patients' wish to hasten death. *Palliat Med.* 2002;16:339–345.
4. Singer PA, Martin DK, Kelner M. Quality end-of-life care: patients' perspectives. *JAMA.* 1999;281:163–168.
5. Ottosson JO. *The Patient-Doctor Relationship* [Swedish]. Stockholm, Sweden: *Natur och Kultur.* 1999:282–308.
6. Thomé B. *Living with Cancer in Old Age: Quality of Life and Meaning.* Thesis. Lund University, Faculty of Medicine; 2003.
7. Cox DR, Hinkley DV. *Theoretical Statistics.* London: Chapman & Hall; 1974.

From the Institute of Health and Care Sciences, Sahlgrenska Academy, University of Gothenburg and Sahlgrenska University Hospital (HW) and Department of Geriatric Medicine (AG), Sahlgrenska University Hospital, Gothenburg, Sweden.

Address correspondence to: Helle Wijk, Sahlgrenska University Hospital, Röda stråket 8, 413 45 Göteborg, Sweden; e-mail: helle .wijk@vgregion.se.

Acknowledgments—This study was facilitated by grants from the Coordinating Board of Swedish Research Councils, the Swedish Medical Research Council, Medical and Social Services Administrations, the Helge Axson Johnson Foundation, and the Hjalmar Svensson Foundation. Thanks are due to Valter Sundh, BSc, for statistical discussions and invaluable help with the data processing.

Altered States
What I've Learned about Death & Disability

Carol Levine

More than a year after the death of Terri Schiavo, discussions about her case remain highly polarized. What principles should guide decisions about people who can no longer speak for themselves? Who should make those decisions, and what do various religious traditions say about such cases? The debates may be provocative, frustrating, or both, but they usually take place on the level of theory, principle, and ideology. As a result, they often neglect the lived experience of persons with disabilities and their caregivers. As someone who has cared for a severely disabled person for nearly seventeen years, I can testify that the reality is unromantic, unpleasant, and often unrewarding. Yet I am unwilling to give it up.

In June I marked my fiftieth wedding anniversary. It was not a celebration. For the past several years I have been living with a man who is not my husband. No disapproving frowns, please. This man and I don't share the same bedroom. He has his own room, complete with hospital bed and all the trappings of a mini-clinic. This man-who-is-not-my-husband and I do share many things: children, grandchildren, a past—although not much of a future. He is my husband, although I see only glimpses of the man I married a half-century ago. It is not by chance, I think, that marriage vows place "in sickness" before "in health," because illness can undermine even longstanding, happy relationships. I do not live with this man-who-is-and-is-not-my husband because of some words I said when I was twenty-one, or because the law says I am responsible for his care, or because my religion says it is my duty. I live *with* him because after all these years I do not know how to live *without* him.

What happened to him happened to me as well. We were both in a terrible automobile accident. I was not injured, but he suffered a near-fatal brain-stem injury. He was in a coma for four months, and had to undergo painful therapy for years. As a result of medical error, his right forearm had to be amputated. He is essentially quadriplegic. Without medication he is in a state of perpetual rage, and even with it, he sometimes becomes disoriented and unreachable. With each medical crisis, we adjust to the "new normal," which is invariably a decline.

In previous generations, people with disabilities were stigmatized, and often hidden away from the outside world. Thanks to advocates for the disabled, that has changed. Inclusion rather than exclusion is the goal. This is a good and just approach, but sometimes in our enthusiasm for accommodating people with disabilities, we can overlook the real challenges these conditions impose. The mantra among advocates for the disabled is "we are all dependent and only temporarily able-bodied." True enough, but how helpful is this notion if you are, say, dependent on a mechanical respirator, not just on the ties that bind a family or a neighborhood? Or, more prosaically, if you are kept waiting on a rainy street corner for a wheelchair-accessible van while the "temporarily able-bodied" jump in cabs?

Accommodations notwithstanding, major disabilities are inherently limiting, in different ways for different people. This is particularly true for people who suffer from cognitive disorders. In *Rescuing Jeffrey,* the story of his seventeen-year-old son's devastating spinal-cord injury, Richard Galli writes: "Jeffrey,' I said, 'you are not your legs. Jeffrey is up here.' I tapped his head. 'Jeffrey is up here, and that means you are still here, all of you." Would he have been able to say that if Jeffrey had suffered a traumatic brain injury? If Jeffrey were in a coma? Or, like Terri Schiavo, in a persistent vegetative state?

Ethicists have suggested that victims of brain injuries must deal with a "drastically altered" sense of self. I cannot say with certainty how my husband perceives himself. As long as he is comfortable, pain-free, and taken care of, he seems to accept his limited life. He even enjoys some of it, like visits from his grandchildren, football on television, and frozen yogurt. But at some level he hates it. He screams and howls in his sleep, and sometimes when he is awake as well. This once sociable, outgoing man now has only a few people in his life—me, our children and grandchildren, the kind and patient home-care aides who take care of him while I work, and underemployed actors I pay to read to him every afternoon.

Yet my husband definitely has a "self," as drastically altered as it is. As I understand it, to have a "self," an "identity," one must be able to perceive one's existence as separate from other people, from sources of pleasure and pain, from the wind and the rain, from the universe. One must be conscious of one's body and mind, however impaired. When my husband was in a coma, he had no "self" in this sense, and afterwards, no memory of the accident, or any of its consequences. I helped him construct a new "self," gave him a narrative of the events that he could integrate into his new identity. But it was a selected narrative—my version of his story—that he now accepts as his own.

I can speak more confidently of my own "drastically altered self." Novelist and essayist Joan Didion calls the year after her husband John Gregory Dunne's sudden death "the year of magical thinking." While rationally she understood that Dunne was dead, at some level this was so unacceptable that she could not bring herself to get rid of his shoes because when he came back he would need them. If magical thinking is common after a loved one's death, how much more powerful it is when the person is not dead but in a coma or persistent vegetative state. How comforting it is to believe that the magic of a kiss, a favorite song, a new drug, a new procedure will restore this precious person to us.

For many years I believed that I could bring back the person I loved by sheer persistence and will. I tried various medical, psychological, and spiritual remedies. My husband was one of the first people in New York to be injected with Botox when it was an experimental drug, not to smooth his wrinkles but to try to release some of the tightness in his legs that was inhibiting physical therapy. A nurse performed "therapeutic touch"—a kind of waving of hands over his body that was supposed to release negative energy. Prayers—many prayers of different religions—were said for him.

Yet all that magical thinking failed, and now I live with the man-who-is-and-is-not-my-husband. The person-who-was-me rarely spoke in meetings, avoided confrontation, and trusted doctors. This person-who-is-now-me rages—politely of course—at a health-care system that saved her husband's life but then abandoned him, at politicians who give bouquets to caregivers and then cut services, and at people who express surprise that "she is still working" (don't they know that insurance doesn't cover "custodial" care?). To all these people I say: Come, be my drastically altered self for a week, including being the night nurse (who never has a full night's sleep), and then we'll talk.

But this person-who-is-now-me is also a better writer, a less fearful speaker, a more determined advocate for her husband, if not for herself. She knows how to reattach a motor under a hospital bed. She knows that the "charge nurse" is the go to person in the ER. She is not afraid to die. She is sometimes, however, afraid to keep on living.

Kristi Kirschner, a rehabilitation physician, recently wrote an article about the dilemmas facing people who suffer debilitating injuries. She notes that while some people initially want to die, most patients ultimately adjust to their condition. She writes about Jeffrey Galli, the young man with a spinal-cord injury, and then allows Jeffrey to respond to her analysis. Now in his early twenties, Jeffrey has a pragmatic view of life. Kirschner writes: "There are other experiences that will be available to Jeffrey because of his injury. He will live life at a slower pace." To this Jeffrey replies: "This was forced on me, it did not become 'available.' I am unable to refuse it." Another benefit of his new condition, Kirschner says, is that "he will learn about interdependency." Jeffrey: "Not learn about, but again, forced to be dependent. And it's not very 'inter.'" Says Kirschner: "Jeffrey feels a strong sense of self-determination—when it comes to his life, he is the 'final authority.'" This Jeffrey does not dispute.

My husband also wants to be the final authority on his life, which includes his death. As confused as he is about some things, he has been very clear and consistent about his wishes about death. He has even planned his own funeral. Advance directives and health-care proxies may be flawed, but they are all we have to turn to in the face of the medical-care system that always seems to have one more test, one more procedure, all designed to delay the inevitable.

As for me, appropriately enough in his centenary year, I turn to Samuel Beckett who wrote in *The Unnameable:* "I can't go on. I'll go on."

CAROL LEVINE, former editor of the Hastings Center Report, directs the Families and Health Care Project at the United Hospital Fund in New York City. This article is based on a presentation at "Reflections on the End of Life: Schiavo Plus One," sponsored by the Fordham Center on Religion and Culture last April.

From *Commonweal,* September 8, 2006, pp. 9–10. Copyright © 2006 by Commonweal Foundation. Reprinted by permission.

UNIT 3
The Dying Process

Unit Selections

11. **Dying on the Streets: Homeless Persons' Concerns and Desires about End-of-Life Care,** John Song et al.
12. **End-of-Life Care around the World: Achievements to Date and Challenges Remaining,** David Clark
13. **Are They Hallucinations or Are They Real? The Spirituality of Deathbed and Near-Death Visions,** L. Strafford Betty
14. **A Spreading Appreciation for the Benefits of Hospice Care,** Kerry Hannon
15. **When Death Strikes without Warning,** Jennifer Couzin

Key Points to Consider

• What is palliative care? Palliative care is often thought to apply to end-of-life issues only, but why not practice palliative care with all patients, whether terminally ill or not? Pain is pain, whether dying or otherwise. Palliative care addresses not only an individual's physical needs but also the spiritual, social, and psychological needs. Is palliative care a familiar term to you?

• Hospice programs are spreading throughout the world. Hospice care is much appreciated by those families who have had the opportunity to benefit from it. What do you know about "hospice"? Have you had a relative or friend enrolled in a hospice program? Was this a positive experience for the family?

• Do the living really talk to the dead? Do they "see" deceased family members and friends? Have you ever had such an experience? Were you hallucinating or were you actually observing such?

• If you could choose, would you prefer a sudden death or a lingering death? What are the pros and cons of each?

Student Website
www.mhhe.com/cls

Internet References

American Academy of Hospice and Palliative Medicine
www.aahpm.org
Hospice Foundation of America
www.hospicefoundation.org
Hospice Hands
http://hospice-cares.com
National Prison Hospice Association
www.npha.org
The Zen Hospice Project
www.zenhospice.org

While death comes at varied ages and in differing circumstances, for most of us there will be time to reflect on our lives, our relationships, our work, and what our expectations are for the ending of life. This is called the dying process. In recent decades, a broad range of concerns has arisen about that process and how aging, dying, and death can be confronted in ways that are enlightening, enriching, and supportive. Efforts have been made to delineate and define various stages in the process of dying so that comfort and acceptance of our inevitable death will be eased. The fear of dying may heighten significantly when actually given the prognosis of a terminal illness by one's physician. Awareness of approaching death allows us to come to grips with the profound emotional upheaval that will be experienced. Fears of the experience of dying are often more in the imagination than in reality. Yet, when the time comes and death is forecast for the very near future, it is reality, a situation that may be more fearful for some than others.

Perhaps you know someone who has communicated with and even "seen" a deceased family member or friend. What is really happening here? Is such an experience a hallucination or is it real? Strafford Betty looks into this "twilight zone" to determine if such is real or a mere hallucination.

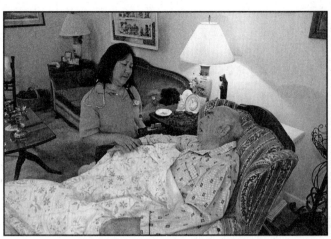

© The McGraw-Hill Companies, Inc./Rick Brady, photographer

The articles by Clark and Hannon address hospice care and the benefits of such. Clark points out the advances around the world of hospice, yet presents challenges which remain. The last article in this section, by Jennifer Couzin, addresses the devastating effect of epilepsy and sudden death.

Dying on the Streets
Homeless Persons' Concerns and Desires about End-of-Life Care

Background: There is little understanding about the experiences and preferences at the end of life (EOL) for people from unique cultural and socioeconomic backgrounds. Homeless individuals are extreme examples of these overlooked populations; they have the greatest risk of death, encounter barriers to health care, and lack the resources and relationships assumed necessary for appropriate EOL care. Exploring their desires and concerns will provide insight for the care of this vulnerable and disenfranchised population, as well as others who are underserved.

Objective: Explore the concerns and desires for EOL care among homeless persons.

Design: Qualitative study utilizing focus groups.

Participants: Fifty-three homeless persons recruited from agencies providing homeless services.

Measurements: In-depth interviews, which were audiotaped and transcribed.

Results: We present 3 domains encompassing 11 themes arising from our investigation, some of which are previously unreported. Homeless persons worried about dying and EOL care; had frequent encounters with death; voiced many unique fears, such as dying anonymously and undiscovered; favored EOL documentation, such as advance directives; and demonstrated ambivalence towards contacting family. They also spoke of barriers to EOL care and shared interventions to improve dying among the very poor and estranged.

Conclusions: Homeless persons have significant personal experience and feelings about death, dying, and EOL care, much of which is different from those previously described in the EOL literature about other populations. These findings have implications not only for homeless persons, but for others who are poor and disenfranchised.

JOHN SONG, MD, MPH, MAT[1,2], DIANNE M. BARTELS, RN, MA, PhD[1,2], EDWARD R. RATNER, MD[1,2], LUCY ALDERTON, MPH[4], BRENDA HUDSON, MS[3], AND JASJIT S. AHLUWALIA, MD, MPH, MS[2,3]

[1]Center for Bioethics, University of Minnesota, N504 Boynton, 410 Church Street S.E., Minneapolis, MN 55455, USA;
[2]Medical School, University of Minnesota, Minneapolis, MN, USA;
[3]Academic Health Center, University of Minnesota, Minneapolis, MN, USA;
[4]Worldwide Epidemiology, GlaxoSmithKline, Mail Stop UP4305, Collegeville, PA 19426-0989, USA.

Background

There remain many deficiencies in how society addresses the needs of dying individuals.[1] One shortcoming is the fundamental assumptions behind end-of-life (EOL) care: it focuses on individuals with loved ones, health care, and a home. Society has not considered homeless persons, who often die without these resources. It is necessary to address EOL care in this population for several reasons. First, the high prevalence of homelessness in the United States, with estimates ranging up to several million,[2] and the disproportionate amount and severity of illness in this population[3,4] is a public health crisis. Homeless persons also suffer high mortality rates—several times the rate of domiciled populations[5-7]—and premature mortality (average ages of death in Atlanta, San Francisco, and Seattle are 44, 41, and 47).[8,9] In addition, homeless persons encounter many barriers to health care[10-12] and, it may be hypothesized, to EOL care. Homeless persons, for example, die with little medical care immediately prior to their deaths.[13] Finally, additional concerns are raised by the unique personal, cultural, and medical characteristics of homelessness. Given the immediacy of basic human needs while living without shelter, homeless persons' concerns beyond daily survival may be different from those of persons who do not worry about food or shelter.

Few studies have addressed EOL care for underserved or disenfranchised persons,[1] and existing work is limited as it reflects the concerns of people with health care and personal resources and relationships. Three studies have previously examined homeless persons and EOL care. One demonstrated that homeless persons are eager to address EOL issues,[14] and a second explored EOL scenarios among homeless persons.[15] A third study addressed ICU care preferences.[16] The first 2 studies, however, are limited by their small and homogeneous samples, and the third focused on one specific aspect of EOL care.

This work represents the first in-depth exploration of a homeless population and their attitudes towards EOL care. We hypothesized that they would have concerns different from those of other previously studied populations. We previously reported how life on the streets influences attitudes towards death and dying (Song et al. submitted for publication) The present paper's objective was to examine how homelessness influences concerns and desires about care at the time of death.

Design

We conducted a qualitative investigation utilizing focus groups of homeless individuals. The study was funded by the NIH/National Institute of Nursing Research and approved by the University of Minnesota Institutional Review Board.

Participants

Participants were recruited from 6 social service agencies that serve homeless persons in Minneapolis and St. Paul, MN. These agencies provide a variety of services, including food, shelter, and health care. Participants were required to be at least 18 years old, speak English, and able to give informed consent. Participants were required to have been homeless at least once in the last 6 months, ascertained by a demographic questionnaire consistent with the federal guidelines.[17]

Participants were recruited through a mixture of random and purposive sampling, utilizing key informants[18]; details of this procedure are detailed elsewhere (Song et al. submitted for publication). Six focus groups were held, with an average of 9 participants per group. Participants were compensated $20. Interim analyses were conducted, and interviews were held until theme saturation was achieved.

Table 1 Interview Guide for Focus Groups

Questions

General questions

Do you have any experience with a serious illness or injury or a close friend or relative who had a serious illness or injury or who has died?

Are you concerned about dying?

Do you think about dying, care while dying, or death? Is this an issue that concerns you?

Is this an issue that you would like to talk about more?

Specific questions

Do you have any one that you can talk to about these issues?

Probes: Do you have family that you are in contact with? Do you have friends that you trust? Do you know any social workers, service providers, or health care providers whom you trust?

What concerns do you have regarding dying, care at the end of life, and death?

Probes: Are you concerned about what happens to your body? Your health care? Pain, symptom management, discomfort? Are you concerned about being stuck on life support? Are you concerned about dying alone?

If you were sick or dying, are there people you trust or love that you can get support from? Who can make decisions for you?

Probes: Do you have family that you are in contact with? Do you have friends that you trust? Do you know any social workers, service providers, or health care providers whom you trust? Have you ever heard of a living will or durable power of health attorney?

Describe a "good death."

Probes: Where would you like to die? Who would you like to have by your side? Who do you need to make peace with? What would you like to have happen to your body? What are you afraid of when dying?

What stands in the way of you having a good death?

Probes: What stands in the way of good health care? What would you need to die in comfort and dignity? What are some problems with services that you have encountered?

What kind of services would you say would be needed so that homeless people might die in comfort and with dignity?

Measurement

Interviews were conducted between July 2003 and January 2004. A semistructured interview guide consisting of open-ended questions was developed through a pilot study,[14] community consultants, and the EOL and homelessness literature (Table 1).

The sessions were audio-taped and investigators took field notes on the group process and nonverbal communication, which served to contextualize the interviews and verify congruence of verbal and nonverbal communication.[18] Audiotapes were transcribed, and Atlas ti software was used to facilitate analysis.

Analysis

Investigators utilized a modified consensual qualitative research (CQR) approach to analyze data, which has proven effective in evaluating complex psychosocial phenomena.[19] This method involves an inductive analytic process to identify themes, which the team derives by consensus and verifies by systematically checking against the raw data.[19] This CQR approach incorporates a 3-step process to identify salient themes; details of CQR utilized by this team are provided elsewhere (Song et al. submitted for publication).

Results

Fifty-three people participated in the 6 focus groups. The mean age of participants was 47, and 35% were female. Thirty-six percent were identified as Native American, 8% reported an advanced degree, and 40% responded that they experienced more than one living situation during the last 6 months (Table 2).

Main outcomes were participants' concerns about and wishes for EOL care. We found 11 themes grouped into 3 domains, by locus of concern: personal themes, relational concerns, and environmental influences (Table 3).

Personal Themes

This domain involves participants' experiences with and attitudes towards EOL care. These results represent internal dynamics and considerations—the experiences that have influenced participants' conceptions about EOL care, including their wishes and concerns about their own care. Within the "personal theme" domain, we found 6 themes: experience with EOL care, fears and uncertainties, advance care planning, preferences/wishes/hopes, spirituality/religion, and veteran status (Table 3).

Experience with End of Life Care

Participants consistently had experiences with serious illnesses and deaths of loved ones or acquaintances, or their own encounters with serious illness. These experiences influenced their beliefs and attitudes towards EOL care. Past experiences with death and EOL care were frequently poor and frightening:

When she (my mom) got sick, they put her in a nursing home, and they denied me access . . . she deteriorated, she lost her hair, she was almost comatose . . . I never got to see her. What they did to her I'll never know. One thing I knew—when she saw me she said, 'Call a taxi; get me out of here.' . . . So everything right now is in a nightmare. I'm trying to find out how she

Table 2 Participant Demographics

Characteristics	%
Age, years	
<35	15
36–45	25
46–55	45
56–65	9
>65	6
Gender	
Female	35
Race	
Hispanic or Latino	2
Not Hispanic or Latino	2
American Indian or Alaskan Native	36
Asian	2
Black or African American	27
Native African	2
Hawaiian/other Pacific Islander	0
White	22
Not reported	7
Years of education	
5–8	8
9–11	39
12–15	32
16+	8
Not reported	13

died . . . nobody told me . . . In my mind I'm thinking she's still alive . . . I never thought I'd lose my mom, or not in this way, not this hideous mess that happened that I can't understand.

This perception of EOL care as being out of the control of patients and family was common: "My mother lacked two weeks being 94 years old when she passed away. She was forced into a nursing home . . . She lost her freedom . . ." So, too, was the feeling that EOL care was unresponsive to the suffering party: "It was a situation where he didn't want to come out of there, living off the machine. When the time came for him to start to die, they wanted us to resuscitate him . . . That kind of weighed heavy on me because I thought I was letting him down. The last of his hours, he was kind of in pain. I just kept asking the doctor to give him something for his pain. They never did."

Because experiences contributed to an attitude that care is imposed, most interventions are seen as an unwanted and invasive: "After I saw my mom die, I'm almost thinking alone would be better. I don't want to be hooked up to tubes and all that crap when it comes time for me to go." Loss of control was a common concern, "Once I got real sick and got [put] in a nursing home. I don't care how old I was, I can't deal with not

Table 3 Domains and Themes of EOL Care Expressed by Homeless People

Domain	Definitions	Representative quote(s)
Personal themes		
Experience with EOL care	Experience with deaths of loved ones, friends, and acquaintances on the streets or personal experiences with illness or injury, and the care received	I've had a lot of tragedy. My girlfriend died in my arms with my baby. She was four months pregnant at the time . . . and she comes back in my dreams. He had a stroke and was on dialysis. Me and him, being about the same age, it made me fear for my life.
Fears and uncertainties	Concerns and fears about dying and EOL care	Me? I'd just like to be remembered by somebody. The only thing I'm worried about is that I don't want to die on the streets. After I've passed, my biggest fear would be not making it back home to Canada and my reservation. . . . they'll throw you in a pauper's grave someplace and nobody's going to mourn you.
Preferences/wishes/hopes	Possibilities related to what would be a "good death"	If that was to happen, I would want it to happen some place where it was noticeable. Yeah, you may be dead there for three, four years . . . I'll be somewhere where nobody could find me. But also, once you see the doctor, the doctor should spend a little more time and get to know you a little bit better and show a little more compassion.
Advance care planning/documentation	Strategies to influence outcomes in the event of death or serious illness	You gotta have it wrote down, or else they'll do just what they want. I'm going to have one of those made out, a living will, because if I end up in the hospital, I don't think I'd want no life support keeping me alive. My will says that if I go into a diabetic coma or if I get hit by a car, they can start life-saving techniques, and then my brother Bob's name is on that. They are to call him and say John's in the hospital, doesn't look good; do you want to come down and sign the papers to pull the plug; we will try to keep him going for some time to see if he improves. If he doesn't improve, then come down. That is exactly how it's worded.
Spirituality/religion	Influence and role that an individual's spirituality or religious convictions has on dying and EOL care	Personally, death comes like peace, but like John said, we look forward to it if we're Christian because I can go and get my reincarnate body and dance without this one.
Veteran status	Thoughts about death and EOL care related to having served in the armed forces	Even though I'm a serviceman, if I was buried in a national cemetery, I feel that my soul would be lost. I went to get medical care, something that they guaranteed me for life. They looked at me and said, 'OK, you have an honorable discharge.' As a matter of fact, I have two. 'Do you have insurance on your job?' and I'm like, whoa. The insurance on my job, OK, when I signed these contracts you didn't say that my insurance would be primary. You said that you would take care of it. So the VA does nothing.
Relational themes		
Relationships with known people	How current relationships with family, friends, and peers affect desires and fears about dying and EOL care	Most of these guys, they don't want their family to know. They ask you what happened. Why are you homeless? What's the problem? But I notice that homeless people, or street punks, whatever you call them, whatever is right for them, prostitutes or whatever, sometimes these type of people, another street person they have known for years and seems more like a family member than their own family. For me that is considered a family member. They'd be there for me, but I wouldn't want them to make all them changes. It takes a lot of money to travel and I don't want them wasting money. Not because I ain't worth the money, but I don't want them.

Table 3 Domains and Themes of EOL Care Expressed by Homeless People (*continued*)

Domain	Definitions	Representative quote(s)
Relationships with strangers	How individuals' relationship with institutions and its representatives influence their views of dying and EOL care	Have a doctor, an intern, or even have a medical student for a doctor, come and work at a shelter for a week to two weeks, just to see how it is, to get woke up at 6:00 in the morning and booted out, and getting a cold bowl of cereal from the branch for breakfast, and just shadowing somebody that has been homeless or is homeless, just to feel what it's like to, if just to say 'I know this guy; he's homeless and this needs to be taken care of right away' and not making him wait. Then they will have an idea of what it's like being homeless.
		The doctor called me a goddamn drug addict and told me to get the hell out of his office.
Communication tools/ strategies	The communication between the subjects and their loved or valued ones, and strategies homeless persons have to communicate with loved ones during a health care crisis or if unable to communicate directly	My sister, I put her name on everything that I have. There can be contact with her and she will communicate with my daughter.
		My living will says my family will have no say or discussion of what is done. Basically, they don't know me, so why should they have a say in whether I live or not.
		I made sure to talk to him (nephew) on the telephone. It just came into my mind. I said, 'I'm going to leave this in your hands. I'm going down hill now.
Environmental		
Environmental barriers/facilitators to good EOL care	Barriers or facilitators identified by subjects to good EOL care	They don't give you proper medical care because they know you are homeless.
		They think because we live in the streets, we're all junkies that don't feel no pain.
		Even if your family is not around at the hospital, there are these great hospice people. If you could spend your last time talking with them . . . that would be a good death.
		Living without life insurance, who's going to put me away—stuff like that?
		I had cancer just last year. My fear was being alone because my children ain't here. But I had support from the people at Listening House, friends.
Participant-suggested interventions	Interventions suggested by participants to improve dying and EOL care for homeless persons	What we do need is a shelter somewhere between Minneapolis and St. Paul that would be fully staffed 24/7 . . . and if you came out and just had surgery, you could go there . . .

EOL end of life.

having my freedom. There's no way. I need to be free . . . once you're in a nursing home or hospital you lose control."

Fears and Uncertainties

Participants expressed many fears and uncertainties similar to those of domiciled people: "Don't prolong my life. I don't want to carry on laying there as a vegetable . . ." However, the derivation of these fears may be different in this population—a combination of experience and the impotence and indignity of homelessness: "I was thinking of my friend Jeff wound up under the bridge. They look at it like another junkie guy, but he was trying really, really hard to work every day. And just to see him treated with little dignity was [not] right . . ."

Another common fear was dying anonymously, which may be unique to this population: "It makes a difference when you're homeless and you're dying by yourself. You're

here by yourself, no one to care"; and, "Me? I just want to be remembered by somebody." A dreaded consequence expressed by many was that their passing, and life, would go unnoticed and without memorialization. Similar fears include not being found and dying in a public place: "I wouldn't want to be under a bridge. If you die somewhere and not be found."

Participants also expressed many misconceptions and uncertainties about surrogate decision-making, persistent vegetative states and heroic treatments, and advance care planning: "A good buddy of mine that used to be a street person . . . fell out and ended up in a coma . . . There [were] doctors and nurses . . . calling, asking anybody to come down and say you were his family, just so you could sign a waiver to pull the plug." This was one of many urban EOL myths expressed by participants.

Another common concern was the final disposal of their body, a fear that appears unique to this population; they believed a homeless, disenfranchised person's body would be anonymously cremated, buried in a common grave, or used in medical experimentation: "I don't know if the city will just take me to the furnace down there and burn me." Participants were not aware of Minnesota state law that forbids cremation without consent of patient or family.

Preferences, Wishes, and Hopes

Participants expressed preferences and hopes, many echoing those articulated in the mainstream EOL literature, such as a wish for reconciliation with loved ones or avoiding heroic interventions. However, the wish for companionship had a unique twist in this disenfranchised population. While some desired reunion with their families, many more simply wanted anyone compassionate at the time of death, whether homeless friends or even anonymous care providers: "I would wish someone to be there, especially since I know my folks won't be."

Given the misconceptions and fears about body disposal, there were explicit and detailed desires that participants' bodies be laid to rest in a personally and culturally acceptable manner. Native Americans, for example, often stated a preference that their body be taken to native lands for proper burial.

Another common desire expressed was that EOL care focus on symptom management, particularly pain control. At the end of a long dialogue on pain control, one participant summed up the prevailing mood: "I'm kind of on the same page as him . . . if I'm dying, just give me my drugs. Make sure I'm loaded; then I'm cool. I'm not going to sell it to anybody; I just want to . . . Let me go in peace."

Finally, participants desired simply to be treated with respect: "deal with us not as some sleaze bag out for trouble, but we are just homeless." A lack of respect fostered fear of dying among subjects: "Right now I'm afraid of dying mostly because I don't have nothing. It's like a disgrace or shame to me to die that way . . . Even though I can't hear it and I won't know it, talking about, 'He was a tramp. He was a no-good tramp.'"

Advance Care Planning

A major finding is the importance of advance care planning and documentation for this isolated population: "My fear is being found on the street, but no one knowing how to help me or who I am." It appears that this desire for advance care planning arises from several concerns. One is, as reflected above, anonymity and estrangement. Given the belief that EOL care is paternalistic and unresponsive, advance care planning was also seen as a way to maintain control: "In '73, I was actually declared brain dead . . . I regained consciousness . . . my only real fear about death is that the doctor tried too aggressively to keep me alive, and because of this, I created a living will."

For some participants advance care planning meant discussion with significant others and/or appointment of a proxy; however, the most cited forms of advance care planning included written documentation of wishes or contact information, personal identification, or written directive or other advance care planning document. One participant voiced a typical strategy to dictate circumstances of his death: "In my wallet, I have a card with my sister's name and a phone number. Do I want to be buried in Minnesota? Hell no!"

When speaking of surrogate decision-makers, nearly all who had thought of this issue or who had appointed one chose surrogates who were not related; they were most often service providers; friends; and, occasionally, romantic partners.

Sprituality/Religion

Spirituality and religion were means of finding comfort and solace when confronting death while homeless: "Can you die alone? I remember when Bill Cosby's son died on the street . . . nobody came to touch him and hold him, but if he's a child of God, then God was holding him and taking him home." Despite the physical reality of dying alone, religion made it possible to believe that, spiritually, one was not alone.

Veteran Status

Many opinions about EOL care related to prior military experience. Participants identified veteran status as either a positive or negative factor. Some, for example, felt reassured they would have care or even a grave provided by the U.S. government: "If I drop dead or die or get my head blown off, if my parents don't do it or my family, put me in the national cemetery, too, with other veterans, my brothers." Others feared poor VA care or did not want burial in a veteran's cemetery.

Relational Themes

A second major domain was "relational themes," which we organized into 3 categories: relationships with known people, relationships with strangers, and communication tools/strategies. This domain captures how current personal and institutional relationships affect attitudes towards EOL care.

Relationships with Known People/Burden to Others

Relationships were described as complex, fractured, or nonexistent. Many were estranged from their family of origin. Some homeless persons viewed dying as an opportunity for reconciliation, though they were uncertain whether this would happen: "Truthfully, I couldn't honestly say who would and who wouldn't [be there]. I'll just have to see when I get there . . . Sometimes when they say they'll be there, they're never there."

A majority of participants did not want contact with their families while dying or after their deaths. There were several reasons for this preference, including the assertion that their families, "abandoning" them in life, had no right to claim a relationship or authority in death: "I got 6 sisters and five brothers . . . but, dead is dead. So don't cry; help me while I breathe, not when I'm stiff and frozen." This rejection extended into surrogate decision-making: "My living will says my family will have no say or discussion of what is done. Basically, they don't know me, so why should they have a say in whether I live or not." Others feared that their families would not be compassionate: "They'd be saying, 'bury him like he lived,' or 'we don't want nothing to do with him.'" Some did not want to be a burden on their families, either emotionally or financially, or feared revealing their circumstances and homelessness: "When I die, don't tell them. I don't want them to know that I'm homeless." Finally, many others did not want their families contacted because they had found, while living on the streets, trusted friends and service providers to serve as surrogates.

Relationships with Strangers

Most respondents commented that society, including police, medical professionals, and social service agency staff, does not treat them with respect or compassion. When discussing physicians, one respondent insisted: "We are homeless. They say, 'well this guy's homeless . . . You ain't got to worry about it.'" They cited slow and poor service at health care facilities, and felt betrayed by the social services system. Based on these experiences, they expected poor care at the EOL: "He'd a died more dignified if they [the counselors] actually sat down and listened to him, instead of saying, 'we're too busy; get out of here . . .'"

However, not all comments were negative. Compassionate providers were described gratefully. Several respondents claimed a particular social service provider as their most trusted confidant and indicated that this individual should be contacted as a surrogate decision-maker. "John," said one respondent, referring to a street case manager, "knows what I want. I trust him."

Communication Tools/Strategies
Those who did wish communication or reconciliation at the EOL had different strategies to insure that this occurred. These strategies were often inventive and adapted to the disenfranchised lives many led. Many, for example, carried phone numbers of loved ones or left them with various social service providers. Although in jest, this comment demonstrates how difficult communication may be: "If I was going to die in three months, I'd probably rob a bank . . . I figure if I robbed a bank, I would get caught. [My family] heard about it in the newspaper and call me up . . ."

Environmental Factors

Our final domain's common thread is the environment in which dying occurs and the structural boundaries of EOL care. We organized it into 2 categories: barriers/facilitators to good EOL care and participant-suggested interventions.

Barriers/Facilitators to Good EOL Care
Health care professionals' attitudes were most often cited as a barrier to good EOL care, while others found care inaccessible or inadequate because of financial or insurance insufficiencies. Because of poverty, even the simplest aspects of EOL care cause worry in this population: "My goal is to get me some type of burial plan. $300 won't bury nobody at this table. Then I wouldn't mind it so much, but right now I'm afraid of dying mostly because I don't have nothing." Inappropriate care also resulted because of preconceptions about homeless persons, such as the denial of pain medication for fear of abuse. Respondents also complained about the lack of respite or hospice facilities and programs; once discharged from the hospital, they only have shelters to go to.

Participant-Suggested Interventions

Finally, participants suggested many interventions to improve care for dying homeless people. Some were educational, directed towards both health care providers and homeless people. Another frequently suggested intervention was some form of advance care planning or document to preserve autonomy: "It's a legal document. Let's say that's your wish, but it's not written anywhere, and someone says, 'keep him on the respirator.' They [would] . . . unless you written it down." Indeed, any kind of identification was considered essential and encouraged for a disconnected population. Finally, homeless participants demanded special accommodations to facilitate dying among this population.

Discussion

In our study, homeless participants demonstrated more differences than similarities in their attitudes and beliefs towards EOL care compared to other populations studied.[20–25] First, many participants have had personal experiences with death, dying, and EOL care. These experiences led them to view EOL care as paternalistic, unresponsive, and poor. Other unique concerns expressed include fear of dying anonymously, without memorialization or remembrance; fear of not being found or identifiable in death; and worry about the final resting place of their bodies. These concerns are all new to the EOL literature.

Another unexpected finding is participants' advocating advance care planning, especially the appointment of surrogate decision-makers and the preparation of advance care documents, such as living wills. These findings are interesting, given the current disfavor toward advance care documents[1] and the intuition that homeless individuals would not value or utilize documentation. According to participants, documents serve different functions among a population that is anonymous, voiceless, or lacks obvious surrogate decision-makers.

Important relational findings were also expressed. Though some participants wished reconcilement and contact, a greater number did not want their families contacted when seriously ill, when dying, or after death. These desires derived from several different reasons, including avoiding emotional and financial burdens on their families, shame, and anger over abandonment. Many had made surrogate decision-making plans that did not include family.

Relationships with institutions also figured prominently in the EOL experiences and desires of homeless persons—which is expected given the role institutions play in the daily lives of homeless persons, providing food, shelter, and other necessities. These relationships were occasionally positive. Participants spoke of trusted service providers, such as shelter personnel, some of whom were even designated as surrogate decision-makers. Most often, though, relationships with systems of care were described as poor, and contributed to give views of dying.

Participants spoke of "environmental" contexts or contributors to EOL care, noting multiple barriers to EOL care, including poor relationships, lack of insurance or finances, poor health care, lack of respect, and lack of knowledge of available resources or rights. Some participants, though, cited factors that led to satisfactory health care experiences or positive expectations of EOL care, such as advance care planning, facilitation of health care by social service workers, and physician advocacy.

Finally, subjects suggested interventions for improving EOL care for homeless or underserved persons. These included patient and provider education, advance care planning, living wills and other documentation, and special programs and facilities for dying or seriously ill homeless persons. A Medline and web search yields no reports of specific efforts focused on dying homeless individuals. Clearly, interventions are needed to serve this population.

The recent NIH state-of-science statement on improving EOL care reported that insufficient research has focused on individuals from different cultural and socioeconomic backgrounds.[1] While there is a growing body of evidence that these individuals may experience disparities in EOL care,[23-29] relatively little attention has been paid to the desires of these populations or interventions to improve their care.[1] Our study provides new and important information on EOL issues among homeless persons, among the most unfortunate of overlooked populations.

Our study's limitations include the selection of subjects from one urban area, a high number of Native Americans represented, and potential selection bias, as our participants are those who accessed service providers. The findings of our study are not necessarily generalizable. Rather, our data are exploratory, examining a previously unknown health-related phenomena: we are among the first to characterize in-depth the EOL concerns and desires of a vulnerable and disenfranchised population from their perspective.

Conclusions

Our study demonstrates that homeless persons have extensive, and often unique, concerns about dying and EOL care. The experiences and circumstances of homelessness inform and influence a view of death and EOL care unlike previously reported findings in the study of EOL care. Our work has implications for further study of this population, as well as study of other underrepresented and underserved populations. This work also suggests examining interventions to improve care for this and other vulnerable populations.

Notes

1. National Institutes of Health State-of-the-Science Conference Statement on Improving End-of-Life Care December 6–8, 2004. Available at www.consensus.nih.gov/2004/2004EndOfLifeCareSOS024html.htm. Accessed March 16, 2006.
2. Burt MR. Homelessness: definitions and counts. In: Baumohl J, ed. Homelessness in America. Phoenix, AZ: Oryx Press, 1996:15–23.
3. Breakey WR, Fischer PJ, Kramer M. Health and mental problems of homeless men and women in Baltimore. *JAMA* 1989; 262:1352–7.
4. Gelberg L, Linn LS. Assessing the physical health of homeless adults. *JAMA* 1989; 262:1973–9.
5. Barrow SM, Herman DB, Cordova PBA. Mortality among shelter residents in New York City. *Am J Public Health* 1999; 89:529–34.
6. Hibbs JR, Benner L. Mortality in a cohort of homeless adults in Philadelphia. *N Engl J Med* 1994; 331:304–9
7. Cheung AM, Hwang SW. Risk of death among homeless women: a cohort study and review of the literature. *CMAJ* 2004; 170(8):1243–7.
8. Hwang SW, Orav EJ, O'Connell JJ, Lebow JM, Brennan TA. Causes of death in homeless adults in Boston. *Ann Intern Med* 1996; 126:625–8.
9. King County Public Health 2004. Available at www.metrokc.gov/HEALTH/hchn/2004-annual-report-HD.pdf. Accessed January 20, 2006.
10. Gallagher TC, Andersen RM, Koegel P, Gelberg L. Determinants of regular source of care among homeless adults in Los Angeles. *Med Care* 1997; 35(8):814–30.
11. Gelberg L, Andersen RM, Leake BD. Healthcare access and utilization. *Health Serv Res.* 2000; 34(6):1273–1314.
12. Gelberg L, Thompson L. Competing priorities as a barrier to medical care among homeless adults in Los Angeles. *Am J Public Health* 1997; 87:217–20.
13. Hwang SW, O'Connell JJ, Lebow JM, Bierer MF, Orav EJ, Brennan TA. Health care utilization among homeless adults prior to death. *J Health Care Poor Underserved* 2001 Feb; 12(1):50–8.
14. Song J, Ratner E, Bartels D. Dying while homeless: Is it a concern when life itself is such a struggle? *J Clin Ethics.* Fall 2005; 16(3):251–61.
15. Tarzian A, Neal M, O'Neil J. Attitudes, experiences, and beliefs affecting end-of-life decision-making among homeless individuals. *J Palliat Med.* Feb 2005, Vol. 8, No. 1: 36–48.
16. Norris W, Nielson E, Engelberg R, Curtis JR. Treatment preferences for resuscitation and critical care among homeless persons. *Chest* 2005; 127(6):2180–7.
17. Stewart B. McKinney Homeless Assistance Act (42 U.S.C. 11431 et seq.)
18. Bernard HR. Research Methods in Cultural Anthropology. Beverly Hills, CA: Sage Publications 1988.
19. Hill CE, Thompson BJ, Williams EN. A guide to conducting consensual qualitative research. *Couns Psychol* 1997; 25:517–72.

20. Singer PA, Martin DK, Kelner M. Quality end of life care: patients' perspectives. *JAMA* 1999; 281:163–8.

21. Steinhauser KE, Clipp CC. In search of a good death: observations of patients, families, and providers. *Ann Intern Med.* 2000; 132:825–31.

22. Vig EK, Pearlman RA. Quality of life while dying: a qualitative study of terminally ill older men. *J Am Geriatr Soc* 2003 Nov; 51(11):1595–601

23. Born W, Greiner KA, Sylvia E, Butler J. Ahluwalia JS. Knowledge, attitudes, and beliefs about end-of-life care among inner-city African Americans and Latinos. *J Palliat Med.* 2004 7(2): 247–56.

24. Blackhall LJ, Murphy ST, Frank G. Ethnicity and attitudes toward patient autonomy. *JAMA* 1995;274:820–5.

25. Caralis PV, Davis B, Wright K, Marcial E. The influence of ethnicity and race on attitudes toward advance directives, life-prolonging treatments, and euthanasia. *J Clin Ethics* 1993;4(2):155–65.

26. Carrese JA, Rhodes LA. Western bioethics on the Navajo reservation. *JAMA* 1995;274:826–9.

27. Daneault S, Labadie J. Terminal HIV disease and extreme poverty: a review of 307 home care files. *J Palliat Care* 1999; 15:6–12.

28. Degenholtz HB, Thomas SB, Miller MJ. Race and the intensive care unit: disparities and preferences for end-of-life care. *Crit Care Med.* 31(5 Suppl):S373–8, 2003 May.

29. Cleeland CS, Gonin R, Baez L et al. Pain and treatment of pain in minority patients with cancer. *Ann Intern Med* 1997;127:813–6.

Corresponding Author: **JOHN SONG,** MD, MPH, MAT; Center for Bioethics, University of Minnesota, N504 Boynton, 410 Church Street S.E., Minneapolis, MN 55455, USA (e-mail: songx006@umn.edu).

Acknowledgements—The authors would like to thank the clients and staff of St. Stephen's shelter; Holy Rosary Church; Listening House; Hennepin County Outreach Services; Health Care for the Homeless, Minneapolis; and Our Saviors Church who were so generous with their time, thoughts, and dedication to serving others. We would also like to thank LeeAnne Hoekstra for administrative support, Tybee Types for transcription, and Karen Howard for manuscript preparation. This study was funded by the National Institute of Nursing Research, National Institutes of Health, grant RO3 NR008586-02.

End-of-Life Care around the World: Achievements to Date and Challenges Remaining

DAVID CLARK

Cicely Saunders' early work was particularly consequential for the way in which it began to forge a peculiarly *modern* philosophy of terminal care—one that combined for the first time a progressive approach to the management of pain and other symptoms with an equal attention to matters of social, psychological, and spiritual concern. This was both the science and the art of caring for patients with advanced disease and it was refined through research and promulgated through education. It quickly led to the establishment of St Christopher's as a center of excellence in a new field of care. Its success was phenomenal and the program soon became the stimulus for an expansive phase of hospice and palliative care development, not only in Britain, but also around the world.

From the outset, ideas developed at St Christopher's were applied differently in other places and contexts. Within a decade it was accepted that the principles of hospice care for cancer patients could be practiced in many settings: in specialist inpatient units, but also in home care and day care services; likewise, hospital units and support teams were established that brought the new thinking about the care of those with advanced malignant disease into the very heartlands of acute cancer medicine. Modern hospice developments took place first in affluent countries, but in time they also gained a hold in poorer countries, often supported by mentoring and "twinning" arrangements with more established hospices in the west.

Prior to the 1970s, cancer pain and the need to improve care of those dying with malignant disease had received little international attention as either clinical or public health problems and were often regarded as inevitable and somewhat intractable problems about which little could be done. As the work of pioneers such as Cicely Saunders, Elisabeth Kübler-Ross, Florence Wald, and others got underway, the spread of modern hospice and palliative care and the creation of the professional field of pain studies encouraged the first International Symposium on Cancer Pain, held in 1978. Research presented at this and subsequent conferences suggested that physicians had the means to relieve even severe cancer pain and that the principal

factors contributing to poor pain management were legal barriers against opioid use and poor dissemination of available knowledge about pain management. In 1982, the World Health Organization (WHO) enlisted the aid of palliative care leaders, cancer pain specialists, and pharmaceutical manufacturers to develop a global Program for Cancer Pain Relief, based on a three-step analgesic ladder with the use of adjuvant therapies, and incorporating the use of strong opioids as the third step. WHO representatives launched an international initiative to remove legal sanctions against opioid importation and use, relying on national coordinating centers to organize professional education and to disseminate the core principles of pain management. The WHO program met with only partial success, however. Opioid consumption between 1984 and 1993 rose dramatically in 10 industrialized countries, but showed much smaller increases in the rest of the world and significant differences in the pattern and the extent of opioid use continued to be observed within and between global regions.

A number of problems remained, including: reluctance on the part of physicians to prescribe strong opioids; fear among health care professionals and the public about addiction and abuse; lack of state and national government engagement with the issue of cancer pain; and a lack of availability of essential drugs due to stringent regulation and economic factors. Recognition of these issues led the WHO to develop its concept of "foundation measures" to promote the implementation of cancer pain relief programs. These highlighted the importance of education, government policy, and drug availability, if cancer pain is to be overcome and palliative care is to be promoted.

From the 1980s, pioneers of hospice and palliative care worked to promote these goals in many countries of the world, building increasingly on international networks of support and collaboration.[1] In 1976, the First International Congress on the Care of the Terminally Ill had been held in Montreal, and was organized every two years thereafter by Balfour Mount and colleagues. In 1980, Josefina Magno and others formed the International Hospice Institute, which in 1999 became the

International Association for Hospice and Palliative Care. In 1988, the European Association for Palliative Care was formed in Milan, Italy, and Vittorio Ventafridda became its first President the following year. In 1990, the well established Hospice Information Service at St Christopher's Hospice in London began its international newsletter which quickly became an invaluable source of information on hospice innovation around the world. In 1999, the Eastern and Central European Palliative Task Force came into being at a congress held in Geneva; it aimed to gather data on hospice and palliative care in the region, share experiences of achievements and obstacles, influence the institutions of government, set standards to meet local needs, and raise awareness. The Foundation for Hospices in Sub-Saharan Africa was established in 1999 to serve hospice developments in the region, later merging with the National Hospice and Palliative Care Organisation in the United States. In the new millennium, the year 2000 saw the creation of the Latin American Association of Palliative Care. In 2001, the Asia Pacific Hospice Palliative Care Network was founded, representing 14 countries. Next came the U.K. Forum for Hospice and Palliative Care Worldwide, which became operational in 2002, with aims to co-ordinate the work of relevant groups in the United Kingdom, to support education, to advocate, to provide information, and to raise funds. The African Association for Palliative Care was founded in 2003, seeking to represent all palliative care interests across the whole continent. The following year, a global alliance of palliative care national associations was formed at a meeting in Korea. There were also many developments at the country level and a substantial literature on national developments in hospice and palliative care records important achievements and many successes in the face of adversity.[2]

The Americas

Hospice services in the United States grew dramatically from the founding organization in New Haven in 1974, to some 3,000 providers by the end of the 20th century. In 1982, a major milestone was the achievement of funding recognition for hospices under the Medicare program. Several key developments occurred in the 1990s. National representative bodies appeared to take a more professionalized approach to their activities, giving greater emphasis to palliative care as a specialized field of activity (the National Hospice Organization became the National Hospice and Palliative Care Organization; the American Academy of Hospice Physicians became the American Academy of Hospice and Palliative Medicine). At the same time, two major foundations developed extensive programs concerned with improving the culture of end-of-life care in American society (the Robert Wood Johnson Foundation created the Last Acts initiative, and the Open Society Institute established the Project on Death in America).

Meanwhile, in neighboring Canada, where Balfour Mount first coined the term "palliative care" in 1974,[3] a Senate report in 2000 stated that no extension of palliative care provision had occurred in the previous five years, and set out recommendations for further development among the country's 600 services.[4]

In Latin America, there was evidence of faltering progress, with palliative care services existing in seven countries, and the greatest amount of development in Argentina.[5] A chief problem here, as in other developing regions, was the problem of poor opioid availability, an issue highlighted in the 1994 Declaration of Florianopolis.[6]

Asia Pacific

The first evidence of hospice developments in the Asia Pacific region came with a service for dying patients in Korea, at the Calvary Hospice of Kangung, established by the Catholic Sisters of the Little Company of Mary in 1965; services had increased to 60 by 1999.[7] In Japan, the first hospice was also Christian, established in the Yodogwa Christian Hospital in 1973; by the end of the century the country had 80 inpatient units.[8] In Australia, the country that established the world's first chair in palliative care, commonwealth and state funds for palliative care increased steadily from 1980 and palliative medicine was recognized as a specialty in 2000; by 2002 there were 250 designated palliative care services.[9] Protocols for the WHO three-step analgesic ladder were first introduced into China in 1991 and there were said to be hundreds of palliative care services in urban areas by 2002.[10]

An extensive review of hospice and palliative care developments in India has mapped the existence of services state-by-state and explored the perspectives and experiences of those involved, with a view to stimulating new development.[11] The study found that 135 hospice and palliative care services exist in 16 states. These are usually concentrated in large cities, with the exception of the state of Kerala, where services are much more widespread. Non-government organizations and public and private hospitals and hospices are the predominant sources of provision. Nevertheless, palliative care provision could not be identified in a total of 19 states and union territories. The development of services in India is generally uneven and for the majority of states, coverage is poor. Barriers to the delivery of palliative care include: poverty; high population need; poor opioid availability; workforce underdevelopment; and limited national palliative care policy. Nevertheless, successful models exist in Kerala for the development of affordable, sustainable community-based hospice and palliative care services,[12] and these may have potential for replication elsewhere.

Africa

Wright and Clark,[13] in a review of hospice and palliative care developments in Africa, have mapped the existence of services country-by-country and explored the perspectives and experiences of those involved. The 47 countries studied could be grouped into four categories of palliative care development: no identified hospice or palliative care activity (21); capacity building activity underway to promote hospice and palliative care delivery (11); localized provision of hospice and palliative care in place, often supported by external donors (11); and hospice and palliative care services achieving some measure of integration with mainstream service providers and gaining wider policy recognition (4). Major difficulties included: opioid availability; workforce development; achieving sustainable critical mass; absorption capacity in relation to major external funding initiatives; coping with the scale of the HIV/AIDS related suffering. The authors concluded that models exist in Uganda, Kenya, South Africa, and Zimbabwe for the development of affordable, sustainable community-based hospice and palliative care services and that the newly formed African Palliative Care Association has huge potential to promote innovation, in a context where interest in the development of hospice and palliative care in Africa has never been greater.

Eastern Europe

In the former communist countries of Eastern Europe and Central Asia, there were few palliative care developments in the years of Soviet domination. Most initiatives can be traced to the early 1990s, after which many projects got underway. These have been documented in detail,[14] and show evidence of some service provision in 23 out of 28 countries in the region. Poland and Russia have the most advanced programs of palliative care, with considerable achievements also made in Romania and Hungary. Nevertheless, in a region of over 400 million people, there were just 467 palliative care services in 2002, more than half of which were found in a single country, Poland. Palliative care in Western Europe made rapid progress from the early 1980s, but by the late 1990s there were still striking differences in provision across different states.[15]

Western Europe

After the foundation of St Christopher's in England, in 1967 the first service outside of the United Kingdom was founded in Norway by *Franciscan AID* in 1974.[16] National concern about care of the dying had resulted in a public debate, and a television program raised wider awareness. Following the work of the Franciscan volunteers, pain clinics were established across Norway and a government publication, *Care for Terminally Ill Patients,* drew attention to issues at the end of life. A National Committee on Terminal Care was established in 1984, and during the same year, the first national conference on end-of-life care was held in Trondheim. During the 1990s, further reports addressed the ways in which palliative care could be incorporated into the health system so that all Norwegians had access to such care whenever and wherever it is needed. By 2006, an estimated 34 services were operational countrywide, which included in-patient care, home care, and day care.

Similar patterns of development can be traced in other western European countries. Services began to appear in Sweden (1977), Italy (1980), Germany (1983), Spain (1984), Belgium (1985), and the Netherlands (1991). In all of these countries the provision of palliative care has moved beyond isolated examples of pioneering services run by enthusiastic founders. Palliative care is being delivered in a variety of settings (domiciliary, quasi-domiciliary, and institutional), though these are not given uniform priority everywhere.

In 1989 and 1992, the European Parliament adopted resolutions on counseling and on care of the terminally ill but thereafter showed little further interest in end-of-life issues until January 2005 when a question was put to the parliament concerning what action the Commission had taken to prepare a strategy for palliative care. The Council of Europe, in contrast, has shown a more concerted interest. Inspired by its 1980 Report of the European Health Committee on "Problems related to death: Care for the dying" and by the Parliamentary Assembly Recommendation 1418 (1999) on "The protection of the human rights and dignity of the terminally-ill and the dying," in 2001 the European Health Committee decided to address the issue of palliative care by setting up a committee of experts which, over a two-year period, prepared a set of European guidelines for the field. Its report[17] was adopted in 2003 by all 45 member countries of the Council of Europe and saw palliative care as an essential and basic service for the whole population. Its recommendations appear to have been used quite actively in some countries with less-developed palliative care systems, particularly in Eastern Europe, where they have served as a tool for advocacy and lobbying.

Policy issues relating to end-of-life care in Europe have also been raised by other non-governmental and inter-governmental organizations. At palliative care conferences in 1995 (Barcelona),[18] 1998 (Poznan),[19] and 2006 (Venice),[20] exhortatory declarations were made, calling for government action on palliative care at the national level and drawing attention to key problems and issues facing palliative care as it develops internationally. By 2003, the European Society for Medical Oncology was giving greater recognition to palliative care.[21] In 2004, the European Federation of Older Persons launched a campaign to make palliative care a priority topic on the European health agenda.[22] The same year, WHO Europe produced an important document on *Better Palliative Care for Older People.* Its aim is "to incorporate palliative care for serious chronic progressive illnesses within ageing policies, and to promote better care toward the end of life."[23] Its companion volume, *Palliative Care: The Solid Facts,* is a resource for policy makers in a context where "the evidence available on palliative care is not complete and . . . there are differences in what can be offered across the European region."[24] Despite the powerful symbolic language of these and other documents however, evidence of their impact remains unclear.[25]

The U.K. group Hospice Information[26] estimated that in 2002 hospice or palliative care initiatives existed, or were under development on every continent of the world, in around 100 countries. The total number of hospice or palliative care initiatives was in excess of 8,000 and these included inpatient units, hospital-based services, community-based teams, day care centers, and other modes of delivery. In 2006, a more detailed picture emerged from the first study ever to attempt an estimate of the global provision of palliative care.[27] In total, 115 of the world's 234 countries have established one or more hospice-palliative care services. Yet only 35 (15%) countries have achieved a measure of integration with other mainstream service providers together with wider policy recognition. Although palliative care services have been found in around half of the world's countries, these countries encompass 88% of the global population. Yet two countries inflate this figure since one-fifth of the world's population is found in China and one-sixth in India, and these are countries with "localized provision" of palliative care services that are not yet scaled up to meet the massive population needs.

When we look at the global need for palliative care, there can be no room for complacency or a false sense of achievement. Around the world, the situation is, in most regards, desperate. Where the need is greatest, the fewest hospice and palliative care services exist. There is unrelieved suffering on a mass scale and the efforts of a handful of activists to promote palliative care globally are often ignored and unsupported. One million people die each week. It is estimated by the World Health Organization that 60% of these could benefit from palliative care. Yet at the moment only a tiny minority of dying people ever receive the support of hospice and palliative care services. At the same time, the scale of the problem is increasing.

The global population is expected to increase by a third in the next 50 years, from six billion to nine billion. Most of the increase will occur in the developing countries. The consequences for the delivery of culturally sensitive and appropriate end-of-life care are enormous. The global burden of cancer will increase from 10 million to 24 million over the next 50 years, and 17 million of these cases will be in developing countries. Of the estimated ten million people who are diagnosed with cancer every year, over half are living in the developing world and many will have incurable disease at the time of diagnosis. By 2020, it is estimated that the incidence of cancer will double. Cancer pain is common. Two-thirds of those with advanced disease and one-third of those undergoing active treatment suffer pain. Until earlier referral and diagnosis occur and standard therapies are able to be deployed for the majority of those with cancer, pain relief and palliative care will remain the most relevant provision for large numbers affected. Meanwhile, both cancer and palliative care remain relatively low priorities on the global health agenda. Around the world there are thought to be over 43 million people with HIV/AIDS, with close to three-quarters of all cases found in sub-Saharan Africa, which also has the highest adult prevalence and the highest number of newly infected adults and children. Most of these people have medical and social problems that could be relieved—or even prevented—with better palliative care.

The gross mismatch between palliative care need and the level of available provision is not just a problem of poverty and under-development, though such factors do play their part. Many countries still have hugely inadequate supplies of appropriate pain medication, even though this can be made available at low cost. Some governments put in place draconian measures to limit the manufacture, sale, transportation, storage, and prescription of strong opioid drugs. Too often the balance between "regulation" and "availability" is tipped in favor of the regulators, to the extent that simple pain relieving measures are largely unavailable. The problem is compounded by clinicians made nervous about prescribing strong pain killers for risk of social opprobrium, or even prosecution. The world of palliative care is divided between the "haves" with access to a range of appropriate medications and the knowledge and will to use them, while the "have nots" are denied even simple formulations available routinely over the counter in most western pharmacies.

Yet we know there appear to be workable solutions. As we saw in Robert Twycross' article, in Kerala in southwest India, hundreds of local communities and volunteers have worked with a few professionals to create a "neighborhood network" for palliative care that is reaching most of those in need. In Uganda, morphine is available free to persons with cancer and AIDS and specially trained nurses are licensed to prescribe it. In Romania, active lobbying recently overturned arcane regulations about pain relieving drugs that stretched back well into the communist era.

Yet palliative care is still underdeveloped globally to an extent that shames us all. Good care at the end of life and a dignified death should be regarded as basic human rights—to which everyone has access when the time comes.

References

1. D. Clark, History, Gender and Culture in the Rise of Palliative Care, in *Palliative Care Nursing. Principles and Evidence for Practice,* S. Payne, J. Seymour, and I. Ingleton (eds.), Open University Press, Maidenhead, pp. 39–54, 2

2. J. Stjernsward and D. Clark, Palliative Care—A Global Perspective, in *Oxford Textbook of Palliative Medicine* (3rd Edition), G. Hanks, D. Doyle, C. Calman, and N. Cherny (eds.), Oxford University Press, Oxford, 2003.

3. B. Mount, The Royal Victoria Hospital Palliative Care Service: A Canadian Experience, in *Hospice Care on the International Scene,* C. Saunders and R. Kastenbaum (eds.), Springer, New York, 1997.

4. S. Carstairs and H. Chochinov, Politics, Palliation and Canadian Progress in End-of-Life Care, *Journal of Palliative Medicine, 4:*3, pp. 396–469, 2001.

5. L. De Lima, Advances in Palliative Care in Latin America and the Caribbean: Ongoing Projects of the Pan American Health Association (PAHO), *Journal of Palliative Medicine, 4:*2, pp. 228–231, 2001.

6. J. Stjernswärd, E. Bruera, D. Joranson, S. Allende, S. Montejo, G. Tristan, L.Q. Castillo, G. Schoeller, T. Pazos, & M.A. Wenk, Opioid Availability in Latin America: The Declaration of Florianopolis, *Journal of Pain and Symptom Management, 10:*3, pp. 233–236, 1995.

7. Y. Chung, Palliative Care in Korea: A Nursing Point of View, *Progress in Palliative Care, 8:*1, pp. 12–16, 1999.

8. T.C. Maruyama, *Hospice Care and Culture,* Ashgate, Aldershot, 1999.

9. R. Hunt, B.S. Fazekas, C.G. Luke, K.R. Priest, and D.M. Roder, The Coverage of Cancer Patients by Designated Palliative Services: A Population-Based Study, South Australia, 1999. *Palliative Medicine, 16,* pp. 403–409, 2002.

10. X.S. Wang, S. Yu, W. Gu, and G. Xu, China: Status of Pain and Palliative Care, *Journal of Pain and Symptom Management, 24:*2, pp. 177–179, 2002.

11. E. McDermott, L. Selman, M. Wright, and D. Clark, *Hospice and Palliative Care Development in India,* poster presented at the 4th Research Congress of the European Association for Palliative Care, Venice, 2006.

12. C. Shabeer and S. Kumar, Palliative Care in the Developing World: A Social Experiment in India, *European Journal of Palliative Care, 13:*2, pp. 76–79, 2005.

13. M. Wright and D. Clark, *Hospice and Palliative Care Development in Africa. A Review of Developments and Challenges,* Oxford University Press, Oxford, 2006.

14. D. Clark and M. Wright, *Transitions in End of Life Care. Hospice and Related Developments in Eastern Europe and Central Asia,* Open University Press, Buckingham, 2003.

15. H. ten Have and D. Clark (eds.), *The Ethics of Palliative Care. 2002; European Perspectives,* Open University Press, Buckingham, 2002.

16. T. Scholberg, The Development of Palliative Care in Norway, *International Journal of Palliative Nursing, 1:*1, pp. 53–56, 1995.

17. Council of Europe, *Recommendation Rec (2003) 24 of the Committee of Ministers to Member States on the Organisation of Palliative Care,* Strasbourg.

18. Barcelona Declaration on Palliative Care, *European Journal of Palliative Care, 3:*1, p. 15, 1995.

19. Poznan Declaration, *European Journal of Palliative Care, 6:*2, pp. 61–65, 1998.

20. The Declaration of Venice, Palliative Care Research in Developing Countries, *Progress in Palliative Care, 14*(5), pp. 215–217, 2006.

21. N.I. Cherny, R. Catane, and P. Kosmidis, ESMO Takes a Stand on Supportive and Palliative Care, *Annals of Oncology, 14:*9, pp. 1335–1337, 2003.

22. See www.eurag-europe.org/palliativ-en.htm, accessed February 9, 2006.

23. E. Davies and I. J. Higginson (eds.), *Better Palliative Care for Older People,* World Health Organization, Copenhagen, 2004.

24. E. Davies and I.J. Higginson (eds.), *Palliative Care: The Solid Facts,* World Health Organization, Copenhagen, 2004.

25. D. Clark and C. Centeno, Palliative Care in Europe: An Emerging Approach to Comparative Analysis, *Clinical Medicine, 6:*2, pp. 197–201, 2006.

26. www.hospiceinformation.info/hospicesworldwide.asp

27. D. Clark and M. Wright, The International Observatory on End of Life Care: A Global View of Palliative Care Development, *Journal of Pain and Symptom Management, 33*(5), pp. 542–546, 2007.

Are They Hallucinations or Are They Real? The Spirituality of Deathbed and Near-Death Visions

L. Stafford Betty, PhD

When I try to unpack the many meanings of the word "spirituality," I try not to forget that the word comes from "spirit," and that one of the main meanings of "spirit" is, as my dictionary puts it, "a supernatural being or essence." Thanatologists have long been aware that people very near death, especially if they have *not* been heavily sedated, frequently "see spirits." French historian Philippe Ariès reports that a thousand years ago throughout Western Europe, most slowly dying people saw such spirits—presumably because sedation was unknown (M. Morse, 1990, p. 60). Even today, with heavy sedation the rule rather than the exception, some hospice nurses report that seeing and communicating with spirits is a "prevalent theme" of the dying patients they provide care for (Callanan & Kelley, 1992, p. 83). Usually these spirits bring comfort and a sense of wonder, not only for the dying, but also for the family of the dying. To put it another way, they "spiritualize" death. They suggest to all concerned that this world is not the only one, but that a "spiritual" world awaits the deceased. What is the nature of these spirits and the world they apparently live in? Is the "romance of death" generated by them a false comfort, a useful fiction, or is there something real and sturdy about them? In this article we will look at the evidence on both sides of the question, then come to a tentative conclusion.

Typical Deathbed or Near-Death Visions

According to Callanan and Kelley, visions of the dying come in two types. The first, and more common, are sightings of spirits who come, for the most part, to greet and encourage those who are dying. Most spirits are recognized by the one dying as a dead relative or friend. These spirits may visit for minutes or even hours; they are not seen by those at the bedside of the dying person, but it is often obvious that the dying person is communicating with an unseen presence or presences. Dozens of such communications are recorded by Callanan and Kelley, of which the following is typical: "Martha described several visitors unseen by others. She knew most of them—her parents and sister, all of whom were dead—but couldn't identify a child who appeared with them" (Callanan & Kelley, pp. 87–88). Martha goes on to explain to her nurse, "They left a little while ago. They don't stay all the time; they just come and go. . . . sometimes we talk, but usually I just know that they're here. . . . I know that they love me, and that they'll be here with me when it's time" (p. 88).

The other type of vision is a transcendental glimpse of the place where the dying think they're going. "Their descriptions are brief—rarely exceeding a sentence or two—and not very specific, but usually glowing" (p. 99). At the end of Tolstoy's famous novella "The Death of Ivan Ilych," Ivan exclaims on his deathbed, "So that's what it is! What joy!" (1993, p. 63)—the last words he ever spoke. His words are typical of visions of this second kind. But since there is no way to ascertain whether this type of vision is veridical or hallucinatory, I won't give much attention to it. Suffice it to say that those who have such visions invariably report them as glimpses of a real world, not as chimeras.

So we will be concentrating on the visions that people close to death have of beings, not of places. Are these visions more than likely veridical? Are they sightings of real beings that any of us, properly equipped, could see, and who exist in their own right whether we see them or not? Or are they hallucinations? Are they as the word is commonly used, sensory perceptions that are unrelated to outside events—in other words, seeing or hearing things that aren't there?

I should add here that two types of people close to death have visions of deceased spirits: (1) those dying slowly, often of cancer, who see spirits at their bedside, and (2) those not necessarily dying who have a potentially fatal experience that culminates in a near-death experience (NDE). Those dying slowly are usually aware of their surroundings and can communicate simultaneously with both the living and the dead— as if they have one foot in this world and one in the next. Those who meet dead relatives or friends during NDEs are completely cut off from our world as they communicate with the deceased. Yet the descriptions of these spirits given by NDErs after their return from the "Other World" are the same as the descriptions given by the slowly dying. The spirits are usually recognizable, loving, and supportive. Sometimes they are described as "takeaway spirits" or "greeters."

The Argument for the Spirit Hypothesis

Social scientists usually have little patience with any theory that takes seriously the reality of beings on the "Other Side." Words used to describe them like "transcendental" or "spiritual" are often looked at with suspicion if not dismissed as nonsense. But there are excellent reasons for taking them seriously. I will list them under four headings.

1. First, persons near death usually insist that the phantasms they see are not hallucinations, but living spirits existing in their own right. This insistence is especially impressive when the dying person is an atheist or materialist who does not believe in life after death. "I'm an atheist. I don't believe in God or Heaven," a 25-year-old woman named Angela, and dying of melanoma, declared to her nurse (Callanan & Kelley, p. 89). Blind and partially paralyzed, she nevertheless had a vision, and it changed her outlook on death. "I don't believe in angels or God," she told her nurse, "but someone was here with me. Whoever it was loves me and is waiting for me. So it means I won't die alone" (p. 90).

Angela's claim is of course easy to dismiss. One can claim, not without reason, that Angela hallucinated a takeaway spirit to ease her despair in the face of eternal extinction. NDErs are typically just as adamant about the reality of the spirits they encounter while out of their body, and social scientists usually react to these claims in the same skeptical fashion. But the sheer volume of such claims by persons near death is impressive. And it is all the more impressive when put alongside similar claims made by other visionaries *not* near death. Conant's study of bereaved but otherwise healthy widows (1996), to take but one example, reveals the same insistence by some of the widows that the spirits who visited them were real. Conant reports that the "vividness of the experience amazed them. The comparison to hallucinations was voiced simultaneously five times and was always rejected. These were *not* hallucinations" (p. 186). Some of the widows "seemed to be amazed by the emotional power of the experience more than by its vividness because of the conviction they had been in contact with the spirit of the deceased [husband]" (p. 187). Not all the widows in the study were confident that the spirits of their

husband actually paid them a visit; most felt that their culture discouraged a "spiritual interpretation" of their visions, and several worried about "the connotation of craziness" (p. 188) that such an interpretation carried. But all agreed that the vision "feels real" (p. 194). And all, even the most skeptical, derived "reassurance that life after death was possible for the deceased . . . as well as for themselves when they would eventually die" (p. 192). I myself am impressed enough by all these visions, especially their feeling of "realness," to keep an open mind about their ontological status. Not so Conant herself. While acknowledging that such visions "served as a safe haven to help mend the trauma of loss, as an inner voice to lessen current social isolation, as an internal reworking of self to meet new realities, and as reassurance of the possibility of immortality" (p. 195), she describes them as "vivid hallucinations." The ontological status of the visions is never discussed. She appreciates that the visions are useful fictions and therefore salutary, but the possibility that they might be real apparently never occurred to her.

Conant's study is especially relevant to our study for two reasons. First, even though she is not studying visions of the dying or potentially dying, the visions of her collection of widows seem to be of the same quality. Though invisible to everyone else, they are convincingly real to the one having the vision, they are recognizable, and they usually convey a message of reassurance. Second, Conant is a cautions, thoroughgoing social scientist with, if anything, a bias against drawing transcendental conclusions based on her research. What she wanted to show was that visions of the deceased should be regarded as successful coping mechanisms, not as delusions that should be discouraged. Her interests run in a completely different direction from mine, yet I find her useful. When two minds so differently attuned find a common ground, there is often something important going on.

2. The second prong of the argument for the reality of spirits comes from a careful analysis of them. The spirits of persons who are identified by NDErs or by the slowly dying have one thing in common: They are almost always spirits of the deceased. You might ask yourself why all these hallucinations are so tidy. Everywhere else hallucinations are higgledy-piggledy. Aunt Adelaide alive on earth is just as likely to be hallucinated as Aunt Jill who died five years before. But these hallucinations, if that's what they are, have sorted themselves out. With uncanny regularity only the dead show up. Why should that be?

The materialist might answer that it would be *illogical* to hallucinate someone you thought was still alive. After all, a person can't be living on earth and living on the Other Side at the same time. If you had a vision of someone alive on this side of the veil, that would be *proof* you were hallucinating and would undercut the benefit you might derive from the hallucination. So the subconscious mind sorts out who's died and who hasn't. It keeps track. And when your time is up, it decks out a nice dead relative for you to hallucinate, a nice dead relative to take care of you when you finally die. Your fear of death vanishes. So the argument goes. But this argument is not as convincing as it might first appear. After all, how logical *are* hallucinations? Hallucinations are made of memory fragments, and those fragments are no more orderly as they come and go in the theater of the mind than the stuff of our daydreams. Zen masters compare the behavior of this mental detritus to a pack of drunken monkeys. And Aldous Huxley refers to them as "the bobbing scum of miscellaneous memories" and as "imbecilities—mere casual waste products of psycho-physiological activity" (1945, pp. 126–127). The materialist's line of reasoning is plausible up to a point, but it overlooks the almost random nature of hallucinations.

But let us grant for the sake of argument that it does have force. I think I can show that whatever force we grant it for the moment is not good enough in the face of the facts. Here is why.

Let us say I am very sick in my hospital bed and have a near-death experience. I see in my vision my grandpa, long dead, and my cousin Manny, whom I think to be very much alive. They present themselves as spirits, and I recognize them as such, but I am confused. For how can Manny be a spirit since he's alive in the flesh? I come out of my NDE, and I express this confusion to the loved ones gathered around me. But they know something I don't know. They know that Manny was killed in an automobile accident two days before. They didn't tell me because they thought it would upset me. There are quite a few cases like this in the literature, and one whole book, a classic, devoted to them (Barrett, 1926). More recently, Callanan and Kelley presented three cases like this in their book on the slowly dying (Chapter Seven), and the Guggenheims (1995) devote a whole chapter to them in their study of after-death communications (ADCs). Here is why I think these cases are so important. If I believe my dear Aunt Mary and Uncle Charlie and my five siblings and my wife and dozens of other relatives and friends, *including my cousin Manny,* are all alive, why should I hallucinate only my cousin Manny from among all these possibilities? Why should my hallucination be so well informed and so selective? It could be a coincidence, but there are too many cases like this for them all to be coincidences. There is always the possibility that I could have known telepathically that Manny, and only Manny from among those I just named, was dead. But if I had never had any powerful telepathic experiences before, isn't this explanation *ad hoc?* I think the best explanation for Manny's appearance alongside my grandpa in my vision is that the newly dead Manny *actually came* (in spirit), along with grandpa, to greet me during my NDE. He was not a hallucination after all. He was not a delusion. He should be taken at face value.

3. The third prong of the argument derives from the physiology of near-death experiences. Recent research by a team of Dutch doctors, led by van Lommel (van Lommel, van Wees, Meyers, & Elfferich, 2001), makes it clear that the typical features of the NDE, including

meetings with deceased relatives, occur while the electro-encephalogram (EEG) is flat-lined—in other words, when the brain is inactive and the whole body is "clinically dead." Van Lommel summarizes the findings:

> From these studies [involving 344 cardiac patients studied over an 8-year period] we know that . . . no electric activity of the cortex of the brain (flat EEG) must have been possible, but also the abolition of brain stem activity like the loss of the cornea reflex, fixed dilated pupils and the loss of the gag reflex is a clinical finding in those patients. However, patients with an NDE [18% of the total] can report a clear consciousness, in which cognitive functioning, emotion, sense of identity, and memory from early childhood was possible, as well as perception from a position out of and above their "dead" body. (van Lommel, no date)

Van Lommel elaborates further: Even though the EEG is flat, people

> experience their consciousness outside their body, with the possibility of perception out of and above their body, with identity, and with heightened awareness, attention, well-structured thought processes, memories and emotions. And they also can experience their consciousness in a dimension where past, present and future exist at the same moment, without time and space, and can be experienced as soon as attention has been directed to it (life review and preview), and even sometimes they come in contact with the "fields of consciousness" of deceased relatives. And later they can experience their conscious return into their body. (van Lommel, no date)

Van Lommel then asks the obvious question: "How could a clear consciousness outside one's body be experienced at the moment that the brain no longer functions during a period of clinical death with flat EEG?" (van Lommel et al., 2001).

What does all this mean for our thesis? It means that the typical elements of the NDE, including meetings with deceased relatives, are not hallucinations. Hallucinations are produced by an *active* brain, one whose wave pattern would be anything but flat. What, then, could account for the visions of deceased loved ones? It appears that the dying person or nearly dead person, free from her physical body for a few moments, enters a world, an ethereal world, close by but undetectable by the physical senses. She looks like a corpse to an outside observer, but she is having the experience of a lifetime—in another dimension. An experience of what? She says an experience of real beings, embodied beings, dead people she recognizes. Is there any good reason to keep our minds closed to this possibility, given the unintelligibility of the alternative?

4. The fourth and last prong of the argument is, like the one we've just looked at, exclusively concerned with the near-death experience, and not the visionary experiences of the slowly dying who do not have an

NDE. Glimpsing spirits of deceased relatives is a standard feature of the NDE, so anything that argues for the veridicality of the NDE *as a whole* gives support for our thesis.

There is quite a bit that does. I will organize it under three headings.

First, many reports of things seen by NDErs having an out-of-body experience (OBE) turn out to be veridical. There are hundreds of examples in the serious literature on NDEs. One woman saw a shoe sitting on an upper-story ledge of her hospital—a shoe invisible from the street or from her room—as she drifted out of the building during her NDE; the shoe, upon inspection, turned out to be exactly where she said it was. Another woman took a trip to see her sister and later reported what her sister was doing and wearing at the time—a report later verified by the surprised sister who wondered how she knew. A five-year-old child described in detail, and with impressive accuracy, what happened when her body was being resuscitated while she, out of her body, watched from near the ceiling of her hospital room. In fact it is common for NDErs to describe their resuscitations while they are clinically dead. Michael Sabom, an Atlanta cardiologist, conducted an experiment involving resuscitation accounts to see how accurate they were:

> Sabom asked twenty-five medically savvy patients to make educated guesses about what happens when a doctor tries to get the heart started again. He wanted to compare the knowledge of "medically smart" patients with the out-of-body experiences of medically unsophisticated patients.
>
> He found that twenty-three of the twenty-five in the control group made major mistakes in describing the resuscitation procedure. On the other hand, none of the near-death patients made mistakes in describing what went on in their own resuscitations. (M. Morse, 1990, p. 120)

It is difficult to account for the accuracy of NDE accounts if NDErs are hallucinating. Why should hallucinations be so accurate? Why should they yield far more accuracy than the accounts of imagined resuscitations provided by "medically savvy" patients relying on their memory?

Second, NDEs are often profoundly life-changing. Melvin Morse did an extensive "Transformations study" to quantify what every NDE researcher already knew: that people who have a deep, well-developed—or "core"—NDE are dramatically transformed by their experience. He reported "amazing results": "After we finished analyzing the data from the more than four hundred people who participated in the research project, we discovered that the near-death experience causes many long-term changes" (M. Morse, 1992, p. 60). He grouped them under four headings: decreased death anxiety, increase in psychic abilities, higher zest for living, and higher intelligence. In the exhaustive study referred to above, van Lommel and his cohorts reported that the "transformational processes after

an NDE were very similar" and encompassed "life-changing insight, heightened intuition, and disappearance of fear of death" (van Lommel et al., 2001, p. 3).

The question that is natural to ask at this point is, Can hallucinations transform the people who have them? D. Morse, a clinical psychologist and hard-nosed materialist until he had his own NDE, has this to say about hallucinations:

> Descriptions given of hallucinations are often hazy and contain distortions of reality, while NDE descriptions are usually normally ordered and lifelike. Hallucinations are often accompanied by anxiety feelings, while NDEs are generally calm and peaceful. Hallucinations afterwards rarely cause life-changing occurrences as do NDEs. (D. Morse, 2000, pp. 48–49)

NDErs, like the widows we surveyed above, typically insist on the "realness" of their experience and that it is this realness that gives them hope of seeing their loved ones again. This quality of "realness," and the transformative quality that derives from it, is verified by van Lommel. He found in follow-up studies that most of his patients who did not have an NDE (the control group) did not believe in an afterlife, whereas those who had one "strongly believed in an afterlife" (no date, p. 8) and showed "positive changes." Furthermore, these changes were more apparent at the eight-year follow-up than the two-year (p. 8). Something deeply and lastingly transformed this second group of people. Which is more likely: That a hallucination did this, or that an overwhelming slap in the face by something very real did it?

Third, near-death researchers, beginning with Moody (1975), have consistently identified the "core features" of the NDE, and claim that these features recur in individuals having very little in common other than their NDE. It appears that NDEs from cultures as different as Japan, India, sub-Saharan Africa, and the West all exhibit these core features. Now, it is known that hallucinations vary radically from person to person—so much so that it would be surprising if one person's hallucination was at all similar to his next-door neighbor's, not to mention someone's from a different culture. How can the similarity in this core experience be explained? If by hallucination, then obviously not by any ordinary hallucination.

Rather than go out on a limb and posit a universal hallucination that all humans carry seed-fashion deep in their brains, most NDE researchers suspect the commonality is explainable by a common environment, or world, that opens up to the NDEr. In other words, they all see much the same thing because the world that opens up to them is not infinitely variable, like hallucinations, but is simply the way it is. It is real, in other words; and reality, while it admits of considerable variation and can be interpreted in a variety of ways, is malleable only up to a point. Beyond that point, all NDErs experience very much the same thing—just as an Inuit and a Zulu, in spite of radically different cultures and geographies, would experience the one world that belongs to us all and be able to talk about it meaningfully to each other. The Zulu and the Inuit might have different feelings about the spirits they met in their respective NDEs, but they would at least be able to say they encountered beings, many whom they recognized, that did not belong to the world of the living.

So again we must choose: Is it more reasonable to explain away the core experience as hallucinatory, or as a reflection of something that is real and is encountered? The only skeptical theory that makes sense is the "seed theory" I mentioned above. It is not a preposterous explanation, but is it the more likely? We must each decide for ourselves. Given the other prongs of the argument presented here, however, it seems much more likely, at least up to this point, that the spirits we see during our NDEs or as we near death after a long illness are what they seem to be: real beings from the world we might be about to enter.

The Weakness in the Spirit Hypothesis

It would be dishonest of me to fail to point out the weak link in the spirit hypothesis I've been defending up to this point. Melvin Morse appreciates it fully and asks the question:

> But we shouldn't forget about the woman who saw Elvis in the light, should we? As one skeptic pointed out, "If these experiences are real and not just dreams, how can you explain Elvis?" Or Buddha? How can NDEs of children be explained where they see pet dogs, or elementary school teachers who are still alive? They show up in some NDEs too. How can they be explained? (M. Morse, 1992, p. 128)

The skeptic asks a good question, and the skeptic in me worries more than a little about the idiosyncratic features of some NDEs, especially as found in children. Morse presents a cornucopia of cases involving children, and quite a few play into the skeptic's hands as he dredges the literature for signs of hallucination. For example, take the NDE of a five-year-old who nearly drowned in a swimming pool. Now a scientist in his forties of distinguished reputation, "Tom" recalls passing down a long tunnel toward the Light. All seems quite normal for an NDE until he sees "God on a throne. People—maybe angels—were below looking up at the throne." He goes on: "I sat on the lap of God, and he told me that I had to go back. 'It's not your time,' he said. I wanted to stay but I came back" (M. Morse, 1990, p. 167). Suffice it to say that very few NDErs report seeing God sitting on a throne. In another case, eight-year-old Michelle had an NDE during a diabetic coma. In typical NDE fashion she felt herself float out of her body and watched the resuscitation effort, later describing it in accurate detail. Eventually she was allowed to make a decision to return or not to return to her body, a typical feature of the NDE. But Michelle expressed her will to return in a novel manner: "In front of me were two buttons, a red one and a green one. The people in white kept telling me to push the red button. But I knew I should push the green one because the red one would mean I wouldn't come back. I pushed the green one instead and woke up from the coma" (M. Morse, 1990, p. 39).

Is there really a red and a green button in a world beyond ours? Does God really sit on a throne and talk to little children in that world? Not a chance, I would say. "Then the NDErs must have been hallucinating these bizarre features of the NDE," says the skeptic, "and if these are hallucinations, then doesn't it stand to reason that the entire experience is a hallucination?"

I raised this question to Greyson, editor of the *Journal of Near-Death Studies,* and this was his reply:

> As for Melvin Morse's 8-year-old patient who pushed the green button to return from her coma, I also find it hard to believe that the button was "real." But then I also have difficulty taking as concretely "real" a lot of things described by NDErs, including, in SOME cases, encounters with deceased loved ones and religious figures. I do not think that these are hallucinations, however, or that the experiencers are lying or fabricating memories. What I think is happening is that they are interpreting ambiguous or hard-to-understand phenomena in terms that are familiar to them.
>
> Many NDErs tell us that what they experienced was ineffable—and THAT I believe wholeheartedly. I think that what happens after death is so far beyond our feeble understanding that there is no way for us to describe it accurately in words. Although experiencers may understand fully while they are "on the other side," once they return to the limitations of their physical brains, they have to unconsciously force-fit their memories of incomprehensible events into images they CAN understand. That's why we hear Christians talk about seeing Jesus or Mary, and we hear Hindus talking about yamatoots (messengers of Yama, the god of the dead), and we hear NDErs from "advanced" Western societies—but not NDErs from "primitive" societies—talk about tunnels. (One NDEr who was a truck driver told me about traveling through a chrome tailpipe, an image he could relate to.)
>
> Many NDErs talk about not wanting to return, and yet here they are, so they have to construct some reason to explain their return. Westerners often say that a deceased relative or religious figure told them it was not yet their time, or their work was not finished. That's an acceptable and believable reason for a time-conscious and achievement-oriented Westerner to return. On the other hand, it is common for Indians to say that they were told a mistake had been made, and that the yamatoots were supposed to have taken Ravi Singh the incense-maker, not Ravi Singh the baker. That kind of "bureaucratic bungling," I am told, is more believable in India, as it is typical of the way things often happen in their society. I suspect that an 8-year-old girl with limited understanding had to come up with a concrete image like pushing a green button to return. She did not hallucinate the button, but after the fact her mind came up with that interpretation of what really happened to her to effect her return. It was a misinterpretation rather than a hallucination.

Am I splitting hairs? I don't think so. A hallucination is a perception that occurs in the ABSENCE of any sensory stimulation. I think NDErs DO "see" SOMETHING that is "really" there—but it is so far beyond our understanding that they have to interpret it subsequently in terms of familiar images. It is more like an illusion than a hallucination. If at night you imagine out of thin air that there is a person in your room, that is a hallucination. But if, in the darkness, you misinterpret a hat-rack for a person in your room, that is an illusion, an imprecise interpretation of something that is really there rather than something that sprang up solely from your imagination. That's what I think a lot of NDE imagery is: imprecise interpretations of things that are comprehensible in the bright light of the NDE, but incomprehensible in the dim light of our physical brains. (Personal communication, January 10, 2005)

Greyson has given us a rich, plausible account of the idiosyncratic features of NDEs. But the skeptic might remain dubious. After all, if there really is a world beyond ours, it is hard to imagine what in it would be confused with a green and a red button. To deal with this challenge, I veer slightly away from Greyson's analysis. It seems more plausible to me that the subconscious imagination of the NDEr is *actively supplying material* for the experience; or, alternatively, that someone else over there is actively supplying it for the benefit of the NDEr. In other words, the mysterious world entered into by the NDEr is made more approachable and intelligible—more *friendly* is perhaps a better word—by his own imagination or someone else's (a spirit guide's?) interpretive or artistic power. Whatever be the case, on balance there are, in my judgment, far too many indicators that the NDE is an experience of another world that exists *in the main* independently of the experiencer, even though certain reported features of it might be explainable by a coloring of the experience or by faulty memory of exactly what happened. The claim that the *entire experience* is a hallucinated fictive world strikes me as incredible. Nevertheless, there is room, based on all the evidence at our disposal, for such a claim. It is not a claim with no basis.

A final clarification of my position is in order. I believe that visions of the dying or nearly-dying are a combination of real transcendental material and imaginative projection. For example, Julian of Norwich, very near death when she had her famous visions of the dying Christ, could not have seen Krishna or Vairocana Buddha: They would have had no meaning for her, and the Mind who assisted her in coloring the vision, or alternatively her own imagination, would not have allowed such a thing. Nor could a South American Indian shaman have glimpsed Christ while entranced. But their visions are not purely the stuff of imagination either: were there no transcendental "canvas" to project them onto, there would not have been any vision. As for glimpses of the dying, especially deceased relatives, these visions are much closer to the realities they seem to be. I don't believe they are so much projections outward from dying persons, as projections "toward" them from deceased relatives who come to greet them. If the skeptic insists on reducing all transcendental phenomena to hallucination, we will not be able to agree on much. We *would* agree, however, that all these visions are, to some extent, cultural, personal, and historical. And we also would agree that most hallucinations in normal subjects (as when a moose charges a sleep-deprived sledder in the Arctic) are not grounded in a transcendental world. In contrast to the visions we have been studying, they exist only in the mind of the subject. They are truly hallucinations.

The Relevance of This Study to the Spirituality of Death

I agree with Lucy Bregman, in her article in this issue, that the word "spirituality" is a wonderful word in search of a meaning. As I tried to show in my opening paragraph, I think the word must be anchored in a transcendent world if it is to retain its distinctive meaning. Otherwise it can become a synonym for *mystique* or *romance*—as when we speak of the spirituality of motherhood or of a sunset or of golf. Each of these can provide wonderful experiences, but they are not what we have in mind when we speak of the *spirituality of death*. As Sherwin Nuland (1995) showed us in his award-winning book *How We Die*, death is not usually a time of wonderful experiences. It is frequently, however, a time of healing experiences, as when long estranged relatives or friends are coerced by death's finality into an act of mutual forgiveness. Perhaps it is not stretching too far the meaning of the word *spirituality* to apply it to such meaningful moments. But there is a time when the word is ideally applicable. That is when a person close to death glimpses a world he or she is about to enter—what we will call the spiritual world, a world where spirits reside, and where the dying will reside when he or she becomes a spirit.

My grandmother transmitted to her family something of the excitement of that world shortly before she died. A devout Christian, she became comatose, or apparently comatose, hours before her death at 94. None of us could reach her, even when whispering our love into her ear. But then my mother happened to whisper that she would soon be with Jesus. So suddenly that we were startled, her eyes opened and her face lit up in great excitement. Like Ivan Ilych, she died joyously. She had a foretaste of the eternal world, the world where spirits reside, and her spirit practically jumped out of her body. Hers was a spiritual experience in the truest sense of the word. The *spirituality of death* may mean many things, but Granny epitomized its meaning for all of us.

But I am not concerned with linguistics or etymology. What I have tried to show here is that books are available to get us ready for death. So are the dying. Callanan and Kelley tell the following story:

Bobby [who was dying] had spoken clearly for the first time in three days.

"He told us, 'I can see the light down the road and it's beautiful,'" Bill said.

This glimpse of the other place gives immeasurable comfort to many, and often is perceived as a final gift from the one who died.

"I've never been a religious person, but being there when Bobby died was a real spiritual experience," his sister said later. "I'll never be the same again."

Bill echoed her sentiments at the funeral. "Because Bobby's death was so peaceful, I'll never be as scared of death," he said. "He gave me a little preview of what lay beyond it for him, and, I hope, for me." (p. 102)

Whether dying persons are telling us of their glimpse of the next world or conversing with people we can't see, we should consider ourselves immensely blessed when it happens. If we don't make the mistake of assuming they are "confused," we are likely to feel some of the excitement they convey. For we are witnessing the momentary merging of two worlds that at all other times remain tightly compartmentalized and mutually inaccessible. That merging is what I mean by the spirituality of death

References

Barrett, W. (1926). *Death-bed visions.* London: Methuen.

Callanan, M., & Kelley, P. (1992). *Final gifts.* New York: Bantam.

Conant, R. (1996). Memories of the death and life of a spouse: The role of images and *sense of presence* in grief. In D. Klass, P. Silverman, & S. Nickman (Eds.), *Continuing bonds: New understandings of grief.* Washington, DC: Taylor & Francis.

Guggenheim, B., & Guggenheim, J. (1995). *Hello from heaven!* New York: Bantam.

Huxley, A. (1945). Distractions—I. In C. Isherwood (Ed.), *Vedanta for the western world.* Hollywood: Vedanta Press.

Moody, R. (1975). *Life after life.* New York: Bantam.

Morse, D. (2000). *Searching for eternity.* Memphis: Eagle Wing.

Morse, M. (1990). *Closer to the light.* New York: Ivy.

Morse, M. (1992). *Transformed by the light.* New York: Ivy.

Nuland, S. (1995). *How we die.* New York: Vintage.

Tolstoy, L. (1993). *The Kreutzer Sonata and other short stories.* New York: Dover.

van Lommel, P., van Wees, R., Meyers V., & Elfferich, I. (2001). Near-death experience in survivors of cardiac arrest: A prospective study in the Netherlands. *Lancet, 358*(9298). Retrieved from World Wide Web: . . ./get_xml.asp?booleanTerm=SO=The+Lancet+AND+SU+Near+Death+Experiences&fuzzy Term

van Lommel, P. (no date). A reply to Shermer: Medical evidence for NDEs. Retrieved June 26, 2005 from the World Wide Web: www.skepticalinvestigations.org/whoswho/vanLommel.htm.

A Spreading Appreciation for the Benefits of Hospice Care

Putting terminally ill patients at ease in their final months.

KERRY HANNON

In Robert and Beverly Stack's red-brick rambler in Orange, Va., the dining room has been transformed into a bedroom. It's furnished with a hospital bed and a dresser lined with medications and other supplies—all provided by Hospice of the Rapidan, a nonprofit agency based in Culpeper, Va., that cares for about 300 patients a year.

Robert, an 81-year-old World War II veteran and retired educator, has Alzheimer's disease. Diagnosed in 2000 and recently bedridden after breaking a hip, he's in declining health, and his daily care has become too demanding for his wife of 54 years to handle. "I can't do it all myself anymore," says 71-year-old Beverly. So with a referral from Robert's physician, she and her family made arrangements for hospice care at home.

Robert Stack is one of more than 1 million patients who began hospice care this year in the United States. Covered under Medicare, Medicaid, and most private insurance plans, hospice care is a swiftly growing healthcare field. About 1.4 million people received new or continuing hospice care last year, more than twice as many as did a decade ago, according to the National Hospice and Palliative Care Organization, the Alexandria, Va.-based industry group.

About 1.4 million Americans received new or continuing hospice care last year, more than twice as many as did a decade ago.

A shift toward the broader use of hospice by Alzheimer's patients has partly driven that growth. And new rules may make hospice care even more appealing. As demand has increased, so has the number of hospice programs nationwide. Today, there are more than 4,700 providers, up from about 3,300 five years ago, according to NHPCO. While the majority of providers are nonprofits, the for-profit sector is gathering steam, accounting for 47.1 percent of hospice agencies last year.

Generally speaking, hospice is intended for any person who has a terminal illness and a prognosis of six months or less to live. Depending on the needs of each patient, care can include pain management, medications, medical supplies and equipment, and assistance with the emotional, psychological, and spiritual aspects of dying. A hospice team usually consists of nurses, home health aides, social workers, bereavement counselors, and clergy, as well as a hospice physician and the patient's personal physician.

Hospice care is usually provided in the patient's home. It can also be made available at a special hospice residence designed with a homelike atmosphere, or in assisted living or skilled nursing facilities. The benefit for Medicare and Medicaid patients is remarkably generous. Medicare pays out $601 per patient per day for inpatient hospice care (and $789 per day for the typical patient who gets 24-hour home care), yet there are no copays, deductibles, or out-of-pocket expenses for the beneficiary. Private insurer hospice benefits offer a variety of hospice services, though they're typically not as generous, according to the Hospice Association of America. To get Medicare or private insurance to cover hospice care, a patient needs only a physician's referral.

Hurdles

Until recently, hospice care, which began as a community-based movement back in the 1960s, has been slow to gain a foothold. Perhaps the biggest hurdle, some say, has been doctors' reluctance to recommend it for their dying patients. Hospice is about caring, not curing, which is often a stumbling block for physicians. "They are focused on healing, and by referring someone to hospice care, they feel like something of a failure," says Michelle Hartman, a registered nurse and clinical director of Good Samaritan Hospice, a mission of Concordia Lutheran Ministries in Cabot, Pa. Patients and their families, too, can be resistant to the idea. "By accepting hospice, you are accepting that you are dying," says Kathy Clements, a nurse and executive director of Hospice of the Rapidan. "That's tough to think about."

As a result, referrals to hospice tend to come unnecessarily late in the game—though that's starting to change. The average time in hospice is currently just 20 days. "That makes it difficult for us to do our best work," says Hartman. "With four to six months, we can improve end-of-life care dramatically with pain management, music therapy, massage—and help family members deal with grief issues."

As demand for hospice care surges, Medicare has upped its scrutiny of the program's cost and quality. For the first time since Medicare began paying for hospice care 25 years ago, the Centers for Medicare and Medicaid Services, the federal health agency that administers Medicare, has new rules for providers. The new regulations, which ratchet up quality-of-care standards, go into effect in December. Hospice providers will be required to provide a closer accounting of the care they offer and show the agency they are improving in areas where they have been lacking. The rules also assure hospice patients a say in their treatment plans and the option to choose their own attending physician.

That's good news for patients. "It's a significant improvement and will bring better day-to-day management," says J. Donald Schumacher, NHPCO president and CEO. "The new regulations [ensure] a framework that will reduce disparities in care and ultimately help consumers pick a hospice provider." Initially, quality-of-care data will be available only to each hospice organization and Medicare, but eventually data are expected to be shared with the public, as the federal government has done with such data for nursing homes and hospitals and home health organizations.

The Bad News

But not all the changes are positive. In October, the agency that oversees Medicare also cut the average reimbursement hospices receive by more than 4 percent nationwide. The goal: to trim hospice expenditures by $2.2 billion over five years. Last year, Medicare spent about $10 billion on hospice care, up from nearly $3 billion in 2000.

Those cuts have hospice operators fuming. "I understand the need for Medicare to look seriously at total healthcare expenditures, and I understand the need to manage costs, but these cuts, if fully implemented, will mean that hospices will be forced to scale back care at the bedside or even shut their doors altogether," Schumacher says. Hospice executives argue that although the price tag for the benefit seems high, it pays for itself. In a study published last year in *Social Science and Medicine,* Duke University researchers found that hospice reduced Medicare costs by an average of $2,309 per hospice patient.

Other providers take a more sanguine view. "Hospice has to do its part to conserve Medicare dollars and should not be immune to the same kind of scrutiny done to business practices at hospitals and nursing homes," says Susan Levine, executive director of Hospice of the Valley, a Phoenix nonprofit founded in 1977 and one of the nation's oldest and largest hospices. "Although I do worry that small, rural hospices who never have enough money will suffer, I'm reluctant to believe that

tightening the reimbursement will cause urban and suburban hospices to struggle to survive."

If Schumacher is right, however, the cuts are discouraging news for the mounting numbers of patients seeking hospice. As aging baby boomers face end-of-life situations for themselves and their parents, the number of patients is likely to continue rising. Four out of 5 patients are 65 or older, and one third of all hospice patients are 85 or older, according to NHPCO data.

Cancer patients have traditionally been the primary group entering hospice care, followed by those in the final stages of heart disease. Yet demand is increasingly coming from dementia patients, including those with Alzheimer's disease, who now account for 10.2 percent of hospice admissions nationwide, up from 5.5 percent in 2000.

Alzheimer's patients' pressing need for hospice is due in large measure to the care-intensive later stages of the disease. Patients are often bedridden and unable to communicate or care for themselves. Nursing homes are often ill prepared to handle these patients, who may require multiple medications to ease pain, anxiety, agitation, and sleeplessness. Moreover, the patients can become aggressive if medication is not closely monitored and specially trained care taken in handling routine procedures such as bathing and feeding. As a result, a growing number of patients are turned away from nursing home facilities or removed from their existing one. With no place else to turn, frequently they wind up back under home care or in a hospice facility.

Dealing with Dementia

To handle the volume of patients with end-stage Alzheimer's and related conditions, some hospices have developed specialized programs for people with dementia. Hospice of the Valley, a Phoenix nonprofit founded in 1977, is one of the nation's oldest and largest hospices, and it initiated a special dementia program in 2003. The program's director, Maribeth Gallagher, says its core curriculum focuses on educating both professional caregivers, such as nurses and physicians, and spouses, friends, and volunteers on how to maximize a dementia patient's comfort and quality of life. The hospice currently serves 639 patients with a primary diagnosis of dementia, nearly three times the number of dementia patients it had when the program began.

Unfortunately, Gallagher says, too few hospices have specialized dementia programs, and too few dementia patients are referred to hospice in the first place. One reason is that the vagaries of the disease make it difficult to predict when death is near. Moreover, physicians, families, and caregivers often do not view Alzheimer's disease as a terminal illness because patients with the disease typically live for eight or nine years before dying of, say, an acute infection.

Beverly Stack, too, has trouble thinking of her husband's illness as terminal, but she is grateful that, at the doctor's urging, she made the call to the Hospice of Rapidan. "The nurses are giving me a lot of support," she says. "And that's what I need right now. They're here for him . . . and for me."

When Death Strikes without Warning

After years of neglect, a devastating effect of epilepsy, sudden death, is drawing new scrutiny.

JENNIFER COUZIN

The call came on a Thursday, 21 February 2002, while Jeanne Donalty sat at her desk at work. Her son Chris, a 21-year-old senior at a Florida college, had stopped breathing. His girlfriend found him on his bed, surrounded by the books he'd been studying and a summer job application. Paramedics were unable to revive him, and just like that, Chris Donalty was gone.

Chris Donalty had had epilepsy—he suffered his first seizure in school when he was 9 years old—but his mother at first saw no clear line connecting his death and the disease for which he was being treated. An autopsy found no visible cause of death, and it was shortly after that that Jeanne Donalty discovered a term she had never heard before: SUDEP.

Sudden unexpected death in epilepsy, SUDEP was first written up in *The Lancet* in 1868 by a British physician; he described the phenomenon as "sudden death in a fit." Neurologists today are familiar with SUDEP, which is thought to follow a seizure, and most specialists have lost patients in this way. "Four or five times a year, someone will not come to my clinic because they have a SUDEP death," says Mark Richardson, a neurologist at King's College London. Most victims, like Chris Donalty, are in their 20s or 30s.

SUDEP has been little studied and is rarely discussed in the medical and scientific communities. Families often learn of it only after a relative's death. In the United Kingdom, which is well ahead of the United States in tracking SUDEP, it's estimated that SUDEP strikes at least 500 people a year. It's thought to explain between 8% and 17% of deaths in people with epilepsy. Among those with frequent seizures, the number may be as high as 40%. This increased risk, recognized only recently, underscores that SUDEP is more likely to occur if seizures are more frequent or treatment is inadequate.

Chris Donalty was in that high-risk group: Despite taking his medications as prescribed, he suffered seizures regularly for 2 years before his death. But he never told his parents—because, they now believe, he did not want to lose his driver's license. "I don't know of any other disease that can be fatal where patients aren't aware of" that risk, says his mother.

Driven largely by grieving families, more doctors are discussing risk of SUDEP with patients, and research is picking up. A few studies are focusing on what happens to breathing and heart rhythm during seizures. In the U.K., researchers and advocates hope to set up a nationwide registry of SUDEP cases. The U.S. National Institutes of Health (NIH) will host several dozen specialists at its Bethesda, Maryland, campus this fall in a first-ever meeting on SUDEP. Still, the epilepsy community is divided on what to tell patients about the risk of sudden death—and exactly what should be done about it.

In from the Shadows

Epilepsy, characterized by recurrent seizures caused by abnormal electrical activity in the brain, has long carried a stigma. Some say this may explain why physicians swept SUDEP under the rug: They didn't want to magnify existing fears, especially because no way to prevent it is known. "There was a real concern that the main message should be, 'You can live a completely normal life with epilepsy,'" says Jane Hanna, who helped found the nonprofit Epilepsy Bereaved in Wantage, U.K., after her 27-year-old partner died of SUDEP shortly after he was diagnosed. Even textbooks on epilepsy omitted mention of SUDEP.

But this discretion carried drawbacks, burying historical knowledge of SUDEP cases and slowing clinical investigation, says Lina Nashef, a neurologist at King's College Hospital in London. Until the early 20th century, many people with epilepsy lived in asylums or other institutions, where staff recognized that patients sometimes died during or after seizures. But the collective memory of these deaths faded as antiepilepsy drugs became widely available and patients began living independently. Most who die of SUDEP now do so at home, unobserved.

Nashef began investigating SUDEP as a research project for a postgraduate degree in 1993, interviewing 26 families who had lost someone to sudden death. Although nearly all the deaths occurred without witnesses, Nashef was often told of signs, such as a bitten tongue, that occur after a seizure. The evidence in other cases was more circumstantial: One young man in his late teens, whose seizures were triggered by flickering light from television and computer screens, was found dead at a computer terminal in the library.

Nashef identified a handful of characteristics that the SUDEP victims shared. All but three were battling regular seizures, though sometimes not more than two or three a year. And all had suffered from a particular type, called generalized tonic-clonic or, colloquially, grand mal seizure. Such seizures, the kind most people associate with epilepsy, are accompanied by a loss of consciousness and violent jerking motions and affect large swaths of the brain.

What Goes Wrong?

Digging deeper into SUDEP, Nashef and others have focused on two life-sustaining functions: respiration and heartbeat. Most physicians now believe that SUDEP stems from arrested breathing, called apnea, or heartbeat, called asystole.

One broader question is whether apnea or asystole strike even during seizures that aren't fatal. Neurologists Maromi Nei and her mentor, Michael Sperling, both at Thomas Jefferson University in Philadelphia, provided an early clue in 2000 when they described electrocardiogram patterns from 43 people with epilepsy. Although none died of SUDEP, 17 of these patients had cardiac abnormalities during or right after seizures, including significant arrhythmias and, in one case, no heartbeat at all for 6 seconds.

More recently, Nei and her colleagues investigated hospital records from 21 people who later died, apparently of SUDEP, and compared their heart rhythms with those from the original study, to see whether the SUDEP cohort had some signs of susceptibility. The biggest difference, they reported in 2004, was not the prevalence of arrhythmias but "a greater degree of heart rate change," says Nei, with heart rate soaring by about 80 beats per minute during seizures that struck while they slept. Seizures tend to boost heart rate because they can provoke the autonomic nervous system, especially when the brain regions stimulated are those that trigger such "fight-or-flight" reactions. These data hinted that the phenomenon is exaggerated in those who later die of SUDEP.

"Four or five times a year, someone will not come to my clinic because they have a SUDEP death."

—Mark Richardson, King's College London

Now Nei is implanting devices under the left collarbone of 19 people with intractable epilepsy to gather data on their heart rhythm over a span of 14 months. Neurologist Paul Cooper of Hope Hospital near Manchester, U.K., is beginning a similar study with 200 people.

Both studies follow a related and troubling report in 2004 from *The Lancet*. There, a group of British researchers described cardiac data from 377 seizures in 20 patients gathered over 2 years. Four of the 20 had perilous stretches of asystole and later had pacemakers permanently implanted to jump-start their hearts if needed.

What might be behind this effect? Asystole isn't always dangerous, although it sounds alarming; it can happen even during some fainting spells. A normal heart starts beating again on its own—which leads clinicians to wonder whether the hearts of patients struck by SUDEP may harbor invisible defects. One possibility is that over time, repeated seizures can scar and damage the organ. Another is that a genetic defect may be causing both heart rhythm problems and epilepsy.

Earlier this year, Nashef, King's College geneticist Neeti Hindocha, and their colleagues intrigued epilepsy specialists with a report on a family with a rare form of inherited epilepsy, including two members who died from SUDEP. The researchers, after gathering DNA from the living, found that all 10 family members who had epilepsy also carried a previously undescribed mutation in a gene called *SCN1A*, which was responsible for their disease. A so-called ion channel gene, *SCN1A* helps control electrical signaling between cells. Similar genes have been linked to epilepsy and sudden cardiac death. The authors postulated that the SUDEP deaths in this family were also caused by *SCN1A*, which could have disrupted heart rhythm or brain-stem function in addition to triggering epilepsy. A group at Baylor College of Medicine in Houston, Texas, is now studying whether ion channel genes that can freeze the heart are also present in brain tissue.

If cardiac defects like these are behind SUDEP, "it might be something preventable," says Stephan Schuele, director of the Comprehensive Epilepsy Center at Northwestern Memorial Hospital in Chicago, Illinois. People with gene defects that cause sudden cardiac death, for example, receive pacemakers that can shock their hearts into beating again. Perhaps, doctors say, the same could be done for epilepsy—if they can determine who's at risk of SUDEP to begin with.

Missing Clues

But Schuele, who's looking for other causes of SUDEP, notes that despite a few reports pointing to genetics, "there is no direct evidence" that asystole is killing people with epilepsy. Schuele wonders if the body's way of stopping seizures in the brain could also be disturbing vital brainstem function in some patients. These mechanisms, which are just starting to be explored and involve surges of certain neurotransmitters, may go overboard and cause chaos in the autonomic nervous system, which governs heart rate and respiration.

The detective work is slow and arduous, in part because so few cases of SUDEP have come to light from epilepsy monitoring units in hospitals, where vital signs are recorded—perhaps, Schuele suggests, because health workers are loath to admit that a SUDEP death occurred on their watch. Last

August, neurologists Philippe Ryvlin of the Hospices Civils de Lyon in France and Torbjörn Tomson of the Karolinska Hospital in Stockholm, Sweden, began surveying 180 hospitals in Europe for information on SUDEP deaths or "near-misses" that required resuscitation. Two months ago, they extended their search worldwide, collecting cases from as far away as India and the United States. They expect to conclude their collection and analysis in about a year.

Just four cases have been published. The most detailed, in 1997 on a patient in Bristol, U.K., reported that that person's brain waves went flat before the pulse faded, perhaps causing a failure of the brain region that controls breathing. This suggests that heart failure could be a consequence, not a cause, of SUDEP. Still, "the mechanism of that brain-activated shutdown is very mysterious," says Ryvlin. "Nobody knows what it could be."

There are clues that respiration is key. By monitoring it in hospitalized epilepsy patients, Nashef found that episodes of apnea were common during seizures. And a mouse strain used for decades to test epilepsy drugs has the disconcerting habit of dying from respiratory failure after a severe seizure. That was "generally considered a nuisance," says Carl Faingold, a neuropharmacologist at Southern Illinois University in Springfield, until he and a handful of others realized the mice could be used to study SUDEP. At Boston College, biologist Thomas Seyfried found that putting the mice in an oxygen chamber during seizures prevented death in all of them.

Faingold considered whether the neurotransmitter serotonin, which functions in the brain's respiratory network, might play a role. He gave the mice the antidepressant Prozac, a serotonin booster, and found that though their seizures remained the same, they were at least 90% less likely to die afterward.

Faingold is disappointed that the mouse work has received little attention and no financial support from NIH—his SUDEP research is funded by an epilepsy advocacy group—and its relevance to humans has been questioned. Because no one can predict who will die of SUDEP or when, "if you don't have a way of investigating [SUDEP] in animals, you're very limited," he says.

Acknowledging the Unmentionable

Meanwhile, doctors face a more pressing question: what to tell their patients about SUDEP. "I admit, I am still trying to figure out the best way to do this," says Elizabeth Donner, a pediatric neurologist at the Hospital for Sick Children in Toronto, Canada. She has grown more willing to share the information, but still, "sometimes we worry in telling people about this phenomenon . . . we could actually make their lives worse." Already, one of the toughest aspects of epilepsy is its unpredictability. "When you add in a statement that some people die, and we don't know why and we can't predict it and we can't prevent it, that can be very scary."

U.K. national guidelines in 2004 recommended that physicians discuss SUDEP with everyone who has epilepsy. In reality, a survey of British neurologists published 2 years ago showed, "nobody told anybody anything," says Cooper. Cooper and some other physicians believe that the 30% or so of patients whose epilepsy does not respond to medication—or those reluctant to take it—ought to be told of SUDEP, because they are at a higher risk than people whose epilepsy is controlled. The latter group, he believes, does not need to know about SUDEP.

That perspective doesn't sit well with epilepsy advocates. "Anecdotally, we're aware of deaths every year in people with second or third seizures," says Hanna of Epilepsy Bereaved. "It does worry me a bit if there's going to be some basic clinical practice that just cuts the line with people who seem to have the most serious epilepsy."

Jeanne Donalty still struggles with her family's ignorance of SUDEP while Chris was alive. "I'm not insensitive to how hard this is for a physician," she says. If she had known of SUDEP then, "I would have been upset; . . . who wouldn't be? But I think you have the right to have all the knowledge about the disease that is out there, so that you can make your decisions based on that knowledge." When it comes to sharing information on SUDEP, says Donalty, "to me, it's easy. You tell everybody."

UNIT 4
Suicide

Unit Selections

Key Points to Consider

- Do suicide rates vary around the world? Just how is suicide viewed by individuals in today's society?

- How "rational" is "rational suicide"? Are high-risk individuals such as heavy smokers, overeating or undereating individuals, or race-car drivers suicidal?

- Do you know of someone who committed suicide? Did that individual show any signs of being suicidal? What is meant by the word suicide?

- The topic of suicide is presented on the Internet. One can even find ways to take her/his own life by looking on the Internet. Should such ways to die be so available to anyone who can turn on a computer and Google? What are the ethical issues involved here?

Student Website

www.mhhe.com/cls

Internet References

Articles on Euthanasia: Ethics
http://ethics.acusd.edu/Applied/Euthanasia
Euthanasia and Physician-Assisted Suicide
www.religioustolerance.org/euthanas.htm
Kearl's Guide to the Sociology of Death: Moral Debates
www.trinity.edu/~mkearl/death-5.htm/#eu
The Kevorkian Verdict
www.pbs.org/wgbh/pages/frontline/kevorkian
Living Wills (Advance Directive)
www.mindspring.com/~scottr/will.html
Not Dead Yet
www.notdeadyet.org
Suicide Awareness: Voices of Education
www.save.org
UNOS: United Network for Organ Sharing
www.unos.org
Youth Suicide League
www.unicef.org/pon96/insuicid.htm

The word *suicide,* meaning "self" and "to kill," was first used in English in 1651. Early societies sometimes forced certain members into committing suicide for ritual purposes and occasionally expected such of widows and slaves. There is also a strong inheritance from Hellenic and Roman times of rational suicide when disease, dishonor, or failures were considered unbearable. Attitudes toward suicide changed when St. Augustine laid down rules against it that became basic Christian doctrine for centuries.

In recent years, suicide has attracted increasing interest and scrutiny by sociologists, psychologists, and others in efforts to reduce its incidence. Suicide is a major concern in the United States today, and understanding suicide is important so that warning signs in others can be recognized. To what extent are nonfamily members responsible for the suicides of young adults when they do not intervene?

Just what constitutes suicide is not clear today. Risky behavior that leads to death may or may not be classified as suicide. We have differing attitudes toward suicide. Suicide rates are high in adolescents, the elderly, and males. A person with high vulnerability is an alcoholic, depressed male between the ages of 75 and 84. Suicidal persons often talk about the attempt before the act and display observable signs of potential suicide. Males are more likely to complete suicide than females because they use more lethal weapons such as guns.

For suicidal persons, the act is an easy solution to their problems—a permanent answer to an often temporary set of problems. The public push for suicide prevention can also be a method of resolving the grief caused by a child taking his or her own life, whether as an adolescent or an adult. The father of Ramon Sampedro (played by Javier Basdem in the movie "The Sea Inside") said this about his adult son's wanting to commit suicide because of a diving accident which left him a quadriplegic, "There is only one thing worse than having a child die on you. It's having him want to die." Certainly a suicide not only leaves a void for family members but

© Laurent Hamels/Photoalto/PictureQuest

typically leaves them feeling guilty and asking where *they* went wrong.

Suicide rates around the world are presented from the mid-twentieth century to 2004 in this section. Additionally, how suicide is defined is addressed in "On 'Intention' in the Definition of Suicide." Was it an accident or a suicide?

A relatively new topic regarding suicide has to do with the Internet. Two articles discuss the availability of suicide information on the Internet and the pros and cons of this: "A Search for Death: How the Internet Is Used as a Suicide Cookbook" and "Ethical, Legal, and Practical Issues in the Control and Regulation of Suicide Promotion and Assistance over the Internet." Literally, there are these cookbook approaches to suicide to be found by simply going on the Internet.

When using a gun in a suicidal attempt, do women and men aim the same? Stack and Wasserman address this in "Gender and Suicide Risk: The Role of Wound Site."

Suicide Rates in the World: 1950–2004

KA-YUET LIU, DPHIL

S uicide rates in the world differ greatly across countries. Such geographical variations are central to Durkheim's (1897/1951) argument that social factors have an important role in suicide. In this study I describe the cross-country differences and the trends of suicide rates in 71 countries that had ever reported mortality data to the World Health Organization (WHO) between 1950 and 2004. It updates the findings from the previous studies using the same data source (Bridges & Kunselman, 2003; Levi et al., 2003; Schmidtke et al., 1999) and provides the latest overview on the suicide rates in these countries.

Another aim of this study is to apply a new method to quantify the temporal stability of suicide rates. Since Durkheim, the historical stability of country-specific suicide rates often has been mentioned in the literature (e.g., Lester, 1996). Previous studies attempted to gauge the extent of this stability by measures such as percentage change, ranking, and range (e.g., Levi et al., 2003). These measures, however, in themselves do not provide a meaningful baseline on the magnitude of the overall stability of suicide rates. Random-effect models, in contrast, can estimate the proportions of variance that are due to between-country and within-country differences (Rabe-Hesketh & Skrondal, 2005). This study makes use of this unique feature of random-effect models and provides precise estimates of the historical stability of suicide rates.

Data and Methods

The data are from the WHO's Mortality Database (WHO, 2006). There were 124 WHO member countries that had ever reported data to the WHO between 1950 and 2004.[1] (The term *country* here also refers to territories or regions, as appropriate. Certain regions, such as Hong Kong, submit mortality data to the WHO independently. Separate statistics also are reported for the rural and urban populations in China.) The countries differ in the years that data are available and the extent of misclassifications and underreporting; however, it is unlikely that their magnitude is large enough to generate the epidemiological patterns being observed (Bertolote, Fleischmann, De Leo & Wasserman, 2004; Bridges & Kunselman, 2003; Pescosolido & Mendelsohn, 1986; Sainsbury, 1983).

Among the reporting countries, the 46 countries that ever had fewer than five cases of suicides per year are excluded from the analysis as reliable rates cannot be estimated. The majority of these excluded countries have a population of fewer than 100,000 people. Countries no longer in existence as of 2006 are also excluded. The remaining 71 countries are included in the analysis. The majority of these countries are found in Europe, followed by Asia. No data from African countries are available, reflecting the fact that many African countries do not collect mortality data routinely or do not supply them to international organizations.

Each reporting country codes the causes of deaths according to the *International Classification of Diseases* (*ICD 7–10;* World Health Organization, 1955, 1967, 1975, 1992). Between 1950 and 2004, there were four revisions of the *ICD* (*ICD-7* to *ICD-10*), and the reporting countries differed in the years in which they adopted the different *ICD* revisions. The four *ICD* revisions adopt similar definitions of suicide; in this study, suicide refers to the following *ICD* codes: E963, E970-E979 in *ICD-7,* E950-E959 in *ICD-8* and *ICD-9, and* X60-X84 in *ICD-10.* I use the raw data of the WHO Mortality Database, which contain the annual numbers of deaths by cause of deaths, age group, and gender. The population data in the Mortality Database are used to calculate annual overall, age-and gender-specific suicide rates per 100,000. Regional rates are calculated by dividing the total number of suicides by the population size in each region.[2]

Following Bridges and Kunselman (2003) and Schmidtke et al. (1999), I classify the countries according to the system used by the World Population Prospectus project (United Nations, 2007b). The countries are categorized into major regions and subregions in the world (see Table 1). The United Nations' Human Development Index (HDI) is used as a summary index of the level of development of the countries (United Nations, 2007a). The HDI is calculated based on life expectancy, literacy, education, and standard of living (United Nations, 2007a). Roughly equal numbers of countries are grouped into four levels of development (i.e., lowest, low, high, and highest) according to their HDI.

A random-effects linear regression model was used to detect the trends over time. In each random-effects model, the dependent variable is suicide rates and the independent variable is calendar year. Random-effect modeling corrects the estimation bias due to the clustering of the data (i.e., years nested within countries) (Stata Corporation, 2005). It also partitions

Table 1 Countries by Region and Subregion

Region	Subregion	No. of Countries (N=71)	Countries
Asia (n = 19)	E Asia	6	Hong Kong SAR, Taiwan, Republic of Korea, China: selected rural areas, China: selected urban areas, and Japan
	SC Asia	7	Turkmenistan, Kyrgyzstan, Sri Lanka, Uzbekistan, Iran: cities, Tajikistan, and Kazakhstan
	SE Asia	3	Singapore, Thailand, and the Philippines
	W Asia	4	Israel, Georgia, Armenia, and Azerbaijan
Europe (n = 35)	E Europe	10	Czech Republic, Romania, Slovakia, Belarus, Bulgaria, Ukraine, Russian Federation, Hungary, Republic of Moldova, and Poland
	N Europe	9	Estonia, Ireland, Norway, Denmark, Finland, Latvia, Sweden, United Kingdom, and Lithuania
	S Europe	10	Albania, Serbia and Montenegro, TFYR Macedonia, Portugal, Italy, Croatia, Spain, Greece, Bosnia and Herzegovina, and Slovenia
	W Europe	6	Netherlands, France, Belgium, Germany, Austria, and Switzerland
Latin America and the Caribbean (n = 12)	C America	3	Mexico, El Salvador, and Colombia
	Caribbean	3	Dominican Republic, Cuba, and Puerto Rico
	S America	6	Argentina, Uruguay, Peru, Paraguay-reporting areas, Chile, and Venezuela
North America (n = 2)	N America	2	United States and Canada
Oceania (n = 2)	Australia/ New Zealand	2	New Zealand and Australia

the variance by the different levels, and interclass correlation coefficient (rho) serves as a measure of the proportion of variance attributable to the country level (Stata Corporation, 2005). Alternative model specifications and estimation methods are used to check the robustness of the results. Stata SE Version 9 software was used to perform all the analyses.

Results
Cross-Country Differences in Suicide Rates

The suicide mortality figures for the 20 countries with the highest and lowest suicide rates are reported in Table 2. The Appendix provides the figures of all 71 countries. Overall suicide rates range from 0.5 per 100,000 in the Philippines to 40.2 per 100,000 in Lithuania. Male suicide rates show an even greater range: from 0.5 per 100,000 in the Philippines to 70.1 per 100,000 in Lithuania. In contrast, female suicide rates fall within a narrower range, from 0.3 per 100,000 in Peru to 24.7 per 100,000 in rural China. In most countries, male suicide rates are higher than female suicide rates. China is still the only country where women have a higher suicide rate than men.[3]

Countries at similar levels of development also differ greatly in their suicide rates. Among the countries with the lowest levels of development as measured by the HDI, overall suicide rates range from 0.5 per 100,000 in the Philippines to 33.2 per 100,000 in Sri Lanka. Among the countries with low levels of HDI, the range is 0.5 per 100,000 (Peru) to 35.1 per 100,000 (Belarus). The same range is 3.4 per 100,000 (Greece) to 40.2 per 100,000 (Lithuania) for countries with high levels of HDI, and 8.3 per 100,000 (Spain) to 25.5 per 100,000 (Japan) for countries with the highest levels of HDI.

Regional Patterns of Suicide

The overall and gender-specific suicide rates and the male:female ratios by subregion are reported in Table 3. In general, Europe has higher rates than the other regions, while countries in Latin America and the Caribbean tend to have lower rates. Among the subregions, Western Asia had the lowest overall male and female suicide rates. Eastern Europe has the highest suicide rates as well as the highest male suicide rates and male:female ratios. The highest female suicide rates and the lowest male:female ratios are found in Eastern Asia.

The last two columns of Table 3 show the range of the country-specific suicide rates in each subregion. Some regional

Table 2 Countries with Highest and Lowest Suicide Rates

Country	Year	Region	Subregion	HDI	Suicide Rates Per 100,000			
					All	M	F	M/F
10 Countries with highest suicide rates								
Lithuania	2004	Europe	N. Europe	High	40.2	70.1	14.0	5.0
Belarus	2003	Europe	E. Europe	Low	35.1	63.3	10.3	6.2
Russian Federation	2004	Europe	E. Europe	Low	34.3	61.6	10.7	5.8
Sri Lanka	1986	Asia	S.C. Asia	Lowest	33.2	46.9	18.9	2.5
Kazakhstan	2003	Asia	S.C. Asia	Low	29.2	51.0	8.9	5.7
Slovenia	2003	Europe	S. Europe	High	28.1	45.0	12.0	3.8
Hungary	2003	Europe	E. Europe	High	27.7	44.9	12.0	3.7
Japan	2003	Asia	E. Asia	Highest	25.5	38.0	13.5	2.8
Estonia	2003	Europe	N. Europe	High	25.3	44.3	9.0	4.9
Latvia	2004	Europe	N. Europe	High	24.3	42.9	8.5	5.0
10 Countries with lowest suicide rates								
Philippines	1981	Asia	S.E. Asia	Lowest	0.5	0.5	0.4	1.4
Peru	1983	Latin America and the Caribbean	S. America	Low	0.5	0.7	0.3	2.3
Azerbaijan	2002	Asia	W. Asia	Lowest	1.1	1.8	0.5	4.0
Iran-cities	1987	Asia	S.C. Asia	Lowest	1.7	2.1	1.3	1.6
Armenia	2003	Asia	W. Asia	Low	1.8	3.2	0.5	6.0
Dominican Republic	1985	Latin America and the Caribbean	Caribbean	Lowest	2.1	2.9	1.4	2.1
Georgia	2001	Asia	W. Asia	Lowest	2.2	3.4	1.1	3.0
Tajikistan	2001	Asia	S.C. Asia	Lowest	2.6	2.9	2.3	1.3
Paraguay (reporting areas)	1987	Latin America and the Caribbean	S. America	Lowest	2.7	3.3	2.1	1.6
Mexico	1995	Latin America and the Caribbean	C. America	Low	3.2	5.4	1.0	5.6

patterns seem to exist, but suicide rates still vary extensively within regions. For example, although the suicide rates in Eastern Europe tend to be high, they still range from 12.5 per 100,000 (Romania) to 35.1 per 100,000 (Belarus).

Trends over Time

Comparing each country's overall suicide rates in the first and the last year that they submitted data to the WHO, 64 had a positive increase in suicide rates (last two columns, Appendix). Twenty out of the 71 countries had a more than 30% increase in their overall suicide rates, while 9 countries had a decrease of more than 30%. The five countries with the biggest changes in suicide rates are Sri Lanka, Ireland, Thailand, Colombia, and Poland. Note that Thailand and Colombia both had low base rates of suicide and, therefore, their high percentage increases

represent less of an increase as compared to the other three countries.

Apart from percentage changes, the importance of between-country differences is traditionally represented by the ranking of countries in terms of their suicide rates across different years. The ranking by overall suicide rates of the 20 countries that have been submitting data to the Mortality Database since the 1950s is shown in Table 4. Although there are a few changes in the ranking across the years, the overall pattern appears to be remarkably stable.

The ranking method, however, can only compare a few countries at a time and thus cannot fully use all the information contained in the data. In contrast, random-effect models utilize all the information, including from those countries which reported data for only a few years. Table 5 reports the estimates from the

Table 3   Regional Patterns of Suicide

Region	Subregion	Regional Suicide Rate per 100,000			M/F	Range of Country-Specific Suicide Rates	
		All	M	F		Lowest	Highest
Asia	E Asia	19.1	24.8	13.4	1.9	6.7	25.5
	SC Asia	8.9	13.6	4.3	3.2	0.5	33.2
	SE Asia	4.7	7.1	2.5	2.8	0.5	10.1
	W Asia	3.0	4.9	1.1	4.5	1.1	6.2
Europe	E Europe	26.6	47.1	8.5	5.5	12.5	35.1
	N Europe	10.9	17.2	4.9	3.5	6.9	40.2
	S Europe	8.9	13.9	4.1	3.4	3.4	28.1
	W Europe	15.1	22.6	8.1	2.8	9.3	21.1
Latin America and the Caribbean	C America	3.4	5.6	1.3	4.3	3.2	7.9
	Caribbean	11.8	16.6	7.1	2.3	2.1	18.3
	S America	4.9	7.8	2.0	3.9	0.5	10.3
North America	N America	11.0	17.9	4.3	4.2	11.0	11.6
Oceania	Australia/ New Zealand	11.8	18.8	5.0	3.8	11.8	11.9

Table 4   Ranking among 20 Selected Countries Based on Their Overall Suicide Rates

Country	1960	1970	1980	1990	2000
Hungary	1	1	1	1	1
Denmark	5	4	2	3	2
Austria	2	2	3	4	3
Finland	4	5	4	2	4
Switzerland	6	6	5	5	5
Sweden	7	3	6	7	6
France	8	7	7	6	7
Japan	3	8	8	8	8
Canada	15	12	9	13	9
Hong Kong SAR	9	9	10	15	10
Norway	17	16	11	9	11
United States	11	11	12	14	12
Singapore	14	14	13	11	13
Australia	10	10	14	12	14
New Zealand	12	13	15	10	15
Netherlands	16	17	16	16	16
Portugal	13	15	17	18	17
Italy	18	18	18	19	18
Ireland	20	20	19	17	19
Greece	19	19	20	20	20

random-effects models. The interclass correlation coefficient, *rho*, is found to be larger than 0.9 in all the models. This suggests that the variations in suicide rates, after controlling for the overall time trends, are mainly due to between-country differences rather than within-country fluctuations. The overall suicide rates in these 71 countries appear to have significantly increased, albeit slightly, with years ($b = 0.07, p = 0.014$). When the suicide rates are broken down by gender and age group, however, only the suicide rates among young men (aged 15–34 years) show a significant positive trend over the years. Moreover, the suicide rates of women in their middle-age (aged 35–60 years) and old age (aged over 60 years) have significantly decreased.

Alternative model specifications yield similar estimates on the random components (results not shown). For example, without including year as a covariate, the intraclass correlation *rho* is estimated to be 0.89 in the model for all age groups, which is only slightly lower than the 0.91 as reported in Table 5 (column 3, first row). Allowing different rates of change for each country yields a *rho* estimate of 0.92. The similarity in the estimates of the fixed and the random slopes model suggests the large part of the between-country differences are due to stable country-level differences rather than differences in linear trends. Changing how year is measured (grand mean centered and from first year of observation in the data) does not affect the random component estimates. Allowing fixed nonlinear relationships between suicide rates and year by including a quadratic term also yield very similar results. The *rho* estimates from random effects models fitted to each region (therefore, data from a smaller number of more homogeneous countries are used for each model) are still substantial (0.75–0.91 in the all age group model).

Random effects models with first-order auto regressive disturbance are used to determine if auto-correlated errors are underlying the large within-country dependence. The estimated *rho* in this model for all age groups is 0.94. This suggests the results on intraclass correlation as reported in Table 5 are conservative estimates of the proportion of unexplained variance

Table 5 Parameter Estimates from Random-Effects Models

		All			Men			Women		
		Intercept	Year	Rho	Intercept	Year	Rho	Intercept	Year	Rho
All	β	10.86*	0.07*	0.91	13.87	0.16*	0.93	8.11*	−0.02	0.96
	s.e.	(1.16)	(0.03)		(1.62)	(0.05)		(0.92)	(0.02)	
	p	0.000	0.014		0.000	0.000		0.000	0.229	
15–34	β	11.27*	0.04	0.95	13.95	0.13*	0.93	8.80*	−0.06	0.98
	s.e.	(1.42)	(0.04)		(1.81)	(0.06)		(1.50)	(0.03)	
	p	0.000	0.330		0.000	0.021		0.000	0.089	
35–60	β	19.25*	0.00	0.93	27.46	0.06	0.92	11.87*	−0.07*	0.94
	s.e.	(1.75)	(0.04)		(2.60)	(0.06)		(1.16)	(0.02)	
		0.000	0.968		0.000	0.303		0.000	0.001	
60+	β	27.50*	−0.08	0.97	40.05	−0.04	0.96	18.91*	−0.12*	0.96
	s.e.	(2.66)	(0.05)		(4.01)	(0.08)		(2.14)	(0.04)	
	p	0.000	0.098		0.000	0.668		0.000	0.001	

Note. *$p < 0.05$

Rho is a measure of the proportion of variance that is due to between country-differences χ^2 tests indicate the random-effect components in all of these models are statistically significant.

due to between-country differences. Lastly, maximum likelihood and restricted likelihood estimations yield almost identical results.

Discussion

This study describes the patterns and trends of suicide rates in 71 countries using the latest WHO mortality data and updates the findings from previous studies (Bridges & Kunselman, 2003; Levi et al., 2003; Schmidtke et al., 1999). Similar to the findings from these previous studies, I show that suicide rates vary greatly across countries, even within the same region or at similar levels of development. Within the same country, suicide rates seem to be largely stable over time. Results from the random-effects models show that a great proportion (>90%) of the variance in suicide rates is due to between-country differences. Different model specifications lead to similar conclusions. Although the historical stability of suicide rates has often been remarked on, random-effect modeling represents a novel way to quantify its extent.

Although the overall patterns of country-specific suicide rates are remarkably stable, there appears to be a positive trend in the suicide rates among young (aged 15–34) men in general, as has been previously reported (Cutler, Glaeser, & Norberg, 2001; Gunnell, Middleton, Whitley, Dorling, & Frankel, 2003). Larger social changes are often indicated as underlying such trends. Gunnell et al. (2003) suggest increases in divorces, declines in marriage, and increases in income equality may explain rising suicide rates among younger men in the United Kingdom. Culter et al.'s results suggest the increasing proportion of youths living with stepparents or with single parents may explain the rise in youth suicide.

In contrast, suicide rates among middle (aged 35–60) and older (aged 60+) women had significantly decreased. In addition, certain countries have shown quite substantial changes in their suicide rates across the years. Greater gender equality and a greater acceptance toward working women have been suggested to have contributed to such decreases (Burr, McCall, & Powell-Griner, 1997). Decreasing toxicity of over-the-counter drugs has also been mentioned as a reason for decreases in female suicide rates (Gunnell et al., 2003).

Cross-country differences in the level of suicide rates as well as changes in suicide patterns are likely to be brought about by complex combinations of different factors in each country. Explaining them requires detailed information about each population and is beyond the scope of this paper. However, the epidemiological patterns described in this article do suggest that social factors have a crucial role in suicide. Further cross-cultural, comparative research is needed to understand the mechanisms underlying the stable cross-country differences in suicide.

This study is subject to the following limitations. Underreporting affects the reliability of suicide mortality data, particularly in some countries. Thus some of the residual variance attributed to between-country factors may merely reflect differences in the level of underreporting. However, as mentioned above, it is unlikely that the differences in reporting system are large enough to generate the epidemiological patterns. It is also important to note that the finding on the large proportion of variance attributed to between-country differences should be interpreted in accordance to the historical period that data are available. With a wider window of time or a different period, we may be able to observe larger variations across time relative to the between-country variations.

Appendix   Suicide Rates in 71 Countries

Country	Region	Subregion	HDI	Year	Suicide Rate				Change	
					All	M	F	M/F	%	from
1 Lithuania	Europe	N. Europe	High	2004	40.2	70.1	14.0	5.0	19.5	1981
2 Belarus	Europe	E. Europe	Low	2003	35.1	63.3	10.3	6.2	42.6	1981
3 Russian Federation	Europe	E. Europe	Low	2004	34.3	61.6	10.7	5.8	−0.8	1980
4 Sri Lanka	Asia	S.C. Asia	Lowest	1986	33.2	46.9	18.9	2.5	403.6	1950
5 Kazakhstan	Asia	S.C. Asia	Low	2003	29.2	51.0	8.9	5.7	29.6	1981
6 Slovenia	Europe	S. Europe	High	2003	28.1	45.0	12.0	3.8	−14.1	1985
7 Hungary	Europe	E. Europe	High	2003	27.7	44.9	12.0	3.7	34.8	1955
8 Japan	Asia	E. Asia	Highest	2003	25.5	38.0	13.5	2.8	29.8	1950
9 Estonia	Europe	N. Europe	High	2003	25.3	44.3	9.0	4.9	−31.2	1981
10 Latvia	Europe	N. Europe	High	2004	24.3	42.9	8.5	5.0	−25.9	1980
11 Ukraine	Europe	E. Europe	Low	2004	23.8	43.0	7.3	5.9	0.5	1981
12 China: selected rural areas	Asia	E. Asia	Lowest	1999	22.5	20.4	24.7	0.8	218.7	1987
13 Belgium	Europe	W. Europe	Highest	1997	21.1	31.2	11.4	2.7	52.8	1954
14 Finland	Europe	N. Europe	Highest	2004	20.3	31.7	9.4	3.4	15.2	1952
15 Switzerland	Europe	W. Europe	Highest	2002	19.8	27.4	12.5	2.2	−6.5	1951
16 Croatia	Europe	S. Europe	High	2004	19.6	30.2	9.8	3.1	−12.1	1985
17 Serbia and Montenegro	Europe	S. Europe	Low	2002	19.3	28.8	10.4	2.8	−16.1	1997
18 Cuba	Latin America & the Caribbean	Caribbean	Low	1996	18.3	24.5	12.0	2.0	65.1	1964
19 Republic of Korea	Asia	E. Asia	High	2002	17.9	24.7	11.2	2.2	96.5	1985
20 France	Europe	W. Europe	Highest	2002	17.8	26.6	9.5	2.8	16.4	1950
21 Austria	Europe	W. Europe	Highest	2004	17.3	27.0	8.2	3.3	−26.0	1955
22 Republic of Moldova	Europe	E. Europe	Lowest	2004	16.7	29.3	5.2	5.7	−15.3	1981
23 Czech Republic	Europe	E. Europe	High	2004	15.5	25.9	5.7	4.6	−25.9	1986
24 Hong Kong SAR	Asia	E. Asia	High	2002	15.3	20.7	10.2	2.0	38.2	1960
25 Poland	Europe	E. Europe	High	2003	15.3	26.7	4.5	5.9	125.6	1959
26 Denmark	Europe	N. Europe	Highest	2001	13.6	19.2	8.1	2.4	−42.4	1951
27 Slovakia	Europe	E. Europe	High	2002	13.3	23.6	3.6	6.5	−11.1	1992
28 Sweden	Europe	N. Europe	Highest	2002	13.2	19.5	7.1	2.8	−18.4	1951
29 Taiwan	Asia	E. Asia	Highest	1969	13.2	15.6	10.5	1.5	−14.1	1959
30 Bulgaria	Europe	E. Europe	Low	2004	13.0	19.7	6.7	3.0	49.8	1964
31 Germany	Europe	W. Europe	Highest	2004	13.0	19.7	6.6	3.0	−25.8	1990
32 Romania	Europe	E. Europe	Low	2004	12.5	21.5	4.0	5.4	14.9	1989
33 New Zealand	Oceania	Australia/New Zealand	High	2000	11.9	19.8	4.2	4.7	32.6	1950
34 Australia	Oceania	Australia/New Zealand	Highest	2002	11.8	18.6	5.1	3.6	−7.1	1950
35 Bosnia and Herzegovina	Europe	S. Europe	Low	1991	11.8	20.3	3.3	6.2	15.6	1985
36 Canada	N. America	N. America	Highest	2002	11.6	18.3	5.0	3.6	50.2	1950
37 Ireland	Europe	N. Europe	Highest	2002	11.5	18.9	4.1	4.6	1950	347.8
38 Portugal	Europe	S. Europe	High	2003	11.0	17.5	4.9	3.6	20.5	1955
39 Norway	Europe	N. Europe	Highest	2003	11.0	16.5	5.6	3.0	69.4	1951
40 United States	N. America	N. America	Highest	2002	11.0	17.9	4.2	4.2	23.7	1950

(continued)

Appendix Suicide Rates in 71 Countries *(continued)*

						Suicide Rate				Change	
41 Uruguay	Latin America & the Caribbean	S. America	Low	1990	10.3	16.6	4.2	3.9	−18.0	1955
42 Singapore	Asia	S.E. Asia	High	2003	10.1	12.5	7.6	1.6	−5.5	1955
43 Netherlands	Europe	W. Europe	Highest	2004	9.3	12.7	6.0	2.1	68.2	1950
44 Kyrgyzstan	Asia	S.C. Asia	Lowest	2004	8.9	15.0	3.0	5.0	−35.3	1981
45 Puerto Rico	Latin America & the Caribbean	Caribbean	Highest	1992	8.7	16.0	1.9	8.5	−21.7	1955
46 Turkmenistan	Asia	S.C. Asia	Lowest	1998	8.6	13.8	3.5	3.9	22.7	1981
47 Spain	Europe	S. Europe	Highest	2003	8.3	12.8	3.9	3.3	41.1	1951
48 El Salvador	Latin America & the Caribbean	C. America	Lowest	1993	7.9	10.4	5.5	1.9	−20.5	1955
49 Thailand	Asia	S.E. Asia	Lowest	2002	7.8	12.0	3.8	3.2	−14.6	1955
50 Italy	Europe	S. Europe	High	2002	7.1	11.4	3.1	3.6	5.3	1951
51 United Kingdom	Europe	N. Europe	High	2002	6.9	10.8	3.1	3.5	−27.9	1950
52 TFYR Macedonia	Europe	S. Europe	Low	2003	6.8	9.5	4.0	2.4	−11.3	1991
53 China: selected urban areas	Asia	E. Asia	Lowest	1999	6.7	6.7	6.6	1.0	−33.5	1987
54 Argentina	Latin America & the Caribbean	S. America	Low	1996	6.4	9.9	3.0	3.3	−13.9	1966
55 Uzbekistan	Asia	S.C. Asia	Lowest	2002	6.2	9.3	3.1	3.0	−13.1	1981
56 Israel	Asia	W. Asia	High	2003	6.2	10.4	2.1	4.9	−17.2	1975
57 Chile	Latin America & the Caribbean	S. America	Low	1994	5.7	10.2	1.4	7.4	19.2	1955
58 Venezuela	Latin America & the Caribbean	S. America	Low	1994	5.1	8.3	1.9	4.4	−1.2	1955
59 Albania	Europe	S. Europe	Low	2003	4.0	4.7	3.3	1.4	68.4	1987
60 Colombia	Latin America & the Caribbean	C. America	Lowest	1994	3.5	5.5	1.5	3.6	165.3	1955
61 Greece	Europe	S. Europe	High	2003	3.4	5.6	1.2	4.5	−7.4	1956
62 Mexico	Latin America & the Caribbean	C. America	Low	1995	3.2	5.4	1.0	5.6	81.9	1958
63 Paraguay: reporting areas	Latin America & the Caribbean	S. America	Lowest	1987	2.7	3.3	2.1	1.6	−9.3	1969
64 Tajikistan	Asia	S.C. Asia	Lowest	2001	2.6	2.9	2.3	1.3	−34.5	1981
65 Georgia	Asia	W. Asia	Lowest	2001	2.2	3.4	1.1	3.0	−64.3	1981
66 Dominican Republic	Latin America & the Caribbean	Caribbean	Lowest	1985	2.1	2.9	1.4	2.1	3.8	1958
67 Armenia	Asia	W. Asia	Low	2003	1.8	3.2	0.5	6.0	−38.1	1981
68 Iran: cities	Asia	S.C. Asia	Lowest	1987	1.7	2.1	1.3	1.6	44.0	1983
69 Azerbaijan	Asia	W. Asia	Lowest	2002	1.1	1.8	0.5	4.0	−75.5	1981
70 Peru	Latin America & the Caribbean	S. America	Low	1983	0.5	0.7	0.3	2.3	−64.7	1966
71 Philippines	Asia	S.E. Asia	Lowest	1981	0.5	0.5	0.4	1.4	−29.0	1963

References

Bertolote, J. M., Fleischmann, A., De Leo, D., & Wasserman, D. (2004). Psychiatric diagnosis and suicide: Revising the evidence. *Crisis, 25*(4), 147–155.

Bridges, F. S., & Kunselman, J. C. (2003). Rates of suicide in the world: 2002 update. *National American Journal of Psychology, 5,* 479–484.

Burr, J. A., McCall, P. L., & Powell-Griner, E. (1997). Female labor force participation and suicide. *Sococial Sciences and Medicine, 44,* 1847–1859.

Cutler, D. M., Glaeser, E. L., & Norberg, K. (2001). Explaining the rise in youth suicide. In J. Gruber (Ed.), *Risky behavior among youths: An economic analysis.* Chicago: University of Chicago Press Series: (NBER-C) National Bureau of Economic Research Conference Report.

Durkheim, E. (1951). In G. Simpson (trans.) *Suicide: A study in sociology.* London: Routledge & Kegan Paul. (Originally published 1951)

Gunnell, D., Middleton, N., Whitley, E., Dorling, D., & Frankel, S. (2003). Why are suicide rates rising in young men but falling in the elderly?—A time-series analysis of trends in England and Wales 1950–1998. *Social Sciences & Medicine, 57*(4), 595–611.

Lester, D. (1996). *Patterns of suicide and homicide in the world.* Comack, NY: Nova Science Publishers.

Levi, F., La Vecchia, C., Lucchini, F., Negri, E., Saxena, S., Maulik, P. K., et al. (2003). Trends in mortality from suicide, 1965–99. *Acta Psychiatrica Scandinavica, 108,* 341–349.

Pescosolido, B. A., & Mendelsohn, R. (1986). Social causation or social construction of suicide? An investigation into social organizations of official rates. *American Sociological Review, 51*(1), 80–100.

Rabe-Hesketh, S., & Skrondal, A. (2005). *Multilevel and longitudinal modeling using Stata.* College Station, TX: Stata Press.

Sainsbury, P. (1983). Validity and reliability of trends in suicide statistics. *World Health Statistics Quarterly, 36*(3–4), 339–348.

Schmidtke, A., Weinacker, B., Apter, A., Batt, A., Berman, A., Bille-Brahe, V., et al. (1999). Suicide rates in the world: Update. *Archives of Suicide Research, 5,* 81–89.

Stata Corporation. (2005). *Stata longitudinal/panel data: Reference manual, release 9.* College Station, TX: Stata Press.

United Nations. (2007a). *Human Development Report 2006.* New York: Author.

United Nations. (2007b). *World Population Prospects: The 2006 Revision Highlights.* New York: Author.

WHO. (1950). *International Statistical Classification of Diseases, Injuries, and Causes of Death,* 7th Rev. Geneva: World Health Organizations.

WHO. (1967). *International Statistical Classification of Diseases, Injuries, and Causes of Death,* 8th Rev. Geneva: World Health Organizations.

WHO. (1975). *International Statistical Classification of Diseases, Injuries, and Causes of Death,* 9th Rev. Geneva: World Health Organizations.

WHO. (1992). *International Statistical Classification of Diseases, Injuries, and Causes of Death,* 10th Rev. Geneva: World Health Organizations.

WHO. (2006). *WHO Mortality Database.* Retrieved September 9, 2006 from www.who.int/healthinfo/statistics/mortdata/en/index.html.

Yip, P. S., & Liu, K. Y. (2006). The ecological fallacy and the gender ratio of suicide in China. *British Journal of Psychiatry, 189,* 465–466.

Notes

1. The latest data used by Bridges and Kunselman (2003) were from 2000. The latest data from Levi et al. (2003) and Schmidtke et al. (1999) were from 1999 and 1997, respectively.

2. The latest available count of suicide in each country and population size in the same year is used to calculate the regional suicide rates.

3. In 1999, China's female suicide rate is higher than the male suicide rate in rural areas, while it is slightly lower than the male rate in urban areas. The large rural population drives the overall male:female ratio in suicide to less than one (Yip & Liu, 2006).

KA-YUET LIU is a post-doctoral researcher at the Institute of Social and Economic Research and Policy at Columbia University.

Address correspondence to Ka-yuet Liu, (ISERP), Columbia University, 420 West 118th Street, 8th Floor, IAB, MC 3355, New York, NY 10027; E-mail: kyl2111@columbia.edu

On "Intention" in the Definition of Suicide

KARL ANDRIESSEN, BSW, GCSUICPREVST

The need for a classification system with uniform definitions and guidelines to classify suicide was early recognized and, subsequently, steadily discussed as an essential ground for the development of contemporary suicidology (Beck, Resnick, & Lettieri, 1974; De Leo, Burgis, Bertolote, Kerkhof, & Bille-Brahe, 2004; Farberow & Shneidman, 1961; Linehan, 1997; Maris, 1981, 1992a; Maris, Berman, & Silverman, 2000; Marusic, 2004; O'Carrol et al., 1996; Silverman & Berman, 2005). In the 1980s the U.S. Centers for Disease Control called together a broad working group of "coroners, medical examiners, statisticians and public health agencies" (Rosenberg et al., 1988, p. 1445) to identify criteria for a definition of *suicide* and to develop guidelines for certification. They put forward that *suicide* is a "(1) death arising from (2) an act inflicted upon oneself (3) with the intent to kill oneself," the so-called Operational Criteria for the Determination of Suicide (OCDS). O'Carrol et al. (1996) countered that it was not yet possible to develop a clinical classification system of suicidal behavior due to the limited knowledge of the causal pathways relevant to clinical and prevention work. Instead, based on the OCDS, they elaborated a nomenclature—a set of precise, defined terms to facilitate clear communication. Recently, Marusic (2004) also proposed to use the criteria of Rosenberg et al. to formulate a nomenclature for all suicidal behaviors. Marusic stated that by applying the criteria "1) intention, 2) act of self-destruction, 3) death" (p. 145), it should be possible to formulate a nomenclature for all fatal and nonfatal suicidal behaviors, including suicidal ideation, call for help, and euthanasia.

De Leo et al. (2004) evaluated the criteria and definition of Rosenberg as well as several other definitions. They found that most definitions of suicide share common aspects. These building bricks of the definition are: (1) behavior with fatal outcome; (2) self-initiated, which includes self-inflicted acts, and active/passive acts; and (3) intention or expectation to die. After thorough consideration they proposed the following modified definitions: "Suicide is an act with a fatal outcome which the deceased, knowing or expecting a potentially fatal outcome, has initiated and carried out with the purpose of bringing about wanted changes" (p. 33). Nonfatal suicidal behavior was defined as "[A] non-habitual act with non-fatal outcome that the individual, expecting to, or taking the risk, to die or to inflict bodily harm, initiated and carried out with the purpose of bringing about wanted changes" (p. 36).

In the recent history of suicidology Stengel (1964) formulated "a suicide attempt is any act of self-damage inflicted with self-destructive intention, however vague and ambiguous" (p. 72). Further, he recommended that clinicians should regard "all cases of potentially dangerous self-poisoning or self-inflicted injury as suicidal attempts" (p. 72). Independent from this source, the notion of "potentially" was now included in the modified definition of suicide (De Leo et al., 2004). In addition, in an early discussion chaired by Shneidman the issue of intentions was addressed: "Many acts of self-injury, which are lumped together under the concept of suicide, do not have self-extinction as their goal" (Kubie, 1969, p. 83). "Sometimes, the conscious and unconscious goals may be precisely the reverse" (p. 82). Shneidman's work was later to culminate in the formulation of the "ten commonalities of suicide" (Shneidman, 1996, p. 131). Among others, these included: purpose: to seek a solution; goal: cessation of consciousness; and cognitive state: ambivalence.

The Distinction between Accidental and Suicidal Behavior

Rosenberg et al. (1988) argued that, of the different aspects of the definition, it is more difficult to determine suicidal intention than to determine whether death was self-inflicted. Because the suicidal person has died, it is not possible to identify fully his/her intentions. As a help, Rosenberg et al. provided a list of criteria to consider in the assessment of suicidal intentions. Because of the uncertainty, suicide has become the "residual" category in the so-called natural, accidental, suicide, homicide (NASH) system (De Leo et al., 2004; Maris et al., 2000). This means that there should be either positive evidence of suicide or, alternatively, that the other categories (natural, accidental, and homicidal [and not determined]) can be excluded (O'Carrol et al., 1996).

Mayo (1992) referred to intentionality as the "most subtle feature of the definition" (p. 95). De Leo et al. (2004) called intention "the most contentious aspect of the definitional debate on suicide and non-fatal suicidal behaviours" (p. 29). Indeed, it has been argued that "intention" does not reach scientific standards and that the concept would be too vague to be included in a definition. However, it is now well recognized that suicidal people can have multiple intentions at the same time, that intentions may evolve during the suicidal process of an individual person, and that the suicidal person can be ambivalent regarding the intent to die. Death can be one of the intentions, and at the same time death can be the method to reach another goal. Nobody knows what it is to be dead. So how can someone *wish* to be dead? "Contemplation of his [one's] own death remains a remote, elusive, unreal and abstract concept" (Kubie, 1967, p. 461); however, in the perception of the person death can be "just a more appealing option than living" (De Leo et al., 2004, p. 30).

While the agent of the action allows to distinguish between homicide and suicide, the concept of intention distinguishes between accidental and suicidal behavior. Thus it is essential in a definition of suicide (De Leo et al., 2004; Farberow & Shneidman, 1961; Litman, 1984; Marusic, 2004; Mayo, 1992). To operationalize *intention* these authors proposed the use of measurement scales such as the Suicide Intent Scale, or psychological autopsy studies. Also, the criteria and questionnaire of Rosenberg et al. (1988) are useful in this context.

The Distinction between *Because* and *in Order to*

Despite these observations there is little research that offers a more solid empirical view on the issue of intentions. Several authors have pointed to the fact that intentions are often confused with motives (Hjelmeland & Knizek, 1999; Silverman & Berman, 2005). Maris et al. (2000) defined (the basically legal concept) *motive* as "the cause or reason that moves the will and induces action," and *intent* is "the purpose a person has in using a particular means (e.g., suicide) to effect a result" (p. 37).

Hjelmeland and Knizek (1999) reviewed the psychological literature on the meanings of intentions and motives. Though some authors used *motives* (or reasons) and *intentions* as synonyms, generally the recommendation was to distinguish between the two. In line with the definitions of Maris et al. (2000), Hjelmeland and Knizek argued that "intentional acts satisfy motives," and intentions are related to what the person wants while motives are related to "the reason for the desire" (p. 277). The act is expressed by the intentions. As such, to explain behavior intentions more than motives are closely related to the act. The causal explanation of behavior looks to the past (the external observer's point of view), while the teleological perspective looks for an explanation in the future (the actor's perspective), to what is to be accomplished by the act (Hjelmeland & Knizek, 1999). Interestingly, support for this distinction is found in another scientific field. Beachler (1979) referred to the Austrian/American philosopher Alfred Schütz (1899–1959), who became influential for phenomenological sociology. Starting from the *verstehende* sociology of Weber, Schütz (1932) stated that social activities must be understood by the sense that subjects give to their actions. A crucial issue in the action theory that he developed throughout his life, and first presented in *The Phenomenology of the Social World,* was the distinction between the *um-zu-motiv* and the *weil-motiv* (Beachler, 1979, p. 53; Barber, 2002). The latter consist of the circumstances that have influenced a person's decision to act, or the "past factors that preceded that past decision" (Barber, 2002). This be–*cause* explanation is always retrospective. The first is the opposite, namely the "in order to" perspective. With this, a person projects an action as completed in the future, and looks at what will be realized. Both perspectives can be applied to suicidal behavior; however, the "in order to" would be more closely related to understand the action. The "decision" to act suicidal is only one choice among many options when faced with unbearable experiences. And as long as there is no action, there is no because (Beachler, 1979). Understanding the intentions behind the behavior is possible via the "in order to" perspective. In addition, Barber (2002) correctly mentioned that the observed behavior or the outcome does not necessarily equal the intended outcome. Unforeseen influences may alter the course and the outcome of an action. Also, the easy availability of lethal means may influence the outcome (Hawton, 2002; Hawton et al., 2001). Otherwise said, medically serious suicide attempts are not necessarily equal with high suicide intent. Thus research on intentions (e.g., applying questionnaires or interviews) is needed in all at-risk populations.

Examples of Recent Research

Bearing in mind that the population who dies by suicide is different to, and partly overlapping with, the population that does not die as a result of its suicidal behavior, the intentions of the latter may give some indication of intentions that can be present in the first group as well. We must, however, be aware that the two populations are only partly overlapping (Farberow & Shneidman, 1961). Kerkhof and Arensman (2004) reported that 44% of those who died by suicide have attempted suicide before. Prospectively, 10% to 15% of the people who attempted suicide eventually die by suicide (Maris, 1981, 1992b), and the risk is highest in the first year after a suicide attempt.

In this perspective, interesting research has been done on nonlethal suicidal behavior. It is not a coincidence that the second and updated edition of Mark Williams' 1997 book *The Cry of Pain* was renamed *Suicide and Attempted Suicide* (Williams, 2001), echoing the seminal work of Stengel. Williams (2001, p. 76) included a table from a study of 1986 in the UK regarding twelve "reasons for taking overdoses." Each participant was allowed to mark all items that were applicable to their case. In this study, reasons included both motives and intentions. The top three reasons cited were: "the situation was so unbearable (motive) that I had to do something (intention) and didn't know what else to do" (67% of participants), "I wanted to die" (intention) (61%), and "I wanted to escape (intention) from an impossible situation (motive)" (58%). Ambivalence was obviously present in this population. These answers, together with a few others, resemble well the "ten commonalities of suicide" (Shneidman, 1996). The total number of percentages of the twelve items was 418%. This means that the participants provided an average of four reasons for their suicidal behavior.

Intentions of nonfatal suicidal behavior were also included in the large WHO/Euro Multi-Centre Study on Suicidal Behaviour (Hjelmeland & Hawton, 2004). A list of 14 possible intentions and the Suicidal Intent Scale were applied in 14 regions. Information was gathered on 1,646 persons aged 15 years or more. The fourteen intentions could be grouped in "care seeking," "influencing others," "temporary escape," and "final exit" (p. 74). A major result from this study is that the "parasuicidal patients" across the different regions and countries reported similar intentions (Hjelmeland et al., 2002). Further it was found that intentions did not vary much across gender and age. However, it is noted that *intentions* in this study included *motives* as well. The top three intentions were: "the situation was so unbearable (motive) that I could not think of any other alternative" (76.3% in women, 71.2% in men), "my thoughts were so unbearable, I could not endure them any longer" (motive) (67.7% and 63.6%), and "I wanted to die" (intention) (59.3% and 64.5%). Again, ambivalence and multiple intentions (and motives) per person were found (p. 385). Also, the suicidal intention as reported in the 14-item list correlated with the results of the Suicidal Intent Scale (p. 388). In addition, there was a positive correlation between the national and regional suicide rates and the frequency of the reply "wanted to die" only in women, and not in men (p. 390). This finding supports the hypothesis that, at least partly, and maybe more in women than in men, the intentions of persons who didn't die of their suicidal behavior could be present in suicide deaths as well. Indeed, a study cited by Hjelmeland et al. (2002) found that "patient-attributed reasons for nonfatal suicidal behavior (such as suicidal desire and preparation) predicted a number of suicide criteria" (p. 391). Of course, identifying risk criteria does not mean that suicidal behavior, fatal or nonfatal, is predictable (Goldney, 2000; Kerkhof & Arensman, 2004).

Obviously, the review above is not an exhaustive overview of the literature. The aim, rather, was to present a few examples of how *intentions* have been addressed in research. As a whole, I argue that, despite limitations of the concept, *intention* is an essential component of the definition of suicide and attempted suicide primarily because it enables one to distinguish between accidental and suicidal behavior. As such, the issue of intentions in the definition of fatal and non-fatal suicidal behavior is germane to death certification, statistics of lethal and nonlethal suicidal behavior, research, prevention, and clinical work. Though intention is an important, even indispensable, element to understand suicidal behavior, little research has focused on this issue. In addition, because motives and intentions are related to different explanatory perspectives (e.g., retrospective versus prospective), future research should clearly distinguish between them both with regard to suicides and attempted suicides. The study of intentions then might contribute to a better understanding of the relation (continuum and/or group similarities/differences) between nonfatal suicidal behavior and suicide, and to a better understanding of the suicidal act.

References

Barber, M. (2002). Alfred Schutz. In E. Zalta (Ed.), *The Stanford encyclopedia of philosophy* (Winter 2002 ed.). Accessed November 25, 2005, from http://plato.stanford.edu/entries/schutz

Beachler, J. (1979). *Suicides* (B. Cooper, Trans.). New York: Basic Books. (Original work published 1975)

Beck, A., Resnik, H., & Lettieri, D. (Eds.). (1974). *The prediction of suicide.* Bowie: Charles Press Publishers.

De Leo, D., Burgis, S., Bertolote, J., Kerkhof, A., & Bille-Brahe, U. (2004). Definitions of suicidal behaviour. In D. De Leo, U. Bille-Brahe, A. Kerkhof, & A. Schmidtke (Eds.), *Suicidal behaviour: Theories and research findings* (pp. 17–39). Göttingen: Hogrefe & Huber.

Farberow, N., & Shneidman, E. (Eds.). (1961). *The cry for help.* New York: McGraw-Hill.

Goldney, R. (2000). Prediction of suicide and attempted suicide. In K. Hawton & K. van Heeringen (Eds.), *The international handbook of suicide and attempted suicide* (pp. 585–595). Chichester: Wiley.

Hawton, K. (2002). United Kingdom legislation on pack sizes of analgesics: Background, rationale, and effects on suicide and deliberate self-harm. *Suicide and Life-Threatening Behavior, 32,* 223–229.

Hawton, K., Simkin, S., Deeks, J., Cooper, J., Johnston, A., Waters, K., et al. (2004). UK legislation on analgesic packs: Before and after study of long-term effects on poisoning. *British Medical Journal, 329,* 1076–1080.

Hjelmeland, H., & Hawton, K. (2004). Intentional aspects of nonfatal suicidal behaviour. In D. De Leo, U. Bille-Brahe, A. Kerkhof, & A. Schmidtke (Eds.), *Suicidal behaviour: Theories and research findings* (pp. 67–78). Göttingen: Hogrefe & Huber.

Hjelmeland, H., Hawton, K., Nordvik, H., Bille-Brahe, U., De Leo, D., Fekete, S., et al. (2002). Why people engage in parasuicide: A cross-cultural study of intentions. *Suicide and Life-Threatening Behavior, 32,* 380–393.

Hjelmeland, H., & Knizek, B. L. (1999). Conceptual confusion about intentions and motives of nonfatal suicidal behavior: A discussion of terms employed in the literature of suicidology. *Archives of Suicide Research, 5,* 275–281.

Kerkhof, A., & Arensman, E. (2004). Repetition of attempted suicide: Frequent, but hard to predict. In D. De Leo, U. Bille-Brahe, A. Kerkhof, & A. Schmidtke (Eds.), *Suicidal behaviour: Theories and research findings* (pp. 111–124). Göttingen: Hogrefe & Huber.

Kubie, L. (1967). Multiple determinants of suicide. In E. Shneidman (Ed.), *Essays in self-destruction* (pp. 455–462). New York: Science House.

Kubie, L. (1969). A complex process. In E. Shneidman (Ed.), *On the nature of suicide* (pp. 81–86). San Francisco: Jossey Bass.

Linehan, M. (1997). Behavioral treatments of suicidal behavior: Definitional obfuscation and treatment outcomes. In D. Stoff & J. Mann (Eds.), *Neurobiology of suicide* (pp. 302–328). New York: Annals of the New York Academy of Sciences.

Litman, R. (1984). Psychological autopsies in court. *Suicide and Life-Threatening Behavior, 14,* 88–95.

Maris, R. (1981). *Pathways to suicide.* Baltimore: Johns Hopkins University Press.

Maris, R. (1992a). How are suicides different? In R. Maris, A. Berman, J. Maltsberger, & R. Yufit (Eds.), *Assessment and prediction of suicide* (pp. 65–87). New York: Guilford.

Maris, R. (1992b). The relationship of nonfatal suicide attempts to completed suicide. In R. Maris, A. Berman, J. Maltsberger, & R. Yufit (Eds.), *Assessment and prediction of suicide* (pp. 362–380). New York: Guilford.

Maris, R., Berman, A., & Silverman, M. (2000). The theoretical component in suicidology. In R. Maris, A. Berman, & M. Silverman (Eds.), *Comprehensive textbook of suicidology* (pp. 26–61). New York: Guilford.

Marusic, A. (2004). Toward a new definition of suicidality? Are we prone to Fregoli's illusion? *Crisis, 25,* 145–146.

Mayo, D. (1992). What is being predicted?: Definitions of "suicide." In R. Maris, A. Berman, J. Maltsberger, & R. Yufit (Eds.), *Assessment and prediction of suicide* (pp. 88–101). New York: Guilford.

O'Carrol, P., Berman, A., Maris, M., Moscicki, E., Tanney, B., & Silverman, M. (1996). Beyond the tower of Babel: A nomenclature for suicidology. *Suicide and Life-Threatening Behavior, 26,* 237–252.

Rosenberg, M., Davidson, L., Smith, J., Berman, A., Buzbee, H., Gantner, G., et al. (1988). Operational criteria for the determination of suicide. *Journal of Forensic Science, 33,* 1445–1456.

Shneidman, E. (1996). *The suicidal mind.* Oxford: Oxford University Press.

Shütz, A. (1932). *Der sinnhafte aufbau der sozialen welt.* Vienna: Springer, 1932.

Silverman, M., & Berman, A. (2005, September). *What's in a name? Advancing a nomenclature for Suicidology.* Paper presented at the XXIII World Congress, International Association for Suicide Prevention, Durban, South Africa.

Stengel, E. (1964). *Suicide and attempted suicide.* Harmondsworth: Penguin Books.

Williams, M. (2001). *Suicide and attempted suicide.* London: Penguin Books.

KARL ANDRIESSEN is Coordinator of the Suicide Prevention Project of the Flemish Mental Health Centres in Belgium and Vice-chair of the Flemish Working Group on Suicide Survivors. He is a Belgian IASP National Representative, Chair of IASP Taskforce Postvention, and recipient of the 2005 IASP Farberow Postvention Award.

The first version of this paper was written as part of the course work in the first year of the Masters of Suicidology, with due thanks to Prof. Diego De Leo, Dr. Karolina Krysinska and Mrs. Jacinta Hawgood at the Australian Institute for Suicide Research and Prevention, Griffith University, Brisbane, Australia. In addition, the author wished to thank the anonymous reviewers for their valuable suggestions.

Address correspondence to Karl Andriessen, MHC Suicide Prevention Project, FDGG, Martelaarslaan 204b, 9000 Gent, Belgium; E-mail: karl.andriessen@telenet.be

Ethical, Legal, and Practical Issues in the Control and Regulation of Suicide Promotion and Assistance over the Internet

Brian L. Mishara, PhD and David N. Weisstub, JD, LLD

There has been growing concern about the numerous reports of suicides following contact with websites that incite people to suicide and provide detailed information on suicide methods (Alao, Yolles, & Armenta, 1999; Australian IT, 2004; Baume, Cantor, & Rolfe, 1997; Becker & Schmidt, 2004; Dobson, 1999; Mehlum, 2000; Rajagopal, 2004; Reany 2004; Richard, Werth & Rogers, 2000; Thompson, 1999). The ethical, legal, and practical issues in the control and regulation of suicide promotion and assistance over the Internet are the focus of this article.

Media Reports

There are numerous reports in the media and scientific journals of suicides purportedly related to contact with Internet sites. Typical examples include the suicide that instigated the introduction of a bill in the Danish Parliament in February 2004 to ban websites that encourage and provide information about suicide. The son of a Danish journalist was apparently encouraged to end his life by a website which gave him information he used to kill himself. Two studies (Becker, El-Faddagh, & Schmidt, 2004; Becker, Mayer, Nagenborg, El-Faddagh, & Schmidt, 2004) that reported on a 17-year-old female suicide attempter concluded that websites may trigger suicidal behavior in predisposed adolescents. Several newspaper articles tell of distraught parents who blamed their child's suicide on Internet sites (Shepherd, 2004), and there was much media coverage of a 21-year-old man from Arizona who killed himself by overdose while chatting online with friends who egged him on.

Multiple suicides by people who meet on chat sites appear to be increasing. One much-publicized example concerned Louis Gillies from Glasgow who met Michael Gooden from East Sussex (England) in May 2002 on a suicide "newsgroup" (Innes,

2003). While on a cliff ready to jump, Gillies was talked out of killing himself by a friend on his cell phone, but Gooden refused to talk and jumped. Gillies was charged with aiding and abetting a suicide; he killed himself in April 2003 just before the trial was about to begin.

Meeting suicide companions online appears to be most prevalent in Japan (Japan, 2004) where, between February and early June 2003, at least 20 Japanese died in suicide pacts with companions they met on the Internet, many by strikingly similar carbon monoxide poisonings (Harding, 2004; "Seven Die in Suicide Pacts," 2004). It is believed that the first "wave" of Internet suicide pacts occurred in 2000 in South Korea when there were three cases. In March 2003, an Austrian teenager and a 40-year-old Italian who met on a suicide chat jointly committed suicide near Vienna ("Pair Planned Suicide," 2003). The man had also contacted two young Germans online, but police alerted their families before they could carry out their suicides.

Legal Provisions and Law Reform Projects

Many countries have laws prohibiting aiding and abetting suicide; however, we are not aware of any case where Internet activity has been pursued in a court of law for aiding or abetting suicide. That said, on February 13, 2005, Gerald Krein was arrested in Oregon for solicitation to commit murder after it was alleged that he used his Internet chat room to entice up to 31 lonely single women to kill themselves on Valentine's Day. The arrest followed a report to police by a woman in the chat room who said another participant talked about killing her two children before taking her own life (Booth, 2005).

So why have not current laws against aiding and abetting suicide been applied to Internet activities, given the compelling nature of specific case histories when people died by suicide in a manner communicated over the Internet and following a series of Internet contacts in which they were encouraged to kill themselves? It may be helpful to examine legal jurisprudence regarding standards for determining causality in such matters. When individuals are deemed to be responsible for having caused harm to another person, their actions are usually in close temporal and physical proximity to the victim's death. For example, a person who strikes another person who subsequently dies from the blow may be deemed responsible because that action had an immediate physical consequence for the victim. In addition, scientific and medical evidence must indicate according to reasonable probabilities that the action in question was causally related to the consequences (Bonger, 2002).

Scientific research on the influence of the media on suicides has concentrated on television and newspapers and their influence on population suicide rates. There are several excellent reviews of research in this area (e.g., Hawton & Williams, 2001; Pirkis & Warwick Blood, 2001; Stack, 2000, 2003, 2005). It is clear that news media depictions of deaths by suicide have a risk of increasing suicides among those who have contact with those media. Generally, the more the publicity, the higher the contagion effect (it has been reported that the suicide of Marilyn Monroe resulted in 197 additional suicides [Phillips, 1974]); however, there are no empirical data on changes in the risk of suicide that may be related to contacts with Internet sites. Nevertheless, it appears from numerous cases reported in the media that contact with Internet sites and with chat rooms preceded deaths by suicide and the methods used were precisely those described in the Internet contact. In sum, these case reports do not meet the requirements for scientific proof that Internet sites cause suicide, but they suggest that a relationship may exist.

Despite the compelling case reports, it can be argued that had the victims not contacted a specific suicide site, they may have still killed themselves. The suicide risk of people who contact suicide sites may have pre-dated their contact. In addition, if a person had not used a method found on a site, other methods are easily available.

Another challenge in determining a causal relationship is the difficulty in generalizing from epidemiological population statistics to individual cases. According to population statistics, it has been demonstrated that media publicity on suicide results in a small but significant increase in the number of people who die by suicide following the media reports. It is not possible, however, to generalize from these population data to determine if any one specific individual's death was facilitated by his or her having read a newspaper article or having watched a specific television program about suicide. The nature of epidemiological research is such that, given the great number of people at risk of committing suicide and the very small number who actually die by suicide, it is impossible to determine that one specific individual is likely to have died as a result of media exposure and that the death could have been avoided by non-exposure.

To date we do not have any epidemiological data on the relationship between contact with the Internet and suicides. All we have is a number of case histories in which there appears to be a link. It is dubious that one could make a good scientific or legal case for the causal relationship between Internet activities and suicide without conducting further research.

Self-Regulation

Even if one could prove that there is a risk associated with certain Internet sites, one must weigh that risk against possible dangers of compromising freedom of expression by attempting to control access to the site. In most countries, there is little or no control of Internet content because of constitutional guarantees of freedom of expression. EU decision number 276-1999, "The European Union Safer Internet Plan" (European Union, 1999), essentially proposes that Internet organizations and Internet service providers (ISPs) act responsibly to control what is available and limit or deny access to sites that are illegal or dangerous. Many countries, including Great Britain, Canada, the United States, and New-Zealand, attempt to control Internet content by self-regulation since guarantees of freedom of speech apparently preclude censorship or government control of access to sites. The use of self-regulation has been criticized for being ineffective, since those who produce the sites and distribute them are also being asked to censor them. It also has been criticized by persons who are concerned about the defence of freedom of expression, since there is no verification of which sites are blocked or censored and no explicit guidelines about what should be banned.

Filtering Techniques

An alternative to self-regulation is rating systems that use filtering techniques to block access to certain sites on personal computers. A primary issue is who actually rates the sites so that filter programs can identify sites to block. The World Wide Web Consortium (W3C) has developed the Platform for Internet Content Selection (PICS) standards in which creators of sites rate their own sites according to specific criteria. Yet ratings of sites, even if accurate, are useless if they are disregarded. Software used to filter sites by blocking access is only effective if they are used and they block target sites and do not block other permissible sites. For this reason, filtering software is mostly used by parents who attempt to control access to sites by minors; for example, sites depicting child pornography, violence, and racial hatred. But filters have limited intelligence to discriminate between desirable and undesirable sites. If filters block access to certain words or terms, for example "suicide" or "suicide methods," they may also block sites that provide helpful information in suicide prevention, such as the site of Befrienders International which offers help over the Internet to suicidal individuals (www.befrienders.org)

Blocking Access to Sites

A number of countries attempt to block access by all individuals to specific Internet content and sites, including Algeria, Bahrein, China, Germany, Iran, North Korea, Saudi Arabia, Singapore, South Korea, Sweden, United Arab Emirates, and Vietnam. For example, in Saudi Arabia all 30 of the ISPs go through a central node, and material and sites containing pornography, believed to cause religious offense, and information on bomb making are blocked. Germany requests that ISPs block media that is morally harmful to youth, including that which is "pornographic, depicts extreme violence, war mongering, racist, fascist or has anti-Semitic content." They have had success in blocking German sites with this material but have been less successful in blocking sites originating outside of Germany. Sweden has laws that require blocking of information instigating rebellion, racial agitation, child pornography, illegal description of violence, and material that infringes upon copyright laws.

In several countries, including the United States, Great Britain, and New Zealand, laws were passed to block certain Internet content but those laws were overturned by the courts because of constitutional guarantees of freedom of expression. Australia is the only country that currently has laws to specifically restrict sites that promote suicide or provide information on suicide methods.

Recent Modifications to the Australian Criminal Code

Public concern about the vulnerability of Australian youth recently gave rise to the enactment of amendments to the Australian Criminal Code making Internet activity intentionally relating directly or indirectly to the incitement of suicide a distinct crime (Commonwealth of Australia, 2004a). The Australian legislation also refers to the promotion of a particular method of committing suicide or providing instruction.

The parliamentary debate highlighted the vulnerability of young adults as a particular group based on both the level of Internet usage and their suicide rates (Commonwealth of Australia, 2004b, 2004c). It was argued that because of those factors there is a moral obligation on the part of society to provide protection. The legislators cited the failure of private ISPs to regulate themselves, thereby mandating government to do so. While acknowledging the division in public opinion, the Australian government argued that public protection trumped issues of liberty and freedom of expression.

There was strong vocal opposition, including from the Green Party. The critics said that the ambiguity of "intentionality" could give rise to unintended results and could render the law impossible to apply. The point was argued that given the volume of suicide items incorporated into daily activity on the Internet, it could be foreseen that ISPs could readily find themselves vulnerable to the legislation despite their efforts to control content, if an aggressive pattern of catchments would take place. It was submitted that attacking the causes of suicide, rather than operating with a wide net of surveillance and intervention, would be more likely to succeed in reducing the threat.

Other interventions addressed the foolhardiness of attempting to restrict information about matters such as suicide and voluntary euthanasia. The key issue, from the point of view of the opposition, was not the need to control Internet content, but the extent to which the government is prepared to devote resources to suicide prevention activities.

Ethical Presuppositions

There are several ethical considerations concerning the control of Internet content in order to prevent suicide. First and foremost is the ethical premise that suicide should be prevented (Mishara & Weisstub, 2005). Those who adopt a libertarian perspective might contend that people have the right to choose to end their life by suicide. Also, since suicide is not illegal in most countries, one could argue that suicidal people should have access to material they desire. If this libertarian position is adopted, it is not possible to justify controlling access to information encouraging suicide or providing information or advice on how to exercise the right to end one's life by suicide.

If one adopts a moralist ethical position that suicide must be prevented, and if controlling access to Internet sites can save lives, then controls must be instituted. If one holds a relativist position that some suicides are acceptable and others are not, one may morally justify some form of Internet control, although control of access for only some people is practically impossible. For example, a relativist who believes that terminally ill people should be allowed or have access to means to end their lives but people in good health who suffer from treatable psychiatric problems should not, would have a difficult time controlling access for some people and not others.

The Internet versus Other Mass Media

One of the questions concerning the ethics of controlling access to the Internet is the specificity of the Internet compared to other mass media. The Internet has been characterized as a "pull" technology, as opposed to the so-called push technologies including radio and television. Push technologies include television and radio; they provide access to the media without the user engaging in any specific and explicit attempt to find a specific media content. Television content is available in every home and because of its universal access, television has been regulated in most countries as to content. In contrast to the mass medias of television and radio, Internet users must actively seek out a specific content.

Also, anonymity of the provider can exist on the Internet and there is no ability to verify the authenticity of the information one finds on a website. No government agencies are ensuring that Web content is appropriate and accurate (unlike television and radio which are generally subject to government control). The Web can be extremely graphic in nature and individuals who display their suicidal intentions and behaviors on the Internet can expect possible exposure to thousands throughout the world, providing glorification of their suicidal acts.

The differences between "push" and "pull" technologies may be used to defend the Internet against control by claiming that the Internet is a private service that does not invade people's homes, and that specific content must be sought out by individuals actively searching through cyberspace. The down side, of course, is this same private nature provides for a level of anonymity of both the person contacting the site and the person providing information on a site, which may lead to an "anything goes" environment where there are no controls whatsoever about the authenticity and credibility of information transmitted or provided.

Different Internet Activities

Internet situations involving suicide vary. Some sites passively provide information, which encourage suicide in texts that suggest it is a good idea to end one's life. Other sites provide information on suicide methods, many including specific details about what medications to mix, how to hang oneself, and the strengths and weaknesses of alternative methods with respect to side effects and risks of failure. Yet still other sites involve the exchange of messages from "suicide encouragers" who interact with suicidal people, trying to stimulate them to proceed with their suicidal plans in chat rooms or in e-mail correspondence. "Suicide predators" seek out people who post messages suggesting they may be feeling suicidal but who are not explicitly asking for information or encouragement. These predators offer unsolicited incitation to suicide and may provide information about how to commit suicide without being asked. If one is considering some form of control of Internet activity, it is important to decide which of the above activities one would like to limit.

Vulnerable Populations

One of the major issues in control of the Internet in order to prevent suicides is the protection of minors and other vulnerable populations, such as persons with psychiatric disorders. The most successful attempts to control access over the Internet has involved child pornography sites and pornography aimed at minors, although these initiatives may be criticized for falling short of their goal of totally blocking access. Thus far, very little has been done to protect minors from suicide promotion sites.

In the area of the exposure of minors to extreme violence, research has shown beyond doubt that media exposure to violence is related to increased violent behavior (Bushman & Anderson, 2001); however, there has been little success in attempts to control violence on the Internet.

The Jurisdictional Factor

Even if one were able to resolve the legal and ethical issues, there are a number of practical considerations that make control of Internet suicide promotion activities extremely difficult (Geist, 2002; Smith, Bird, & Bird, 2002). The first is the issue of cross-border jurisdiction. Although countries may be able to control activities of Internet sites that originate within their borders, international jurisprudence makes it difficult to obtain jurisdiction over sites that originate outside the country. Jurisprudence generally distinguishes between passive Internet activity, such as simply operating a website which may be accessed from different countries, and active endeavors which involve sending information, interacting (for example, in a chat room), and doing business in a country. Furthermore, jurisprudence has favored limiting claims of harm to actual impact rather than claims of potential damage.

Two important cases underline the difficulties in cross-border jurisdiction issues. The first case, in Canada, *Braintech Inc. v. Kostivk* (1999), involved a libel complaint concerning a site in Canada. In denying jurisdiction, the judge found that there is a "need for better proof the defendant entered Texas than the mere possibility that someone in Texas may have reached to cyberspace to bring defamation material to a screen in Texas." The ability to access material from a site outside a jurisdiction was not sufficient to allow for jurisdiction in another area (Geist, 2002).

The "Calder test," based on the U.S. case of *Calder v. Jones* (1984) is often used to determine jurisdiction in Internet cases. This test requires that the defendant's intentional tortuous actions are: (1) expressly aimed at the forum state and (2) cause harm to the plaintiff in the forum state, of which the defendant knows is likely to be suffered. This test provides protection for Internet sites and activities which do not explicitly attempt to have an effect outside of their own jurisdiction or intentionally cause harm to an individual in another jurisdiction. Obviously, there is virtue in protecting individuals from being liable in every country in the world for actions, which may be perfectly legal in their own jurisdiction. Still, jurisdiction issues make attempts to control Internet activity extremely difficult.

Conclusion

There remains a great need for scientifically valid data on the extent that Internet sites contribute to the risk of suicide. Specifically, we need to determine if Internet activities increase suicide risk and, if so, which subpopulations are particularly vulnerable. Spectacular media reports of suicides following Internet contact and case reports of individuals who died by suicide using methods they found on the Internet or in pacts with people they met over the Internet, as impressive as they may seem, do not constitute scientific proof that Internet activities provoke suicides. One could try to build a case for the relationship between Internet activities and suicide using psychological autopsy methods. Qualitative assessments of the content of Internet contacts where seemingly vulnerable individuals appeared to be forcefully encouraged to kill themselves has high face validity; however, we need to develop more creative methodologies, perhaps inspired by the studies of the relationship between suicide reporting in other media and suicide rates. One of the greatest challenges is to determine if individuals who kill themselves after Internet contacts would have died by suicide if they did use the Internet.

It is also important to clarify the ethical basis upon which any form of suicide prevention activity is undertaken before applying one's beliefs to controlling Internet suicide promotion. Furthermore, any action to control Internet suicide promotion must consider the different forms of Internet activities, which range from passive posting of information on a website to interacting in a chat room or seeking out vulnerable individuals as an Internet predator.

Any attempt to control the Internet must be viewed along with the control and freedom of other media, unless special characteristics of the Internet are judged to lead to special laws or consideration. It can be argued that, unlike other media, the internet lacks quality control, and this may justify legislative intervention. Most keep in mind, however, that editors of newspapers, like Web masters, are free to publish what they please, even if it may incite suicides. If a journalist publishes a "dangerous" article, she may evoke the ire of readers and sales may decline (or increase due to the controversy). When a website or chat does something people do not like, users can simply not frequent that site. In this regard it is interesting to compare the Internet to published works. If one were to publish the philosopher David Hume's writings recommending suicide on an Australian Internet site, would this be banned? If so, would it be considered as more dangerous than publishing his book and selling it in a bookstore? Internet sites provide information on means to kill oneself in an often clear but informal manner; however, if the same information is available in medical textbooks, what would justify control of this information over the Internet while permitting the sale of medical textbooks and their availability in libraries?

The fact that the Internet allows for global access leads to complex jurisdiction issues and practical difficulties. Given the rapidly changing state of technologies which lead to the continued development of new ways to circumvent control, it may not be practically possible to ban sites, censor material, or limit access. Even if data to document that high risks of suicide are related to specific Internet activities were available, and even if a country decides to prevent access to suicide sites, the only way to ensure even a minimal level of success would be to install draconian censorship measures. Regardless, it is not certain that the controls would be effective. Therefore, alternatives to control and censorship should be considered, such as developing increased suicide prevention activities on the Internet to counterbalance Internet suicide promotion activities. Persons involved in suicide prevention should be encouraged to enter chat discussions to dissuade suicidal persons from killing themselves and encourage them to seek help. Finally, public education could be enhanced to facilitate ways and means to obtain help from the Internet in the interest of suicide prevention.

References

Alao, A. O., Yolles, J. C, & Armenta, W. (1999). Cybersuicide: The internet and suicide. *American Journal of Psychiatry, 156,* 1836–1837.

Australian IT. (2004). Crackdown on suicide chat rooms. Retrieved from http://australianit.news.com.au/wireless/story/0,8256,10340811,00.html

Baume, P., Cantor, C. H., & Rolfe, A (1997). Cybersuicide: The role of interactive suicide notes on the internet. *Crisis, 18,* 73–79.

Becker, K., & Schmidt, M. H. (2004). Letters to the editor: Internet chat rooms and suicide. *Journal of the American Academy of Child and Adolescent Psychiatry, 43,* 246.

Becker, K., El-Faddagh, M., & Schmidt, M. H. (2004). Cybersuizid over Werther-Effekt online: Suizidchatrooms und-foren im Internet. *Kindheit und Entwicklung, 13,* 14–25.

Becker, K., Mayer, M., Nagenborg, M., El-Faddagh, M., & Schmidt, M. H. (2004). Parasuicide online: Can suicide websites trigger suicidal behavior in predisposed adolescents? *Nordic Journal of Psychiatry, 58,* 111–114.

Bonger, B. (2002). *The suicidal patient: Clinical and legal standards of care* (2nd ed.). Washington, DC: American Psychological Association.

Booth, J. (2005, February 14). St-Valentine's Day mass suicide pact fears. *Times ONLINE.* Retrieved from www.timesonline.co.uk/article/0,,3-1484028,00.html

Braintech Inc. v. Kostivk, 171 D.L.R. (4+h) 46, British Columbia, Canada (1999).

Bushman, B. J., & Anderson, C. A. (2001). Media violence and the American public. *American Psychologist, 56,* 477–489.

Calder v. Jones, 465 U.S. 783 (1984).

Commonwealth of Australia. (2004a). Criminal Code Amendment. *Telecommunications Offences and Other Measures—Suicide Related Material Offences (Bill no. 2).*

Commonwealth of Australia. (2004b). *House of Representatives Official Hansard, no. 12.* (Wednesday, 4 August 2004, 30035–32038)

Commonwealth of Australia. (2004c). *House of Representatives Official Hansard, no. 12.* (Wednesday, 11 August 2004, 32473–32480)

Dobson, R. (1999). Internet sites may encourage suicide. *British Medical Journal, 319,* 337.

European Union. (1999). *The European union safer Internet plan.* Brussels: Author. (EU-Decision Number 276–1999)

Geist, M. (2002). *Internet law in Canada* (3rd ed.). Concord: Captus Press.

Harding, A. (2004, December 9). Japan's Internet "suicide clubs." *BBC News.* Retrieved from http://news.bbc.co.uk/go/pr/fr/2/hi/programmes/newsnight/4071805.stm

Hawton, K., & Williams, K. (2001). The connection between media and suicidal behaviour warrants serious attention. *Crisis, 22,* 137–140.

Innes, J. (2003, October 1). Coroner calls for police watch on web chat rooms. *The Scotsman.* Retrieved from http://news.scotsman.com/top ics.cfm?tid=746&id=1086122003>

Japon: Suicide collectif par Internet. (2004, November 13). *Le Devoir,* p. B6.

Mehlum, L. (2000). The Internet, suicide, and suicide prevention. *Crisis, 21,* 186–188.

Mishara, B. L., & Weisstub, D. N. (2005). Ethical issues in suicide research. *International Journal of Law and Psychiatry, 28,* 23–41.

Pair planned suicide online police. (2003, April 9). *New Report RE; Europe.* http://iafrica.com/news/worldnews/227377.htm

Phillips, D. P. (1974). The influence of suggestion on suicide: Substantive and theoretical implications of the Werther effect. *American Sociological Review, 39,* 340–354.

Pirkis, J., & Warwick Blood, R. (2001). Suicide and the media. *Crisis, 22,* 146–154.

Rajagopal, S. (2004). Suicide pacts and the Internet: Complete strangers may make cyberspace pacts. [electronic version]. *British Medical Journal, 329,* 1298–1299. Retrieved January 6, 2005, from www.bmj.com.

Reany, P. (2004, December 6). Internet pourrait encourager les suicides collectifs. *Le Devoir,* p. B6.

Richard, J., Werth, J. L., & Rogers, J. R. (2000). Rational and assisted suicidal communication on the internet: A case example and discussion of ethical and practice issues. *Ethics and Behavior, 10,* 215–238.

Seven die in suicide pacts, bringing death toll to 22. (2004, September 22). *New York Herald Tribune,* p. 3.

Shepherd, J. (2004, March 6). Suicide blamed on chatrooms. *Birmingham Post.* Retrieved from http://icbirmingham .icnetwork.co.uk/0100news/0100localnews/tm_objectid=14022 277%26method=full%26siteid=50002-name_page.html

Smith, G. H., Bird, & Bird. (2002). *Internet Law and Regulation* (3rd ed.). London, UK: Sweet & Maxwell.

Stack, S. (2000). Media impacts on suicide: A quantitative review of 293 findings. *Social Science Quarterly, 81,* 957–971.

Stack, S. (2003). Media coverage as a risk factor in suicide. *Journal of Epidemiology and Community Health, 57,* 238–240.

Stack, S. (2005). Suicide in the media: A quantitative review of studies based on nonfictional stories. *Suicide and Life-Threatening Behavior, 35,* 121–133.

Thompson, S. (1999). The Internet and its potential influence on suicide. *Psychiatric Bulletin, 23,* 449–451.

BRIAN MISHARA is Director of the Centre for Research and Intervention on Suicide and Euthanasia, and Professor in the Department of Psychology at the University of Quebec at Montreal. **DAVID N. WEISSTUB** is Philippe Pinel Professor of Legal Psychiatry and Biomedical Ethics at the University of Montreal, Canada.

Address correspondence to Brian L. Mishara, PhD, CRISE/UQAM, C.P. 8888. Succ. Centre-Ville, Montreal (Quebec) Canada, H3C 3P8; E-mail: mishara.brian@uqam.ca.

A Search for Death: How the Internet Is Used as a Suicide Cookbook

Rheana Murray

Literature Review

While reasons for suicides have long been analyzed, the Internet presents a comparatively unexamined influence. Recent news stories have begun to direct attention to the emergence of chat rooms, message boards and other resources on the web as a possible factor in the rise of suicide rates. As the Internet has become an increasingly vital technological development, some people have begun to worry about "suicide websites," a term that refers to websites that promote, encourage and/or offer methods to commit suicide.

Alao and colleagues (2006) address the role of the Internet on suicides in a manuscript composed of three parts. The first describes how the Internet can help users commit suicide; the second looks at cases in which this has happened; and the last explores how the Internet could be used to help suicidal users back to stable mental health. The authors include interesting and pertinent information about suicide websites, and they report that there are more than 100,000 of them that deal with suicide methods. Some sites do not allow entrance to anyone intending to persuade users to not commit suicide. Suicide notes, death certificates, color photographs of people committing suicide, messages supporting suicide or encouraging individuals to carry out planned suicides can all be found on these websites. Some of the websites are very graphic, even including "the best way to point a gun into the mouth for maximum effect," according to the journal article (Alao 490). The article "Cybersuicide: Review of the Role of the Internet on Suicide" also acknowledges that chat rooms, as well as websites, can provide information on suicide.

Few researchers have considered the idea that suicide websites might decrease suicides, but the second part of "Cybersuicide," though brief, insists that the Internet is also a potential source of help for suicidal people. Alao and colleagues refer to the possibility of online counseling, although they do not include evidence that proves its success (490).

Tam, Tang and Fernando (2007) also introduce the idea that the Internet may serve a double purpose when it comes to suicide, both harming and helping. They note that the Internet romanticizes suicide and that it "provides services and information ranging from general information to online orders of prescription drugs or other poisons that bypass government regulations and custom controls." This, the authors say, "bridges the gaps of locality and accessibility" (453). A suicidal person can use the Internet to learn methods to commit suicide. The person learns what a particular method calls for, be it chemicals, weapons, rope, drugs, etc. Then, inching closer to death, the person can use the Internet to *buy* the tools. CNN reporters Gutierrez and McCabe (2005) illustrate this process in the story of Suzy Gonzales, a 19 year-old college student from Florida, who killed herself by swallowing potassium cyanide. Through an online suicide message board, Gonzales learned how to pose as a jeweler to obtain the lethal cocktail.

While the article by Tam and colleagues makes the problem of suicide websites clear, it goes on to raise the interesting dilemma that the Internet could also help people escape their suicidal impulses. The authors provide little evidence, however, offering the idea as more of an opportunity than a reality. They mention self-help sites for suicidal persons and the potential for therapeutic chat rooms. Yet, once again, evidence of effectiveness is sparse.

Madelyn Gould, Patrick Jamieson and Daniel Romer (2003) researched suicide contagion from the news as well as fiction. Their research suggested a strong relationship between reports of suicide in the media and increased suicide rates. According to Gould (1271), "the magnitude of the increase in suicides following a suicide story is proportional to the amount, duration, and prominence of media coverage." Celebrities' suicides are 14.3 times more likely to result in a copycat effect than suicides of non-celebrities.

Gould and colleagues analyzed suicide stories from 1998 in the nine most widely circulated newspapers in the United States, tracking the number of suicide stories each paper published, the percentage of stories that were placed in the first nine pages, and the percentage of stories that referred to suicide in the headline. *The Los Angeles Times* reported the most suicides, 176, and *USA Today* reported the fewest, only 35. Interestingly, *USA Today* was the paper that most frequently placed the suicide article within the first nine pages, doing so 91.4% of the time, and *Newsday* did so the least. *The Washington Post* was the paper that referred to suicide in the headline most frequently, and *USA Today* did so the least. Gould and colleagues also included the most recently released recommendations for journalists covering suicides and the need for guidelines for fictional programming.

Studies by Katja Becker and colleagues (2004) further support Gould's report that suicides increase proportionally to the amount, duration and prominence of media coverage. They illustrate the Internet's influence on users, particularly adolescents. In a *Nord J Psychiatry* article, Becker and colleagues say suicide contagion is real and prevalent. Reasons include "inadvertent romanticizing of suicide or idealizing it as a heroic deed" (112).

Brian Mishara and David Weisstub (2007) discussed the ethical and legal implications of various ways to prevent using the Internet as an aid to committing suicide, considering self-regulation and blocking access to suicide websites. Viewpoints from a libertarian perspective and also from a moralist ethical position are analyzed. Mishara and Weisstub compare the Internet to other mass media in relation to censorship. Their research raises interesting questions and viewpoints without resolving qualms concerning Internet censorship.

In an article on "Internet Chat Rooms and Suicide" (2005), Becker and Schmidt discuss a 17 year-old female who visited suicide web forums to find suicide methods and a 15 year-old female who reported that "the Internet inspired her to commit suicide as a problem-solving strategy" (229). The article discusses the availability and ease associated with suicide websites, and how many portray suicide as a legitimate, even respectable solution to life's problems. "Ambivalence, an often-precarious balance between a chosen life and a chosen death, which is considered common to suicide attitude, may tip in the direction of death in response to suicide chat rooms," the article states (229). This warning makes for an adequate summary of the entire article.

Methods and Objectives

This paper aims to explain the existence of websites, newsgroups and online message boards that promote, condone, encourage and/or discuss suicide from a pro-suicide or pro-choice angle. Research involving human participants was conducted, and this project was approved by the Institutional Research Board (IRB) at the College of Charleston.

Interviews were conducted on two groups of participants: 1) people that use suicide websites and 2) creators and supporters of H.R. 940, a current bill aiming to make it illegal to help someone commit suicide via the Internet. To gather participants, I used a convenience sample. Participation was voluntary and communication occurred primarily through e-mail.

Group 1: My objective in interviewing people that use suicide websites, newsgroups and/or message boards was to understand the cause and objective of their participation, and how they are affected by the websites. The following questions were asked:

1. Why did you start using (website's name)?
2. Does (website's name) promote and/or encourage suicide and/ or suicidal tendencies?

3. Does (website's name) offer methods of committing suicide?
4. Are you aware of suicides connected with the Internet?
5. If so, do you feel regret upon hearing about suicides in the news?
6. Are you aware of suicides that have been linked to (website's name)?
7. Do you have any ethical issues with the website's content?
8. Are you concerned with the possibility that a law could force (website's name) to shut down?
9. How do you feel toward people who scorn (website's name)?

Each interview's significance lies within the responses, which serve as the primary research for this paper along with text drawn from suicide websites, newsgroups, and message boards. Results are qualitative and often based on case studies.

Group 2: My objective in interviewing creators of H.R. 940, also called "Suzy's Law," was to understand the origin of the bill and its components, so my readers will understand its intent. The following questions were asked of the bill's creators:

1. Explain the law.
2. When did the law come about?
3. How are you trying to get the law considered and passed?
4. Why did you create this law?
5. Are there similar laws that exist now?
6. How long do you think the Internet's influence on suicides has been a problem?
7. Do you think this law will be successful?
8. How does the law avoid impeding on free speech?

Findings

Following the established information revealed in the preceding literature review, I investigated suicide websites for my own research. I found several, and focused on three that appeared to be the most prevalent and frequented online spaces for suicidal people, the alt.suicide.holiday Usenet newsgroup (ASH), the alt.suicide.methods Usenet newsgroup (ASM) and alt.suicide .bus.stop, a channel in Internet Relay Chat (IRC) and known as ASBS.

None of these groups qualifies as a website, so the term "suicide website" loses its precision here, but the term is conventionally used to categorize ASH, ASM, ASBS. ASH, which has sustained many transformations and replacements since it was created in the 1950s, did begin as an actual website as opposed to a message board or chat room. Although the three groups are often called "sister sites," ASH is considered the original, and was first to appear. The creator of the original website, ash.xanthia.com, froze the site in 2002 and removed it in 2003 because, he wrote, "it represents a social space which no longer exists."

However, the popular Dutch journalist Karen Spaink offered to archive the ASH website materials on her own website, ash.spaink.net, which continues to provide an inactive copy of the former ASH site. Several sites have emerged to take the place of ASH, including ASM and ASBS, and a new site that uses the name ASH. This active version of ASH consists of message boards in which members post about life, depression and suicide-related topics. According to Google, the group has high activity, and "talk about why suicides increase at holidays" is the description. While sources, as well as the name itself, imply that the creation of ASH stemmed from intentions to brew discussion of suicides around holidays, it is no longer a topic of discussion, and certainly not the focal point of the boards it may once have been. As of April 3, 2008, ASH has 2459 subscribers.

ASM is also a Usenet newsgroup through Google, and was inspired by the infamous "Methods File," an extensive compilation of detailed suicide methods featured on the original ASH website. Members of ASM particularly discuss ways to commit suicide, saving less relevant discussion, such as the source of an individual's suicidal impulses, for the ASH newsgroup. However, members of one group are often members of the other, and conversations overlap. ASM also has high activity, according to Google, and is described as "discussions about how to do yourself in." As of April 3, 2008, ASM has 1994 subscribers.

ASBS, unlike ASH and ASM, is a channel in Internet Relay Chat (IRC) found at ashbusstop.org. The site offers live chat with other members, as opposed to message boards. ASBS provides more than the newsgroups, going far beyond interactive chatting and message boards. The website offers a plethora of information about suicide, a seemingly endless consideration of preparation and aftermath. There are pages that examine the purpose of living, offering pro-life and pro-death viewpoints, and information about euthanasia. The "Tying Loose Ends" page reminds people contemplating suicide to consider pets, bills, funeral plans and more. There are links to animal shelters, lists of funeral homes, as well as detailed instructions of how to close e-mail accounts and erase all ASH-related information from a personal computer, so that family members cannot discover the person's identity as an asher. The "How to Write a Suicide Note" page includes an introduction of suicide notes, with history and statistics, and detailed advice on how to write a note, whether the writer wants closure or revenge, to tell his or her story, or simply to provide an explanation. This page covers the five stages of receiving catastrophic news so that a note-writer can better understand the emotional state of his or her friends and family.

The "Methods" section of ASBS includes a page about the morality of publishing suicide websites, a page about how to compare different suicide methods, and features a Lethality-Time-Agony Method calculator (LTA). The calculator allows people to enter numbers in a space next to each factor—lethality, time and agony—to register the importance he or she assigns to that factor. The sum of the numbers must be 100. For example, if a suicidal person feels that lethality is the most important, but is not worried about experiencing agony, and mildly cares about the time the suicide takes, he or she might assign lethality 70 points, time 30 points, and agony 0 points. By typing these numbers in the calculator, and clicking the calculate button, a list of recommended suicide methods appears.

Table 1 Methods of Suicide from Ashbusstop.org

Method	Lethality (%)	Time (min)	Agony
Carbon Monoxide	71	21.5	18
Overdose Rx drugs	12.3	129	8.5
Overdose non-Rx drugs	6	456	22.5
Overdose illegal drugs	43.96	116.25	5.25
Household toxins	77.5	24	54.5
Cyanide	97	1.8	51.5
Gunshot of head	97	2.5	13
Gunshot of chest	89.5	7	21.7
Gunshot of abdomen	65	69	74
Shotgun to head	99	1.7	5.5
Shotgun to chest	96.4	1.4	16
Explosives	96.4	1.6	3.75
Electrocution	65.5	2.4	72
Set fire to self	76.5	57	95
Structure fire	73	52.5	91.5
Cut throat	51.5	15.5	86
Cut wrists/arms/legs	6	105	71
Stab of chest	58.5	96	76
Stab of abdomen	12.5	252	78
Auto crash	78.5	20.5	30
Jump from height	93.44	4.56	17.78
Hit by train	96.18	17.92	7.08
Hit by truck/auto	70	19	63
Hanging	89.5	7	25.5
Plastic bag over head	23	7	23
Drowning: ocean/lake	63	18.5	79
Drowning: bathtub	21.5	18.5	79
Drowning: pool	21.5	18.5	79

At the bottom of the page, a chart lists 28 suicide methods and their predicted lethality, the time each would take to complete, and a numeric measure of agony. See Table 1.

Upon entering ASH, ASM and ASBS, there is a warning that explains that the pages deal with serious topics intended for mature audiences. People visiting the ASH or ASM newsgroups are welcomed with an "Adult Content Warning" and must click an "I am at least 18 years old" button to proceed. ASBS instructs users to proceed only after reading a "Terms of Use" section and agreeing to not raise any complaints, verified by clicking the "I agree . . . let me in" button.

I interviewed ten people who use the ASH, ASM and ASBS groups. A convenience sample was used to select participants, and questions were asked and answered through direct e-mail to insure privacy. Users of any of these forums call themselves "ashers," since all three stem from the original ASH website. (From here on, I will refer to ASH, ASM and ASBS collectively as ASH to avoid redundancy.) Ashers use a set of terms that are unique to "ashspace," which they use as a term for these suicide forums. Other significant terms include "catch the bus" or "ctb," which both mean to commit suicide. Ashers tend to find ashspace by researching suicide or suicide methods on the Internet. Many say they were suicidal and ready to die. They began using ASH as a place to vent, to get input on their suicidal ideas and thoughts, and to feel less alone. Frequent responses to question 1, "Why did you start using ASH?" dealt with the isolation a suicidal person feels from the rest of the (non-suicidal) world.

According to an asher who uses the nickname Another-RubberDucky, "I feel like less of a freak," [by using ASH]. Another user, LSD, even referred to the cartoon X-Men, saying, "you know, the mutants were so criticized and left out." Like the outcast monsters, suicidal people feel alone in a world that scrutinizes and scorns them. By sharing her feelings with people in Ashland, LSD said she felt like less of an "alien."

While it was not a frequent explanation for using ASH, two ashers I interviewed said they came to ASH looking for someone to die with. User Joy Miller said, "I would like to find a partner, but there's not that many looking [on ASH]." LSD acknowledged that many people use the Internet to find partners to commit suicide, saying she was even involved in a suicide pact that went astray when the other person in the pact "turned out to be a freak with a suicide fetish that liked to watch people hang in the webcam."

More frequently, people use ASH as a place to talk to people with similar suicidal feelings. An asher who uses the name AndSheWas said, "ASH is not often a discussion about suicide. It's a diary of a spattering of people around the world who have been fortunate enough to find a place to vent their inner feelings. Everyone knows talking about your problems can help." Asher Lyllian Croft summed up the most popular reason people use ASH: "For me, it merely provides a place where I know someone is listening."

AnotherRubberDucky, who came to ASH after years of depression and skin disorders, thinks ASH's attractiveness to its users comes from its nonjudgmental atmosphere. She said:

You'll find that if you talk suicide with a depressed person and you tell them that "it is not an option" or "[it is] a permanent solution to a temporary problem," well, this produces a sort of claustrophobic feeling in the patient. Making suicide in a way, more appealing and inevitable. As soon as you admit that suicide is an option, and that one is not crazy to consider it, the suicidal person can breathe again.

Question 2, "Does ASH promote and/or encourage suicide and/ or suicidal tendencies?" garnered a consistent response: that ASH is pro-choice, not pro-suicide, a viewpoint most participants seemed well-versed in defending. Being pro-choice translates to tolerance of, but not advocacy for, suicide. According to an asher named Maija, "suicide is neither to be encouraged or to be condemned; it's treated as a personal choice." LSD said, "It's not a 'yeah, go kill yourself' thing, but more of a 'we understand' thing."

Furthermore, half of the people interviewed said that ashers actually discourage young people from committing suicide. An asher named CTB said:

One ethical standard that tends to emanate throughout the group is that young people (teens and early twenties) are discouraged from suicide or for that matter even participating in the newsgroup. Many ashers will tell the youngsters to "leave us losers alone and get some life experience. Let your brain develop. If you feel the same way at age 25 then, 'welcome to ash, sorry you're here' (our standard greeting to a newcomer)."

Maija answered with a similar response and added, "The same thing goes for people who seem to have very hasty reasons for committing suicide, such as a breakup that happened just days before." Suicide is viewed as an option on ASH, but a last resort.

Some participants took their answers a step further, going as far as to say that ASH even helps its users to avoid suicide by serving as an outlet for frustration and depression. Another-RubberDucky said, "In truth, I have all the information that I need for my 'final exit' but I like the support that I get from the group. And this is support to continue living, not to kill myself."

Particular threads on the ASH message board support the answer that ASH prevents suicide, at least in some cases. In a 2004 thread entitled, "How does ASH impact suicidal ideation for you," ashers discussed whether ASH made them more or less suicidal. Many said that since joining ASH, their desire to commit suicide has decreased because they had found a place where suicide was accepted.

Even more straightforward is the thread from November 2005, "How ASH saved my life," posted by a former asher, jpatti. Jpatti explained that she had not used ASH in years and was no longer suicidal, but said "I'm posting because I'm pissed about the CNN thing." An article about Suzy Gonzales and her involvement in ASH had appeared on CNN.com two days before jpatti's thread. She explained how finding a community of suicidal people and being able to talk openly about suicide helped her out of suicidality. She further observed, "Those who claim to be opposed to suicide, under any circumstances, often have a sick way of expressing it—by attacking suicidal people. It's like coming upon a car accident and finding someone bleeding on the side of the road and *kicking* them as hard as you can because you're 'opposed' to car accidents."

Maija, an asher since 1999, is no longer suicidal, but still visits ASH. "It is always nice to discuss subjects that are taboo elsewhere, and in general to have in-depth conversations with very intelligent and thoughtful people," she said. "These, especially the latter, are the reasons why I still read ASH almost every day and occasionally post as well." Maija's loyalty to ASH wasn't unique; most of the ashers I interviewed seemed to rely heavily on ASH as an outlet or even as a hangout. On the message boards, dozens of new threads appear every day, and not all relate to suicide. Some are random questions or thoughts, or polls to get to know each other—signaling a desire for friendship. As asher AndSheWas said, "Ash is my lifeline."

Ashers' responses to my questions as well as the tone and language used in the message boards reveal a nonchalant and accepting attitude toward suicide. Suicide isn't feared. It is discussed, dissected, awaited and anticipated. It's also something that can happen at any time. One interviewee, Robert Brown, ended an e-mail by politely adding that if I have any more questions, I should feel free to ask. Brown said he planned to kill himself that night, but that an old friend just called and made plans to stop by later that week to give him a tattoo. "So I should be here another week," he wrote. An argument could even be made that the language ashers use makes suicide less daunting and more natural. Saying "I'm going to catch the bus tonight" has a different manner than "I'm going to commit suicide tonight."

Several ashers admitted to knowing of suicides connected with ASH. Although few revealed names, Suzy Gonzales, an asher whose suicide was scrutinized by the media in 2003, was often mentioned. However, by searching the message boards, there are various memorial lists throughout the years. Ashers list names of fellow ashers who have committed suicide, and they discuss whether or not some missing ashers are dead or have simply stopped using ASH. In a post from March 31, 2008, an asher claimed to know of 26 confirmed suicides of ashers. Others simply listed the former usernames of friends they know to have committed suicide. Ashers expressed sadness over the loss of friends, but happiness for the dead. AnotherRubberDucky said, "Loss of life is always sad, but then again, so is intense suffering."

The Case of Suzy Gonzales and the Introduction of H.R. 940

In 2003, the daughter of Mike and Mary Gonzales committed suicide. Their daughter Suzy Gonzales was a frequent member to the ASH website, where she used the nickname Suzy California. Suzy consulted other ashers for advice on how to complete her suicide; she eventually chose to die by drinking a lethal cocktail of potassium cyanide. With the instruction she received through the online group, Suzy learned how to send her family and the police department delayed messages saying she had died, and how to pose as a jeweler to obtain her drug of choice. She ordered the cyanide along with other chemicals, so that the order appeared authentic, from a Massachusetts-based chemical company (Scheeres 2003). On March 23, 2003, she received the chemicals and, without missing a beat, she fed her kitten, rented a hotel room and lay down to die. "If you compared the information given on these sites and what Suzy did, you would see that she followed their recipes of deadly instructions," her parents said.

Mike and Mary Gonzales pursued their impulse to seek legal consequences for those aiding in their daughter's death. It wasn't that easy. "For two years," they said, "we asked law enforcement and legal firms to investigate what happened and they all told us that there were no relevant current laws to act upon."

Enter H.R. 940, a bill the Gonzales' helped develop to prevent stories like their own. The bill, also called "Suzy's Law,"

is backed by California congressman Wally Herger, and was introduced to the United States House of Representatives on February 8, 2007. According to Lindsay Bartlett, who assists in maintaining the H.R. 940 website, the bill "specifically makes it a crime to go on the Internet and tell someone who seems to be thinking of suicide, 'You should go through with it. Here's how to do it and where to get the materials.'"

To publicize the bill and garner support, Mike and Mary Gonzales have appeared on television shows including *Oprah, Dateline, Good Morning America* and various news programs, and granted interviews to several newspapers and magazines, among them the *San Francisco Chronicle, Cosmopolitan, Seventeen* and *Wired*. Across the country, radio stations have also told their story.

Since Suzy Gonzales' death, several threads on ASH have mentioned possible legal action from her parents and the bill they are pursuing. Most feel that their messages continue to be protected by the First Amendment. In relation to Suzy Gonzales, ashers seem to share the belief that her suicide was inevitable; the support she received from ASH was at most an advancing factor in her death, but in no way responsible. In response to a thread entitled, "Should we be banned," started on February 8, 2008, a user named Dan said:

> Suzy Gonzales' parents should realize SUZY is responsible for her own actions and her own suicide. Maybe she found information on how to obtain cyanide, but reading the archives a year ago, I remember that she was saying that she was so desperate as to resort to jumping, and even fantasizing about guillotines. She may have committed suicide regardless of ever finding ASH.

Mike and Mary Gonzales, Lindsay Bartlett, and Wally Herger, on the other hand, remain optimistic, although the bill is in the first step in the legislative process. "We have two years from date of introduction to get the bill voted on and out of the House to the Senate," Mike Gonzales said. From there, the Senate will discuss and debate the bill, and if the Senate chooses to pass the bill, it goes on to the President. "We'll keep revising it until it does become successful," Bartlett said, "We're in for the long haul!"

Conclusion

The Internet has not received nearly as much consideration as other suicide factors. While the literature review provided a great deal of relevant information about suicide and its components, this study has uncovered new information. While my data were qualitative and often based on case studies, the results are nonetheless significant. By exploring the content of suicide websites, newsgroups and message boards, and interviewing the people that use them, I have presented a fresh look into the connection between suicide and the Internet.

Previous research provided grounds for further investigation. My investigation unearthed the same graphic suicide paraphernalia Alao and colleagues (2006) discussed. Their article, "Cybersuicide: Review of the Role of the Internet on Suicide" went on to discuss how the Internet can be a potential source of help for suicidal people, a conclusion that other researchers and myself also reached. Alao and colleagues said that the Internet can be beneficial when suicidal people seek counseling online (490). Tam, Tang and Fernando (2007) called the Internet a "double-edged tool" in relation to suicide, explaining how the Internet could help suicidal people by providing online support groups, etc.

However, each instance of research merely illustrated the Internet's *potential* in serving as a source of help for suicidal people. None of the research thus far has offered compelling evidence that pro-suicide websites ironically help some people avoid suicide. In my research, responses to interviews provided evidence that suicide websites, or at least newsgroups such as ASH, can be beneficial to suicidal people and help them to not commit suicide. This is an unexamined perspective, but one that my research strongly supported.

Suicide has always yielded questions, but it is the high-speed development of the Internet and its effect on the age-old quandary of suicide, that calls for even more and newer research. The existence of suicide websites is verified and, as of now, the law does not interfere in their continuation. In an era in which search engines have replaced dictionaries and "Google it" has become a catchphrase, it is clear that suicide methods are only a click away. Websites, message boards, chat rooms and newsgroups can all harbor suicidal people, foster discussion about the best way to die, and reveal the means. Their effect, however, is not yet clear. It is far too soon to rule out the possibility that they might function to counteract suicidal impulses and hinder attempts.

References

Alao, Adekola, Maureen Soderberg, and Elyssa Pohl. "Cybersuicide: Review of the Role of the Internet on Suicide." *CyberPsychology & Behavior* 9.4 (2006): 489–93.

Becker, Katja, et al. "Parasuicide Online: Can Suicide Websites Trigger Suicidal Behaviour in Predisposed Adolesents?" *Nord J Psychology* 58.2 (2004): 111–14.

Becker, Katja, and Martin Schmidt. "When Kids Seek Help OnLine: Internet Chat Rooms and Suicide." *Reclaiming Children and Youth* 13.4 (2005): 229–30.

Gould, Madelyn, Patrick Jamieson, and Daniel Romer. "Media Contagion and Suicide Among the Young." *American Behavioral Scientist* 46.9 (2003): 1269–80.

Gutierrez, Thelma, and Kim McCabe. "Parents: Online Newsgroup Helped Daughter Commit Suicide." *CNN*. 10 Nov. 2005. 19 Feb. 2008 <www.cnn.com>.

Mishara, Brian, and David Weisstub. "Ethical, Legal, and Practical Issues in the Control and Regulation of Suicide Promotion and Assistance over the Internet." *Suicide and Life-Threatening Behavior* 37.1 (2007): 58–65.

Rhine, Clinton Ernest, et al. "Dimensions of Suicide: Perceptions of Lethality, Time and Agony." *Suicide and Life-Threatening Behavior* 25.3 (1995): 373–80.

Scheeres, Julia. "A Virtual Path to Suicide: Depressed Student Killed Herself With Help From Online Discussion Group." *San Francisco Chronicle* 8 June 2003. 27 Feb. 2008. <www.sfgate.com/cgi-bin/article.cgi?f=/c/a/2003/06/08/MN114902.DTL>.

Tam, J., W. S. Tang, D. J. S. Fernando. "The Internet and Suicide: A Double-Edged Tool." *European Journal of Internal Medicine* 18 (2007): 453–55.

Gender and Suicide Risk: The Role of Wound Site

STEVEN STACK, PHD, AND IRA WASSERMAN, PHD

The association between gender and suicide is one of the most consistent relationships in suicidology. For well over a hundred years the vast majority of research investigations have found that men are typically two to four times more apt than women to complete suicide (e.g., Joiner, 2005, pp. 155–158; Lester, 1972, 2000; Stack, 1982, 2000). In the five nations with the highest suicide rates in the world (Belarus, Latvia, Lithuania, Russia, Ukraine), this ratio ranges from 4.69 (Lithuania) to 6.69 (Belarus) (Joiner, 2005). In the United States, the suicide rate of men is currently four times that of women (data on trends in gender and suicide rates perpetrated with firearms are provided in Table 1). In 2003, the suicide rate for American males was 17.6/100,000 compared to 4.3/100,000 for females (Centers for Disease Control, 2006, p. 56).

A variety of explanations have been advanced to help understand the large gender gap in completed suicide (e.g., for reviews see Canetto & Sakinofsky, 1998; Lester, 2000; Maris, Berman, & Silverman, 2000; Stack, 2000). These explanations contain social-psychological, psychological, sociological, and cultural themes regarding both risk and protective factors. From a sociological perspective, it has been argued that women are higher in social integration than men, and the social support derived from social networks protects women from suicide. Further, since women are more integrated into organized religion than men, religious protections against suicide favor women. Psychological explanations have included the greater incidence of substance abuse among men than women. Alcohol abuse is a risk factor in suicide (e.g., Stack, 2000), and men have been reported to have a rate of alcoholism that is often five times that of women. Nationally, the gender ratio in alcohol-induced deaths is three to one (Centers for Disease Control, 2006, p. 84). Culturally, from an anomie perspective on suicide, there is greater cultural pressure on men than on women to succeed in the labor market. In such a cultural context, occupational and economic failures place men more at risk of suicide than women. Additionally, the cultural system tends to define suicide completions as more acceptable

Table 1 U.S. Female and Male Suicides Perpetrated with Firearms, 1970–2003

Year	Male	Female
1970	58%	30%
1980	63.1%	38.6%
1992	64.6%	38.9%
1996	63%	40%
2003	59%	33%

Sources: Canetto & Sakinofsky, 1998, p. 10; CDC, 2006, p. 73; Maris et al., 2000, p. 151.

for men than women (e.g., Canetto & Sakinofsky, 1998), with men reporting higher levels of suicide acceptability than do women (e.g., Agnew, 1998; Stack, 2000). Men also are often expected to be more stoic and to hide feelings of weakness and vulnerability, and differential emotional transparency has been linked to gender and suicide risk (Canetto & Sakinofsky, 1998). Furthermore, there are important gender differentials in help-seeking behaviors where males are less apt to seek professional help for depression; untreated depression is more lethal than treated depression (e.g., Canetto & Sakinofsky, 1998; Stack, 2000). Part of the gender differential may be the result of social constructionism. For example, women's suicides are more apt than those of men to be misclassified as nonsuicides since women use nonviolent methods more than do men. Nonviolent suicides are more apt to be disguised as accidents, or underdetermined deaths (Canetto & Sakinofsky, 1998). Finally, there is evidence that men are more intent on dying in their efforts at suicide than are women (e.g., Crane et al., 2007; Haw, Hawton, Houston, & Townsend, 2003; Kumar, Mohan, Ranjith, & Chandrasekaran, 2006; Nock & Kessler, 2006; Townsend, Hawton, Harriss, Bale, & Bond, 2001; but for exceptions see, Denning, Conwell, King, & Cox, 2000; Skogman, Alsen, & Ojehagen, 2004).

Table 2 Characteristics of Previous Investigations on Gender and Wound Site in Firearm Suicides

Study	Location	% Head Males	% Head Females	Gun Type	*N* Gun Suicides
Cohle, 1977	Dallas	88.9%	48.4%	Handguns	121
Eisele et al., 1981	Seattle	75%	72%	All	226
Kohlmeier et al., 2001	San Antonio	85.4%	76.2%	All	1,704
Mitchell & Milvenan, 1977	Dallas	53.9%	31%	Shotgun	105
Stone, 1987	Dallas	72%	67%	All	202

The relative merits of these and other explanations for the gender differential in completed suicide are not fully understood (Joiner, 2005; Stack, 2000), and it is beyond the scope of the present investigation to settle the long debate over the complex root causes of the gender differential in suicide. There is, however, a consensus that part of the gender differential is due to the pattern of women choosing guns less often than men (e.g., Canetto & Sakinofsky, 1998; Lester, 2000: see Table 1 for trend data on the proportion of suicides by firearms by gender). In 2003, for example, 59% of males used guns in their suicides compared to 33% of the females. Interestingly, these percentages changed very little from 1970 through 2003.

Clearly, a proximate cause of the gender ratio in suicide is the strong tendency for men to select firearms as a method of suicide. For women, the percentage who choose guns is substantially less. Why women are less apt to choose guns for suicide is not a well-researched area. The present study contributes to the literature by addressing a related, forensics-oriented issue. Several previous investigations have noted that part of the gender differential in suicide may be due to gender differences in the location of gunshot wounds: whether the wounds are in the head (highly lethal) or the body (less lethal) (e.g., Kposowa & McElvain, 2006, p. 436; Lester, 1972, p. 40). The chances of death from gunshot wounds are significantly higher for wounds to the head as opposed to wounds to the body (e.g., Cina, Ward, Hopkins, & Nichols, 1999). In this study, we explored gender as a predictor of gunshot wounds to the head. If gender is related to location of wound site, this may explain part of the gender gap in suicide rates.

Review of Literature

Several previous investigations have noted, typically in passing, that women are more apt than men to shoot themselves in the body when they use guns (Kposowa & McElvain, 2006, p. 436: Lester, 1972, p. 40; Lester, 2000, p. 36; Stone, 1987). In the suicide literature, this argument is based loosely on the notion that given a higher value placed on appearance among women than men, women are less apt to shoot themselves in the head due to fears of disfigurement.

Support for the differential valuing of physical attractiveness among women comes from a variety of sources. Females have a considerably greater incidence of body dissatisfaction and eating disorders than do males (Blaise, 2005; Groesz, Levine, & Muren, 2002; Van Hoeken, Lucas, & Hoek, 1998). For example, the incidence of bulimia nervosa is ten times higher among women than men (American Psychiatric Association, 2005, p. 548; Kaye et al., 2008). At the same time, the socialization of women places considerable emphasis on facial beauty with the associated values of cosmetics (e.g., eye shadow, lipstick, mascara to make eyelashes larger and thicker, eye brow penciling, blush to make cheeks rosy pink, eye liner to accentuate the base of the eye, and foundation cosmetics to tone skin and even its appearance). Such socialization begins early on, from at least kindergarten (e.g., Blaise, 2005), and continues into adulthood. Glamour magazines, beauty pageants, advertising expenditures by the multibillion dollar cosmetics industry, and other media images such as those on billboards and television reinforce the value of female facial beauty (Blaise, 2005; Groesz et al., 2002), which is apt to be compromised by a gunshot to the head. This is not to say that men do not value beauty for themselves. Indeed, men value building muscle structures in the arms, legs, and body (e.g., Cahill & Mussap, 2007); however, gunshot wounds to the head do not destroy these muscle structures.

The empirical basis for linking gender with suicide wound sites, as they refer to fear of disfigurement, apparently rests on rather old and limited data (e.g., from Dallas [Stone, 1987] and Los Angeles [Lester, 1972]). In the present investigation we tested the hypothesis concerning gender and location of wound in suicides with more extensive and recent data from a large mid-Western County. A bibliographical search through Medline and sociological abstracts found five previous studies with some empirical findings on gender and wound site in firearm suicides (Cohle, 1977; Eisele, Reay, & Cook, 1981; Kohlmeier, McMahon, & DiMaio, 2001; Mitchell & Milvenan, 1977; Stone, 1987). These five studies are summarized in Table 2. In Mitchell and Milvenan's (1977) study restricted to 105 suicides by shotgun, 54% of men versus 31% of women shot themselves in the head. In a related investigation of 121 suicides by handguns, 89% of men and 48% of women shot themselves in the head (Cohle, 1977). Stone (1987) investigated 202 firearm suicides in Dallas (both long guns and handguns). Stone determined that 72% of the men compared to 67% of the women shot themselves in the head. An investigation of 226 firearm suicides in Seattle also noted a gender difference. Eisele et al. (1981) determined that 75% of the men and 72% of the women shot themselves in the head in their suicides. Finally, in the largest study to date, a gender differential was documented in San Antonio, Texas. Using data from a 15-year period on 1,704 gunshot suicides, Kohlmeier et al. (2001) determined that 85.4% of the men and 76.2% of the women shot themselves in the head.

Schmeling, Strauch, and Rothschild (2001) investigated 19 female gunshot suicides in Berlin. Two of these involved wounds to the chest and 17 wounds to the head. However, the rigorous interpretation of these findings with regard to a gender differential is not possible since there was no male control group.

A limitation of the previous investigations is that they report the findings on gender and wound site largely in passing in the context of much larger epidemiological reports. As a consequence, there is typically no multivariate analysis. The present investigation adds to the literature in several ways. First, it presents epidemiological findings based on data for a region of the nation (Midwest) which has been neglected in the previous investigations (nearly all previous studies were done in the state of Texas). To the extent that gender roles vary by region of the nation, the gender gap in wound site may vary accordingly. Second, the present investigation uses recent data. It is possible that, given changes in gender roles, there is less of a gender gap in wound site today than in previous eras. Third, we used multivariate analysis in order to ascertain if the relationship between gender and wound site will hold up under controls.

The central hypothesis to be tested is that among those who suicide with guns, men will be more apt than women to shoot themselves in the head. While we cannot rigorously test the reasons behind any such gendered difference, it is assumed that part of any gender differential may be explained by the fear of disfigurement thesis (Cohle, 1977, p. 2; Eisele et al., 1981, p. 484; Kohlmeier et al., 2001; Kposowa & McElvain, 2006, p. 434; Lester, 1972, p. 40; 2000, p. 36; Schmeling et al., 2001; Stone, 1987). In addition, such a gender difference would also be consistent with the gender differential in suicidal intent (e.g., Crane et al., 2007; Haw et al., 2003; Kumar et al., 2006; Nock & Kessler, 2006; Townsend et al., 2001).

The need for controls is warranted for such reasons as cohort effects on gender roles. For example, to the extent that younger women are less accepting than older women of traditional gender role stereotypes and expectations, they may be less apt to be concerned about disfigurement in their suicides. In like manner, different races may have different degrees of adherence to the fear of disfigurement and suicidal intent. We introduced controls for these demographic factors to ascertain if they may render as spurious any zero order relationship between gender and wound site.

Finally, previous research has suggested that men and women differ somewhat in the types of firearms used in gun suicides (Cohle, 1977; Mitchell & Milvenan, 1977). The weapon of choice is the handgun for both men and women in gun suicides; however, men are much more likely than women to pick long guns as a second choice. For example, in the largest study to date, females used long guns in 13% of their gun suicides, while men used long guns in 24% of their gun suicides. Females are smaller than males, which makes it more difficult to position a long gun to facilitate head shooting. Further, the odds of shooting oneself in the head as opposed to the body diminish as you go from handguns to long guns. Long guns are heavier and their length makes it more awkward and difficult to shoot oneself in the head than the body. For example, the respective percentages of head shooters goes from a high of 82% for those using handguns, down to 67% for those using rifles, and down to 47% for those opting to use shotguns (Eisele et al., 1981). Hence, since males are more likely than females to choose long guns, gender differences in head shooting may diminish under a control for type of firearm employed.

Methods

Data on suicide were collected from the files of an urban medical examiner's office. The data refer to a county in the Midwest. Files for the period 1997–2005 were searched to locate suicides committed with firearms. All files where the weapon used in the suicide was a firearm (e.g., shotgun, rifle, handgun) are included. A total of 1,412 suicide case files were investigated. The files contained demographic information, an investigator's report, and toxicology report. Some files also contained additional information including copies of any suicide note. In all, 807 firearm suicides were found.

The dependent variable is wound site. It is a dichotomous variable where 1 = *wound is located in the head* (e.g., forehead, left temple, right temple, mouth). All other locations (e.g., left chest, right chest, stomach) are coded as zeroes. Since the dependent variable is a dichotomy, logistic regression techniques are appropriate (Menard, 2002).

The core independent variable is gender where 1 = *female* and 0 = *male*. Controls are introduced for demographic factors, which are available in the files of the medical examiner. Age is coded as years. Race is coded as a binary variable where 1 = *Caucasian* and 0 = *all other races*.

Long guns are defined as rifles and shotguns. Rifles include lever action, bolt action, and automatic weapons. Shotguns include single barrel, double barrel, automatic, and semi-automatic weapons. Handguns include revolvers

Table 3 The Association between Gender and Wound Site in Gunshot Suicides: Multiple Logistic Regression Results (*N*=807 Firearm Suicides)

Variable	Coefficient	Standard Error	Odds Ratio
Gender (female)	−0.630*	.258	0.53
Caucasian	0.413*	.212	1.51
Age	0.003	0.005	0.997
Constant	1.73	0.263	
−2L Likelihood=667.9*			

*$p<.05$

Table 4 Type of Gun Used by Gender of Suicide Victim (*N*=807 Gun Suicides, 1997–2005)

Firearm Type	Males	Females
Handguns	64.6% (*n*=452)	80.4% (*n*=86)
Shotguns	22.0% (*n*=154)	10.3% (*n*=11)
Rifles	13.4% (*n*=94)	9.3% (*n*=10)
Totals	100% (*n*=700)	100% (*n*=107)

$\alpha=10.912, p<.01$

and clip-based weapons. Type of gun is coded as 1=*handgun* and 0=*long guns.*

Results

A total of 85.15% of the gunshot suicides of males involved wounds to the head; 14.85% shot themselves in the body. For women, 75.47% shot themselves in the head and 24.53% involved the body as a wound site. These differences were statistically significant ($\alpha=6.36$, $p < 0.01$). The results of the multiple logistic regression analysis are provided in Table 3. The coefficient for gender is significant, being more than twice its standard error. Controlling for the other predictors, women are 47% (OR=.53) less apt to shoot themselves in the head than are men. Controlling for the other predictor variables, Caucasians are 1.51 times more apt than other races to shoot themselves in the head. The coefficient for race is nearly twice its standard error. Finally, controlling for the other predictors, the coefficient for age is not significant. Its coefficient is essentially equal to its standard error.

Table 5 The Effect of Gender on Head Shooting for Handgun Suicides (*N*=538)

Wound Site	Males	Females
Gunshot to the Head	88.9% (*n*=402)	79.1% (*n*=68)
Gunshot to the Body	11.1% (*n*=50)	20.9% (*n*=18)
Totals	100% (*n*=452)	100% (*n*=86)

$\alpha=6.372, p<.05$

Table 6 The Effect of Gender on Head Shooting for Long Gun Suicides (*N*=269)

Wound Site	Males	Females
Gunshot to the Head	81.9% (*n*=203)	71.4% (*n*=15)
Gunshot to the Body	18.1% (*n*=45)	28.6% (*n*=6)
Totals	100% (*n*=248)	100% (*n*=21)

$\alpha=1.37, p>.05.$

The results on the distribution of type of firearm by gender is provided in Table 4. As anticipated, men are more likely than women to have long guns as a second choice weapon in gun suicides. The percentage of men using long guns in their gun suicides (35.4%) is nearly double that of women (19.6%). With regard to handgun suicides (*N*=538), 88.9% of males compared to 79.1% of females shot themselves in the head (Table 5). This difference is statistically significant. For the effect of gender on head shooting in suicides by long guns (*N*=269), shotgun and rifle suicides were combined given the small numbers of females using these weapons (Table 6). While the difference in percent for gun shots to the head is in the predicted direction, 81.9% for males and 71.4% for females, it does not meet the requirements for statistical significance.

Conclusion

While there have been many competing explanations for the large gender differential in suicide completions, the relative merits of these explanations are still not fully clear (e.g., Joiner, 2005; Kposowa & McElvain, 2006; Lester, 2000; Stack, 2000). The present paper draws attention to a neglected factor in this debate: wound site. Using a multivariate analysis of 807 gunshot suicides in an urban county in the Midwest, we found that, controlling for demographics, women are 47% less likely than men to shoot themselves in the head, as opposed to the body. While previous studies have reported a gender differential, they have not controlled for the covariates of wound site. The present research does so and, thus, provides a firmer basis for the generalization linking gender to wound site.

The association between gender and wound site is subject to interpretation, but it is consistent with what has been termed the "beautiful corpse thesis" (Schmeling et al., 2001): that to the extent that women are more concerned about physical appearances, especially facial beauty, than men (e.g., Blaine, 2005; Groesz et al., 2002), we would expect women to be less apt than men to shoot themselves in the head. The study results are also consistent with the thesis that men have a stronger suicidal intent (e.g., Crane et al., 2007; Kumar et al., 2006; Nock & Kessler, 2006).

Our results are consistent with the notion that firearm choice (handgun vs. long gun) follows a gendered pattern (see Tables 4–6). Since men are more apt to choose long guns than women, and since long guns make it more difficult to shoot oneself in the head, the gender differential in wound location is actually lowered given men's differentially high selection of long guns. As anticipated, even with controlling for type of firearm, men were more apt to shoot themselves in the head in the case of handguns. However, the gender differential in head shooting did not hold up in the case of long guns, firearms that make head shooting somewhat more difficult for those involved.

Future research is needed for rural areas. All previous investigations, like the present one, have been based on highly urban populations. To the extent that rural gender role stereotypes are more traditional than urban ones, we would expect to find more of a gender gap in wound site in rural areas than in urban areas. Other forensics-oriented factors also may help to explain part of the gender gap in suicide. In particular, the caliber of the weapon may follow a gendered pattern (e.g., to the extent that women select lower caliber weapons than men, women would be expected to have lower risk of suicide).

References

Agnew, R. (1998). The approval of suicide: A social-psychological model. *Suicide & Life-Threatening Behavior, 28,* 205–225.

American Psychiatric Association. (2005). Diagnostic and Statistical Manual of Mental Disorders (4th ed.). Washington, DC: Author.

Blaise, M. (2005). A feminist, poststructuralist study of children "doing" gender in an urban kindergarten classroom. *Early Childhood Research Quarterly, 20,* 85–108.

Cahill, S., & Mussap, A. J. (2007). Emotional reactions following exposure to idealized bodies predict unhealthy body change attitudes and behaviors in women and men. *Journal of Psychosomatic Research, 62,* 631–639.

Canetto, S., & Sakinofsky, I. (1998). The gender paradox in suicide. *Suicide and Life-Threatening Behavior, 28,* 1–23.

Centers for Disease Control. (2006). *Deaths: Final data for 2003. National Vital Statistics Reports, 54*(13), 1–120.

Cina, S., Ward, M., Hopkins, A., & Nichols, C. A. (1999).

Multifactorial analysis of firearm wounds to the head with attention to anatomic location. *American Journal of Forensic Medicine and Pathology, 20,* 109–115.

Cohle, S. (1977). Handgun suicides. *Forensic Science Gazette, 8,* 2.

Crane, C., Williams, J.M.G., Hawton, K., Arensmen, E., Hjelmeland, H., et al. (2007). The association between life events and suicide intent in self poisoners with and without a history of deliberate self-harm: A preliminary study. *Suicide and Life-Threatening Behavior, 37,* 367–378.

Denning, D. G., Conwell, Y., King, D., & Cox, C. (2000). Method choice, intent & gender in completed suicide. *Suicide and Life-Threatening Behavior, 30,* 282–288.

Eisele, J. W., Reay, D. T., & Cook, A. (1981). Sites of suicidal gunshot wounds. *Journal of Forensic Science, 26,* 480–485.

Groesz, L. M., Levine, M. P., & Murnen, S. K. (2002). The effect of experimental presentation of thin media images on body satisfaction: A Meta analytic review. *International Journal of Eating Disorders, 31,* 1–16.

Haw, C., Hawton, K., Houston, K., & Townsend, E. (2003). Correlates of relative lethality and suicidal intent among deliberate self-harm patients. *Suicide and Life-Threatening Behavior, 44,* 353–364.

Joiner, T. (2005). *Why people die by suicide.* Cambridge: Harvard University Press.

Kaye, W. H., Bulik, C., Plotnicow, K., Thornton, L., Devlin, B., et al. (2008). The genetics of anorexia nervosa collaborative study. *International Journal of Eating Disorders, 41,* 289–300.

Kohlmeier, R. E., McMahon, C. A., & DiMaio, V.J.M. (2001). Suicide by firearm: A 15-year review. *The American Journal of Forensic Medicine and Pathology, 22,* 337–340.

Kposowa, A. K., & McElvain, J. P. (2006). Gender, place, & method of suicide. *Social Psychiatry & Psychiatric Epidemiology, 41,* 435–443.

Kumar, C.T.S., Mohan, R., Ranjith, G., & Chandrasekaran, R. (2006). Gender differences in medically serious suicide attempts: A study from south India. *Psychiatry Research, 144,* 79–86.

Lester, D. (1972). *Why people kill themselves.* Springfield, OH: Chs. Thomas.

Lester, D. (2000). *Why people kill themselves* (4th ed.). Springfield, OH: Chs. Thomas.

Maris, R., Berman, A., & Silverman, M. (2000). *Comprehensive textbook of sucicidology.* New York: Guilford.

Menard, S. (2002). *Applied logistic regression analysis,* Thousand Oaks, CA: Sage.

Mitchell, J. S., & Milvenan, J. (1977). Shotgun suicides. *Forensic Science Gazette, 8,* 3.

Nock, M. K., & Kessler, R. F. C. (2006). Prevalence of risk factors for suicide attempt vs. suicide gestures: Analysis of the national comorbidity study. *Journal of Abnormal Psychology, 115,* 616–623.

Schmeling, A., Strauch, H., & Rothschild, M. A. (2001). Female suicides in Berlin with the use of firearms. *Forensic Science International, 124,* 178–181.

Skogman, K., Alsen, M., & Ojehagen, A. (2004). Sex differences in risk factors for suicide after attempted suicide: A follow-up study of 1052 suicide attempters. *Social Psychiatry & Psychiatric Epidemiology, 39,* 113–120.

Stack, S. (1982). Suicide: A decade review of the sociological research. *Deviant Behavior, 4,* 41–66.

Stack, S. (2000). Suicide: A fifteen-year review of the sociological literature, Part I: Cultural and economic factors. *Suicide and Life-Threatening Behavior, 30,* 145–162.

Stone, L. C. (1987). Observations and statistics relating to suicide weapons. *Journal of Forensic Sciences, 32,* 711–716.

Townsend, E., Hawton, K., Harriss, L., Bale, E., & Bond, A. (2001). Substances used in deliberate self-poisoning 1985–1997: Trends and associations with age, gender, repetition, and suicide intent. *Social Psychiatry and Psychiatric Epidemiology, 36,* 228–234.

Van Hoeken, D., Lucas, A. R., & Hoek, H. W. (1998). Epidemiology. In H. W. Hoek, J. L. Treasure, & M. A. Katzman (Eds.), *Neurobiology in the treatment of eating disorders* (pp. 97–126). New York: Wiley.

STEVEN STACK is with the Center for Suicide Research and Wayne State University; and IRA WASSERMAN is with Eastern Michigan University.

This is a revised version of a paper read at the annual meetings of the Michigan Sociological Association held in Mt. Pleasant, MI, October 6–7, 2006. We would like to thank Dr. Carl J. Schmidt of the Wayne County Medical Examiner's Office for providing the data for the analysis.

Address correspondence to Steven Stack, PhD, Center for Suicide Research, 6341 Parkview Drive, Troy, Michigan 48098; E-mail: steven_stack@hotmail.com

UNIT 5

Animals and Death

Unit Selections

Key Points to Consider

- Do you remember your first death experience? Was it that of a person or an animal? How did you react? How did your parents relate to this experience? Did your family have a "service" for the deceased animal, followed by earth burial or did one of your parents simply dispose of the animal without ceremony? Now that you are an adult and look back on that experience, how did you feel about how the situation was handled?

- If and when you have children of your own (if you do not already have them), how will you deal with the death of your child's pet or the death of any other animal which she/he may encounter (roadkill, for example)?

- Veterinarians are often asked to euthanize animals. How do they deal with these traumatic situations with the animal's owner often present? Do veterinary medicine schools prepare veterinary students to relate to individuals in end-of-life situations?

- Should we have hospice facilities for dying animals, as we do for dying humans? Would you be inclined to place your dog or cat in a hospice facility, if the animal is indeed at end-stage of its fatal illness?

Student Website

www.mhhe.com/cls

Internet References

The Humane Society of the United States
    www.humanesociety.org/about/departments/faith/francis_files/the_grief_over_a_pets_death_.html
Pet Loss Support Page
    www.pet-loss.net/emotions.shtml

The first encounter that many children have with death is with that of an animal. It may be a pet or a dead bird or wild animal on the roadway. If that experience is indeed an animal, how do we as adults deal with the topic? The death of an animal presents a good opportunity for parents to help children learn their lessons of death by answering questions. If a family pet, the child may have had the pleasure of watching the animal grow from a small puppy, kitten, or guinea pig into a large dog, cat, or guinea pig. With non-human animals having shorter life spans than humans, children often observe a pet going through the life cycle, with the omega being death. Thus, a pet's death is a realistic orientation to death.

In this section of the anthology, we present articles on animals and death. One of the pieces, "Treat People Like Dogs" addresses the idea of euthanasia and palliative care. How and when to "put down" one's animal is not an easy question to answer, thus one often relies heavily on the veterinarian's advice on this. An individual does not want to have the animal euthanized too soon and take away some of its life while it has some quality to it, yet at the same time one does not want to wait too long and let the animal suffer beyond that which should not have been. Afterward, one may feel guilty if she/he felt that action occurred too soon or the same if it was too late. A not so win-win situation.

"When a Cherished Pet Dies" addresses the issue of the impact of the death of a pet on the elderly. Often, an elderly person's best friend and companion may be her/his dog or cat or some other animal. When that animal dies, it can be devastating to the individual.

Next, the rather fascinating story of Oscar the Cat who, in a nursing home setting, seemed to sense when death was approaching for one of the residents is presented in Henry's piece. Lastly, there are available today some hospice programs for pets, thus an animal can experience palliative care just as we humans can. This topic is addressed in Souza's "Veterinary Hospice" article.

© Digital Vision

Treat People Like Dogs

KAREN OBERTHALER, V.M.D.

When I say I'm a veterinary oncologist, I am usually met with a bemused, slightly incredulous reaction. I'm often asked, "Do people really treat their pets for *cancer?*" As a matter of fact, they do. Not only do I administer radiation and chemotherapy to cats and dogs (not to mention the occasional ferret and hedgehog) on a daily basis, but I work in one of the most sophisticated veterinary hospitals in the country, with a neurosurgeon, a dermatologist, an ophthalmologist, and a host of other specialists. Pet owners routinely rack up $10,000 bills to save the life of an animal that they consider a beloved member of the family.

This may seem extreme, but it's not even close to what many Americans do for their (human) relatives. A breathtaking $66.8 billion each year—almost a third of all Medicare dollars—is spent treating patients in the last two years of their lives. Too often, expensive procedures are tried simply so medical providers can cover themselves against potential lawsuits from bereaved family members who want to make sure everything possible was done. The fact that insurance generally covers all of this makes it more likely that doctors and patients pile on excessive and nonessential tests and procedures.

About 90 percent of my animal patients are geriatric—and, as odd as this sounds, the veterinary world may hold lessons for the broader health-care system. While pet insurance exists, only roughly 3 percent of owners carry it; even then, clients pay a substantial portion of costs themselves. That means they usually want to know the rationale behind each test. I explain what I think is going on, what I want to look for, and which tests I need to perform to find it. I rank the diagnostics from most to least essential and lay out approximate costs. My clients then choose what they want done, with an understanding of the relative importance, risk, and cost of each option. This step-by-step approach may seem time-consuming, but it dramatically reduces the number of expensive, unnecessary tests. And the process is more gratifying.

As odd as this sounds, the veterinary world may hold lessons for the broader health-care system.

When facing the death of a loved one—human or animal—the real challenge is coming to grips with the reality of the situation. Since my approach draws me closer to families, it's easier to suggest that the best course of treatment may be relieving pain rather than fighting a disease. Owners are less likely to fear that you're giving up on their beloved pet if they trust you. When I'm asked about performing tests, and I know the results won't change the outcome, I say so. If your golden retriever's cancer is too far advanced for surgery, getting a biopsy may be a pricey—and superfluous—exercise.

No family wants to subject its already sick pet to uncomfortable tests or dump thousands of dollars into dead-end diagnostics. So why do we do that to our grandparents? Clearly the stakes are different: we're talking about the people who brought us into the world. Vets, also, are not saddled with the threat of career-ending malpractice lawsuits. While most pets are treated like children, legally animals are property—I can't be sued for more than their face value. We're also not buried under paperwork, which accounts for our ability to spend more time with clients.

I'm not advocating that people and their families be allowed to dictate their care entirely. But there is something to be said for inviting them deeper into the process. In some ways, veterinary practice today is not that different from the practice of human medicine before insurance companies dictated policy and the threat of lawsuits guided decisions. Which might explain why the question I'm asked with the second-most frequency is "Do you think *I* could be treated in this hospital?"

OBERTHALER is on staff at NYC Veterinary Specialists.

When a Cherished Pet Dies

"After several months I am still so distraught over the death of my dog, Pixie, I can't even talk about her. I miss watching TV with her on my lap and I miss her companionship."

—Diane, 74-years-old

Pets can be an important part of life, holding a special place in the heart. A pet can be a faithful companion, an integral part of one's home life and daily schedule. A pet can provide unconditional love that many people, particularly older adults, may get from no one else. When a special pet dies, this loss can have a significant impact on a person's health and well-being. Today, there is a growing public awareness about the anguish people can feel when a cherished pet dies, and more community resources are available to help those grieving a pet.

How Do Older People Benefit from Having a Pet?

Pets can provide their owners with a sense of purpose and fulfillment, companionship, affection, acceptance and friendship. Pets rely on their owners for food, water, exercise and medical care, which may give the owner a feeling of responsibility and of being needed. In return, pets often express contentment through their chirps, wags, licks or purrs. A pet may provide opportunities for physical contact, such as touching, hugging, cuddling, and can even be a sleep partner. Owners talk to, spend time with, and have fun with a pet. Through these interactions, a pet can become an integral part of everyday life. For many, a pet can hold the rank of "valued friend" or "close family member."

Caring for and providing a loving home to an animal can help an older person remain active and healthy. This active involvement with an animal can help lower blood pressure, decrease stress, reduce bone loss, lower cholesterol levels, and improve blood circulation. A pet may also provide an opportunity to meet and socialize with others, such as gathering with other pet owners in the park or conversing with the staff at the vet's office. Thus, a pet can help lessen or prevent feelings of isolation and loneliness.

How Might the Death of a Pet Affect Older People?

Losing a cherished pet means losing a significant relationship. Your pet loss can feel overwhelming, particularly if you are experiencing other losses, many of which are common to the aging process.

It is not unusual, for example, for older adults to have long-time friends, a spouse, and a pet die all within a short time of each other. Your pet may have been the one link left to your past, or perhaps was your loyal companion during an otherwise lonely time. Or you may have moved from your old neighborhood to a new environment, and your pet may have been a source of strength during the transition to your new home. For those coping with a chronic illness, your pet may have comforted you, by staying nearby or licking your hand. For others, your pet may have been trained to help you with daily activities. For example, just as a seeing-eye dog is specifically trained to help someone with vision impairment get around, your pet may have been trained to be able to move easily and fetch things in the house for you or alert others in case you needed help in an emergency.

The loss of your pet may change your outlook on your life. For example, you may lose a sense of purpose in your day if you experience feelings of emptiness or sadness when no longer having a dog to walk, a bird to talk to or a cat to brush. In addition, the loss of a beloved pet can remind you of your own vulnerability and mortality. This can lead to feelings of worry about getting another pet, wondering if the pet will become orphaned if you have a prolonged hospitalization or die.

What Are Common Feelings When a Pet Dies?

Grieving is a natural response to the loss of an attachment. It is normal to grieve a pet that has been a part of your life. There is no right or wrong way to express your feelings related to the loss of a beloved pet. Some people are outwardly emotional while others emote privately. Some will grieve for days or weeks while others may take months or even years to recover from the loss of a beloved animal friend. Your own reactions and feelings connected to this loss will likely depend on the nature of the relationship you had with your pet, how long the pet was part of your life, if the death was sudden or gradual, and the situation in which the pet died.

When a pet dies, it is not unusual for a person to experience a range of feelings. When the loss of a pet occurs under particularly stressful circumstances, the emotional response can be quite intense. For example, you may experience anger or helplessness if a precious pet needs to be given away because of financial limitations, ill health or because of a move to a new place that does not accept pets, like a nursing home or assisted living facility. You might experience anguish if faced with the difficult decision to euthanize a pet. Or, if your pet died from an accident, you may feel guilt if you believe you could have been more protective. Holiday and birthday celebrations may feel less joyful after the loss of a pet. After a pet dies, you might feel sad each year on the anniversary marking the date your pet came into your heart and home.

If your sadness or pain seems to grow over time, or you find the loss of your pet affecting your ability to get things done on a daily basis, it is probably time to seek professional counseling to help you cope with your continued grief.

Why Are Feelings about Losing a Pet Often Hidden?

You might feel upset and sad about the loss of your pet and find yourself hiding these feelings from others. You may believe it is inappropriate, silly or weak to be so concerned about an animal's death. Or you may have been raised believing that showing emotion is improper making it difficult for you to express personal feelings. If you feel embarrassed, ashamed, or uncomfortable about your emotional reaction to your pet's death, trying to ignore or disguise your grief is common.

In addition, sometimes otherwise well-meaning people may say careless things like, "You can always get another one." This might be true, yet this statement does not acknowledge the uniqueness of your pet and the special relationship you enjoyed. Feeling misunderstood, you might decide not to share the sadness you feel.

Our society does not always recognize the depth of feeling that can accompany the loss of a pet. Thus, many communities offer no way or only very limited ways to share the loss of a pet with others (e.g., rituals, ceremonies, or memorials). Without an organized opportunity to remember a pet, many people feel uncomfortable expressing grief.

Grieving the loss of a pet, while difficult, can be a healthy process. Holding back may leave you with a heavy heart for a prolonged period of time.

How Can I Cope with the Loss of My Pet?

It is common to feel sorrow with the loss of a pet. It is important to realize that things will get better over time. Here are some things you can do to cope with the loss of your pet:

Talk about your feelings for your pet with others who are compassionate, sensitive and understanding.

Remember your pet by creating a scrapbook about them, place a framed picture of them in a special place, or write a story or poem about them.

Participate in a support group, counseling session, Internet chat room or call a pet loss hotline. Your veterinarian or local Humane Society can recommend counselors or support groups that might help you.

Consider holding a memorial service, buying a burial site, or putting a stone marker in your garden or in a room in your house.

Make a memorial contribution in your pet's name to a favorite charity or to an animal rescue organization. Saying good-bye can give you an opportunity to express your feelings, reach some closure, and to think about the role of the pet in your life.

Volunteer with a charity or religious group that you are affiliated with to keep yourself busy and with other people. Animal shelters and animal organizations need people to walk, pet, and care for abandoned animals.

Increase your interaction with family, friends and social groups in your community.

Read books and magazines about pet loss and how to deal with your feelings of grief.

Book Profiles Furry Angel of Death: Oscar the Cat

RAY HENRY

The scientist in Dr. David Dosa was skeptical when first told that Oscar, an aloof cat kept by a nursing home, regularly predicted patients' deaths by snuggling alongside them in their final hours.

Dosa's doubts eroded after he and his colleagues tallied about 50 correct calls made by Oscar over five years, a process he explains in a book released this week, "Making Rounds With Oscar: The Extraordinary Gift of an Ordinary Cat." (Hyperion, $23.99) The feline's bizarre talent astounds Dosa, but he finds Oscar's real worth in his fierce insistence on being present when others turn away from life's most uncomfortable topic: death.

"People actually were taking great comfort in this idea, that this animal was there and might be there when their loved ones eventually pass," Dosa said. "He was there when they couldn't be."

Dosa, 37, a geriatrician and professor at Brown University, works on the third floor of the Steere House, which treats patients with severe dementia. It's usually the last stop for people so ill they cannot speak, recognize their spouses and spend their days lost in fragments of memory.

He once feared that families would be horrified by the furry grim reaper, especially after Dosa made Oscar famous in a 2007 essay in the *New England Journal of Medicine*. Instead, he says many caregivers consider Oscar a comforting presence, and some have praised him in newspaper death notices and eulogies.

"Maybe they're seeing what they want to see," he said, "but what they're seeing is a comfort to them in a real difficult time in their lives."

The nursing home adopted Oscar, a medium-haired cat with a gray-and-brown back and white belly, in 2005 because its staff thinks pets make the Steere House a home. They play with visiting children and prove a welcome distraction for patients and doctors alike.

After a year, the staff noticed that Oscar would spend his days pacing from room to room. He sniffed and looked at the patients but rarely spent much time with anyone—except when they had just hours to live.

He's accurate enough that the staff—including Dosa—know it's time to call family members when Oscar stretches beside their patients, who are generally too ill to notice his presence. If kept outside the room of a dying patient, he'll scratch at doors and walls, trying to get in.

Nurses once placed Oscar in the bed of a patient they thought gravely ill. Oscar wouldn't stay put, and the staff thought his streak was broken. Turns out, the medical professionals were wrong, and the patient rallied for two days. But in the final hours, Oscar held his bedside vigil without prompting.

Dosa does not explain Oscar scientifically in his book, although he theorizes the cat imitates the nurses who raised him or smells odors given off by dying cells, perhaps like some dogs who scientists say can detect cancer using their sense of scent.

At its heart, Dosa's search is more about how people cope with death than Oscar's purported ability to predict it. Dosa suffers from inflammatory arthritis, which could render his joints useless. He worries about losing control of his life in old age, much as his patients have lost theirs.

Parts of his book are fictionalized. Dosa said several patients are composite characters, though the names and stories of the caregivers he interviews are real and many feel guilty. Donna Richards told Dosa that she felt guilty for putting her mother in a nursing home. She felt guilty for not visiting enough. When caring for her mother, Richards felt guilty about missing her teenage son's swimming meets.

Dosa learns to live for the moment, much like Oscar, who delights in naps and chin scratches or the patient who recovers enough to walk the hall holding the hand of the husband she'll eventually forget.

The doctor advises worried family members to simply be present for their loved ones.

Richards was at her mother's bedside nonstop as she died. After three days, a nurse persuaded her to go home for a brief rest. Despite her misgivings, Richards agreed. Her mother died a short while later.

But she didn't die alone. Oscar was there.

Veterinary Hospice

Ways to Nurture Our Pets at the End of Life

AMY SOUZA

Kramer, a black poodle/terrier mix with warm brown eyes, has silky black ears and a slightly tousled tuft of hair above his triangular face that makes him resemble his *Seinfeld* namesake. He has lived with Frank and Carol Miller for eight of his nine years, ever since the couple adopted him from a local shelter. To an outsider, Kramer appears healthy and vibrant, as a dog his age should. But the Millers see what a stranger cannot: slight stubble on his chin and thinning back hair caused by chemotherapy, and a slight thickening around the waist from taking prednisone.

Last September, during a routine dental cleaning, Kramer's vet discovered a mass on the dog's tongue. The news was dire. Though pathologists were unable to pinpoint exactly what type of tumor Kramer has, they know it's an aggressive immune-cell cancer. Because of the tumor's location, radiation was not an option, but vets estimated that with surgery and chemotherapy, Kramer could live for one more year. The Millers were told not to expect a cure.

Seven months and many treatments later, it's unclear whether their beloved pet will make it to another September. Whatever happens, the Millers are determined to do everything they can to keep Kramer healthy, happy and by their sides for as long as possible. So, they are taking his care into their own hands.

In a small room bordering the sitting area of their Maryland home, near a small refrigerator holding Kramer's medications, Carol maintains a calendar to keep track of Kramer's treatments. She has filled in each day of the month: "C" for chemo; "P" for prednisone; and "1," "2" or "3" for the particular homeopathic remedy he is to receive that day. The drugs keep Kramer's tumor in check, minimizing his discomfort and allowing him to eat.

The Millers haven't given it a name, but essentially what they're giving Kramer is hospice care.

What Is Veterinary Hospice?

Veterinary hospice has existed for more than a decade, but it is far from mainstream. That appears to be changing, however, as more and more practitioners begin to focus on end-of-life care and discover a huge demand for their services. It's not surprising: An increasing number of people with pets are willing to give subcutaneous fluids or learn how to inject pain medication, especially if it means a few more months, weeks or days with their pets.

Dr. Liz Palmer of Charlottesville, Virginia, opened a mobile end-of-life care practice a year and a half ago. Though she has never marketed her services, Palmer has an extensive client list. After a local newspaper published an article about her business, she received more phone calls than she could handle. Other hospice providers report similar experiences; when people read or hear about their services, they receive an influx of calls.

"There's a Catch-22 right now, and that is we don't have very many people who see themselves as providers in this area, and there are a lot of potential users of animal hospice who have no idea that it exists," says Dr. Amir Shanan, who has offered veterinary hospice for more than 10 years in his Chicago general practice. "Pet owners don't ask about hospice services, and veterinarians don't offer information because, they say, pet owners aren't asking about it."

Part of the reason is that neither general-practice vets nor the general public know exactly how to define pet hospice. The confusion stems, in part, from the term itself, because "hospice" also refers to a standard of care provided to dying humans. Pet hospice takes many forms, however: a couple like the Millers tending to their dying pet, veterinarians who travel to people's homes, or even a physical location where animals live out their final days. In the broadest sense, hospice is a philosophy of caring for a dying animal in a loving, appropriate manner, while also supporting the pet's family.

Many people agree that the best place for a pet to die is at home, surrounded by familiar sights and smells and the people who love them. Veterinarians focused on hospice or end-of-life care aim to make the time before death comfortable for animals by teaching people how to administer medications and fluids, and helping them decide when euthanasia is warranted.

During more than 25 years as a general practitioner, Palmer says she never had time to deal with end-of-life care properly. "I was so focused on treating disease, spay/neuter and primary care," she says. "When I was trying to figure out what I was doing [with this new business], I was trying to find a word for it. It's care in the end of life, but I also consider it ending life. I'm involved in the dying process."

During an initial visit, Palmer conducts a thorough exam, particularly to detect pain, but she believes it's equally important to assess an animal's environment. "I really pay attention to how much an animal has to struggle to get through daily life. I like to go to homes, to sit on the couch and observe. I like to see the obstacles a pet faces and give the owners the 'What are you going to do if . . .' scenarios," Palmer says. "I look at the quality of life of the owner, too. I don't want the relationship to be a frustrating burden. That's not good for the animal or the human."

Making Tough Choices

As animal guardians, we must make choices for our pets, but on the whole, the veterinary profession—while excellent at offering medically oriented solutions—is not well equipped to help people make end-of-life decisions. These decisions are fraught with emotions and bring up all sorts of practical, ethical and existential questions. What value do we place on life? Does that extend to animals as well as humans? What constitutes suffering? How do we know when euthanasia is warranted?

The Argus Institute at Colorado State University's veterinary teaching hospital has on-site counselors who are available around the clock to assist people facing difficult medical decisions about their pets. Dr. Jane Shaw directs the institute and teaches veterinary communication at the school. Students often ask her what to do if someone doesn't want to euthanize a pet.

"We ask questions of the client and can discover whatever barriers are there," Shaw says. "There's a subset of clients, mostly because of spiritual reasons, for whom euthanasia is not an option. For other people who desire a natural death for their pet, we walk them through what that death might look like. In many disease conditions, the death is not peaceful, and we have to have pretty frank conversations about that. Euthanasia is a controlled process and, done appropriately, is peaceful. Natural death is completely unknown, and that makes some vets uncomfortable. They're worried about the animal's welfare and the client's welfare."

In non-emergency cases, quality-of-life scales can help people evaluate their animals. One widely used scale, created by oncologist Dr. Alice Villalobos, asks people to rate their pet from 1 to 10 in six areas: hurt, hunger, hydration, happiness, mobility, and more good days than bad. "Every member of the family should do the scale separately, because there's always one person who has blinders on," Villalobos says.

Dr. Nancy Ruffing, a mobile hospice veterinarian in Pittsburgh, Pennsylvania, supplements Villalobos's scale with a handout containing her own words of wisdom about end-of-life decisions. "A lot of people don't want to make it a numerical decision," she says. Yet, assessing a pet's quality of life is crucial, and she considers it a big part of her job. "Owners have to have some type of a mental plan for what to do at the end of life, but you have to look at your pet critically when they're having a good day so you can recognize the subtle differences on a bad day," Ruffing says. "You really have to be in tune with your pet, and that starts at the beginning."

To End Life or Let Life End?

Gail Pope, founder of BrightHaven, a residential hospice on 10 acres in Santa Rosa, California, believes strongly in letting an animal's life play out to the very end. It's a stance she arrived at slowly. For many years, Pope worked at a conventional veterinary office and was schooled in conventional practices, including the idea that euthanasia constituted a normal end to an animal's life. She and her husband started BrightHaven in 1996 with the simple goal of caring for elderly and infirm animals.

When one of their resident cats, Mariah, began showing signs that she was about to die, Pope panicked. She was alone and couldn't leave the other animals, so she called a vet to come euthanize the cat—a notion that now makes Pope shake her head. "It's the old thought of 'She's dying, hurry up, let's kill her.'"

Her veterinarian promised to send someone out during the lunch hour, and in the meantime Pope phoned a friend and animal communicator who instructed her to carry Mariah outside to an oak tree and sit with her in her arms. "I was terrified. I didn't know what was going to happen," she says.

Pope remained agitated, but Mariah was calm. The cat died quietly in Pope's lap. She says, "My friend told me, 'Mother Nature designed this,' and that has stuck with me to this day." Over the next few years, as Pope moved toward administering alternative medicine, such as homeopathy, and feeding animals a natural diet, she saw amazing things happen. Animals came to BrightHaven to die, but more and more of them instead grew healthier and livelier. Now, she says, her cats routinely live into their 20s.

Though Pope is not opposed to euthanasia in cases when she feels it is absolutely warranted, her philosophy and practice are to allow for natural death with few to no drugs other than natural remedies. Euthanasia is often employed too quickly, she says, and in an effort to relieve suffering, people actually may be ending their animals' lives prematurely.

Pope's position is atypical in the pet hospice community but it is shared by some, including Kathryn Marocchino of Nikki Hospice Foundation for Pets in Vallejo, California. Marocchino thinks that in many instances, people would rather not euthanize an ill animal, but they're not presented with any other option, such as hospice care.

"There is intense debate in the community around what is hospice for animals," says Marocchino, who helped organize a pet hospice symposium in 2008. "Hospice to vets means, 'I will do everything to help you, but I have a quality of life scale, and when the dog reaches a certain number, it's time for euthanasia.'"

At the symposium, Marocchino says only two veterinarians in attendance had ever witnessed the natural death of an animal. This fact suggests to her that euthanasia is used too frequently and too readily by veterinarians. "They're not giving death a chance," Marocchino says. "Euthanasia should be a last resort."

The majority of people working in pet hospice, however, do believe that euthanasia is a necessary—and humane—tool. Some of them worry that the larger veterinary community, and the general public, will misinterpret the term "pet hospice," believing that death without euthanasia is a fundamental tenet.

"Hospice is not about replacement of euthanasia," says Dr. Robin Downing, owner of the Downing Center for Animal Pain Management in Windsor, Colorado. "In 23 years of practicing oncology, I have a fairly high conviction that the number of animals who die a natural death is few and far between. Most animals reach a point where they are actively in distress, and we have an obligation to let them leave while they still know who they are and who their family is. The only time a client has expressed regret to me is the regret that they waited too long."

The subject of death prompts strong feelings in most humans, and there are no easy answers for doctors or people with pets when confronting an animal's final days. As the veterinary hospice field grows, it is crucial that practitioners remain open to divergent opinions and values, says Shanan, who this year co-founded the International Association for Animal Hospice and Palliative Care. "We must humbly accept that the subjective experience of dying is a great mystery," Shanan says. "Also, we are acting as proxy for the wishes of a patient who is not of our species. It is very easy to err no matter what guiding principle we choose to follow."

Hoping for a Miracle

A few weeks ago during a walk at a nearby lake, Kramer became short of breath and had to be carried home. The Millers made an appointment with the vet, who x-rayed the dog's lungs to see if the cancer had spread there. (It hadn't.) Two days later at the same lake, Kramer acted like his old self, chasing geese twice his size.

"Animals don't know they're dying," Carol Miller says. "Toward the very end I think they might, but they don't get anxious about it all the time like we do. Sometimes when I'm upset, he looks up at me like, 'What's wrong? What can I do for you to make you feel better?'"

Above all, the Millers don't want Kramer to suffer. One form of chemo made him violently ill, and neither Frank nor Carol wants that to happen again. Their oncologists presented options for new treatments, and the Millers chose one that seems to be working.

"We are enjoying every precious day," Carol says. "Kramer's spirits are high." But if the drugs lose effectiveness and his cancer spreads, they've decided to stop chemotherapy and continue herbal treatments and prednisone until Kramer's body gives out or he indicates to them that it's time to go. They still hope for a miracle, but the Millers are practical and know they must plan. They've contacted a mobile veterinarian, who, when the time comes, will perform euthanasia in their home.

UNIT 6

Ethical Issues Regarding Dying and Death

Unit Selections

Key Points to Consider

- The question, "What is a good death?" has been asked for centuries. What would constitute a good death in this time of high-tech medical care? Does the concept of a good death include the taking of a life? Defend your answer.

- Does the role of the health-care provider include taking life or providing the means for others to do so? Why or why not?

- Are constraints required to prevent the killing of persons we do not consider worthwhile contributors to our society? Explain.

- Should limits be placed on the length of life as we consider the expenses involved in the care of the elderly and the infirm?

Student Website

www.mhhe.com/cls

Internet References

Articles on Euthanasia: Ethics
   http://ethics.acusd.edu/Applied/Euthanasia
Euthanasia and Physician-Assisted Suicide
   www.religioustolerance.org/euthanas.htm
Kearl's Guide to the Sociology of Death: Moral Debates
   www.Trinity.Edu/~mkearl/death-5.html#eu
The Kevorkian Verdict
   www.pbs.org/wgbh/pages/frontline/kevorkian
Living Wills (Advance Directive)
   www.mindspring.com/~scottr/will.html
Not Dead Yet
   www.notdeadyet.org
UNOS: United Network for Organ Sharing
   www.unos.org

One of the concerns about dying and death that is pressing hard upon our consciences is the question of helping the dying to die sooner with the assistance of the physician. Public awareness of the horrors that can visit upon us by artificial means of ventilation and other support measures in a high-tech hospital setting has produced a literature that debates the issue of euthanasia—a "good death." As individuals think through their plans for care when dying, there is a steady increase in the demand for control of that care. The recent case of Terri Schiavo had brought national attention to the need for more clarity in end-of-life directives and the legitimacy of passive euthanasia.

Another controversial issue is physician-assisted suicide. Is it the function of the doctor to assist patients in their dying—to actually kill them at their request? The highly publicized suicides in Michigan, along with the jury decisions that found Dr. Kevorkian innocent of murder, as well as the popularity of the book *Final Exit,* make these issues prominent national and international concerns. Legislative action has been taken in some states to permit this, and the issue is pending in a number of others. We are in a time of intense consideration by the courts, by the legislatures, and by the medical and nursing professions of the legality and the morality of providing the means by which a person can be given the means to die. Is this the role of health-care providers? The pro and contra positions are presented in several of the unit's articles. Although the issue is difficult and personally challenging, as a nation we are in the position of being required to make difficult choices. There are no "right" answers; the questions pose dilemmas that require choice based upon moral, spiritual, and legal foundations.

What Living Wills Won't Do
The Limits of Autonomy

ERIC COHEN

In the aftermath of the Terri Schiavo case, it seems clear that most Americans are uncomfortable at the prospect of politicians' intervening in family decisions about life and death. This is not only understandable, but usually wise. Americans understand that eventually they will have to make medical decisions for loved ones, and that such decisions are wrenching. Most people have little faith that the state—or the courts—can make better judgments than they can. And they are usually right.

But it is precisely the complexity of these life-and-death decisions that sometimes makes state involvement inevitable. The state was involved in the Schiavo case long before Congress intervened, from the time Terri's parents went to court in Florida to challenge her husband's fitness as a guardian back in 1993. State judiciaries must decide when family members clash, or when doctors and families disagree, or when surrogates wish to override a loved one's living will. And state legislatures have a responsibility to set the parameters for judicial decisions in particular cases. They must decide the admissibility of casual conversations in determining a person's prior wishes, or the appropriate weight to give a person's desires (such as requests for assisted suicide) even when they are clearly expressed.

For decades, we have deluded ourselves into believing that living wills would solve our caregiving problems; that healthy individuals could provide advance instructions for what to do if they became incompetent; that such a system would ensure that no one is mistreated and that everyone defines the meaning of life for himself until the very end. But it is now clear that living wills have failed, both practically and morally.

In the March–April 2004 issue of the *Hastings Center Report,* Angela Fagerlin and Carl E. Schneider survey the social science data, and their conclusions are damning: Most people do not have living wills, despite a very active campaign to promote them; those who do usually provide vague and conflicting instructions; people's opinions often change from experience to experience; and people's instructions are easily influenced by how a given scenario is described. These are not problems that any reform can fix. A person simply can't grasp in the present every medical and moral nuance of his own future case.

Most people do not have living wills, despite a very active campaign to promote them; those who do usually provide vague and conflicting instructions.

The dream of perfect autonomy—everyone speaking for himself, never deciding for another—should fade each time we change a parent's diaper, or visit a grandparent who does not recognize us, or sell an uncle's property to pay for the nursing home. After all, the only fully autonomous death—with every detail governed by individual will—is suicide. And suicide is hardly a basis for dealing more responsibly with the burdens of caregiving.

As the baby boomers age, we are entering a period when long-term dementia will often be the prelude to death, and when caregivers will regularly have to make decisions about how or whether to treat intervening illnesses like infections, heart trouble, or cancer. When should we accept that death has arrived, and when does stopping treatment entail a judgment that Alzheimer's patients are "better off dead"? What do we owe those who are cognitively disabled and totally dependent?

On these hard questions, the most vocal critics of Congress and "the religious right" in the Schiavo case have revealed the shallowness of their own thinking. Defending the "right to privacy" ignores the moral challenge of deciding how we should act in private, as both patients and caregivers. Asserting that "the state should stay out" of these decisions ignores the fact that some hard cases will always end up in court; that legislatures have a civic responsibility to pass the laws that courts apply; and that a decent society should set some minimum moral boundaries, such as laws against euthanasia and assisted suicide. And claiming that we should "defer to medical experts" ignores the potential conflict between the ideology of living wills and the ethic of medicine, since some people will leave instructions that no principled physician could execute.

In the end, the retreat to moral libertarianism and liberal proceduralism is inadequate. We need, instead, a moral philosophy, a political philosophy, and a medical philosophy that clarify our roles as caregivers, citizens, and doctors attending to those who cannot speak for themselves.

Any moral philosophy of care should begin with the premise that disability—even profound disability—is not grounds for seeking someone's death. But seeking death and accepting death when it arrives are very different matters. And while we should not seek death, neither should we see extending life at all costs as the supreme goal of care.

Imagine, for example, that a person with advanced Alzheimer's is diagnosed with cancer, and there is a burdensome treatment (like radiation) that might extend the person's remaining life from three months to six months. In this case, family members seem morally justified in rejecting the treatment, even knowing that an earlier death is the likely result. But they don't reject treatment *so that* the patient will die; they reject it so that the patient will not suffer excessively as death arrives. They choose minimum discomfort, not death. By contrast, if the same Alzheimer's patient gets an infection that is easily treated by antibiotics, it is hard to see any moral ground for withholding treatment. Holding back ordinary care is not the same as euthanasia, but it is still a choice that hastens death as its aim.

In reality, many dementia cases involve multiple illnesses, with uncertain prognoses, and a menu of treatment options. Often, there are various morally justifiable choices. Personal values do matter. But what is always needed is a moral framework that governs such private decisions, based on the belief that every life is equal, and no life should be treated as a burden to be relinquished, including one's own.

Given the infinite complexity of these clinical situations, the scope of the law should always be limited. What is legally permissible is not always morally right, but what is morally wrong should not always be outlawed. Nevertheless, it is foolish to ignore the extent to which the current legal framework shapes how people make private decisions, or to ignore the proper role of the state in setting certain minimum boundaries. Legally, no competent person should ever be forced to accept medical treatment in the present that he does not want. Legally, no one should have the right to commit suicide or procure assistance in doing

so, and no one should be killed or forced to die against his will or that of his guardians. And legally, guardians should not be forced to implement living wills that aim at death as their goal.

As for the courts that are called upon to settle certain cases, they will need some political guidance or governing principles to do so. For example, what if a tenured professor of bioethics, unable to bear the loss of his cognitive powers, leaves written instructions not to treat any infections if he ever suffers dementia? Decades later, now suffering from Alzheimer's, the former professor is mentally impaired but seemingly happy. He can't recognize his children, but he seems to enjoy the sunset. He's been physically healthy for years, but then gets a urinary tract infection. All his family members believe he should be treated.

Should the state intervene to prohibit antibiotics—to protect the incompetent person's "right to die"? Or should the state leave the family members alone, so they can do what they believe is in the best interests of the person the professor now is? If Andrew Sullivan and other critics are worried about "theocons" using the power of the state to undermine the right to self-determination, are they willing to use the power of the state to impose death when families choose life? Is this what their idea of "autonomy" really requires?

And this leads us, finally, to the ethics of medicine. We have already gone very far in turning medicine into a service industry and doctors into technicians who simply use their skills to do our bidding. The physicians who perform abortions when the life and health of the mother are not in danger, or the cosmetic surgeons who give breast implants to healthy women, or the doctors who prescribe growth hormone for kids of average height are not really practicing medicine; they are serving desires. Most doctors take their medical oath seriously, struggling daily and often heroically to provide for those entrusted to their care. But some have succumbed to various forms of utilitarianism, or simply believe that people with cognitive disabilities are already humanly dead. In cases like Terri Schiavo's—a disabled woman, not dead or dying, whose feeding was keeping her alive without imposing additional burdens—it is hard to see how any doctor could ethically remove a feeding tube. And if we are to respect medicine as a moral profession, no court should compel doctors of conscience to do so.

As America ages and dementia becomes a common phenomenon, the dilemmas that the Schiavo case thrust onto the nightly news will only become more urgent and more profound. As a society, we will need to navigate between two dangers: The first is the euthanasia solution, and the prospect of treating the old and vulnerable as burdens to be ignored, abandoned, or put to sleep at our convenience. The second is that the costs of long-term care will suffocate every other civic and cultural good—like educating the young, promoting the arts and sciences, and preserving a strong defense.

We will face imperfect options, as societies always do. In navigating the dangers, we will need to rely on more than the gospel of autonomy, and we will need to confront the failure of living wills and the ideology they rest upon: that deciding for others is always to be avoided. In reality, deciding for others is what many of us will be required to do as parents age or spouses decline, and we will do well to accept this burden with moral sobriety rather than pretending it does not exist.

ERIC COHEN is editor of the *New Atlantis* and resident scholar at the Ethics and Public Policy Center.

The Comfort Connection

Dr. Diane Meier is quietly leading a revolution to treat patients (and their families, too) as living, breathing, feeling individuals. And why is that so shocking?

JOANNE KENEN

When a loved one dies, the first thing you usually receive from a doctor is a bill. When a patient of Diane Meier, M.D., dies, the family receives a call or a note.

"She was with me when my wife died at home," says Bert Gold, of New York City, still missing Sylvia, his wife of 57 years. "She took me into the living room and put her arms around me and started to cry. She thanked me for letting her take care of Sylvia. Imagine."

Meier, 55, of the Mount Sinai School of Medicine in New York City, is one of the leading exponents of a new and growing discipline known as palliative care. Palliative care means soothing the symptoms of a disease, regardless of whether a patient is seeking a cure. It's a concept that's totally transforming the way doctors and hospitals treat seriously ill patients. The idea of easing pain and improving the quality of a patient's life may not seem radical, but classic medical training focuses on attacking the disease. Most doctors simply don't have time to be super-sensitive Marcus Welbys checking up on patients to see how they feel. Even if they *do* have the time, they lack the advanced training of palliative-care doctors and nurses to ease symptoms such as anxiety, pain, or severe nausea. Most are better equipped to deal with microorganisms than matters of comfort.

When people first hear about palliative care, they often confuse it with hospice care. It's not. Hospice focuses on terminally ill patients: people who no longer seek treatments to cure them and expect to live about six months or less. Palliative-care teams—consisting of everyone from social workers to physical therapists—can follow patients for days, months, or years.

Thanks in large part to the training and outreach programs Meier runs as the head of the Center to Advance Palliative Care (CAPC) in New York City, the number of hospitals with palliative-care programs has nearly doubled, from 632 in 2000 to 1,240 in 2005. Palliative care has the potential to change the way doctors and nurses address pain and emotional distress—not to mention how they help patients and families sort through their choices as life nears its end.

Bert Gold is doing pretty well for a man who recently turned 91. A retired professor of social work, he lives at home. But he is frail. He takes a lot of medicines. He falls sometimes. He lost a big toe five years ago and still deals with pain and an awkward gait.

Bert visits Meier in her office today before going back to the foot surgeon, and Meier spends more than an hour with him—yes, an hour—reviewing his symptoms, his diet, his medications, his mood. Open or stubborn wounds can be dangerous for elderly patients, but Meier, who has worked with Bert for 12 years, also worries that the pain has isolated him, kept him home watching television instead of going to the Y for his regular bridge game.

"Are you having fun?" she asks.

"No," he says, frowning.

"You're not?"

"No. I'm not depressed, but I'm not having fun."

Meier keeps listening. She offers some advice, more in the spirit of a friend than a doctor. She gently reminds him that even if he doesn't like his wheelchair, it can get him out to a movie now and then. They talk about his diet, good-naturedly negotiating over . . . prunes. Though he flat out refuses to eat them for breakfast, he agrees to have them at lunch. Bert smiles. He has been listened to by a doctor who took the time to treat him not as a collection of symptoms, but as a person who deserves to get the best he can out of life, even at 91.

Meier believes strongly that palliative care should not be the "death team," and she sees patients early in the course of a disease. On one recent day, two palliative-care nurses at Mount Sinai were treating a French-speaking African woman in her 30s dying of AIDS, and a man in his 80s with cancers of the skin, prostate, bladder, and pancreas, who now had relentless hiccups from the march of his tumors through his belly.

"Sometimes something like that—hiccups—will get us in the door, to then say, 'What else is going on? How's life when you're at home and not in the hospital,'" says Sue McHugh-Salera, a palliative-care nurse at Mount Sinai.

Which brings us to another of palliative care's radical-but-shouldn't-be concepts: family meetings. That's right—actually sitting down with patients and their families to discuss the good, the bad, and the scary. Ira Byock, M.D., a longtime leader in hospice care who now heads palliative care at Dartmouth, recalls a man who had been languishing in the ICU for months. The patient was "stable," but no one had helped his family see the chasm between the clinical realities and their hopes for a miracle. So the man's doctor called in the palliative-care team, and Byock set up family meetings to discuss the patient's condition and the family's expectations.

"We couldn't change the fact that he was not going to survive," says Byock. "But when he did die, his family's sadness—as deep as it was—was free of the doubts, the 'could haves' and 'should haves,' that often complicate grief."

Although most of the programs, such as Meier's, are consultant teams, moving through the hospitals and clinics, a few have dedicated inpatient units, such as the 11-bed section at the Massey Cancer Center at Virginia Commonwealth University in Richmond. It's peaceful, without the jarring bustle of a typical hospital floor. Families have their own lounge, with a TV, a computer, games for the kids, and cookie dough in the fridge. Some patients will go home when their symptoms are under control. Some will shift to home hospice. Others will die on the unit, with a lot of hands-on care and fine-tuning of medications. All will have received more focus on their comfort than they would get in a traditional hospital environment.

Traditional doctors focus only on the disease; Meier shifts the balance to quality of life.

Meier's goal is to improve the treatment of seriously ill patients, but she sells hospitals on the idea that palliative care can cut costs. CAPC estimates that hospitals can save up to $3,000 per patient, in part by moving people out of the ICU sooner, avoiding a flurry of tests when it's too late, and slowing the revolving door between nursing homes and emergency rooms.

But not everyone is sold on the benefits. Some health-policy experts are skeptical of the savings (they want more detailed data); others wonder if palliative care should even be its own entity, or whether all physicians should provide the caring, coordination, and communication that Meier gives to her patients. Meier agrees—to a point:

"It's like saying, 'Shouldn't cardiology not have to be there; shouldn't every doctor know how to handle hypertension, congestive heart failure, angina?' Of course every doctor should. But nobody would argue that we don't need specialists to handle the more complex aspects of cardiology."

Palliative-care specialists are needed, she says, to step in and manage the challenging cases that other doctors don't have the skills, or perhaps the time, to manage themselves. "It's the rare primary care practitioner who can do repeated 90-minute family meetings, because they've got 50 patients in the waiting room," she says.

So Meier keeps pushing for more programs. Thirty percent of U.S. hospitals and 70 percent of teaching hospitals now offer palliative care. The more hospitals buy into the philosophy, she says, the better it will be for patients. Too many are stuck in a medical nowhere-land, forced to choose between comfort care and emotional support in a hospice—or a chance to keep fighting their illness. "It's not human nature to accept death and agree to give up on life," says Meier. With palliative care, we don't have to.

JOANNE KENEN is a health writer in Washington, D.C. Learn more about palliative care at www.getpalliativecare.org.

Ethics and Life's Ending

An Exchange

ROBERT D. ORR AND GILBERT MEILAENDER

Feeding tubes make the news periodically, and controversies over their use or non-use seem unusually contentious. But feeding tubes are not high technology treatment; they are simple, small-bore catheters made of soft synthetic material. Nor are they new technology; feeding tubes were first used in 1793 by John Hunter to introduce jellies, eggs, sugar, milk, and wine into the stomachs of patients unable to swallow. Why does this old, low-tech treatment generate such controversy today? The important question is not whether a feeding tube *can* be used, but whether it *should* be used in a particular situation.

Too often in medicine we use a diagnostic or therapeutic intervention just because it is available. This thoughtless approach is sometimes called the technological imperative, i.e., the impulse to do everything we are trained to do, regardless of the burden or benefit. Kidney failure? Let's do dialysis. Respiratory failure? Let's use a ventilator. Unable to eat? Let's put in a feeding tube. By responding in this way, the physician ignores the maxim "the ability to act does not justify the action." Just because we know how to artificially breathe for a patient in respiratory failure doesn't mean that everyone who cannot breathe adequately must be put on a ventilator. Such a response also represents a failure to do the moral work of assessing whether the treatment is appropriate in a particular situation.

The moral debate about the use or non-use of feeding tubes hinges on three important considerations: the distinction between what in the past was called "ordinary" and "extraordinary" treatments; the important social symbolism of feeding; and a distinction between withholding and withdrawing treatments.

It was recognized many years ago that respirators, dialysis machines, and other high-tech modes of treatment are optional. They could be used or not used depending on the circumstances. However, it was commonly accepted in the past that feeding tubes are generally not optional. Part of the reasoning was that feeding tubes are readily available, simple to use, not very burdensome to the patient, and not very expensive. They were "ordinary treatment" and thus morally obligatory.

Ordinary [versus] Extraordinary

For over four hundred years, traditional moral theology distinguished between ordinary and extraordinary means of saving life. Ordinary means were those that were not too painful or burden-some for the patient, were not too expensive, and had a reasonable chance of working. These ordinary treatments were deemed morally obligatory. Those treatments that did involve undue burden were extraordinary and thus optional. This distinction was common knowledge in religious and secular circles, and this language and reasoning was commonly applied in Western society.

As medical treatments became more complicated, it was recognized that this distinction was sometimes not helpful. The problem was that the designation appeared to belong to the treatment itself, rather than to the situation. The respirator and dialysis machine were categorized as extraordinary while antibiotics and feeding tubes were classed as ordinary. But real-life situations were not that simple. Thus began a change in moral terminology first officially noted in the *Declaration on Euthanasia* published in 1980 by the Catholic Church's Sacred Congregation for the Doctrine of the Faith in 1980: "In the past, moralists replied that one is never obligated to use 'extraordinary' means. This reply, which as a principle still holds good, is perhaps less clear today, by reason of the imprecision of the term and the rapid progress made in the treatment of sickness. Thus some people prefer to speak of 'proportionate' and 'disproportionate' means."

This newer and clearer moral terminology of proportionality was used in secular ethical analysis as early as the 1983 President's Commission report, *Deciding to Forgo Life-Sustaining Technologies*. The "ordinary/extraordinary" language, however, continues to be seen in the medical literature and heard in the intensive care unit. Reasoning on the basis of proportionality requires us to weigh the burdens and the benefits of a particular treatment for a particular patient. Thus a respirator may be proportionate (and obligatory) for a young person with a severe but survivable chest injury, but it may be disproportionate (and thus optional) for another person who is dying of lung cancer. The same is true for (almost) all medical treatments, including feeding tubes. There are two treatments that always remain obligatory, as I shall explain below.

A second aspect of the discussion about the obligation to provide nutritional support, especially in secular discussions but also in religious debate, was the symbolism of food and water—feeding is caring; nutrition is nurture; food and water are not treatment, and therefore they are never optional. The reasoning commonly went as follows: we provide nutritional support for vulnerable infants because this is an important part of "tender loving care." Shouldn't we provide the same for vulnerable adults as well?

Certainly when a patient is temporarily unable to swallow and has the potential to recover, artificially administered fluids and nutrition are obligatory. Does that obligation change if the prognosis is poor?

This aspect of the debate continued through the 1970s and '80s. It appeared to be resolved by the U.S. Supreme Court in its 1990 decision in *Cruzan v. Director, Missouri Department of Health* when five of the nine Justices agreed that artificially administered fluids and nutrition are medical treatments and are thus optional. Since *Cruzan* medical and legal professions have developed a consensus that feeding tubes are not always obligatory. This debate is ongoing, however, and in some minds the symbolism of feeding remains a dominant feature.

Starvation

A parallel concern to the symbolism entailed in the use of fluids and nutrition is the commonly heard accusation, "But you will be starving him to death!" when discontinuation of a feeding tube is discussed. This is incorrect. Starvation is a slow process that results from lack of calories and takes several weeks or months. When artificially administered fluids and nutrition are not used in a person who is unable to swallow, that person dies from dehydration, not starvation, and death occurs in five to twelve days. Dehydration is very commonly the last physiologic stage of dying, no matter what the cause.

"But that is no comfort! Being dehydrated and thirsty is miserable." Yes and no. Being thirsty is miserable, but becoming dehydrated need not be. The only place in the body where thirst is perceived is the mouth. There is good empirical evidence that as long as a person's mouth is kept moist, that person is not uncomfortable, even if it is clear that his or her body is becoming progressively dehydrated.

I said earlier that there are two treatments that are never optional: these are good symptom control and human presence. Therefore, when a person is becoming dehydrated as he or she approaches death, it is obligatory to provide good mouth care, along with other means of demonstrating human caring and presence, such as touching, caressing, gentle massage, hair-brushing, talking, reading, and holding.

Withholding [versus] Withdrawing

A third feature of the debate over feeding tubes is the issue of withholding versus withdrawing therapy. Thirty years ago, it was common teaching in medicine that "it is better to withhold a treatment than to withdraw it." The thinking was that if you stop a ventilator or dialysis or a feeding tube, and the patient then dies from this lack of life support, you were the agent of death. Therefore, it would be ethically better not to start the treatment in the first place. Then, if the patient dies, death is attributable to the underlying disease and not to your withdrawal of life support.

Slowly, with help from philosophers, theologians, attorneys, and jurists, the medical profession came to accept that there is no moral or legal difference between withholding and withdrawing a treatment. In fact, it may be ethically better to withdraw life-sustaining treatment than it is to withhold it. If there is a treatment with a very small chance of helping the patient, it is better to give it a try. If it becomes clear after a few days or weeks that it is not helping, then you can withdraw the treatment without the original uncertainty that you might be quitting too soon, and now with the comfort that comes from knowing you are not the agent of death.

However, even if there is no professional, moral, or legal difference, it still may be psychologically more difficult to withdraw a treatment that you know is postponing a patient's death than it would have been not to start it in the first place. Turning down the dials on a ventilator with the expectation that the patient will not survive is more personally unsettling than is merely being present with a patient who is actively dying. Withdrawal of a feeding tube can be even more unsettling, especially if the professional involved has any moral reservations about the distinction between ordinary and extraordinary means, or about the symbolism of artificially administered fluids and nutrition.

Some develop this part of the debate with moral concern about intentionality. They contend that your intention in withdrawing the feeding tube is that the patient will die, and it is morally impermissible to cause death intentionally. In actuality, the intention in withdrawing any therapy that has been proven not to work is to stop postponing death artificially.

With these aspects of the debate more or less settled, where does that leave us in making decisions about the use or non-use of feeding tubes? The short-term use of a feeding tube for a patient who is unable to swallow adequate fluids and nutrition for a few days, because of severe illness or after surgery or trauma, may be lifesaving and is almost always uncontroversial. Such usage may even be morally obligatory when the goal of treatment is patient survival and a feeding tube is the best way to provide needed fluids and nutrition.

A feeding tube is sometimes requested by a loved one as a last-gasp effort to postpone death in a patient who is imminently dying and unable to swallow. This is almost always inappropriate. Good mouth care to maintain patient comfort and hygiene is obligatory, but in such cases maintenance of nutrition is no longer a reasonable goal of treatment. In fact, introduction of fluids may even lead to fluid overload that can cause patient discomfort as the body's systems are shutting down.

Long-Term Use

The situation that can generate ethical quandaries, front-page news, and conflicts in court is the long-term use of feeding tubes. And these situations are not as neatly segregated into proportionate or disproportionate usage.

Long-term use of a feeding tube remains ethically obligatory for a patient who is cognitively intact, can and wants to survive, but is permanently unable to swallow, an example being a patient who has been treated for malignancy of the throat or esophagus. Protracted use of a feeding tube is also morally required in most instances when it is uncertain whether a patient will regain awareness or recover the ability to swallow—for instance, immediately after a serious head injury or a disabling stroke.

Long-term use of a feeding tube becomes controversial in patients suffering from progressive deterioration of brain function (e.g., Alzheimer's dementia), or in patients with little or no likelihood of regaining awareness after illness or injury (e.g., the permanent vegetative state). Thus, the most perplexing feeding-tube questions involve patients who are unable to take in adequate fluids and nutrition by themselves but who have a condition that by itself will not soon lead to death. The reasoning is, the patient has no fatal condition; he or she can be kept alive with the simple use of tube feedings; therefore we are obligated to use a feeding tube to keep this person alive.

Alzheimer's dementia is the most common type of brain deterioration, afflicting five percent of individuals over sixty-five and perhaps as many as 50 percent of those over eighty-five. It is manifested by progressive cognitive impairment, followed by physical deterioration. This process generally takes several years, often a decade, and is ultimately fatal. In its final stages it almost always interferes with the patient's ability to swallow. Eventually the individual chokes on even pureed foods or liquids. Continued attempts at feeding by mouth very commonly result in aspiration of food or fluid into the airway, frequently leading to pneumonia. Aspiration pneumonia will sometimes respond to antibiotics, but other times it leads to death. Such respiratory infections are the most common final event in this progressive disease.

Feeding tubes have been commonly used in the later stages of Alzheimer's. The reasoning has been that this patient is not able to take in adequate fluids and nutrition and he is not imminently dying. Several assumptions then follow: a feeding tube will improve his comfort, will prevent aspiration pneumonia, and will ensure adequate nutrition which will in turn prevent skin breakdown and thus postpone his death. However, empirical evidence, published in the *Journal of the American Medical Association* in 1999, has shown each of these assumptions to be incorrect: using a feeding tube in a patient with dementia does not prevent these complications, nor does it prolong life.

In addition, there are several negative aspects to using a feeding tube in a person with advanced cognitive impairment. There are rare complications during insertion, some merely uncomfortable, some quite serious. Having a tube in one's nose is generally uncomfortable; even having one coiled up under a dressing on the abdominal wall can be annoying. Because the demented patient doesn't understand the intended purpose of the feeding tube, he or she may react by trying to remove it, requiring either repeated re-insertions or the use of hand restraints. In addition, using a feeding tube may deprive the patient of human presence and interaction: hanging a bag of nutritional fluid takes only a few seconds, as opposed to the extended time of human contact involved in feeding a cognitively impaired person.

End Stage Alzheimer's

There is a slowly developing consensus in medicine that feeding tubes are generally not appropriate for use in most patients nearing the end stage of Alzheimer's disease. This belief can be supported from a moral standpoint in terms of proportionality. And yet feeding tubes are still rather commonly used. A recently published review of all U.S. nursing home patients with cognitive impairment found that an average of 34 percent were being fed with feeding tubes (though there were large state-to-state variations, from nine percent in Maine, New Hampshire, and Vermont to 64 percent in Washington, D.C.).

The cases we read about in the newspaper—in which families are divided and court battles fought—most often involve patients in a permanent vegetative state (PVS). This is a condition of permanent unawareness most often caused by severe head injury or by the brain being deprived of oxygen for several minutes. Such deprivation may be the result of successful cardiopulmonary resuscitation of a patient whose breathing or circulation had stopped from a cardiac arrest, near-drowning, strangulation, etc. In a PVS patient, the heart, lungs, kidneys, and other organs continue to function; given good nursing care and artificially administered fluids and nutrition, a person can live in this permanent vegetative state for many years.

A person in a PVS may still have reflexes from the spinal cord (grasping, withdrawal from pain) or the brain stem (breathing, regulation of blood pressure), including the demonstration of sleep-wake cycles. He may "sleep" for several hours, then "awaken" for a while; the eyes are open and wander about, but do not fix on or follow objects. The person in a PVS is "awake, but unaware" because the areas of the upper brain that allow a person to perceive his or her environment and to act voluntarily are no longer functioning.

Uncertainty

Some of the clinical controversy about nutritional support for persons in a PVS is due to uncertainty. After a head injury or resuscitation from a cardiac arrest, it may be several weeks or months before a patient can rightly be declared to be in a PVS—months during which the provision of nutritional support via feeding tubes is often very appropriate. Loved ones usually remain optimistic, hoping for improvement, praying for full recovery. The length of time from brain damage to declaration of a PVS can extend, depending on the cause of the brain injury, from one month to twelve months. And just to muddy the waters even further, there are rare instances of delayed improvement after many months or even a few years, so that the previously unaware patient regains some ability to perceive his or her environment, and may even be able to say a few words. These individuals are now in a "minimally conscious state." More than minimal delayed improvement is exceedingly rare. (Treatment decisions for persons in a minimally conscious state are perhaps even more controversial than are those for PVS patients, but that discussion must wait for another time.)

The greatest ethical dilemma surrounding the use or non-use of nutritional support for persons in a PVS arises from the fact that they are not clearly dying. With good nursing care and nutrition, individuals in this condition have survived for up to thirty-five years. Those who advocate continued nutritional support argue thus: this person is alive and not actively or imminently dying; it is possible to keep him alive with minimal effort; this human life is sacred; therefore we are obligated to continue to give artificially administered fluids and nutrition.

It is hard to disagree with the various steps in this line of reasoning. (Some utilitarians do disagree, however, claiming that a patient in a PVS is "already dead" or is a "non-person." Those who believe in the sanctity of life must continue to denounce this line of thought.) Let us stipulate the following: the person in a PVS is alive; he can be kept alive for a long time; his life is sacred. But does the obligation to maintain that severely compromised human life necessarily follow from these premises?

Let's first address the issue of whether he is dying. One could maintain that his physical condition is such that he will die soon but for the artificial provision of fluids and nutrition. Thus the permanent vegetative state could be construed to be lethal in and of itself. However, that fatal outcome is not inevitable since the saving treatment is simple. How does this differ from the imperative to provide nourishment for a newborn who would die without the provision of fluids and nutrition? There are two differences. Most newborns are able to take in nutrition if it is placed in or near their mouths. PVS patients can't swallow, so the nutrition must be delivered further down the gastrointestinal tract. As for sick or premature infants, they have a great potential for improvement, growth, and development. The PVS patient has no such potential.

Kidney Failure

Rather than a newborn, a better analogy for this aspect of the discussion would be a person with kidney failure. The kidney failure itself is life-threatening, but it is fairly easily corrected by dialysis three times a week. If the person has another condition that renders him unaware of his surroundings, or a condition that makes life a continuous difficult struggle, most would agree that the person is ethically permitted to stop the dialysis even if that means he will not survive. The ultimate cause of death was treatable, so that death could have been postponed, possibly for years. However, other mitigating circumstances may make the dialysis disproportionate, and so one should be allowed to discontinue this death-postponing treatment in a person who is not imminently dying.

Someone coming from a mechanistic perspective can easily and comfortably decide that a person in a PVS with no potential for recovery has no inherent value and is even an emotional drain on loved ones and a financial drain on society. But what about a person of faith? Does the sanctity of life, a basic tenet of Christianity, Judaism, and Islam, dictate that life must always be preserved if it is humanly possible to do so? Our moral intuitions tell us the answer is no.

It might be possible to postpone the death of a patient from end-stage heart failure by doing one more resuscitation. It might be possible to postpone the death of someone with end-stage liver disease by doing a liver transplant. It might be possible to postpone the death of someone with painful cancer with a few more blood transfusions or another round of chemotherapy. But these therapies are often not used—because the burden is disproportionate to the benefit. Thus the timing of death is often a matter of choice. In fact, it is commonly accepted that the timing of 80 percent of deaths that occur in a hospital is chosen.

Believers do not like to use the words "choice" and "death" in the same sentence. Doing so recalls acrimonious contests about the "right to life" versus the "right to choose" that are the pivotal point in debates about abortion, assisted suicide, and euthanasia. And certainly belief in the sanctity of human life obligates believers to forgo some choices. But does this belief preclude all choices? No: life is full of difficult choices. This is true for believers and nonbelievers alike. Believers may have more guidance about what choices to make and perhaps some limits on options, but we still are faced with many choices—such as choices about the use or non-use of feeding tubes.

When engaging in moral debate on matters of faith, it is important not to focus exclusively on one tenet of faith to the exclusion of others. In debating the use of feeding tubes—or of any mode of treatment for that matter—one must not ignore the concepts of finitude and stewardship by focusing only on the sanctity of life.

If belief in the sanctity of human life translated automatically into an obligation to preserve each human life at all costs, we would not have to debate proportionate and disproportionate treatments. We would simply be obligated to use all treatments available until they failed to work. However, because of the Fall, human life is finite. All of us will die. Since that is inevitable, God expects us to care wisely for our own bodies and for those of our loved ones, and also for our resources. Healthcare professionals similarly must be wise stewards of their skills and services.

Taking into consideration the scriptural principle of stewardship and the tradition of proportionate treatment, I conclude that there must be some degree of discretion in the use or non-use of feeding tubes. There are clearly situations where a feeding tube must be used. There are other situations where a feeding tube would be morally wrong. But there are many situations where the use of a feeding tube should be optional. And this means that one individual of faith might choose to use a tube when another might choose not to use it.

Personal Values

Because of the patient's personal values, someone might choose to continue artificially administered fluids and nutrition for a loved one in a permanent vegetative state for many years. Another might choose to continue for one year and then to withdraw it if there was no sign of awareness. Still another might choose to stop after three months or one month.

What might those discretionary personal values include? Such things, among others, as an assessment of how to deal with uncertainty, concern about emotional burden on loved ones, and cost of care. Though beliefs in the sanctity of human life and in the obligation to care for vulnerable individuals are not optional for persons of faith, an assessment of whether or not to use a given technology requires human wisdom and thus entails some discretion.

Gilbert Meilaender

There is much to agree with in Robert D. Orr's measured discussion of the moral issues surrounding the use of feeding tubes, there are a few things that seem to me doubtful or in need of clarification, and then there is one major issue that requires greater precision.

Accepted Claims

It may be useful to note first some claims of Dr. Orr that few would dispute.

- Feeding tubes are a rather low-tech form of care.
- Our ability to do something does not mean that we should do it.
- Any distinction between "ordinary" and "extraordinary" care (if we wish to use that language) cannot simply be a feature of treatments but must be understood as patient-relative. What is ordinary treatment for one patient

may be extraordinary for another, and what is ordinary treatment for a patient at one point in his life may become extraordinary at another point when his illness has progressed to a new stage.

- There is no crucial moral difference between withholding or withdrawing a treatment. (Dr. Orr actually writes that there is "no moral or legal difference" between these. The issue of legality is, I suspect, sometimes more complicated, but I take him to be correct insofar as a strictly moral judgment is involved.)
- There are circumstances, some noted by Dr. Orr, in which the use of feeding tubes seems clearly required and is relatively uncontroversial.
- Patients in a persistent vegetative state are not dying patients. (I don't quite know how to combine this with Dr. Orr's statement a few paragraphs later that the permanent vegetative state "could be construed to be lethal in and of itself." In general, I don't think his article ever really achieves clarity and precision on this question, and it will turn out to be a crucial question below.)
- A commitment to the sanctity of human life does not require that we always do everything possible to keep a person alive.

There are also places where Dr. Orr's discussion seems to me to be doubtful or, at least, underdeveloped. Among these are the following:

- The idea that the terms "proportionate" and "disproportionate" are more precise than the (admittedly unsatisfactory) language of "ordinary" and "extraordinary" is, at best, doubtful. On what scale one "weighs" benefits and burdens is a question almost impossible to answer. Even more doubtful is whether we can "weigh" them for someone else. My own view is that when we make these decisions for ourselves, we are not in fact "weighing" anything. We are deciding what sort of person we will be and what sort of life will be ours. We are making not a *discovery* but a *decision*. And if that is true, then it is obvious that we have not discovered anything that could necessarily be transferred and applied to the life of a different patient. In general, the language of "weighing" sounds good, but it is almost impossible to give it any precise meaning.
- No *moral* question was resolved by the Supreme Court's *Cruzan* decision. It established certain legal boundaries, but it did no more than that.
- I suspect that—despite the growing consensus, which Dr. Orr correctly describes—he is too quick to assume that the "symbolism" issue can be dispensed with, and too quick to assume that feeding tubes are "treatment" rather than standard nursing care. A consensus may be mistaken, after all. It is hard to see why such services as turning a patient regularly and giving alcohol rubs are standard nursing care while feeding is not. To take an example from a different realm of life, soldiers are combatants, but the people who grow the food which soldiers eat are not combatants (even though the soldiers could not continue to fight without nourishment). The reason is simple:

they make not what soldiers need to fight but what they need, as we all do, in order merely to live. Likewise, we might want to think twice before endorsing the view that relatively low-tech means of providing nourishment are treatment rather than standard nursing care.

Intention

- Dr. Orr's discussion of the role of "intention" in moral analysis is, putting it charitably, imprecise. Obviously, if a treatment has been shown not to work, in withdrawing it we do not intend or aim at the patient's death. We aim at caring for that person as best we can, which hardly includes providing treatment that is useless. But the crucial questions will turn on instances in which the treatment is not pointless. If we stop treatment in such cases, it is harder to deny that our aim is that the patient should die.
- Dr. Orr's seeming willingness to allow the state of a patient's cognitive capacities to carry weight—or even be determinative—in treatment decisions is troubling. Obviously, certain kinds of higher brain capacities are characteristics that distinguish human beings from other species; however, one need not have or be exercising those capacities in order to be a living human being. Allowing the cognitive ability of a patient to determine whether he or she is treated will inevitably lead to judgments about the comparative worth of human lives.

If Dr. Orr is correct in arguing that the use of feeding tubes in end-stage Alzheimer's patients is of no help to those patients and may sometimes be burdensome to them, we would have no moral reason to provide them with tube feeding. This judgment, however, has nothing at all to do with "proportionality." It has to do, simply, with the two criteria we ought to use in making treatment decisions—usefulness and burdensomeness. If a treatment is useless or excessively burdensome, it may rightly be refused.

This brings us to the most difficult issue, which clearly troubles Dr. Orr himself, and which is surely puzzling for all of us; the patient in a persistent vegetative state. We cannot usefully discuss this difficult case, however, without first getting clear more generally on the morality of withholding or withdrawing treatment. As I noted above, on this issue the language of proportionality is unlikely to be of much use for serious moral reflection.

Morality of Treatment

At least for Christians—though, in truth, also much more generally for our civilization's received medical tradition—we begin with what is forbidden. We should never aim at the death of a sick or dying person. (Hence, euthanasia, however good the motive, is forbidden.) Still, there are times when treatment may rightly be withheld or withdrawn, *even though* the patient may then die more quickly than would otherwise have been the case. How can that be? How can it be that, as a result of our decision, the patient dies more quickly, yet we do not aim at his death? This is quite possible—and permissible—so long as we aim to dispense with the treatment, not the life. No one need live in a way that seeks to ensure the longest possible life. (Were that a moral requirement, think of all the careers that would have to be prohibited.) There may be many circumstances in which we foresee that decisions we make may shorten our life, but we do not suppose that in so deciding we are aiming at death or formulating a plan of action that deliberately embraces death as a good. So in medical treatment decisions the question we need to answer is this: Under what circumstances may we rightly refuse a life-prolonging treatment without supposing that, in making this decision, we are doing the forbidden deed of choosing or aiming at death?

The answer of our medical-moral tradition has been the following: we may refuse treatments that are either *useless* or *excessively burdensome.* In doing so, we choose not death, but one among several possible lives open to us. We do not choose to die, but, rather, how to live, even if while dying, even if a shorter life than some other lives that are still available for our choosing. What we take aim at then, what we refuse, is not life but treatment—treatment that is either useless for a particular patient or excessively burdensome for that patient. Especially for patients who are irretrievably into the dying process, almost all treatments will have become useless. In refusing them, one is not choosing death but choosing life without a now useless form of treatment. But even for patients who are not near death, who might live for a considerably longer time, excessively burdensome treatments may also be refused. Here again, one takes aim at the burdensome treatment, not at life. One person may choose a life that is longer but carries with it considerable burden of treatment. Another may choose a life that is shorter but carries with it less burden of treatment. Each, however, chooses life. Neither aims at death.

Rejecting Treatments

It is essential to emphasize that these criteria refer to treatments, not to lives. We may rightly reject a treatment that is useless. But if I decide not to treat because I think a person's life is useless, then I am taking aim not at the treatment but at the life. Rather than asking, "What if anything can I do that will benefit the life this patient has?" I am asking, "Is it a benefit to have such a life?" If the latter is my question, and if I decide not to treat, it should be clear that it is the life at which I take aim. Likewise, we may reject a treatment on grounds of excessive burden. But if I decide not to treat because it seems a burden just to have the life this person has, then I am taking aim not at the burdensome treatment but at the life. Hence, in deciding whether it is appropriate and permissible to withhold or withdraw treatment—whether, even if life is thereby shortened, we are aiming only at the treatment and not at the life—we have to ask ourselves whether the treatment under consideration is, for this patient, either useless or excessively burdensome.

Against that background, we can consider the use of feeding tubes for patients in a persistent vegetative state. (I set aside here the point I noted above—that we might want to regard feeding simply as standard nursing care rather than as medical treatment. Now we are asking whether, even on the grounds that govern treatment decisions, we have good moral reason not to feed patients in a persistent vegetative state.)

Is the treatment useless? Not, let us be clear, is the life a useless one to have, but is the treatment useless? As Dr. Orr notes—quite rightly, I think—patients "can live in this permanent vegetative state for many years." So feeding may preserve for years the life of this living human being. Are we certain we want to call that useless? We are, of course, tempted to say that, in deciding not to feed, we are simply withdrawing treatment and letting these patients die. Yes, as Dr. Orr also notes, these patients "are not clearly dying." And, despite the sloppy way we sometimes talk about these matters, you cannot "let die" a person who is not dying. It is hard, therefore, to make the case for treatment withdrawal in these cases on the ground of uselessness. We may use those words, but it is more likely that our target is a (supposed) useless life and not a useless treatment. And if that is our aim, we had better rethink it promptly.

Is the treatment excessively burdensome? Alas, if these patients could experience the feeding as a burden, they would not be diagnosed as being in a persistent vegetative state. We may wonder, of course, whether having such a life is itself a burden, but, again, if that is our reasoning, it will be clear that we take aim not at a burdensome treatment but at a (presumed) burdensome life. And, once more, if that is our aim, we had better rethink it promptly.

Choosing Life

Hence, although these are troubling cases, Dr. Orr has not given us good or sufficient arguments to make the case for withdrawing feeding tubes from patients in a persistent vegetative state. I have not suggested that we have an obligation always and at any cost to preserve life. I have simply avoided all comparative judgments of the worth of human lives and have turned aside from any decisions which, when analyzed carefully, look as if they take aim not at a dispensable treatment but at a life. "Choosing life" does not mean doing whatever is needed to stay alive as long as possible. But choosing life clearly means never aiming at another's death—even if only by withholding treatment. I am not persuaded that Dr. Orr has fully grasped or delineated what it means to choose life in the difficult circumstances he discusses.

MR. ORR is the Director of Ethics and a professor of family medicine at the University of Vermont College of Medicine. **MR. MEILAENDER** is a member of the President's Council on Bioethics. From "Ethics & Life's Ending: An Exchange," by Robert D. Orr and Gilbert Meilaender, *First Things,* August/September 2004, pages 31–38.

As seen in *Current,* October 2005, pp. 24–30; originally in *First Things Journal,* August/September 2004, pp. 31–38. Copyright © 2004 by Institute on Religion and Public Life. Reprinted by permission.

When Students Kill Themselves, Colleges May Get the Blame

ANN H. FRANKE

Experts estimate that more than a thousand students at American colleges and universities will commit suicide this year. After a death, the grieving family will pack up the victim's belongings and, within a matter of months, lose touch with the institution. A few families, however, will return with their lawyers to charge that the institution bears legal responsibility.

While the number of such lawsuits remains very small, they are growing in frequency. Five years ago college lawyers discussed among themselves perhaps one or two pending suicide cases at any given moment. Today the cases total about 10 nationwide, with the prospect that many more suicides could, over time, move into the courts. Although a study of student suicides committed between 1980 and 1990 at 12 large Midwestern universities, published in 1997, found that college students killed themselves at a lower rate than others of their same age in the general population, whenever a death does occur, the potential for institutional liability looms larger today than ever before.

Whose responsibility is it to put the pieces together? When and how should well-meaning people intervene?

These are awful lawsuits. They can exacerbate grief, guilt, and blame on all sides. The cases can drag on for years. The courts have, so far, provided little guidance on the legal tests for institutional responsibility. We have only a fairly small number of reported decisions (many court decisions are unpublished), and the outcomes of each of those cases have turned less on general legal principles than on close analyses of the facts.

The current wave of litigation will likely lead to some clarification. In the meantime, we might usefully look at the types of claims that the families typically assert. Evaluating previous allegations can help us re-examine campus policies and procedures with two goals in mind: preventing deaths and, should a suicide occur, preventing institutional liability.

The most common claims have been:

The institution put the student in harm's way. Take the example of when a college holds a student in custody for some reason. In 1992 a Michigan court held that a state university might bear some responsibility for the 1982 suicide of a student who hanged himself with his socks and belt while detained for about 35 minutes in a campus-security, short-term holding cell. The institution had in effect at the time a policy that no prisoner should be left unattended unless he (in the vocabulary of the era) was first searched and relieved of objects that might be used to harm himself or others. The message for today is that all institutions owe a heightened duty of suicide prevention to those who may be in their custody.

Custodial suicides are, fortunately, rare. More common is the allegation that the institution negligently created unreasonable access to the means of suicide. To understand that allegation, it is helpful to review the most common methods of student suicide. According to the study of Midwestern universities, those methods are hanging or asphyxiation, jumping, gas inhalation, chemical poisoning (including drugs and cyanide), firearms, and, to a lesser degree, vehicles, knives, and drowning. If cyanide from the chemistry lab or a gun from an unlocked cabinet in the public-safety office were used in the suicide death of a student, the family could seek to blame the institution.

For example, in the 1990s the mother of a college football player who committed suicide argued that the athletics department's carelessness in casually dispensing large quantities of prescription medications, including Darvocet and Tylenol #3, contributed to her son's death. The young man had died from a self-inflicted gunshot wound, yet the family argued that the drugs were a phase in his general deterioration, and the Arkansas Supreme Court found that argument plausible enough to send the case back to the trial court for further proceedings.

Take note. From a public-health perspective, as well as a legal one, it is prudent to keep under lock and key dangerous substances and objects that might appeal to students as a means of suicide. Colleges should lock their roofs, towers, and other high perches from which depressed students can jump.

Sometimes differentiating suicide from an accidental death can be tricky. A student's fatal alcohol or drug overdose, for

Some Suicide Warning Signs among Young Adults

Behaviors Requiring Immediate Response

- Indicating intent to harm themselves (talking, threatening)
- Seeking availability of or obtaining ropes, weapons, pills, or other ways to kill themselves
- Talking or writing about death, dying, or suicide

Associated Behaviors Requiring Evaluation

- Feeling hopeless
- Expressing rage or anger; seeking revenge
- Acting recklessly or impulsively or engaging in risky activities, seemingly without thinking
- Feeling trapped, like there's no way out, or nothing else will help
- Increasing alcohol or drug use or abuse
- Withdrawing from friends, school activities, community, and family
- Expressing anxiety, agitation, an inability to sleep, or sleeping all the time
- Exhibiting dramatic mood changes
- Expressing loss of interest or reason for living; no sense of purpose or meaning in life
- Acting "immaturely" and/or displaying disregard for others' safety, feelings, or property

Source: M. Silverman, "College Student Suicide Prevention," *College Health Spectrum* (March 2004).

themes of despair in a student's poetry. Whose responsibility is it to put these pieces together? When and how should well-meaning people intervene?

Many institutions conduct educational programs to raise campus awareness about suicide and increase the possibility that fellow students, residence-hall workers, and faculty members will help the student into treatment. Good online screening programs—available through organizations like the Jed Foundation and Screening for Mental Health—reach students directly, providing a rough evaluation of their own suicide risk and encouraging them to seek treatment. Although such programs are not legal necessities, they certainly can advance student well-being.

Some colleges have also created committees that meet weekly to evaluate the behavior of students who pose potential risks to themselves or others. A leading program at the University of Illinois at Urbana-Champaign enlists many people across the campus, including public-safety officers, residence-hall administrators, and faculty members, to report any signs that a student might be considering self-harm to a suicide-prevention task force. The task force has the authority to require students to attend four mandatory assessment sessions at the counseling center, sessions that have proved very effective in reducing students' suicidal thoughts and intentions.

Administrators sometimes worry that any program to increase student safety may also increase the institution's liability, should a problem fall through the cracks. College lawyers can help structure programs to minimize that possibility. For example, should an institution conduct a screening program and retain in its records, without following up, information that a specific student is at high risk of suicide, then the prospect of its liability for that student's suicide is greatly increased. To protect against that, a screening program could clearly state that it is voluntary and anonymous, and that the institution will not keep a record of the results or follow up with the student.

The institution failed to respond appropriately to warning signs. Family members could argue that the institution knew, or at least should have known, that the student was at high risk of suicide. With the clarity of hindsight, they will point to steps that the institution should have taken, including, most pointedly, notifying them about the problem.

Issues of how to notify parents about a student's potential for self-harm have confounded many administrators. Some campus mental-health providers argue strenuously that they enjoy a legally privileged and confidential relationship with their patients. (The specifics vary by state and by type of profession.) A dean of students may feel that the Family Educational Rights and Privacy Act, which restricts the information that colleges can release about students, inhibits her from picking up the phone. The student's consent can, of course, avert the impasse. Experienced student-affairs staff members and counselors can usually build sufficient trust with a disturbed student to persuade him to contact his family. But sometimes the student adamantly refuses.

Administrators should then begin a collaborative analysis of the situation. The element of collaboration spreads the burden of

example, might have arisen from ignorance or miscalculation, or it might have been an intentional act of self-harm. After such deaths, the families may point to lax enforcement of institutional policies against drug and alcohol abuse. Do the trash cans in the first-year dorms overflow with beer bottles every Monday morning? If so, whether they view the death as accidental or intentional, the grieving parents may allege that the institution recklessly contributed to the student's alcohol poisoning. An institution that fails to enforce its existing policies faces an uphill battle in court.

The institution failed to recognize suicide warning signs. Depression can impair an individual's ability to seek help, and fewer than 20 percent of students who seriously consider suicide have received either therapy or antidepressant medication. Campus mental-health professionals are often not on the front lines of these problems, as suicidal students frequently don't come to see them, leaving to others the task of catching the cues and enlisting assistance for such students. A residence-hall adviser may notice signs of a student's emotional deterioration. An English professor may become concerned by the dark the decision whether to notify the family beyond the shoulders of just one individual. As a substantive matter, both the therapist–patient privilege and FERPA contain exceptions for emergencies, and a risk of self-harm counts as an emergency. In fact, some prudent student-health and counseling centers disclose on their websites, in their brochures, and on their patient paperwork that in emergency situations they may contact others.

From a legal standpoint, the safest course is to notify the family of a genuinely suicidal student unless previously known indicators, like a history of child abuse, suggest that parental notification would be harmful. Sometimes it just comes down to picking your lawsuit. A student's suit for invasion of privacy is, by most any reckoning, preferable to a suit over a suicide. Be ready, however, for the unexpected. One college, after making the decision to contact the family of an international student, ran into the unanticipated difficulty that the overseas parents did not speak English.

Hospitalization can be another appropriate response to a suicidal student. One large private university had 18 student psychiatric hospitalizations during a five-week period at the beginning of a recent fall semester. A national provider of student health insurance reported a rate of psychiatric hospitalizations in 2002 of 3.4 per 1,000 students.

Such numbers reflect the important role that community resources play in responding to student mental-health needs. The counseling center at Northwestern University, for example, devotes considerable attention to coordinating care with the hospitals and community mental-health practitioners who may be treating a student. Hospitalization may be easier if a suitable facility is nearby and the student has health insurance, or if the state has a flexible involuntary-commitment law.

Whether or not a college plays an active part in hospitalizing the student, it may be that a suicidal student's mental health is too fragile for him or her to function on the campus. Involuntary medical withdrawal is a good option in such situations, and it is prudent to have rules in place establishing the standards and procedures for that withdrawal, as well as for the return of such students to the campus. Washington and Lee University, Cornell University, and the University of North Carolina at Greensboro are among the institutions with involuntary-medical-withdrawal protocols available on their websites.

Perhaps the most important message about a college's liability for student suicide is to know your personal and institutional limits as a helper. An institution can work to resolve some problems internally, but others are beyond its scope and call for the intervention of families and external resources. A counseling center struggling even to meet its nonemergency appointment load should not lead students and parents to think that it provides full emergency care. A faculty member can do more harm than good by providing, over an extended period, a shoulder for a depressed student to cry on rather than aiding the student in getting treatment. If the student is relying on the professor for general comfort, then that student may be disinclined to get the medical help that he or she really needs.

The institution mishandled the emergency response to a suicide attempt. If a young man reports that his girlfriend is locked in her dorm room sending instant messages saying farewell and announcing plans to end it all, will the institution respond swiftly and effectively? The best approach is to contact local emergency services or to respond immediately with trained campus public-safety officers or medical personnel. College personnel should not, in any event, leave the student alone.

Institutions should plan for such emergencies in advance and develop operating procedures, conducting drills of imaginary student-suicide scenarios and working through the communications and response issues that might involve student-affairs and counseling staff members, residence-hall personnel, and public-safety officers. During what may be the last moments of a student's life, the institution's emergency response needs to be credible and to follow established protocols.

Fewer than 20 percent of students who seriously consider suicide have received either therapy or antidepressant medication.

After a suicide, sensitive outreach to the family is crucial. Senior campus officials should attend the funeral and express condolences in writing. The college should involve the family in planning college-sponsored memorial services and other activities in the name of the student, as well as maintain contact over an extended period. Most families welcome the occasional phone call just to say "We're thinking of you." The student's birthday and the anniversary of the death will be especially hard for them, so a note or call on those occasions would be particularly appropriate. Caring outreach will not increase the risk of institutional liability, and demonstrations of genuine concern can help keep the family's grief from turning to rage at the institution.

ANN H. FRANKE is vice president for education and risk management at United Educators Insurance and a former counsel to the American Association of University Professors.

UNIT 7
Funerals

Unit Selections

Key Points to Consider

- Describe how the funeralization process can assist in coping with grief and facilitate the bereavement process. Distinguish between grief, bereavement, and funeralization.

- Discuss the psychological, sociological, and theological/philosophical aspects of the funeralization process. How does each of these aspects facilitate the resolution of grief?

- Describe and compare each of the following processes: burial, cremation, environmentally friendly alternatives, cryonics, and body donation for medical research. What would be your choice for final disposition of your body? Why would you choose this method, and what effects might this choice have upon your survivers (if any) and the stewardship for the earth's resources? Would you have the same or different preferences for a close loved one such as a spouse, child, or parent? Why or why not?

Student Website
www.mhhe.com/cls

Internet References

Cryonics, Cryogenics, and the Alcor Foundation
www.alcor.org
Funeral Consumers Alliance
www.funerals.org
Funerals and Ripoffs
www.funerals-ripoffs.org/-5dProf1.html
The Internet Cremation Society
www.cremation.org

Decisions relating to the disposition of the body after death often involve feelings of ambivalence—on one hand, attachments to the deceased might cause one to be reluctant to dispose of the body, while on the other hand, practical considerations make the disposal of the body necessary. Funerals or memorial services provide methods for disposing of a dead body, remembering the deceased, and helping survivors accept the reality of death. They are also public rites of passage that assist the bereaved in returning to routine patterns of social interaction. In contemporary America, 79 percent of deaths involve earth burial and 21 percent involve cremation. These public behaviors, along with the private process of grieving, comprise the two components of the bereavement process.

This unit on the contemporary American funeral begins with a general article on the nature and functions of public bereavement behavior by Michael Leming and George Dickinson. Leming and Dickinson provide an overview of the present practice of funeralization in American society, including traditional and alternative funeral arrangements. They also discuss the functions of funerals relative to the sociological, psychological, and theological needs of adults and children.

© Skip Nall/Getty Images

The remaining articles in this section reflect upon the many alternative ways in which funerals, rituals, and final dispositions for the deceased may be constructed.

The Contemporary American Funeral

MICHAEL R. LEMING AND GEORGE E. DICKINSON

Paul Irion (1956) described the following needs of the bereaved: reality, expression of grief, social support, and meaningful context for the death. For Irion, the funeral is an experience of significant personal value insofar as it meets the religious, social, and psychological needs of the mourners. Each of these must be met for bereaved individuals to return to everyday living and, in the process, resolve their grief.

The psychological focus of the funeral is based on the fact that grief is an emotion. Edgar Jackson (1963) indicated that grief is the other side of the coin of love. He contends that if a person has never loved the deceased—never had an emotional investment of some type and degree—he or she will not grieve upon death. As discussed in the opening pages of Chapter 2, evidence of this can easily be demonstrated by the number of deaths that we see, hear, or read about daily that do not have an impact on us unless we have some kind of emotional involvement with those deceased persons. We can read of 78 deaths in a plane crash and not grieve over any of them unless we personally knew the individuals killed. Exceptions to the preceding might include the death of a celebrity or other public figure, when people experience a sense of grief even though there has never been any personal contact.

In his original work on the symptomatology of grief, Erich Lindemann (1944) stressed this concept of grief and its importance as a step in the resolution of grief. He defined how the emotion of grief must support the reality and finality of death. As long as the finality of death is avoided, Lindemann believes, grief resolution is impeded. For this reason, he strongly recommended that the bereaved persons view the dead. When the living confront the dead, all of the intellectualization and avoidance techniques break down. When we can say, "He or she is dead, I am alone, and from this day forward my life will be forever different," we have broken through the devices of denial and avoidance and have accepted the reality of death. It is only at this point that we can begin to withdraw the emotional capital that we have invested in the deceased and seek to create new relationships with the living.

On the other hand, viewing the corpse can be very traumatic for some. Most people are not accustomed to seeing a cold body and a significant other stretched out with eyes closed. Indeed, for some this scene may remain in their memories for a lifetime. Thus, they remember the cold corpse, not the warm, responsive person. Whether or not to view the body is not a cut-and-dried decision. Many factors should be taken into account when this decision is made.

Grief resolution is especially important for family members, but others are affected also—the neighbors, the business community in some instances, the religious community in most instances, the health-care community, and the circle of friends and associates (many of whom may be unknown to the family). All of these groups will grieve to some extent over the death of their relationship with the deceased. Thus, many people are affected by the death. These affected persons will seek not only a means of expressing their grief over the death, but also a network of support to help cope with their grief.

Sociologically, the funeral is a social event that brings the chief mourners and the members of society into a confrontation with death. The funeral becomes a vehicle to bring persons of all walks of life and degrees of relationship to the deceased together for expression and support. For this reason in our contemporary culture the funeral becomes an occasion to which no one is invited but all may come. This was not always the case, and some cultures make the funeral ceremony an "invitation only" experience. It is perhaps for this reason that private funerals (restricted to the family or a special list of persons) have all but disappeared in our culture. (The possible exception to this statement is a funeral for a celebrity—in which participation by the public may be limited to media coverage.)

At a time when emotions are strong, it is important that human interaction and social support become high priorities. A funeral can provide this atmosphere. To grieve alone can be devastating because it becomes necessary for that lone person to absorb all of the feelings into himself or herself. It has often been said that "joy shared is joy increased;" surely grief shared is grief diminished. People need each other at times when they have intense emotional experiences.

A funeral is in essence a one-time kind of "support group" to undergird and support those grieving persons. A funeral provides a conducive social environment for mourning. We may go to the funeral home either to visit with the bereaved family or to work through our own grief. Most of us have had the experience of finding it difficult to discuss a death with a member of the family. We seek the proper atmosphere, time, and place. It is during the funeral, the wake, the shivah, or the visitation with the bereaved family that we have the opportunity to express our condolences and sympathy comfortably.

Anger and guilt are often deeply felt at the time of death and will surface in words and actions. They are permitted within the funeral atmosphere as honest and candid expressions of grief, whereas at other times they might bring criticism and reprimand. The funeral atmosphere says in essence, "You are okay, I am okay; we have some strong feelings, and now is the time to express and share them for the benefit of all." Silence, talking, feeling, touching, and all means of sharing can be expressed without the fear of their being inappropriate.

Another function of the funeral is to provide a theological or philosophical perspective to facilitate grieving and to provide a context of meaning in which to place one of life's most significant experiences. For the majority of Americans, the funeral is a religious rite or ceremony (Pine, 1971). Those grievers who do not possess a religious creed or orientation will define or express death in the context of the values that the deceased and the grievers find important. Theologically or philosophically, the funeral functions as an attempt to bring meaning to the death and life of the deceased individual. For the religiously oriented person, the belief system will perhaps bring an understanding of the afterlife. Others may see only the end of biological life and the beginning of symbolic immortality created by the effects of one's life on the lives of others. The funeral should be planned to give meaning to whichever value context is significant for the bereaved.

"Why?" is one of the most often asked questions upon the moment of death or upon being told that someone we know has died. Though the funeral cannot provide the final answer to this question, it can place death within a context of meaning that is significant to those who mourn. If it is religious in context, the theology, creed, and articles of faith confessed by the mourners will give them comfort and assurance as to the meaning of death. Others who have developed a personally meaningful philosophy of life and death will seek to place the death in that philosophical context.

Cultural expectations typically require that we dispose of the dead with ceremony and dignity. The funeral can also ascribe importance to the remains of the dead. In keeping with the specialization found in most aspects of American life (e.g., the rise of professions), the funeral industry is doing for Americans that necessary task they no longer choose to do for themselves.

The Needs of Children and Their Attendance at Funerals

For children, as well as for their elders, the funeral ceremony can be an experience of value and significance. At a very early age, children are interested in any type of family reunion, party, or celebration. To be excluded from the funeral may create questions and doubts in the minds of children as to why they are not permitted to be a part of an important family activity.

Another question to be considered when denying the child an opportunity to participate in postdeath activities is what goes through the child's mind when such participation is denied. Children deal with other difficult situations in life, and when denied this opportunity, many will fantasize. Research suggests that these fantasies may be negative, destructive, and at times more traumatic than the situation from which the children are excluded.

Children also should not be excluded from activities prior to the funeral service. They should be permitted to attend the visitation, wake, or shivah. (In some situations it would be wise to permit children to confront the deceased prior to the public visitation.) It is obvious that children should not be forced into this type of confrontation, but, by the same token, children who are curious and desire to be involved should not be denied the opportunity.

Children will react at their own emotional levels, and the questions that they ask will usually be asked at their level of comprehension. Two important rules to follow: Never lie to the child, and do not over answer the child's question.

At the time of the funeral, parents have two concerns about their child's behavior at funerals. The first concern is that the child will have difficulty observing the grief of others—particularly if the child has never seen an adult loved one cry. The second concern is that parents themselves become confused when the child's emotional reactions may be different than their own. If the child is told of a death and responds by saying, "Oh, can I go out and play?" the parents may interpret this as denial or as a suppressed negative reaction to the death. Such a reaction can increase emotional concern by the parents. However, if the child's response is viewed as only a first reaction, and if the child is provided with loving, caring, and supportive attention, the child will ordinarily progress into an emotional resolution of the death.

The final reasons for involving children in postdeath activities are related to the strength and support that children give other grievers. They often provide positive evidence of the fact that life goes on. In other instances, because they have been an important part of the life of the deceased, their presence is symbolic testimony to the immortality of the deceased. Furthermore, it is not at all unusual for children to change the atmosphere surrounding bereavement from one of depression and sadness to one of laughter, verbalization, and celebration. Many times children do this by their normal behavior, without any understanding of the kind of contribution being made.

How Different Religions Pay Their Final Respects

From mummies to cremation to drive-up wakes, funeral rituals reflect religious traditions going back thousands of years as well as up-to-the-minute fads.

WILLIAM J. WHALEN

Most people in the United States identify themselves as Protestants; thus, most funerals follow a similar form. Family and friends gather at the funeral home to console one another and pay their last respects. The next day a minister conducts the funeral service at the church or mortuary; typically the service includes hymns, prayers, a eulogy, and readings from the Bible. In 85 percent of the cases today, the body is buried after a short grave-side ceremony. Otherwise the body is cremated or donated to a medical school.

But what could be called the standard U.S. funeral turns out to be the funeral of choice for only a minority of the rest of the human race. Other people, even other Christians, bury their dead with more elaborate and, to outsiders, even exotic rites.

How your survivors will dispose of your body will in all likelihood be determined by the religious faith you practiced during your life because funeral customs reflect the theological beliefs of a particular faith community.

For example, the Parsi people of India neither bury nor cremate their dead. Parsis, most of whom live in or near Bombay, follow the ancient religion of Zoroastrianism. Outside Bombay, Parsis erected seven Towers of Silence in which they perform their burial rites. When someone dies, six bearers dressed in white bring the corpse to one of the towers. The Towers of Silence have no roofs; within an hour, waiting vultures pick the body clean. A few days later the bearers return and cast the remaining bones into a pit. Parsis believe that their method of disposal avoids contaminating the soil, the water, and the air.

Out of the Ashes

The Parsis' millions of Hindu neighbors choose cremation as their usual burial practice. Hindus believe that as long as the physical body exists, the essence of the person will remain

nearby; cremation allows the essence, or soul, of the person to continue its journey into another incarnation.

Hindus wash the body of the deceased and clothe it in a shroud decorated with flowers. They carry the body to a funeral pyre, where the nearest male relative lights the fire and walks around the burning body three times while reciting verses from Hindu sacred writings. Three days later someone collects and temporarily buries the ashes.

On the tenth day after the cremation, relatives deposit the ashes in the Ganges or some other sacred river. The funeral ceremony, called the *Shraddha,* is then held within 31 days of the cremation. Usually the deceased's son recites the prayers and the invocation of ancestors; that is one reason why every Hindu wants at least one son.

Prior to British rule in India, the practice of suttee was also common. Suttee is the act of a Hindu widow willingly being cremated on her husband's funeral pyre. Suttee was outlawed by the British in 1829, but occasionally widows still throw themselves into the flames.

Like the Hindus, the world's Buddhists, who live primarily in China, Japan, Sri Lanka, Myanmar, Vietnam, and Cambodia, usually choose cremation for disposing of a corpse. They believe cremation was favored by Buddha. A religious teacher may pray or recite mantras at the bedside of the dying person. These actions are believed to exert a wholesome effect on the next rebirth. Buddhists generally believe that the essence of a person remains in an intermediate state for no more than 49 days between death and rebirth.

While Hindus and Buddhists prescribe cremation, the world's 900 million Muslims forbid cremation. According to the Qu'ran, Muhammad taught that only Allah will use fire to punish the wicked.

If a Muslim is near death, someone is called in to read verses from the Qu'ran. After death, the body is ceremonially washed, clothed in three pieces of white cloth, and placed in a simple wooden coffin. Unless required by law, Muslims will not allow embalming. The body must be buried as soon as possible after death—usually within 24 hours. After a funeral service at a mosque or at the grave side, the body is removed from the coffin and buried with the head of the deceased turned toward Mecca. In some Muslim countries the women engage in loud wailing and lamentations during the burial.

Some Islamic grave sites are quite elaborate. The Mogul emperor Shah Jahan built the world-famous Taj Mahal as a mausoleum for his wife and himself. The Taj Mahal, which is one of the finest examples of Islamic architecture, was finished in 1654. It took 20,000 workers about 22 years to complete the project.

The Baha'i faith, which originated in Persia in the nineteenth century as an outgrowth of the Shi'ite branch of Islam, also forbids cremation and embalming and requires that the body not be transported more than an hour's journey from the place of death. Because Bahaism has no ordained clergy, the funeral may be conducted by any member of the family or the local assembly. All present at the funeral must stand during the recitation of the Prayer for the Dead composed by Baha'u'llah. Several million Baha'is live in Iran, India, the Middle East, and Africa; and an estimated 100,000 Baha'is live in the United States.

In Judaism, the faith of some 18 million people, the Old Testament only hints at belief in an afterlife; but later Jewish thought embraced beliefs in heaven, hell, resurrection, and final judgment. In general, Orthodox Jews accept the concept of a resurrection of the soul and the body while Conservative and Reform Jews prefer to speak only of the immortality of the soul.

Orthodox Judaism prescribes some of the most detailed funeral rites of any religion. As death approaches, family and friends must attend the dying person at all times. When death finally arrives, a son or the nearest relative closes the eyes and mouth of the deceased and binds the lower jaw before rigor mortis sets in. Relatives place the body on the floor and cover it with a sheet; they place a lighted candle near the head.

Judaism in its traditional form forbids embalming except where required by law. After a ritual washing, the body is covered with a white shroud and placed in a wooden coffin. At the funeral, mourners symbolize their grief by tearing a portion of an outer garment or wearing a torn black ribbon. The Orthodox discourage flowers and ostentation at the funeral.

The Jewish funeral service includes a reading of prayers and psalms, a eulogy, and the recitation of the Kaddish prayer for the dead in an Aramaic dialect. Like other Semitic people, Jews forbid cremation. Orthodox Jews observe a primary mourning period of seven days; Reform Jews reduce this period to three days. During the secondary yearlong mourning period, the Kaddish prayer is recited at every service in the synagogue.

Dearly Beloved

Christianity, the world's largest religion, carries over Judaism's respect for the body and firmly acknowledges resurrection, judgment, and eternal reward or punishment.

These Christian beliefs permeate the liturgy of a Catholic funeral. Older Catholics remember the typical funeral of the 1940s and '50s: the recitation of the rosary at the wake, the black vestments, the Latin prayers. They probably recall the *"Dies Irae,"* a thirteenth-century dirge and standard musical piece at Catholic funerals prior to the liturgical changes of the Second Vatican Council in the 1960s.

Nowadays, those attending a Catholic wake may still say the rosary, but often there is a scripture service instead. The priest's vestments are likely to be white or violet rather than black. Prayers tend to emphasize the hope of resurrection rather than the terrors of the final judgment.

As death approaches, the dying person or the family may request the sacrament of the Anointing of the Sick. Once called Last Rites or Extreme Unction, this sacrament is no longer restricted to those in imminent danger of death; it is regularly administered to the sick and the elderly as an instrument of healing as well as a preparation for death.

Sacred Remains

The Catholic Church raises no objections to embalming, flowers, or an open casket at a wake. At one time Catholics who wished to have a church funeral could not request cremation. In 1886 the Holy Office in Rome declared that "to introduce the practice (of cremation) into Christian society was un-Christian and Masonic in motivation." Today Catholics may choose the option of cremation over burial "unless," according to canon law, "it has been chosen for reasons that are contrary to Christian teaching."

The church used to deny an ecclesiastical burial to suicides, those killed in duels, Freemasons, and members of the ladies' auxiliaries of Masonic lodges. Today the church refuses burial only to "notorious apostates, heretics, and schismatics" and to "sinners whose funerals in church would scandalize the faithful." Catholics who join Masonic lodges no longer incur excommunication, although they still may not receive Communion.

The church has also softened its position on denying funeral rites to suicides. Modern pastoral practice is based on the understanding that anyone finding life so unbearable as to end it voluntarily probably was acting with a greatly diminished free will.

For Roman Catholics, the Mass is the principal celebration of the Christian funeral; and mourners are invited to receive the Eucharist. Most Protestant denominations, except for some Lutherans and Episcopalians, do not incorporate a communion service into their funeral liturgies. The Catholic ritual employs candles, holy water, and incense but does not allow non-Christian symbols, such as national flags or lodge emblems, to rest on or near the coffin during the funeral. In many parishes the pastor encourages the family members to participate where appropriate as eucharistic ministers, lectors, and singers. In the absence of a priest, a deacon can conduct the funeral service but cannot preside at a Mass of Christian burial.

The revised funeral liturgy of the Catholic Church is meant to stress God's faithfulness to people rather than God's wrath toward sinners. The Catholic Church declares that certain men and women who have lived lives of such heroic virtue that they are indeed in heaven are to be known as saints. The church also teaches that hell is a reality but has never declared that anyone, even Judas, has actually been condemned to eternal punishment.

Unlike Protestant churches, Catholicism also teaches the existence of a temporary state of purification, known as purgatory, for those destined for heaven but not yet totally free from the effects of sin and selfishness. At one time some theologians suggested that unbaptized babies spent eternity in a place of natural happiness known as limbo, but this was never church doctrine and is taught by few theologians today.

At the committal service at the grave site, the priest blesses the grave and leads the mourners in the Our Father and other prayers for the repose of the soul of the departed and the comfort of the survivors. Catholics are usually buried in Catholic cemeteries or in separate sections of other cemeteries.

Dressed for the Occasion

The funeral rite in the Church of Jesus Christ of Latter-day Saints, which is the fastest growing church in the United States, resembles the standard Protestant funeral in some ways; but one significant difference is in the attire of the deceased. Devout Mormons receive the garments of the holy priesthood during their endowment ceremonies when they are teens. These sacred undergarments are to be worn day and night throughout a Mormon's life. When a Mormon dies, his or her body is then attired in these garments in the casket. At one time Mormon sacred garments resembled long johns, but they now have short sleeves and are cut off at the knees. The garments are embroidered with symbols on the right and left breasts, the navel, and the right knee, which remind the wearer of the oaths taken in the secret temple rites.

Mormons who reached their endowments are also clothed in their temple garb at death. For the men, this includes white pants, white shirt, tie, belt, socks, slippers, and an apron. Just before the casket is closed for the last time, a fellow Mormon puts a white temple cap on the corpse. If the deceased is a woman, a high priest puts a temple veil over her face; Mormons believe the veil will remain there until her husband calls her from the grave to resurrection. Mormons forbid cremation.

Freemasons conduct their own funeral rites for a deceased brother, and they insist that their ceremony be the last one before burial or cremation. Thus, a separate religious ceremony often precedes the Masonic rites. Lodge members will bury a fellow Mason only if he is a member in good standing and he or his family has requested the service.

All the pallbearers at the Masonic services must be Masons, and each wears a white apron, white gloves, a black band around his left arm, and a sprig of evergreen or acacia in his left lapel. The corpse is clothed in a white apron and other lodge regalia.

Masonry accepts the idea of the immortality of the soul but makes no reference to the Christian understanding of the resurrection of the soul and the body. The Masonic service speaks of the soul's translation from this life to that "perfect, glorious, and celestial lodge above" presided over by the Grand Architect of the Universe.

In Memoriam

Other small religious groups have much less elaborate and formalized funeral services. Christian Scientists, for example, have no set funeral rite because their founder, Mary Baker Eddy, denied the reality of death. The family of a deceased Christian Scientist often invites a Christian Science reader to present a brief service at the funeral home.

Unitarian-Universalists enroll many members who would identify themselves as agnostics or atheists. Therefore, in a typical Unitarian Universalist funeral service, the minister and loved ones say little about any afterlife but extol the virtues and good works of the deceased.

Salvation Army officers are buried in their military uniforms, and a Salvationist blows taps at the grave side. In contrast, the Church of Christ, which allows no instrumental music during Sunday worship, allows no organs, pianos, or other musical instruments at its funerals.

The great variety of funeral customs through the ages and around the world would be hard to catalog. The Egyptians mummified the bodies of royalty and erected pyramids as colossal monuments. Viking kings were set adrift on blazing boats. The Soviets mummified the body of Lenin, and his tomb and corpse have become major icons in the U.S.S.R.

In a funeral home in California, a drive-up window is provided for mourners so that they can view the remains and sign the book without leaving their cars. In Japan, where land is scarce, one enterprising cemetery owner offers a time-share plan whereby corpses are displaced after brief burial to make room for the next occupant. Complying with the wishes of the deceased, one U.S. undertaker once dressed a corpse in pajamas and positioned it under the blankets in a bedroom for viewing.

The reverence and rituals surrounding the disposal of the body reflect religious traditions going back thousands of years as well as up-to-the-minute fads. All of the elements of the burial—the preparation of the body, the garments or shroud, the prayers, the method of disposal, the place and time of burial—become sacred acts by which a particular community of believers bids at least a temporary farewell to one of its own.

From *U.S. Catholic,* September 1990, pp. 29–35. Copyright © 1990 by Claretian Publications. Reprinted by permission.

Green Graveyards—A Natural Way to Go

Back-to-nature burials in biodegradable caskets conserve land.

BARBARA BASLER

In lovely woods just outside the tiny town of Westminster, S.C., discreetly scattered among the tall pines and poplars, are 20 graves, many hand-dug by Billy Campbell.

The graves, mounds of earth dotted with wildflowers and bathed in dappled sunlight, are marked with flat stones engraved with the names of the dead—from a rock-ribbed Southern Baptist to a gentle New Age hippie.

Campbell, the town's only doctor, is an ardent environmentalist. He buries patients, friends and strangers—without embalming them—in biodegradable caskets, or in no caskets at all, in the nature preserve he created along Ramsey Creek.

The burials are legal and meet all state regulations and health requirements. But in the beginning, many in this conservative town of 2,700 people were skeptical, even angry, about the Ramsey Creek Preserve, where the dead protect the land of the living.

"We weren't doing anything weird or outlandish," Campbell says, "but people accused us of throwing bodies in the creek or laying them out for buzzards to eat." He recalls one irate woman, apparently convinced of the bodies-in-the-creek rumor, who "told me I was a rich doctor who could buy bottled water, but she would have to drink my dead men's soup."

In the six years since the burial ground opened, Westminster has come, slowly but surely, to accept it. And now, Campbell's idea—nurtured in the backwoods of South Carolina—is spreading to rich, trendy Marin County, Calif.

Campbell, 49, and his new partner Tyler Cassity—a 34-year old entrepreneur who owns cemeteries in three states—are scheduled to open the new burial preserve this summer on a hillside in the shadow of the Golden Gate Bridge.

Campbell says he and Cassity hope to work with conservation groups to open similar natural burial grounds across the country, each crisscrossed—like Ramsey Creek—with hiking trails. "What we are doing is basically land conservation," Campbell says. "By setting aside a woods for natural burials, we preserve it from development. At the same time, I think we put death in its rightful place, as part of the cycle of life. Our burials honor the idea of dust to dust."

At Ramsey Creek, burial in a simple casket costs about $2,300. The National Funeral Directors Association says the average conventional funeral costs about $6,500. That includes mortuary services, embalming, a casket and a cement vault or box for the casket, which is often required for a cemetery burial. A cemetery plot adds even more to the cost.

"The mortuary-cemetery business is a $20-billion-a-year industry, and if we could get just 10 percent of that," Campbell says, "we'd have $2 billion a year going toward land conservation on memorial preserves where people could picnic, hike or take nature classes."

> **"We put death in its rightful place, as part of the cycle of life. Our burials honor the idea of dust to dust."**
>
> —Billy Campbell

A native of Westminster—his family's roots here go back to the Revolutionary War—Campbell studied to be an ecologist, then switched to medicine. Soft-spoken and wry, Campbell concedes he's a bit of an eccentric, but then "small Southern towns are good places for eccentrics," he says. Westminster, after all, was home to the Guns, Cabinets and Nightcrawlers store, "and I think that's a whole lot stranger than Ramsey Creek," he laughs.

The folksy, erudite doctor and the hip young businessman who owns Hollywood Forever, a celebrity cemetery where Rudolph Valentino and Cecil B. DeMille are buried, believe they have the potential to revolutionize the funeral industry and conserve a million acres of land over the next 30 years.

Campbell and Cassity, who has been a consultant to HBO's television series *Six Feet Under,* think the idea of burials that protect, rather than consume, green space will appeal to boomers, including those who want their cremated ashes scattered or buried. In Marin County, they plan to designate three of the site's 32 acres for interments and conserve the rest.

In place of the perpetual care fund of the conventional cemetery, "where money is set aside to mow the grass and battle back any natural growth," Campbell says, funds in memorial preserves will be used to restore the land.

Campbell's Ramsey Creek—the first "green" burial site in America—has inspired another in Florida, and a third has recently opened in Texas.

Campbell remembers that when his father died, he wanted to bury him in a simple, dignified biodegradable wood box. But his father was buried in the only wood box the funeral home offered—an eye-popping, ornate oak casket the funeral director assured him was the same model that held actor Dan Blocker, who played Hoss Cartwright on the TV hit *Bonanza*.

"You know, I didn't take any real comfort in that," Campbell says.

Over the years Campbell has spoken to environmental groups, birdwatchers and native-plant associations and found that "the idea of the preserve resonates with a lot of very different people" who aren't all young, liberal environmentalists.

"Ramsey Creek is unusual. It's different. And people will talk," says Jerry Smith, the owner of Moon's Drug Store & Gift Shop on Main Street. "But I think it's fantastic, myself."

Indeed, what is New Age and cutting edge to some is simply old-fashioned common sense to others. Sherrill Hughes, who lives in Westminster, buried her husband Rowland in Ramsey Creek Preserve with his favorite country music playing.

"Nobody would call him an environmental person," Hughes says. "Rowland grew up hard in West Virginia, and he liked plain and simple. He was a good provider, but he didn't like to waste money." When Rowland said he wanted to be buried in a plain pine box, Hughes says she told him she didn't think they did that anymore. "Then," she says, "my daughter heard about Ramsey Creek."

Campbell and his wife, Kimberly, can tell the story of everyone buried in Ramsey Creek—from the stillborn baby Hope, the first burial on the site, to the interior decorator who left instructions for an elaborate funeral with black-plumed horses to be led by Kimberly. "His relatives nixed that, though," Campbell says. "They said, 'Those horses bite, and we can't take any chances.'"

Kimberly operates the Ramsey Creek business from a room in Billy Campbell's Foothills Family Medicine office on Main Street. He treats the patients, she sells the gravesites. "Billy doesn't discuss Ramsey Creek during medical appointments," Kimberly says.

Twenty people are already buried at Ramsey Creek, and 50 other families, some from as far away as California and New York, have bought plots there.

Campbell says when he first announced the opening of his green cemetery in 1998, the local newspaper referred to it as "tree-hugger heaven," and the local funeral director—a man he grew up with—tried to get the state authorities to shut it down. "Now, several funeral homes work with us to help store or transport bodies to Ramsey Creek," Campbell says.

Bob Fells, a spokesman for the International Cemetery and Funeral Association, says the industry is always open to new ideas. "Many cemeteries," he says, "have undeveloped acreage. So it would be easy to leave the trees and rocks and dedicate that area as a green cemetery that follows the rules for green burials. We're all about consumer choice."

Campbell's company, Memorial Ecosystems, sets aside 25 percent of the Ramsey Creek burial price for conservation and for development projects like nature classes and plant surveys. It's a for-profit company, and "so far, we're about breaking even," he says. "But as word spreads, people come, and we are growing."

Jim Nichols, a computer software salesman from Greenville, S.C., buried his younger brother Chris in Ramsey Creek after the 28-year-old died of cancer in May. "Chris was what you might call a hippie, and he was very conscious of the environment," Nichols says. "When he was dying, he said he wanted to be buried here."

Standing in front of the grave, listening to the sounds of the birds and the rushing creek, Nichols recalls, "My father and I were leery, but the first time we came out here, we knew it was right for Chris. It's beautiful and peaceful. It's full of life, not death."

When he died they buried Chris in a coffin his father had made, wrapped in quilts sewn by his great-grandmothers. His dog Briar was at the graveside, along with 70 friends and family members.

"Now, my wife and I, my parents and my two uncles all plan to be buried here," Nichols says. "Ramsey Creek changed our minds about burials and death."

Reprinted from *AARP Bulletin*, July/August 2004, pp. vol. 45, no. 7, March 4, 2005, by Barbara Basler (staff). Copyright © 2004 by American Association for Retired Persons (AARP). Reprinted by permission.

Social Workers' Final Act of Service: Respectful Burial Arrangements for Indigent, Unclaimed, and Unidentified People

GRACIELA M. CASTEX

Although little discussed in the professional literature, social workers have long been involved in identifying resources and making final arrangements for clients who die without an estate or heirs to assume economic responsibility; who may have been institutionalized; who are unknown to the community; or whose body may be unclaimed for burial. This task can be demanding, if only because social workers must often locate resources quickly if they are to prevent a client from being buried with no ceremony of interment and frequently in an unmarked grave or in a grave marked only by a number in ground set aside for the burial of indigents—a "potter's field."

A person's respectful final disposition is important for the living, for the deceased, and, it may be argued, for the health of the larger society. Knowledge that respectful final arrangements have been made may offer psychological comfort to a client at the end of life, help a grieving family and friends during a time of sorrow and remembrance, and also mark the community's recognition of and respect for our common humanity. This article highlights the challenges faced by many social workers as they attempt to prevent undignified burials when requested to make final arrangements for terminally ill or deceased people, especially those who are indigent, unclaimed, or unknown. ("Burial" here refers to any form of final disposition: interment burial at sea, cremation, and so forth; "indigent" is a legal term often used in reference to people whose estates lack the resources to pay for final arrangements independently.)

Death is destiny for all of us; for most of humanity, there seems to be an almost universal impulse to attend the final mystery, the final journey, of death with ceremonies of respect and remembrance, implementing local traditions and commonly seeking religious or spiritual guidance and solace (Ariès, 1974; Kastenbaum, 2004). Remembrances of the dead connect us to the past and honor the influence of those who have departed in helping us become what we are today. Observances of respect for the departed touch our common humanity; common sentiments such as "there but for the grace of God go I" and "as I am, so you will be" reinforce humility and empathy. In sum, as important as they are for emotional reasons, respectful death rites and burial practices are threads in the fabric of community that holds a society together.

Absent substantial policy reform at state and national levels, the need for "preventive" services to ensure respectful burials for all people may increase dramatically in the future. In part, an increase in indigent burials is a result of population increase, especially among the older-age cohorts. But the primary cause of an indigent burial is poverty at death.

Therefore, demography is only part of the story. Various social and political factors contribute to indigence at death; examples include the current financing of the U.S. medical system, which leaves 46 million people without insurance coverage (DeNavas-Walt, Proctor, & Lee, 2005); the political climate, which supports the diminishment of social safety nets; increasing numbers of incarcerated individuals with very long sentences, resulting in prison deaths; changes in family structure resulting in fewer offspring or other relatives available to make final arrangements; increasing numbers of immigrant residents who may have few social supports and no extended family in the United States; homelessness and all that it implies regarding lack of social attachments and unmet basic needs; and a system of payment for long-term care (assisted living, nursing, hospice, and so forth) that virtually guarantees the impoverishment of many people at death.

Private Pain, Public Bodies

Every place where groups of human beings live will be faced with burying people who have no resources or friends or relatives to attend to their final arrangements or who may be entirely unknown to the community. The number of individuals who currently die in such circumstances in the United States is not well documented; no national data on indigent burials or unclaimed bodies are collected, and data collected at the state level are often erratic and incomplete (personal communication with M. Jones, public affairs specialist, National Center for Health Statistics, June 26, 2006). In 2004, about 2.4 million people died in the United States; in addition, there are approximately 26,000 stillbirths annually. The precise number of indigent burials in the United States, however, or of those who are unclaimed or unknown, is undetermined because the data are not collected (Centers for Disease Control and Prevention [CDC], 2003; Miniño, Heron, & Smith, 2006; National Institutes of Health [NIH], 2003).

A hint of the number of indigent burials for the nation as a whole is, however, offered by extrapolation from the experience of New York City, which with 8 million residents makes up almost 3 percent of the U.S. population. About 3,000 (5 percent) of New York City's 60,000 annual deaths require some form of city burial assistance, of which about 1,500 adults and 1,000 or more infant and stillborn children are buried annually on Hart Island, the local potter's field (Corn, 2000; New York City Department of Health and Mental Hygiene, 2005). Extending New York City's experience to the nation, one might crudely estimate more than 100,000 potter's field burials annually (5 percent of the 2.4 million U.S. deaths)—perhaps too high a number, but there are at least tens of thousands of publicly assisted burials annually.

The limited state data available, and projections from a survey conducted by the Department of Veterans Affairs in 2003 (Schulman, Ronca, & Bucuvalas, Inc., 2003), suggest that even the 100,000-plus estimate may be reasonable: Michigan, for example, subsidizes 6,000 to 7,000 indigent burials each year, one-third of which occur in Wayne County (Detroit); Ohio paid for 2,000 in the year 2000 (Brickey, 2005); and Maricopa County (Phoenix), Arizona, pays for about 300 burials per year (Maricopa County Office of Management and Budget, 2000). Some regions face special challenges; for example, more than 200 immigrants died crossing the Arizona desert from Mexico in the fiscal year ending September 30, 2005, a third of whom will never be identified (Carroll, 2005; "Deaths on Border," 2005).

Although such examples illustrate the experience of a few jurisdictions for which data are available, it would be a mistake to view indigent burials as primarily a product of the anonymity or localization of poverty in urban environments. The need for social workers to provide burial assistance may arise in a rural county in North Carolina or Minnesota, perhaps for a migrant farm worker or nursing home resident.

Lack of assets at death is likely to become more common as members of the rapidly growing elderly population exhaust their retirement savings, as income distribution becomes increasingly skewed in favor of those who are wealthy, and as support for such a basic concept as social insurance faces increasing challenge. Thus, a social context that, perhaps unintentionally, promotes financial depletion at death increases the challenge facing a social worker seeking out resources to avoid a client's anonymous burial in a local potter's field, the lowest common denominator of indigent burial options funded out of the public purse.

Response of Governments to a Societal Need

Funeral and burial expenses in the United States are customarily the responsibility of the estate of the deceased or of the deceased's family. However, there may be no estate or family or the family may be unable or unwilling to pay the final expenses. Yet, the remains must be disposed of, and some government entity must ultimately assume the responsibility of ensuring a proper disposal.

In other words, whatever the time and place, what of those whose families could not and cannot afford what they regard as an appropriate disposition? What of unknown or unclaimed bodies? Who takes responsibility for their burial? Any city and most villages, whether modern or ancient, had, have, and will have people die who are poor or unknown, and recognition of the undeniable need for communities to provide for their burial is ancient (Parkes, Laungani, & Young, 1997). In the United States, state governments have generally assumed this responsibility or assigned the task to local governments. In New York State, for example, Section 4200 of the Public Health Law mandates that "every body of a deceased person, within this state, shall be decently buried or incinerated within a reasonable time after death" (New York State Cemetery Board, 2001, p. 38).

Legal scholar Virginia Murray underlined the principle that in U.S. jurisprudence, most states have legislation guaranteeing that "all persons, including paupers and prisoners, are entitled to a decent burial. Sanctity of the dead is so basic a principle that it is referred to as a "right of the dead and a charge on the quick" (Trope & Echo-Hawk, as cited in Murray, 2000, para. 2). Even so, although the law recognizes that the living must pay to ensure the rights of the dead, no governing entity at the local, state, or national level has consistently been enthusiastic about assuming the financial burden of this responsibility.

Some jurisdictions go to lengths to discourage situations in which government burials might subsidize what many people would consider standard elements of a funeral. In 2001, for example, York County, Nebraska, clarified existing guidelines regarding county burials and explicitly banned independent arrangements by family members with mortuaries or cemeteries to provide additional services such as flowers, headstones, or clergy fees (Wilkinson, 2001).

Furthermore, state policies and regulations are usually implemented in piecemeal fashion by a patchwork of town, city, county, and state agencies. In many cases, state governments dictate what local authorities are required to do, creating what is all too often a partially funded or completely unfunded mandate to bury the dead. Confusion resulting from ad hoc local responses to a state mandate can be extreme: In New Jersey, for example, in 2003 the legislature had to step in and require that county governments, not municipalities, pick up the charges for indigent burials. Furthermore, the responsible county would be that in which the deceased person resided, not that in which he or she had died; certain counties with large, regional hospitals were in effect subsidizing the indigent burial expenses of other counties (Dressel, 2003).

State reimbursement to localities for indigent burials, when it exists, has rarely kept up with inflation. In 2001, the state of Ohio eliminated a $750 reimbursement to localities. The state of Washington did the same in 1993, although it requires that "[the county] shall provide for the final disposition of any indigent person including a recipient of public assistance who dies within the county and whose body is unclaimed by relatives or church organizations" (Brickey, 2005; Crumley, 2002; Revised Code of Washington, 1993, c 4, § 36.39.030). In other states, funeral homes must accept indigent burials at a loss.

Potter's Field: A Pauper's Grave

In the United States, people planning a funeral seem to have many choices when selecting a respectful final disposition. For example, one may be interred in the earth, buried at sea, cremated, or entombed; have a green (ecologically respectful) burial; be donated for scientific research; or be cryogenically preserved. One may or may not be embalmed; one's organs may be donated to others. Eventually, the final remains may be kept in a plot, crypt, niche, urn, or tomb. Objects commonly merchandized for funerary use include caskets, clothing, grave liners, guest books, flowers, memorial jewelry, balloons, grave markers, and so forth, depending on the customs and belief systems of the deceased and his or her family. The hallmark of the indigent burial is lack of choice and, all too often, the lack of respect and dignity.

Interment and the Classic Potter's Field

The term "potter's field" derives from a New Testament Bible story (Matthew 27:3–10) in which a plot of land owned by a potter outside the walls of the city of Jerusalem is purchased "as a burial place for foreigners" with the tainted 30 pieces of silver that Judas received (and returned) for betraying Jesus (New York City Department of Corrections, 1967). In time, however, the term took on other connotations: "Potter's field: A public burial place (as in a city) for paupers, unknown persons, and criminals" (Gove, 1976).

One of the most visually dramatic examples of the dehumanization of anonymous burials at a U.S. potter's field may be observed at City Cemetery on New York City's Hart Island, which was opened in 1869 and brings the efficiency and scale of the Industrial Revolution to the medieval pauper's grave. Every weekday will find teams of men who are incarcerated stacking unpainted plywood coffins, often of tiny children, eight or 10 deep in trenches These mass graves are then backfilled with earthmoving equipment until the ground is leveled, and backhoes move on to create the next trench (Hunt & Sternfeld, 1998; Risen, 2002). Even when faced with such images, however, the dehumanization of indigent, unknown, or unclaimed deceased individuals was not the intent of the architects of the original potter's field, or of any subsequent version.

Of course, most potter's fields in the United States do not operate on such an industrial scale. In Bradenton, Florida, for example, the 150 or so indigent funerals annually are handled by local funeral homes for a county fee of $400, with burial in a county cemetery and numbers on a concrete strip for a headstone. The newspaper reports on one such recent burial, of a 37-year-old woman who died of a heart attack after working a 14-hour shift as a short-order cook. Family and friends were unable to raise the $5,000 an average Manatee County, Florida, private funeral cost in 2005. The woman was buried at county expense in a particleboard casket sealed with duct tape. The funeral home did, however, generously donate a service complete with flowers, for which it received no reimbursement, before burial in the county potter's field (Cullinan, 2005).

Obviously, the Florida funeral and disposition was more respectful, and appears to have been more emotionally fulfilling for family, than burial in an anonymous trench on Hart Island. This difference illustrates the challenges facing the social worker advocating for an indigent client. There are no clearcut paths to a desired solution when values, norms, rules, regulations, reimbursements, and services offered can vary from state to state, town to town, and even funeral home to funeral home.

Burial Options, Costs, and Indigence: The Example of Cremation

One might assume that a key element in addressing the problem of indigence at death and respectful final dispositions would be a reduction in the cost of final dispositions. Although funeral costs have sometimes been criticized as excessive, this issue is separate from provision for the burials of indigent people. Respectful and inexpensive options exist, although options may be limited by the preferences of the deceased and prevailing customs or religious practices. Costs for modest burials are commonly trivial compared with the medical costs of a final illness. What constitutes a respectful final disposition, however, not only varies by community, but also may change over time for a community.

The key word is "respectful." Ensuring a final disposition will inevitably be assigned to an agency of the community, be that a parish in the Middle Ages or colonial America or a county government in the 21st century. Requirements or perceptions of common decency, health, and public order ultimately transcend the costs of particular burial practices. There will always be a need for intervention to ensure any final disposition, much less a respectful burial, for some clients.

Consider the option of cremation. The practice is certainly less expensive than interment, and cremations are increasingly regarded as respectful. In 2004, for example, about 30 percent of the final dispositions in the United States were cremations; interments constituted virtually all of the remaining burials, and there are predictions that the proportion of cremations will increase in the future (Cremation Association of North America [CANA], 2006). A change in burial practices favoring cremation will not in most cases, however, divert the road away from potter's field. Cremations cost less than interments, but most indigent burials involve people with, at most, a few hundred dollars in assets. The need for assistance will continue.

Although more inexpensive burial practices only marginally affect the volume of indigent burials, a social worker may be called on to intervene in a more subtle manner; a crematory may itself become a sort of potter's field. A survey conducted a decade ago by CANA found that 5.7 percent of cremated remains in 1996 to 1997 were never picked up, and 2.4 percent of cremated remains delivered to a cemetery were placed in a common grave. Of the remains that were never picked up, 46 percent were "placed in storage on the premises"; 32 percent were "disposed of in a proper and legal way"; and the remaining 22 percent were "placed in a permanent vault." Vague language leaves room for much interpretation in what, for crematory operators, are ad hoc solutions to a problem imposed on them (CANA, 1998).

Changes in burial practices are unlikely to substantially affect the larger policy issues regarding the final disposition of human remains. In addition, there may be an issue respecting religious diversity; some religious communities do not customarily practice cremation.

The Road to Potter's Field: The Growing Need for Social Work Intervention

Although a lack of data obscures the absolute number of people who spend eternity in some form of pauper's grave in the United States, in looking at the total number of people who die, their ages, and their economic circumstances, one can quickly begin to piece together a grim reality. Social workers often provide services to those who are most vulnerable in society and most at risk of not having the resources to afford a burial, much less a funeral.

The social work community has always worked with members of groups such as elderly people, those who are incarcerated, newly arrived immigrants, homeless people, and so forth. However, a number of changes in the size of certain component groups of U.S. society appear likely to greatly affect both the number and the distribution of indigent burials. For example, the tripling of the population of those incarcerated for the long term—that is, over a 20-year period—merits special attention. Those 1.5 million prisoners will make substantial although often yet undetermined, demands on the social services delivery system in many areas, not the least of which will likely be provisions for final arrangements.

Poverty and age at death tend to be reinforcing. The group that will grow the most in numbers, elderly people, constitute the age cohorts most likely to die and those second most likely to live in circumstances of economic deprivation. Members of the cohorts with the second highest mortality, the infant children of (by definition) young families, have the highest rates of poverty, particularly if the family is headed by a single mother (DeNavas-Walt et al., 2005).

The dynamic interrelationship of demographic changes and family structure that reinforce poverty are, of course, exacerbated by a number of unrelated trends that also tend to impoverish these same clients. Especially significant are the reduction in the number of people covered by defined-benefit (fixed amount per month) corporate pension systems; rising medical costs combined with declining health and life insurance coverage for the most at-risk populations; the declining supports provided by family systems at all ages; and an increase in the poverty rate for children, whose parents may not be able to pay for burials or health insurance for all family members. Many social workers would add still more. All reinforce the likelihood that the financial resources of decedents will be exhausted at the time of death.

Age at Death

One's life may end on its first day, at age 25 in an auto accident, or during one's 100th year. The CDC reported that 2,443,908 people died in 2003 in the United States, and NIH reported that there are at least an additional 26,000 stillbirths annually (to be counted as a death by the collectors of vital statistics, one must be born alive; although as of 2007, NIH calls stillbirths "fetal mortalities," they still do not contribute to the total count of deaths) (MacDorman, Hoyert, Matin, Munson, & Hamilton, 2007). As is typical of people living in industrialized societies, most mortalities occur as stillbirths (26,000), as infant mortalities in the first year of life (1.2 percent, or 28,458 in 2003), or after 65 years of age (74 percent, or 1,803,827 in 2003). As a cohort group, the death rate in the first year of life, even excluding stillbirths, is not equaled until about age 60 (Hoyert, Heron, Murphy, & Kung, 2006; NIH, 2003).

Poverty and Age

In the United States, a large number of people are born into poverty, live in poverty, and die in poverty; many millions never have the opportunity to accumulate significant assets during their lives. Others are poor only at some point in their lives. In 2004, 12.7 percent of the national population, 37 million people, lived in poverty, officially defined as an annual household income of $15,219 for a family of three. The poverty rate rose to 17.8 percent of households with children that year, encompassing 13 million children plus their parents and caretakers. The poverty rate jumped to 28.4 percent if the family was headed by a single woman. A single mother is unlikely to be able to save much for emergencies, retirement, or the final arrangements for a child (DeNavas-Walt et al., 2005).

For those age 65 and older, more than 6 million of 35 million people (17 percent) lived in households with incomes of less than $14,000 (about $1,200 per month)—about 25 percent above the official poverty threshold for this age group (DeNavas-Walt et al., 2005). The numbers of poor people with children and the numbers of elderly people who live in financially stringent circumstances are both quite large—these are households in which, by definition, some members cannot work and are therefore likely to be financially challenged.

Some regional, racial, and ethnic groups also have poverty rates, and death rates, much higher than national averages. These are among the groups most at risk of indigence at death.

Incarcerated People

On July 1, 2004, there were 2,131,180 people—one in 143 residents—incarcerated in the United States. Of those, 1,410,405 were incarcerated in state and federal prisons, up from 487,593 in 1985 as prison terms have increased dramatically as a result of draconian drug laws, three-strikes laws, and the like (Harrison & Beck, 2005). Comparing 2003 with 1995, the greatest percentage increases in the inmate population were for people 55 years of age or older (85 percent), followed by those ages 45 to 54 (77 percent), with the two groups totaling about 251,000 prisoners (Harrison & Beck, 2004).

The release of death statistics lags incarceration statistics, but there were 3,311 deaths in state and federal prisons in 2001: 57 were killed by another person and 60 were executed. With an aging population of inmates, prison "nursing homes" are a current reality (*Sourcebook of Criminal Justice Statistics*, 2004, Table 6.76.2004). Inmates have long faced the prospect of having their unclaimed remains buried in prison potter's fields, often with no marker or ceremony.

Social Work Intervention
Before and after the Death of a Client

The role of social workers reaches beyond the significant contributions made to clients and loved ones in the process of assisting with the complex issues surrounding death and dying. In many cases, social workers may prevent an individual potter's field burial by implementing a range of interventions designed to secure a dignified and respectful final disposition.

Legal requirements. Learn the legal requirements and local regulations and practices regarding indigent, unknown, or unclaimed bodies in the state and local community in which you practice.

Although each state develops its own policies, responsibility has usually been passed on to some local entity, usually a county or city government. Knowledge of local practice helps establish the parameters of interventions. It is important to establish a time frame for action—how long do you have to locate family or resources before the deceased is removed for a potter's field burial?

Government agencies. Contact the Social Security Administration, state or local human resources departments, federal and state Departments of Veterans Affairs, and other public assistance programs available in your area as soon as possible. At a minimum, almost every U.S. resident is entitled to receive a $255 social security death benefit.

VA burial benefits. A *veteran* is "a person who served in the active military, naval, or air service and who was discharged or released under conditions other than dishonorable" (U.S. Department of Veterans Affairs, 2003, para. 2). No veteran need be buried in a potter's field. The VA itself asks to be contacted to check whether any unclaimed person, male or female, qualifies for veteran's burial benefits; the VA checks identities against a database. All veterans are entitled to a variety of burial-related benefits, as in some cases are their spouses and even some dependents. So when contacting the VA, spousal information may also be helpful. Note that a man's spouse may be a veteran, even if he is not.

Collect and revise client Information. Collection and periodic revision of personal, financial, medical, and end-of-life information for a client might avoid later difficulties. Many agencies are using electronic documentation to facilitate this process, and gathering key information is already a standard part of the intake process for most assisted-living facilities, nursing homes, and so forth. Examples of pertinent information include death notification contact information; the location of wills; prearranged funeral and burial plans; segregated funds earmarked for burial expenses; wishes of the deceased regarding his or her care after death; information regarding cash, wages due or anticipated, income, savings, securities, bonds, insurance policies (including travel, auto, and credit cards), and retirement funds and accounts; client's real estate assets; vehicles owned; livestock; collections of potential monetary or emotional value; labor union membership (which may include death benefits); armed forces information (including spousal service for both genders); membership in professional, civic, or fraternal organizations; and legal residence status in the United States or other nations (U.S. citizens and residents may have accrued benefits on social insurance programs of other countries by living or working there; this is most common for refugees from Europe). Request and record all other names the client may have used—maiden name, married names other than the current name, nickname, birth name used before adoption, or name change as a result of an abusive relationship may be among the key information to be obtained.

Accessing local resources. Depending on where one practices, many organizations offer burial assistance for their members or for members of the public. Many religious organizations, such as the Jewish Federation and the St. Vincent DePaul Society, for example, have special programs for assisting coreligionists in need; professional and labor organizations, such as Actor's Equity, and fraternal and sororal groups such as the Masons, Eastern Star, and

the Knights of Columbus may all have burial benefits for members and families. Local groups may also bury individuals with dignity, such as the Garden of Angels in Desert Lawn Memorial Park outside Los Angeles, which provides burial and funeral services for abandoned babies (Roche, 2000). In many communities, organizations that advocate for the most vulnerable residents compile and distribute publications with titles such as "A Guide to Burial Assistance"; these often serve as a helpful introduction to local resources and contacts at key government agencies.

Bureau of Indian Affairs. For those deceased clients who are, or might be, members of a legally recognized Native American tribe or Alaska Native community, social workers should contact a representative of the group's governing body, from which burial assistance might be available. For example, the Cherokee Nation may provide substantial burial assistance in a means-tested program; information is available from www.cherokee.org.

Foreign nationals. If the client needing a place of eternal rest is an immigrant, it might be helpful to contact the consulate of his or her native country (if known). A consulate may be able to offer suggestions and concrete resources to assist in a burial or in contacting family members living abroad. For example, Mexican consulates have brochures available in English and Spanish offering detailed advice and suggestions to people assisting in the provision of final arrangements for Mexican nationals.

Scientific identification resources. Before an unidentified client is interred or cremated, try to ensure that key data necessary for identification—typically, photographs, fingerprints, DNA samples, dental records, and visual records—have been collected and preserved.

Posting and seeking information on websites to identify unknown people. Many states, communities, and private organizations, through police departments or other government agencies, have a Web page with photos, drawings, or other unique markers or possessions, including dental information, of deceased individuals to aid in identification. The Mexican government is testing such a system for filing missing-persons reports in Mexico or in consulates located in the United States (Carroll, 2005). For example, one such well-established site is the Doe Network: International Center for Unidentified and Missing Persons (www.doenetwork.org), which also links to the North American Missing Persons Network. A social worker can assist by posting information about a missing person or in searching for loved ones or friends of an unknown person. These sites may also be very useful after natural disasters. In time, these types of registries may grow in sophistication, completeness, and importance in the search for missing people and in the identification of relatives or friends of unclaimed people or of unclaimed bodies.

Encouraging community generosity. Actively encourage the generosity of individuals, community groups, or other private, religious, or governmental groups who might donate goods and services or participate in fundraising for a particular burial. For example, on May 21, 2005, more than 200 people attended a funeral mass in Rockaway, New York, for an unidentified three-year-old child who had been found on a nearby beach with broken ribs and vertebrae. The child was named John Valentine Hope by the officiating pastor, who commented that the tragedy of a violent death was worsened by a "violence of silence" by the boy's parents, who never claimed him. "It's the violence of silence that makes this mystery continue," he said. The ceremony did offer comfort to the community, however (Kilgannon, 2005, p. 38).

Final Thoughts
Implications for Policy

Although advocacy for broad-based policy reformulation transcends the primary aims of this article, policy changes could alleviate future distress for clients and workers. Success in the profession's continuing efforts to address some issues—such as poverty, income inequality, and benefit levels—will help avoid some indigent burials. In addition, social workers could educate and influence clients, the general public, and policymakers by advocating on the following issues.

Acknowledgement and discussion. Public discussion of indigent burials; the risks of an indigent burial for the individual; local, state, and national issues relating to indigent burials; and the scope of the numbers of people potentially affected may raise public awareness of the issue. Death and burial should not be veiled, entering public discussion only in times of crisis.

Increase the social security death benefit. Beginning in September 1960, the Social Security Administration allowed the one-time, lump-sum death payment of $255 to be assigned to funeral homes. The estates of all people who have met the qualifications for social security protection qualify for this payment, which has not been increased for more than 40 years (Social Security Administration, 2004). If the final payment had been indexed for inflation, the value of this lump-sum death payment would have risen to at least $1,000. Such a final payment would go a long way toward avoiding indigent burials (DeNavas-Walt et al., 2005, p. 30). Social workers could include death benefit entitlement among social security policy debates.

Veterans benefit enhancement. Although veterans are guaranteed a respectful burial somewhere, if they wish to be buried in a particular location, perhaps on a family plot in a private cemetery, the VA may subsidize the burial with a small amount of money (up to $600) and a marker or headstone. This subsidy, too, has not been raised in decades (U.S. Department of Veterans Affairs, 2003). Enhancement would facilitate burial in cemeteries close to family and friends.

Clarification of state and local responsibilities. Many laws and implementing regulations regarding indigent burials are obsolete and based on outdated assumptions. If proposals to clarify responsibility for final dispositions come before legislative bodies, input from social workers might support protection for future clients. At the least, unfunded mandates might be opposed.

Social workers have a unique opportunity to ensure a respectful funeral and burial for clients. Securing a dignified and respectful disposition of a person's body will in many cases allow family and loved ones the opportunity to grieve and mourn by having an identifiable permanent resting place to honor their loved one. Most of us "would want to feel that our loved one is 'all right' even though

dead" (Kastenbaum, 2005, p. 6). Death marks both an ending and a beginning for family, friends, and community; our treatment of the dead also serves as a marker for our respect for the living. In earlier times, this observation would have been almost a truism. As William E. Gladstone so famously remarked more than 125 years ago, "Show me the manner in which a nation cares for its dead, and I will measure with mathematical exactness the tender mercies of its people, their respect for the laws of the land and their loyalty to high ideals" (Murray, 2000).

References

Ariès, P. (1974). *Western attitudes towards death from the Middle Ages to the present.* Baltimore: Johns Hopkins University Press.

Brickey, H. (2005, February 20). Grave consequences. *The Blade.* Retrieved July 5, 2007, from www.toledoblade.com/apps/pbcs .dll/section?Category=ARCHIVES

Carroll, S. (2005, May 21). Mexico database to ID border-crosser bodies. *Arizona Republic.* Retrieved August 10, 2005, from www.wkconline.org/resources/word/Carroll-Bodies.doc

Centers for Disease Control and Prevention. (2003). *U.S. standard certificate of death* (Rev. 11/2003). Retrieved June 25, 2006, from cdc.gov/nchs/data/dus/DEATH11-03final.pdf

Corn, L. (2000). New York City's potter's field: A visit to Hart Island's City Cemetery in Bronx County: *New York Genealogical and Biographical Society Newsletter,* Summer. Retrieved January 24, 2005, from www.newyorkfamilyhistory .org/modules.php?name=Sections&op=printpage&artid=60

Cremation Association of North America. (1998). *1996/1997 cremation container, disposition and service survey.* Chicago: Author. Retrieved June 26, 2006, from http:// cremationassociation.org/docs/dreport.pdf

Cremation Association of North America. (2006). *Confirmed 2003 statistics.* Chicago: Author. Retrieved June 26, 2006, from http://cremationassociation.org/docs/WebConfirmed.pdf

Crumley, A. (2002, May 10). Coroner's office making the best of a difficult situation. *The Courthouse Journal, 18,* 17–18. (Reprinted from "Coroner's office making the best of a difficult situation," by A. Crumley, April 27, 2002, *Port Orchard Independent*)

Cullinan, K. (2005, July 20). Indigent burials on the increase. *Sarasota Herald-Tribune.* Retrieved August 15, 2005, from www.heraldtribune.com/apps/ pbcs.dll/section?CATEGORY= HELP05&template=ovr2

Deaths on border of Arizona strain morgue's capacity. (2005, September 4). *New York Times,* p. A21.

DeNavas-Walt, C., Proctor, B. D., & Lee, C. H. (2005). *Income, poverty, and health insurance coverage in the United States: 2004* (Current Population Reports P60-229). Washington, DC: U.S. Census Bureau.

Dressel, W. G. (2003, January 29). *Indigent burial costs.* Trenton: New Jersey State League of Municipalities. Retrieved September 9, 2003, from www.njslom.org//m1012903b.html

Gove, P. B. (Ed.). (1976). *Webster's third new international dictionary of the English language, Unabridged.* Springfield, MA: G. & C. Merriam.

Harrison, P. M., & Beck, A. J. (2004, November). Prisoners in 2003 (NCJ205335). *Bureau of Justice Statistics Bulletin.* Retrieved May 5, 2005, from www.ojp.usdoj.gov/bjs/abstract/p03.htm

Harrison, P. M., & Beck, A. J. (2005, April). Prison and jail inmates at midyear 2004 (NCJ208801). *Bureau of Justice Statistics Bulletin*. Retrieved May 5, 2005, from www.ojp.usdoj .gov/bjs/pub/pdf/pjim04.pdf

Hoyert, D. L., Heron, M. P., Murphy, S. L., & Kung, H. (2006). Deaths: Final data for 2003. *National Vital Statistics Reports, 54*(13). Hyattsville, MD: National Center for Health Statistics.

Hunt, M., & Sternfeld, J. (1998). *Hart Island*. Zurich: Scalo Editions.

Kastenbaum, R. (2004). Why funerals. *Generations: Journal of the American Society on Aging, 28(2),* 5–10.

Kilgannon, C. (2005, May 22). Honoring an unknown child found on a beach, and a long-lost Vietnam War pilot. *New York Times*, p. 38.

MacDorman, M. F., Hoyert, D. L., Matin, J. A., Munson, M. L., & Hamilton, B. E. (2007). Fetal and perinatal mortality, United States, 2003. *National Vital Statistics Reports, 55(6)*. Retrieved February 23, 2007, from www.cdc.gov/nchs/data/nvsr/nvsr55/ nvsr55_06.pdf

Maricopa County Office of Management and Budget. (2000, February 17). *Indigent burial rates in Maricopa County* [Research Report] (Catalog No. 00-006). Phoenix, AZ: Author.

Miniño, A. M., Heron, M. P., & Smith, B. L. (2006). Deaths: Preliminary data for 2004. *National Vital Statistics Reports, 54*(19). Retrieved June 25, 2006, from www. cdc.gov/nchs/data/ nvsr/nvsr54/nvsr54_19.pdf

Murray, V. H. (2000). A "right" of the dead and a charge on the quick: Criminal laws relating to cemeteries, burial grounds and human remains. *Journal of the Missouri Bar, 56*(2). Retrieved September 1, 2005, from www.mobar.org/journal/2000/marapr/ murray.htm

National Institutes of Health. (2003, November 19). NICHD funds major effort to determine extent and causes of stillbirth. *NIH News*. Retrieved August 24, 2005, from www.nichd.nih.gov/ news/releases/stillbirth.cfm

New York City Department of Corrections. (1967). *Potter's Field historical resume: 1869–1967*. New York: Author. Retrieved January 15, 2005, from www.correctionhistory.org/html/ chronicl/hart/html/hartbook2.html

New York City Department of Health and Mental Hygiene, Bureau of Vital Statistics. (2005). *Summary of vital statistics 2004, The City of New York*. New York: Author.

New York State Cemetery Board. (2001). *Cemetery and crematory operations: Relevant laws, administrative rules & regulations of the New York State Cemetery Board*. Albany, NY: Author.

Parkes, C., Laungani, P., & Young, B. (1997). *Death and bereavement across cultures*. London: Routledge.

Revised Code of Washington. Disposal of remains of indigent persons, c 4, § 36.39.030 (1993).

Risen, C. (2002). Hart Island. *The Morning News*. Retrieved August 27, 2005, from www.themorningnews.org/archives/new_york_new_ york/hart_island.php

Roche, T. (2000). A refuge for throwaways. *Time, 155*(7). Retrieved July 5, 2007, from www.time.com/time/magazine/ article/0,9171,996127,00.html

Schulman, Ronca, & Bucuvalas, Inc. (2003). *2003 VBA survey of medical examiners' and coroners' process in identification of unclaimed remains for veteran status*. Silver Spring, MD: Author.

Social Security Administration. (2004). *Social Security handbook: Your basic guide to social security programs*. Baltimore: Author. Retrieved June 26, 2006, from www.ssa.gov/OP_Home/ handbook/ssa-hbk.htm

Sourcebook of Criminal Justice Statistics. (2004). *Table 6.76.2004: Number and rate (per 100,000 prisoners) of deaths among state and federal prisoners: By cause of death, 2001*. Albany, NY: Author. Retrieved August 13, 2005, from www.albany.edu/ sourcebook/pdf/t6762004.pdf

U.S. Department of Veterans Affairs. (2003). *Burial of unclaimed, indigent veterans*. Retrieved May 5, 2004, from www.vba .va.gov/bln/21/topics/indigent/index.htm

Wilkinson, M. (2001, November 14). Requirements for county burials clarified. *York News-Times*. Retrieved July 18, 2005, from www.yorknewstimes.com/stories/111401/1oc_1114010019 .shtml

GRACIELA M. CASTEX, EdD, ACSW, LMSW, is associate professor, Social Work Program, Lehman College, City University of New York, 250 Bedford Park Boulevard, West Bronx, NY 10468-1589; e-mail: graciela.castex@lehman.cuny.edu.

UNIT 8

Bereavement

Unit Selections

Key Points to Consider

- Discuss how the seven stages of grieving over death can also be applied to losses through divorce, moving from one place to another, or the amputation of a limb (arm or leg). What is the relationship between time and the feelings of grief experienced within the bereavement process?

- Describe the four necessary tasks of mourning. What are some of the practical steps one can take in accomplishing each of these tasks? How can one assist friends in bereavement?

- What are the special problems encountered in the death or a child and in a perinatal death? How can one assist friends in this special type of bereavement?

- How can one know if one is experiencing "normal" bereavement or "abnormal" bereavement? What are some of the signs of aberrant bereavement? What could you do to assist people experiencing abnormal grief symptoms?

- Provide a list of "dos" and "don'ts" for dealing with children who have experienced a death.

- How are bereavement needs of children and young adults different than those of adults?

Student Website

www.mhhe.com/cls

Internet References

Bereaved Families of Ontario Support Center
www.bereavedfamilies.net
The Compassionate Friends
www.compassionatefriends.org
Practical Grief Resources
www.indiana.edu/~famlygrf/sitemap.html
Widow Net
www.widownet.org

In American society many act as if the process of bereavement is completed with the culmination of public mourning related to the funeral or memorial service and the final disposition of the dead. For those in the process of grieving, the end of public mourning only serves to make the bereavement process a more individualized, subjective, and private experience. Private mourning of loss for most people, while more intense at its beginning, continues throughout their lifetime. The nature and intensity of this experience is influenced by the relationship of the mourner to the deceased, the age of the mourner, and the social context in which bereavement takes place.

This unit on bereavement begins with two general articles on the bereavement process. The first article, by Michael Leming and George Dickinson, describes and discusses the active coping strategies related to the bereavement process and the four tasks of bereavement. The second article, by Kenneth Doka, provides an alternative perspective on the understanding of the bereavement process. The third article, by Charles Corr, enhances and broadens the concept of disenfranchised grief in significant ways and explains that there are aspects of most losses that are indeed disenfranchised.

The article by Therese Rando ("The Increasing Prevalence of Complicated Mourning") illustrates the principles described

© Getty Images/Purestock

by Leming, Dickinson, and Doka by providing a critique of America's health-care industry for its lack of involvement in the post-death grieving experience. The final articles are focused upon bereavement and coping strategies employed by a special population of grievers.

The Grieving Process

Michael R. Leming and George E. Dickinson

Grief is a very powerful emotion that is often triggered or stimulated by death. Thomas Attig makes an important distinction between grief and the grieving process. Although grief is an emotion that engenders feelings of helplessness and passivity, the process of grieving is a more complex coping process that presents challenges and opportunities for the griever and requires energy to be invested, tasks to be undertaken, and choices to be made (Attig, 1991).

Most people believe that grieving is a diseaselike and debilitating process that renders the individual passive and helpless. According to Attig (1991, p. 389):

It is misleading and dangerous to mistake grief for the whole of the experience of the bereaved. It is misleading because the experience is far more complex, entailing diverse emotional, physical, intellectual, spiritual, and social impacts. It is dangerous because it is precisely this aspect of the experience of the bereaved that is potentially the most frustrating and debilitating.

Death ascribes to the griever a passive social position in the bereavement role. Grief is an emotion over which the individual has no control. However, understanding that grieving is an active coping process can restore to the griever a sense of autonomy in which the process is permeated with choice and there are many areas over which the griever does have some control.

Coping with Grief

The grieving process, like the dying process, is essentially a series of behaviors and attitudes related to coping with the stressful situation of a change in the status of a relationship. Many individuals have attempted to understand coping with dying as a series of universal, mutually exclusive, and linear stages. Not all people, however, will progress through the stages in the same manner.

Seven behaviors and feelings that are part of the coping process are identified by Robert Kavanaugh (1972): shock and denial, disorganization, volatile emotions, guilt, loss and loneliness, relief, and reestablishment. It is not difficult to see similarities between these behaviors and Kübler-Ross's five stages (denial, anger, bargaining, depression, and acceptance) of the dying process. According to Kavanaugh (1972, p. 23), "these seven stages do not subscribe to the logic of the head as

much as to the irrational tugs of the heart—the logic of need and permission."

Shock and Denial

Even when a significant other is expected to die, at the time of death there is often a sense in which the death is not real. For most of us our first response is, "No, this can't be true." With time, our experience of shock diminishes, but we find new ways to deny the reality of death.

Some believe that denial is dysfunctional behavior for those in bereavement. However, denial not only is a common experience among the newly bereaved but also serves positive functions in the process of adaptation. The main function of denial is to provide the bereaved with a "temporary safe place" from the ugly realities of a social world that offers only loneliness and pain.

With time, the meaning of loss tends to expand, and it may be impossible for one to deal with all of the social meanings of death at once. For example, if a man's wife dies, not only does he lose his spouse, but also his best friend, his sexual partner, the mother of his children, a source of income, and so on. Denial can protect an individual from some of the magnitude of this social loss, which may be unbearable at times. With denial, one can work through different aspects of loss over time.

Disorganization

Disorganization is the stage in the bereavement process in which one may feel totally out of touch with the reality of everyday life. Some go through the 2- to 3-day time period just before the funeral as if on "automatic pilot" or "in a daze." Nothing normal "makes sense," and they may feel that life has no inherent meaning. For some, death is perceived as preferable to life, which appears to be devoid of meaning.

This emotional response is also a normal experience for the newly bereaved. Confusion is normal for those whose social world has been disorganized through death. When Michael Leming's father died, his mother lost not only all of those things that one loses with a death of a spouse, but also her caregiving role—a social role and master status that had defined her identity in the 5 years that her husband lived with cancer. It is only natural to experience confusion and social disorganization when one's social identity has been destroyed.

Volatile Reactions

Whenever one's identity and social order face the possibility of destruction, there is a natural tendency to feel angry, frustrated, helpless, and/or hurt. The volatile reactions of terror, hatred, resentment, and jealousy are often experienced as emotional manifestations of these feelings. Grieving humans are sometimes more successful at masking their feelings in socially acceptable behaviors than other animals, whose instincts cause them to go into a fit of rage when their order is threatened by external forces. However apparently dissimilar, the internal emotional experience is similar.

In working with bereaved persons over the past 20 years, Michael Lemming has observed that the following become objects of volatile grief reactions: God, medical personnel, funeral directors, other family members, in-laws, friends who have not experienced death in their families, and/or even the person who has died. Mild-mannered individuals may become raging and resentful persons when grieving. Some of these people have experienced physical symptoms such as migraine headaches, ulcers, neuropathy, and colitis as a result of living with these intense emotions.

The expression of anger seems more natural for men than expressing other feelings (Golden, 2000). Expressing anger requires taking a stand. This is quite different from the mechanics of sadness, where an open and vulnerable stance is more common. Men may find their grief through anger. Rage may suddenly become tears, as deep feelings trigger other deep feelings. This process is reversed with women, notes Golden. Many times a woman will be in tears, crying and crying, and state that she is angry.

As noted earlier, a person's anger during grief can range from being angry with the person who died to being angry with God, and all points in between. Golden's mentor, Father William Wendt, shared the story of his visits with a widow and his working with her on her grief. He noticed that many times when he arrived she was driving her car up and down the driveway. One day he asked her what she was doing. She proceeded to tell him that she had a ritual she used in dealing with her grief. She would come home, go to the living room, and get her recently deceased husband's ashes out of the urn on the mantle. She would take a very small amount and place them on the driveway. She then said, "It helps me to run over the son of a bitch every day." He concluded the story by saying, "Now that is good grief." It was "good" grief because it was this woman's way of connecting to and expressing the anger component of her grief.

Guilt

Guilt is similar to the emotional reactions discussed earlier. Guilt is anger and resentment turned in on oneself and often results in self-deprecation and depression. It typically manifests itself in statements like "If only I had . . . ," "I should have . . . ," "I could have done it differently . . . ," and "Maybe I did the wrong thing." Guilt is a normal part of the bereavement process.

From a sociological perspective, guilt can become a social mechanism to resolve the **dissonance** that people feel when unable to explain why someone else's loved one has died. Rather than view death as something that can happen at any time to anyone, people can **blame the victim** of bereavement and believe that the victim of bereavement was in some way responsible for the death—"If the individual had been a better parent, the child might not have been hit by the car," or "If I had been married to that person, I might also have committed suicide," or "No wonder that individual died of a heart attack, the spouse's cooking would give anyone high cholesterol." Therefore, bereaved persons are sometimes encouraged to feel guilt because they are subtly sanctioned by others' reactions.

Loss and Loneliness

Feelings of loss and loneliness creep in as denial subsides. The full experience of the loss does not hit all at once. It becomes more evident as bereaved individuals resume a social life without their loved one. They realize how much they needed and depended upon their significant other. Social situations in which we expected them always to be present seem different now that they are gone. Holiday celebrations are also diminished by their absence. In fact, for some, most of life takes on a "something's missing" feeling. This feeling was captured in the 1960s love song "End of the World."

> Why does the world go on turning?
>
> Why must the sea rush to shore?
>
> Don't they know it's the end of the world
>
> Cause you don't love me anymore?

Loss and loneliness are often transformed into depression and sadness, fed by feelings of self-pity. According to Kavanaugh (1972, p. 118), this effect is magnified by the fact that the dead loved one grows out of focus in memory—"an elf becomes a giant, a sinner becomes a saint because the grieving heart needs giants and saints to fill an expanding void." Even a formerly undesirable spouse, such as an alcoholic, is missed in a way that few can understand unless their own hearts are involved. This is a time in the grieving process when anybody is better than nobody, and being alone only adds to the curse of loss and loneliness (Kavanaugh, 1972).

Those who try to escape this experience will either turn to denial in an attempt to reject their feelings of loss or try to find surrogates—new friends at a bar, a quick remarriage, or a new pet. This escape can never be permanent, however, because loss and loneliness are a necessary part of the bereavement experience. According to Kavanaugh (1972, p. 119), the "ultimate goal in conquering loneliness" is to build a new independence or to find a new and equally viable relationship.

Relief

The experience of relief in the midst of the bereavement process may seem odd for some and add to their feelings of guilt. Michael Leming observed a friend's relief 6 months after her husband died. This older friend was the wife of a minister, and her whole life before he died was his ministry. With time, as she built a new world of social involvements and relationships of which he was not a part, she discovered a new independent person in herself whom she perceived was a better person than she had ever before been.

Relief can give rise to feelings of guilt. However, according to Kavanaugh (1972, p. 121): "The feeling of relief does not imply any criticism for the love we lost. Instead, it is a reflection of our need for ever deeper love, our quest for someone or something always better, our search for the infinite, that best and perfect love religious people name as God."

Reestablishment

As one moves toward reestablishment of a life without the deceased, it is obvious that the process involves extensive adjustment and time, especially if the relationship was meaningful. It is likely that one may have feelings of loneliness, guilt, and disorganization at the same time and that just when one may experience a sense of relief, something will happen to trigger a denial of the death.

What facilitates bereavement and adjustment is fully experiencing each of these feelings as normal and realizing that it is hope (holding the grieving person together in fantasy at first) that will provide the promise of a new life filled with order, purpose, and meaning.

Reestablishment occurs gradually, and often we realize it has been achieved long after it has occurred. In some ways it is similar to Dorothy's realization at the end of *The Wizard of Oz*—she had always possessed the magic that could return her to Kansas. And, like Dorothy, we have to experience our loss before we really appreciate the joy of investing our lives again in new relationships.

Four Tasks of Mourning

In 1982 J. William Worden published *Grief Counseling and Grief Therapy*, which summarized the research conclusions of a National Institutes of Health study called the Omega Project (occasionally referred to as the Harvard Bereavement Study). Two of the more significant findings of this research, displaying the active nature of the grieving process, are that mourning is necessary for all persons who have experienced a loss through death and that four tasks of mourning must be accomplished before mourning can be completed and reestablishment can take place.

According to Worden (1982), unfinished grief tasks can impair further growth and development of the individual. Furthermore, the necessity of these tasks suggests that those in bereavement must attend to "grief work" because successful grief resolution is not automatic, as Kavanaugh's (1972) stages might imply. Each bereaved person must accomplish four necessary tasks: (1) accept the reality of the loss, (2) experience the pain of grief, (3) adjust to an environment in which the deceased person is missing, and (4) withdraw emotional energy and reinvest it in another relationship (Worden, 1982).

Accept the Reality of the Loss

Especially in situations when death is unexpected and/or the deceased lived far away, it is difficult to conceptualize the reality of the loss. The first task of mourning is to overcome the

natural denial response and realize that the person is dead and will not return.

Bereaved persons can facilitate the actualization of death in many ways. The traditional ways are to view the body, attend the funeral and committal services, and visit the place of final disposition. The following is a partial list of additional activities that can assist in making death real for grieving persons.

1. View the body at the place of death before preparation by the funeral director.
2. Talk about the deceased person and the circumstances surrounding the death.
3. View photographs and personal effects of the deceased person.
4. Distribute the possessions of the deceased person among relatives and friends.

Experience the Pain of Grief

Part of coming to grips with the reality of death is experiencing the emotional and physical pain caused by the loss. Many people in the denial stage of grieving attempt to avoid pain by choosing to reject the emotions and feelings that they are experiencing. As discussed by Erich Lindemann (1944), some do this by avoiding places and circumstances that remind them of the deceased. Michael Leming knows one widow who quit playing golf and quit eating at a particular restaurant because these were activities that she had enjoyed with her husband. Another widow found it extremely painful to be with her dead husband's twin, even though he and her sister-in-law were her most supportive friends.

Worden (1982, pp. 13–14) cites the following case study to illustrate the performance of this task of mourning:

> One young woman minimized her loss by believing her brother was out of his dark place and into a better place after his suicide. This might not have been true, but it kept her from feeling her intense anger at him for leaving her. In treatment, when she first allowed herself to feel anger, she said, "I'm angry with his behavior and not him!" Finally she was able to acknowledge this anger directly.

The problem with the avoidance strategy is that people cannot escape the pain associated with mourning. According to Bowlby (cited by Worden, 1982, p. 14), "Sooner or later, some of those who avoid all conscious grieving, break down—usually with some form of depression." Tears can afford cleansing for wounds created by loss, and fully experiencing the pain ultimately provides wonderful relief to those who suffer while eliminating long-term chronic grief.

Assume New Social Roles

The third task, practical in nature, requires the griever to take on some of the social roles performed by the deceased person or to find others who will. According to Worden (1982), to abort this task is to become helpless by refusing to develop the skills necessary in daily living and by ultimately withdrawing from life.

An acquaintance of Michael Leming's refused to adjust to the social environment in which she found herself after the death of her husband. He was her business partner, as well as her best and only friend. After 30 years of marriage, they had no children, and she had no close relatives. She had never learned to drive a car. Her entire social world had been controlled by her former husband. Three weeks after his funeral she went into the basement and committed suicide.

The alternative to withdrawing is assuming new social roles by taking on additional responsibilities. Extended families who always gathered at Grandma's house for Thanksgiving will be tempted to have a number of small Thanksgiving dinners at different places after her death. The members of this family may believe that "no one can take Grandma's place." Although this may be true, members of the extended family will grieve better if someone else is willing to do Grandma's work, enabling the entire family to come together for Thanksgiving. Not to do so will cause double pain—the family will not gather, and Grandma will still be missed.

Reinvest in New Relationships

The final task of mourning is a difficult one for many because they feel disloyal or unfaithful in withdrawing emotional energy from their dead loved one. One of Michael Leming's family members once said that she could never love another man after her husband died. His twice-widowed aunt responded, "I once felt like that, but I now consider myself to be fortunate to have been married to two of the best men in the world."

Other people find themselves unable to reinvest in new relationships because they are unwilling to experience again the pain caused by loss. The quotation from John Brantner at the beginning of this chapter provides perspective on this problem: "Only people who avoid love can avoid grief. The point is to learn from it and remain vulnerable to love."

However, those who are able to withdraw emotional energy and reinvest it in other relationships find the possibility of a newly established social life. Kavanaugh (1972, pp. 122–123) depicts this situation well with the following description:

At this point fantasies fade into constructive efforts to reach out and build anew. The phone is answered more quickly, the door as well, and meetings seem important, invitations are treasured and any social gathering becomes an opportunity rather than a curse. Mementos of the past are put away for occasional family gatherings. New clothes and new places promise dreams instead of only fears. Old friends are important for encouragement and permission to rebuild one's life. New friends can offer realistic opportunities for coming out from under the grieving mantle. With newly acquired friends, one is not a widow, widower, or survivor—just a person. Life begins again at the point of new friendships. All the rest is of yesterday, buried, unimportant to the now and tomorrow.

Disenfranchised Grief

KENNETH J. DOKA

Introduction

Ever since the publication of Lindemann's classic article, "Symptomatology and Management of Acute Grief," the literature on the nature of grief and bereavement has been growing. In the few decades following this seminal study, there have been comprehensive studies of grief reactions, detailed descriptions of atypical manifestations of grief, theoretical and clinical treatments of grief reactions, and considerable research considering the myriad variables that affect grief. But most of this literature has concentrated on grief reactions in socially recognized and sanctioned roles: those of the parent, spouse, or child.

There are circumstances, however, in which a person experiences a sense of loss but does not have a socially recognized right, role, or capacity to grieve. In these cases, the grief is disenfranchised. The person suffers a loss but has little or no opportunity to mourn publicly.

Up until now, there has been little research touching directly on the phenomenon of disenfranchised grief. In her comprehensive review of grief reactions, Raphael notes the phenomenon:

There may be other dyadic partnership relationships in adult life that show patterns similar to the conjugal ones, among them, the young couple intensely, even secretly, in love; the defacto relationships; the extramarital relationship; and the homosexual couple.... Less intimate partnerships of close friends, working mates, and business associates, may have similar patterns of grief and mourning.

Focusing on the issues, reactions, and problems in particular populations, a number of studies have noted special difficulties that these populations have in grieving. For example, Kelly and Kimmel, in studies of aging homosexuals, have discussed the unique problems of grief in such relationships. Similarly, studies of the reactions of significant others of AIDS victims have considered bereavement. Other studies have considered the special problems of unacknowledged grief in prenatal death, [the death of] ex-spouses, therapists' reactions to a client's suicide, and pet loss. Finally, studies of families of Alzheimer's victims and mentally retarded adults also have noted distinct difficulties of these populations in encountering varied losses which are often unrecognized by others.

Others have tried to draw parallels between related unacknowledged losses. For example, in a personal account, Horn compared her loss of a heterosexual lover with a friend's loss of a homosexual partner. Doka discussed the particular problems of loss in nontraditional relationships, such as extramarital affairs, homosexual relationships, and cohabiting couples.

This article attempts to integrate the literature on such losses in order to explore the phenomenon of disenfranchised grief. It will consider both the nature of disenfranchised grief and its central paradoxical problem: the very nature of this type of grief exacerbates the problems of grief, but the usual sources of support may not be available or helpful.

The Nature of Disenfranchised Grief

Disenfranchised grief can be defined as the grief that persons experience when they incur a loss that is not or cannot be openly acknowledged, publicly mourned, or socially supported. The concept of disenfranchised grief recognizes that societies have sets of norms—in effect, "grieving rules"—that attempt to specify who, when, where, how, how long, and for whom people should grieve. These grieving rules may be codified in personnel policies. For example, a worker may be allowed a week off for the death of a spouse or child, three days for the loss of a parent or sibling. Such policies reflect the fact that each society defines who has a legitimate right to grieve, and these definitions of right correspond to relationships, primarily familial, that are socially recognized and sanctioned. In any given society these grieving rules may not correspond to the nature of attachments, the sense of loss, or the feelings of survivors. Hence the grief of these survivors is disenfranchised. In our society, this may occur for three reasons.

1. The Relationship Is Not Recognized

In our society, most attention is placed on kin-based relationships and roles. Grief may be disenfranchised in those situations in which the relationship between the bereaved and deceased is not based on recognizable kin ties. Here the closeness of other non-kin relationships may simply not be understood or appreciated. For example, Folta and Deck noted, "While all of these studies tell us that grief is a normal phenomenon, the intensity of which corresponds to the closeness of the relationship, they fail to take this (i.e., friendship) into account. The underlying assumption is that closeness of relationship exists only among spouses and/or immediate kin." The roles of lovers, friends, neighbors, foster parents, colleagues, in-laws, stepparents and stepchildren, caregivers, counselors, co-workers, and room-mates (for example, in nursing homes) may be long-lasting and intensely interactive, but even though these relationships are recognized, mourners may not have full opportunity to publicly grieve a loss. At most, they might be expected to support and assist family members.

Then there are relationships that may not be publicly recognized or socially sanctioned. For example, nontraditional relationships, such as extramarital affairs, cohabitation, and homosexual relationships have tenuous public acceptance and limited legal standing, and they face negative sanctions within the larger community. Those involved in such relationships are touched by grief when the relationship is terminated by the death of the partner, but others in their world, such as children, may also experience grief that cannot be acknowledged or socially supported.

Even those whose relationships existed primarily in the past may experience grief. Ex-spouses, past lovers, or former friends may have limited contact, or they may not even engage in inter-action in the present. Yet the death of that significant other can still cause a grief reaction because it brings finality to that earlier loss, ending any remaining contact or fantasy of reconciliation or reinvolvement. And again these grief feelings may be shared by others in their world such as parents and children. They too may mourn the loss of "what once was" and "what might have been." For example, in one case a twelve-year-old child of an unwed mother, never even acknowledged or seen by the father, still mourned the death of his father since it ended any possibil-ity of a future liaison. But though loss is experienced, society as a whole may not perceive that the loss of a past relationship could or should cause any reaction.

2. The Loss Is Not Recognized

In other cases, the loss itself is not socially defined as signifi-cant. Perinatal deaths lead to strong grief reactions, yet research indicates that many significant others still perceive the loss to be relatively minor. Abortions too can constitute a serious loss, but the abortion can take place without the knowledge or sanc-tions of others, or even the recognition that a loss has occurred. It may very well be that the very ideologies of the abortion con-troversy can put the bereaved in a difficult position. Many who affirm a loss may not sanction the act of abortion, while some who sanction the act may minimize any sense of loss. Similarly, we are just becoming aware of the sense of loss that people experience in giving children up for adoption or foster care, and we have yet to be aware of the grief-related implications of surrogate motherhood.

Another loss that may not be perceived as significant is the loss of a pet. Nevertheless, the research shows strong ties between pets and humans, and profound reactions to loss.

Then there are cases in which the reality of the loss itself is not socially validated. Thanatologists have long recognized that significant losses can occur even when the object of the loss remains physically alive. Sudnow for example, discusses "social death," in which the person is alive but is treated as if dead. Examples may include those who are institutionalized or comatose. Similarly, "psychological death" has been defined as conditions in which the person lacks a consciousness of exis-tence, such as someone who is "brain dead." One can also speak of "psychosocial death" in which the persona of someone has changed so significantly, through mental illness, organic brain syndromes, or even significant personal transformation (such as through addiction, conversion, and so forth), that signifi-cant others perceive the person as he or she previously existed as dead. In all of these cases, spouses and others may experi-ence a profound sense of loss, but that loss cannot be publicly acknowledged for the person is still biologically alive.

3. The Griever Is Not Recognized

Finally, there are situations in which the characteristics of the bereaved in effect disenfranchise their grief. Here the person is not socially defined as capable of grief; therefore, there is little or no social recognition of his or her sense of loss or need to mourn. Despite evidence to the contrary, both the very old and the very young are typically perceived by others as having little comprehension of or reaction to the death of a significant other. Often, then, both young children and aged adults are excluded from both discussions and rituals.

Similarly, mentally disabled persons may also be disen-franchised in grief. Although studies affirm that the mentally retarded are able to understand the concept of death and, in fact, experience grief, these reactions may not be perceived by others. Because the person is retarded or otherwise mentally disabled, others in the family may ignore his or her need to grieve. Here a teacher of the mentally disabled describes two illustrative incidences:

> In the first situation, Susie was 17 years old and away at summer camp when her father died. The family felt she wouldn't understand and that it would be better for her not to come home for the funeral. In the other situation, Francine was with her mother when she got sick. The mother was taken away by ambulance. Nobody answered her questions or told her what happened. "After all," they responded, "she's retarded."

The Special Problems of Disenfranchised Grief

Though each of the types of grief mentioned earlier may cre-ate particular difficulties and different reactions, one can legiti-mately speak of the special problem shared in disenfranchised grief.

The problem of disenfranchised grief can be expressed in a paradox. The very nature of disenfranchised grief creates additional problems for grief, while removing or minimizing sources of support.

Disenfranchising grief may exacerbate the problem of bereavement in a number of ways. First, the situations mentioned tend to intensify emotional reactions. Many emotions are asso-ciated with normal grief. Bereaved persons frequently experi-ence feelings of anger, guilt, sadness and depression, loneliness, hopelessness, and numbness. These emotional reactions can be complicated when grief is disenfranchised. Although each of the situations described is in its own way unique, the literature uniformly reports how each of these disenfranchising circumstances can intensify feelings of anger, guilt, or powerlessness.

Second, both ambivalent relationships and concurrent crises have been identified in the literature as conditions that complicate grief. These conditions can often exist in many types of disenfranchised grief. For example, studies have indicated the ambivalence that can exist in cases of abortion, among ex-spouses, significant others in nontraditional roles, and among families of Alzheimer's disease victims. Similarly, the literature documents the many kinds of concurrent crises that can trouble the disenfranchised griever. For example, in cases of cohabiting couples, either heterosexual or homosexual, studies have often found that survivors experience legal and financial problems regarding inheritance, ownership, credit, or leases. Likewise, the death of a parent may leave a mentally disabled person not only bereaved but also bereft of a viable support system.

Although grief is complicated, many of the factors that facilitate mourning are not present. The bereaved may be excluded from an active role in caring for the dying. Funeral rituals, normally helpful in resolving grief, may not help here. In some cases the bereaved may be excluded from attendance. In other cases they may have no role in planning those rituals or in deciding whether even to have them. Or in cases of divorce, separation, or psychosocial death, rituals may be lacking altogether.

In addition, the very nature of the disenfranchised grief precludes social support. Often there is no recognized role in which mourners can assert the right to mourn and thus receive such support. Grief may have to remain private. Though they may have experienced an intense loss, they may not be given time off from work, have the opportunity to verbalize the loss, or receive the expressions of sympathy and support characteristic in a death. Even traditional sources of solace, such as religion, are unavailable to those whose relationships (for example, extramarital, cohabiting, homosexual, divorced) or acts (such as abortion) are condemned within that tradition.

Naturally, there are many variables that will affect both the intensity of the reaction and the availability of support. All the variables—interpersonal, psychological, social, physiological— that normally influence grief will have an impact here as well. And while there are problems common to cases of disenfranchised grief, each relationship has to be individually considered in light of the unique combinations of factors that may facilitate or impair grief resolution.

Implications

Despite the shortage of research on and attention given to the issue of disenfranchised grief, it remains a significant issue. Millions of Americans are involved in losses in which grief is effectively disenfranchised. For example, there are more than 1 million couples presently cohabiting. There are estimates that 3 percent of males and 2–3 percent of females are exclusively

homosexual, with similar percentages having mixed homosexual and heterosexual encounters. There are about a million abortions a year; even though many of the women involved may not experience grief reactions, some are clearly "at risk."

Disenfranchised grief is also a growing issue. There are higher percentages of divorced people in the cohorts now aging. The AIDS crisis means that more homosexuals will experience losses in significant relationships. Even as the disease spreads within the population of intravenous drug users, it is likely to create a new class of both potential victims and disenfranchised grievers among the victims' informal liaisons and nontraditional relationships. And as Americans continue to live longer, more will suffer from severe forms of chronic brain dysfunctions. As the developmentally disabled live longer, they too will experience the grief of parental and sibling loss. In short, the proportion of disenfranchised grievers in the general population will rise rapidly in the future.

It is likely that bereavement counselors will have increased exposure to cases of disenfranchised grief. In fact, the very nature of disenfranchised grief and the unavailability of informal support make it likely that those who experience such losses will seek formal supports. Thus there is a pressing need for research that will describe the particular and unique reactions of each of the different types of losses; compare reactions and problems associated with these losses; describe the important variables affecting disenfranchised grief reactions; assess possible interventions; and discover the atypical grief reactions, such as masked or delayed grief, that might be manifested in such cases. Also needed is education sensitizing students to the many kinds of relationships and subsequent losses that people can experience and affirming that where there is loss there is grief.

***

KEN DOKA, PhD, is a professor of gerontology at the College of New Rochelle in New York. He became interested in the study of death and dying quite inadvertently. Scheduled to do a practicum in a facility that housed juvenile delinquents, he discovered that his supervisor had changed the assignment. Instead, Doka found himself counseling dying children and their families at Sloan-Kettering, a major cancer hospital in New York. This experience became the basis of two graduate theses, one in sociology entitled "The Social Organization of Terminal Care in Two Pediatric Hospitals," and the other in religious studies entitled "Pastoral Counseling to Dying Children and Their Families." (Both were later published.) His doctoral program pursued another long-standing interest: the sociology of aging. In 1983, Dr. Doka accepted his present position at the College of New Rochelle where he specializes in thanatology and gerontology.

Active in the Association for Death Education and Counseling since its beginnings, Dr. Doka was elected its president in 1993. In addition to articles in scholarly journals, he is the author of *Death and Spirituality* (with John Morgan, 1993), *Living with Life-Threatening Illness* (1993) and *Disenfranchised Grief: Recognizing Hidden Sorrow* (1989), from which the following selection is excerpted. His work on disenfranchised grief began in the classroom when a graduate student commented, "If you think widows have it rough, you ought to see what happens when your ex-spouse dies."

From *Disenfranchised Grief: Recognizing Hidden Sorrow*, Lexington Books, 1989, pp. 3–11. Copyright © 1989 by Kenneth J. Doka. Reprinted by permission of the author.

Enhancing the Concept of Disenfranchised Grief

Doka (1989a, p. 4) defined disenfranchised grief as "the grief that persons experience when they incur a loss that is not or cannot be openly acknowledged, publicly mourned, or socially supported." He suggested that disenfranchisement can apply to unrecognized relationships, losses, or grievers, as well as to certain types of deaths.

This article contends that disenfranchisement in bereavement may have a potentially broader scope than has been hitherto recognized. That claim is defended by exploring further the implications of disenfranchisement and by suggesting ways in which certain understandings or misunderstandings of the dynamic qualities of grief, mourning, and their outcomes may be open to disenfranchisement or may participate in disenfranchisement.

The aims of this argument are to enhance the concept of disenfranchised grief in itself and to deepen appreciation of the full range of all that is or can be experienced in bereavement.

Charles A. Corr, PhD

In 1989 Doka (1989a) first proposed the concept of "disenfranchised grief." His suggestion had an immediate appeal to many and the concept of disenfranchised grief has since been widely accepted by practitioners, educators, and researchers in the field of death, dying, and bereavement. In particular, it has been applied in ways that seek to elucidate and validate the experiences of a broad range of bereaved persons.

In his initial proposal, Doka described the concept of disenfranchised grief, identified those aspects of the grief experience that he understood to have been subject to disenfranchisement, provided examples of many ways in which disenfranchisement has occurred, and indicated why attention should be paid to the concept of disenfranchised grief. This article seeks to enhance understanding of the concept of disenfranchised grief and by so doing to deepen appreciation of the full range of all that is or can be experienced in bereavement. The present analysis begins with a review of Doka's original description of the concept of disenfranchised grief. Thereafter, the inquiry is guided by two primary questions: 1) What exactly is meant by the disenfranchisement of grief?; and 2) What is or can be disenfranchised in grief? Responding to these questions may help to enrich understanding of Doka's seminal concept in particular, and of bereavement in general. On that basis, it may also be possible for helpers to identify better ways in which to assist grievers of all types, especially those whose experiences have been disenfranchised.

Disenfranchised Grief: The Original Concept

In his original work, Doka (1989a, p. 4) defined "disenfranchised grief" as "the grief that persons experience when they incur a loss that is not or cannot be openly acknowledged, publicly mourned, or socially supported." In addition, he suggested that grief can be disenfranchised in three primary ways: 1) the relationship is not recognized; 2) the loss is not recognized; or 3) the griever is not recognized. Some comments on each of these three types of disenfranchisement may help to clarify Doka's original proposal.

Disenfranchised Relationships

Why don't you just stop crying and grieving for that person who died. He wasn't even close to you.

I just don't see why you should be so upset over the death of your ex-husband. He was a bum, you hated him, and you got rid of him years ago. Why cry over his being gone for good?

With respect to a *relationship* that is disenfranchised, Folta and Deck (1976, p. 235) have noted that "the underlying assumption is that the 'closeness of relationship' exists only among spouses and/or immediate kin." Unsuspected, past, or secret relationships may simply not be publicly recognized or socially sanctioned. Disenfranchised relationships can include associations which are well-accepted in theory but not appreciated in practice or in particular instances, such as those between friends, colleagues, in-laws, ex-spouses, or former lovers. Disenfranchised relationships may also include nontraditional liaisons such as those involving extra-marital affairs and homosexual relationships. In referring to these as instances of disenfranchised grief, the implication is that such relationships have often been or may be deemed by society to be an insufficient or inappropriate foundation for grief.

Disenfranchised Losses

Why do you keep on moaning over your miscarriage? It wasn't really a baby yet. And you already have four children. You could even have more if you want to.

Stop crying over that dead cat! He was just an animal. I bet that cat wouldn't have been upset if you had been the one to die. If you stop crying. I'll buy you a new kitten.

In the case of a *loss* which is disenfranchised, the focus of the disenfranchisement appears to arise from a failure or unwillingness on the part of society to recognize that certain types of events do involve real losses. For example, until quite recently and perhaps still today in many segments of society, perinatal deaths, losses associated with elective abortion, or losses of body parts have been disenfranchised. Similarly, the death of a pet is often unappreciated by those outside the relationship. And society is only beginning to learn about grief which occurs when dementia blots out an individual's personality in such a way or to such a degree that significant others perceive the person to be psychosocially dead, even though biological life continues. As one husband said of his spouse with advanced Alzheimer's disease, "I am medically separated from my wife—even though she is still alive and we are not divorced." To say that loss arising from a "medical separation" of this type is disenfranchised is to note that society does not acknowledge it to be sufficient to justify grief—or at least not sufficient to justify grief of the type that society associates with a physical death.

Disenfranchised Grievers

I don't know why that old guy in Room 203 keeps moaning and whimpering about the death of his loud-mouthed daughter who used to visit him every week.

With his poor memory and other mental problems, he hardly even knew when his daughter came to visit anyway.

I told Johnnie he should grow up, be a man, and stop whining about his grandfather's death. He's too young to really remember much about his grandfather or even to understand what death really means.

In the case of a disenfranchised *griever,* disenfranchisement mainly has to do with certain individuals to whom the socially-recognized status of griever is not attached. For example, it is often asserted or at least suggested that young children, the very old, and those who are mentally disabled are either incapable of grief or are individuals who do not have a need to grieve. In

this case, disenfranchisement applies not to a relationship or to a loss, but to the individual survivor whose status as a leading actor or protagonist in the human drama of bereavement is not recognized or appreciated.

Disenfranchising Deaths

That teenager who killed himself must not have had all his marbles. His family is probably all screwed up, too. Don't be sorry for them. Just stay away from them.

It's just too bad that actor died of AIDS. God punished him for having all that sex. And now his boyfriends will probably wind up with all his money. They sure don't need us to feel sorry for them.

In his original concept, Doka (1989a) added that some types of deaths in themselves may be "disenfranchising." He offered as examples deaths involving suicide or AIDS. The point seems to have been that our society is repelled or turns away from certain types of death, mainly because their complexities are not well understood or because they are associated with a high degree of social stigma. As a result, the character of the death seems to disenfranchise what otherwise might have been expected to follow in its aftermath. But not all societies at all points in time would or have disenfranchised deaths associated with suicide or AIDS. In other words, what is disenfranchised in one social context may not be disenfranchised in another social context. This clearly recalls Doka's fundamental point that disenfranchised grief is always founded on a specific society's attitudes and values.

Why Pay Attention to Disenfranchised Grief?

The purpose of drawing attention to the meaning of disenfranchised grief and to the ways in which it can be implemented can be seen in Doka's (1989a, p. 7) observation that, "The very nature of disenfranchised grief creates additional problems of grief, while removing or minimizing sources of support." Additional problems arise that go beyond the usual difficulties in grief because disenfranchised grief typically involves intensified emotional reactions (for example, anger, guilt, or powerlessness), ambivalent relationships (as in some cases of abortion or some associations between ex-spouses), and concurrent crises (such as those involving legal and financial problems). In circumstances of disenfranchised grief there is an absence of customary sources of support because society's attitudes make unavailable factors that usually facilitate mourning (for instance, the existence of funeral rituals or possibilities for helping to take part in such rituals) and opportunities to obtain assistance from others (for example, by speaking about the loss, receiving expressions of sympathy, taking time off from work, or finding solace within a religious tradition).

Clearly, issues associated with disenfranchised grief deserve attention. They indicate that social outlooks often embody a judgmental element (whether explicitly articulated or not) and the short-term concerns of the group when dealing with some bereaved persons. That is, societies which disenfranchise grief appear to act on specific values or principles at the expense of an overarching interest in the welfare of all of their members. In these ways, disenfranchised grief can be seen to be an important phenomenon. It is also a phenomenon that is lived out in different ways in different societies, easily observed by those who pay attention to social practices, and hurtful to individual members of society if not to society itself. For all of these reasons, it is worth exploring further what is meant by saying that some grief is disenfranchised and what is or can be disenfranchised in grief.

What Is Meant by Saying That Some Grief Is Disenfranchised?

As has been noted, grief always occurs within a particular social or cultural context. The concept of disenfranchised grief recognizes that in various spoken and unspoken ways social and cultural communities may deny recognition, legitimation, or support to the grief experienced by individuals, families, and small groups.

It is important to recognize that the grief under discussion here is not merely silent, unnoticed, or forgotten. Any griever may keep silent about or decide not to reveal to the larger society the fact of his or her grief, or some of its specific aspects. Failing to disclose or communicate to others what one is experiencing in grief does not of itself mean that such grief is or would be disenfranchised. Society might be fully prepared to recognize, legitimize, and support grief that an individual, for whatever reason, holds in privacy and does not share.

Further, even when an individual is willing to share his or her grief, some grief experiences may still go unnoticed or be forgotten by society. Thus, Gyulay (1975) wrote of grandparents following the death of a grandchild as "forgotten grievers." She meant that all too often attention associated with the death of a child is focused on the child's parents or siblings to the exclusion of grandparents. In fact, however, bereaved grandparents often find themselves grieving both the death of their grandchild and the loss experienced by an adult who is simultaneously their own child (or son/daughter-in-law) and the child's parent (Hamilton, 1978). Typically, when this two-fold grief of grandparents is brought to the attention of members of society, it is not disenfranchised but acknowledged and respected.

In short, the concept of disenfranchised grief goes beyond the situation of mere unawareness of grief to suggest a more or less active process of disavowal, renunciation, and rejection. Not surprisingly, the word "disenfranchise" takes its origin from the term "enfranchise," which has two basic historical meanings: 1) "To admit to freedom, set free (a slave or serf)"; and 2) "To admit to municipal or political privileges" (*Oxford English Dictionary*, 1989, Vol. 5, p. 246). In the most familiar sense of this term, to enfranchise is to set an individual free from his or her prior condition by admitting that person to the electoral franchise or granting permission to vote for representatives in a government. Disenfranchisement applies to those who are

not accorded a social franchise extended by society to individuals who are admitted to full participation in the community.

A more contemporary meaning of enfranchisement is to be granted a franchise or license to offer for sale locally some national or international product or service. For example, one might purchase or be awarded a franchise to sell a certain brand of fast food or automobile, or to advertise one's local motel as a member of a national chain of motels. Often one has to earn or somehow pay for the use of a franchise, and there may also be obligations to uphold certain service standards or to deliver a product of a certain type in a certain way. When the use of a franchise has not been earned or implemented properly, it may come into dispute or even be withdrawn by those in authority. In all of these examples, it is the permission to behave in a certain way (to vote, to act as a franchisee or agent of a franchise holder) that is central to both enfranchisement and disenfranchisement.

In the case of bereavement, enfranchisement applies in particular to those who are recognized by society as grievers. These are individuals who are free to acknowledge their losses openly, mourn those losses publicly, and receive support from others—at least within that society's accepted limits. Disenfranchised grief goes beyond the boundaries of what is regarded as socially accepted grief. It is therefore denied the legitimacy and freedom that comes with social sanction and approval (Doka, 1989b; Pine et al., 1990).

What Is or Can Be Disenfranchised in Grief?
Bereavement

Doka is clearly correct in recognizing that disenfranchisement can apply to relationships, losses, and grievers. These are, in fact, the three key *structural elements* that define the meaning of the term "bereavement." Thus, what Doka has really defined is "disenfranchised bereavement." For that reason, it may help to begin our exploration of how disenfranchisement applies to grief by reminding ourselves of how we understand the root concept of bereavement.

The word "bereavement" is widely understood to designate the objective situation of one who has experienced a significant loss. If there were no significant person or object to which an individual was attached, there would be no bereavement. For example, when a parent threatens to take away from a child a much-disliked serving of spinach as a "punishment" for the child's refusal to clean his or her plate at dinner, the child is not likely to experience a loss or to grieve. Further, if the object were a significant one to the child, but the child perceived (as a result of previous parental behavior patterns) that the threatened loss would not come about in fact, again there would be no bereavement or grief. Finally, if there were no individual to grieve a loss—as when someone threatens to or actually does take away a significant object, but the threat and the loss are not effectively communicated to the individual to whom they would presumably have been directed—again there is no bereavement or grief. A griever is effectively absent when the threat is merely an empty gesture made in his or her absence or when, for some other reason, there is no awareness or experience of a significant loss—as during the period between the death of a loved one in a far-off land and the communication of that fact to the survivor.

In short, the noun "bereavement" and the adjective "bereaved" only apply to situations and individuals in which there exists an experience such that one believes oneself to have been deprived of some important person or object. Both "bereavement" and "bereaved" (there is no present participial form, "bereaving," in standard English today) are words that derive from a verb not often used today in colloquial English. That word is "reave"; it means "to despoil, rob, or forcibly deprive" (*Oxford English Dictionary,* 1989, Vol. 13, p. 295). In short, a bereaved person is one who has been deprived, robbed, plundered, or stripped of something. This indicates that the stolen person or object was a valued one, and suggests that the deprivation has harmed or done violence to the bereaved person. In our society, all too many bereaved persons can testify that dismissal or minimization of the importance of their losses are familiar components of the experience of survivors, with or without added burdens arising from disenfranchisement.

We could explore further each of the central elements identified by Doka in describing his concept of disenfranchised grief. Such an exploration might produce: 1) a rich and varied portrait of the many types of *relationships* in which humans participate, including those fundamental relationships called "attachments" which serve to satisfy the basic needs of human beings; 2) a panorama of *losses* which may affect relationships involving human beings—some permanent, others temporary, some final, others reversible; and/or 3) a list of many different types of *grievers*. If we did this, it would become apparent (among other things) that loss by death is but one category of loss, and that certain types or modes of death are more likely to be disenfranchised than others. And we might also learn that while disenfranchising the bereaved involves costs of different types for individuals and societies themselves, enfranchising the disenfranchised might also involve costs of other types (Davidowitz & Myrick, 1984; Kamerman, 1993).

All of the above are ways to enrich appreciation of the concept of disenfranchised grief. Most involve simply accepting the conceptual scheme as it was originally proposed by Doka and applying it to specific types of relationships, losses, and grievers. Applications of this type have been prominent in written reports and conference presentations in recent years (e.g., Becker, 1997; Kaczmarek & Backlund, 1991; Schwebach & Thornton, 1992; Thornton, Robertson, & Mlecko, 1991; Zupanick, 1994).

In this article, it seems more useful to try to enhance or enlarge the concept of disenfranchised grief by examining it critically in relationship to the *dynamic components* of the bereavement experience, especially as it is related to grief, mourning, and their outcomes.

Grief

Stop feeling that way! You'll be better off if you just pack up all those bad feelings and throw them away with the garbage.

In reactions to being "reaved" or to perceiving themselves as having been "reaved," those who have suffered that experience typically react to what has happened to them. In normal circumstances, one would be surprised if they did not do so. Failure to react would seem to imply that the lost person or object was actually not much prized by the bereaved individual, that the survivor is unaware of his or her loss, or that other factors intervene. "Grief" is the reaction to loss. The term arises from the grave or heavy weight that presses on persons who are burdened by loss (*Oxford English Dictionary,* 1989, Vol. 6, pp. 834–835).

Reactions to loss are disenfranchised when they—in whole or in part; in themselves or in their expression—are not recognized, legitimated, or supported by society. How many times have grieving persons been told: "Don't feel that way"; "Try not to think those thoughts"; "Don't say those things (about God, or the doctor, or the person who caused the death)"; "You shouldn't act like that just because someone you loved died." Sometimes any reaction is judged to be inappropriate; in other circumstances, some reactions are accepted while others are rejected. In some cases, it is the existence of the reaction that is disenfranchised; in other examples, it is only the expression of the reaction that meets with disapproval. Through what amounts to a kind of "oppressive toleration" society often presses a griever to hold private his or her grief reaction in order not to trouble or disturb others by bringing it out into the open or expressing it in certain ways. The effect of any or all of these practices is to disenfranchise either some aspects of the grief or some modes in which they are manifested.

Grief as Emotions?

I can understand why you're feeling upset about your mother's death. You can be sad if you want to. But you've got to start eating again and getting a good night's sleep.

My co-worker used to be a such a great guy. But ever since his younger sister died, he comes to work and sometimes it's like he's wandering around in a fog and not concentrating on the job. I told him today that he needs to pull himself together and get focused on his work again.

My friend was always such a cheery person at the Senior Citizen's Center. But ever since her grandchild died, she keeps asking all those difficult questions about why God let such a bad thing happen to an innocent child. I told her that it was OK to be sad, but she just had to accept God's will and stop questioning it.

In each of these examples, feelings of grief are legitimized but other aspects of the grief reaction are disenfranchised. One might also argue that something very much like this form of disenfranchisement can be found in much of the professional literature on bereavement. For example, quite often grief is described or defined as "the emotional reaction to loss." On its face, a definition of this type is at once both obvious and inadequate. Clearly, bereaved persons may or do react emotionally to loss; equally so, they may not or do not merely react emotionally to loss. Careless, unintentional, or deliberate restriction of the meaning of grief to its emotional components is an unrecognized form of disenfranchisement of the full grief experience.

In this connection, Elias (1991) reminded readers that, "Broadly speaking, emotions have three components, a somatic, a behavioral and a feeling component" (p. 177). As a result, "the term *emotion,* even in professional discussions, is used with two different meanings. It is used in a wider and in a narrower sense at the same time. In the wider sense the term *emotion* is applied to a reaction pattern which involves the whole organism in its somatic, its feeling and its behavioral aspects. . . . In its narrower sense the term *emotion* refers to the feeling component of the syndrome only" (Elias, 1991, p. 119).

The importance of feelings in the overall grief reaction to loss is undeniable. Equally undeniable is the importance of other aspects of the grief reaction. These include somatic or physical sensations and behaviors or behavioral disturbances, as Elias has indicated, as well as matters involving cognitive, social, and spiritual functioning. Establishing a comprehensive list of all of these aspects of the grief reaction to loss is not of primary importance here. What is central is the recognition that human beings may and indeed are likely to react to important losses in their lives with their whole selves, not just with some narrowly defined aspect of their humanity. Failure to describe grief in a holistic way dismisses and devalues its richness and breadth.

Grief as Symptoms?

As a psychiatrist and her son-in-law, I tried to talk to your mother about your father's death. She refused and got upset after I told her that her unwillingness to discuss with me her reactions to the death was a classic symptom of pathological grief. She said she had talked to her sister and just didn't want to talk to you or me or her other children about it.

Sadness and crying are two of the main symptoms of grief. Whenever we identify them, we should refer the individual for therapy.

Another form of depicting or categorizing grief in a limiting and negative way involves the use of the language of *symptoms* to designate both complicated and uncomplicated grief. In principal, grief is a natural and healthy reaction to loss. There can be unhealthy reactions to loss. One of these would be a failure to react in any way to the loss of a significant person or object in our lives. However, most grief reactions are not complicated or unhealthy. They are appropriate reactions to the loss one has experienced. In cases of uncomplicated grief—which constitute the vast majority of all bereavement experiences—we ought to speak of signs, or manifestations, or expressions of grief. And we ought to avoid the term "symptoms" in relationship to grief, unless we consciously intend to use the language of illness to indicate some form of aberrant or unhealthy reaction to loss. When we use the language of symptoms to describe all expressions of grief, we have pathologized grief and invalidated or disenfranchised its fundamental soundness as the human reaction to loss.

Mourning

OK, we've had our grief ever since Kerri died. Now that the funeral is over, that's it. There's nothing more we can do and nothing more we need to do. So, let's just put all this behind us and forget it.

Many aspects of what is called grief in bereavement are essentially reactive. They seek to push away the hurt of the loss with denial, or turn back upon it with anger, or reply to its implacability with sadness. Much of this is like a defensive reflex. But there is more to most bereavement experiences than this. The other central element in a healthy bereavement experience is in the effort to find some way to live with the loss, with our grief reactions to that loss, and with the new challenges that are associated with the loss. As Weisman (1984, p. 36) observed, coping "is positive in approach; defending is negative." In brief, coping identifies the efforts that we make to manage perceived stressors in our lives (Lazarus & Folkman, 1984). In the vocabulary of bereavement, this is "mourning"—the attempt to manage or learn to live with one's bereavement. Through mourning grievers endeavor to incorporate their losses and grief into healthy ongoing living.

If we fail to distinguish between grief and mourning in appropriate ways, we run the risk of ignoring the differences between reacting and coping, between seeking to defend or push away our loss and grief, and attempting to embrace those experiences and incorporate them into our lives. This is another form of disenfranchisement insofar as it blurs distinctions between two central aspects of bereavement, misconceives what is involved in mourning an important loss, and refuses to acknowledge and support both grief and mourning.

At the simplest level, the efforts that one makes to cope with loss and grief in mourning are frequently not understood for what they are and thus are not valued by society. For example, a griever will be told not to go over the details of the accident again and again, as if such filling in of the stark outlines of a death is not an essential part of the process of *realization* or making real in one's internal, psychic world what is already real in the external, objective world (Parkes, 1996). Another familiar way of disenfranchising mourning occurs when a bereaved person is advised that the proper way to manage a loss is simply to "put it behind you" or "get beyond it." This assumes that one can simply hop over a stressful event in life, ignore the unwelcome interruption, and go on living without being affected by what has happened. Sometimes, bereaved survivors are even counseled to "forget" the deceased person as if he or she had not been a significant part of their lives. None of these are appropriate elements in constructive mourning.

Note that mourning is a present-tense, participial word. As such, it indicates action or activities of the type expressed by verbs. In the language of nouns, this is "grief work" (a phrase first coined by Lindemann in 1944). Lindemann understood "grief work" in a specific way, but the central point is that the grief work at the heart of mourning is an active, effortful attempt to manage what bereavement has brought into one's life (Attig, 1991, 1996).

Moreover, since the consequences of bereavement typically include both primary and secondary losses, as well as grief and new challenges, there is much to cope with in the whole of one's mourning. Indeed, contrasting loss and grief with the new challenges of bereavement could be said to require an oscillation between "loss-oriented" and "restoration-oriented" processes in mourning (Stroebe & Schut, 1995).

In other words, in his or her mourning a bereaved person is faced with the tasks of integrating into his or her life three major elements: 1) the primary and secondary losses that he or she has experienced, 2) the grief reactions provoked by those losses; and 3) the new challenges involved in living without the deceased person. For example, if my spouse should die I would be obliged to mourn or try to learn to live in healthy ways with her loss (the fact that she has been taken away from me constituting my primary loss), with the secondary losses associated with her death (e.g., being deprived of her company or being without her guidance in some practical matters), with my grief reactions to those losses (e.g., my anger over what has been done to me or my sadness at the apparent barrenness of the life that is now left to me), and with my new situation in life (e.g., after years of marriage I may be unclear how to function as a newfound single person). If any aspect of my losses, grief, or new challenges is disenfranchised, then my efforts to mourn or cope with those aspects of my bereavement will also be disenfranchised.

Mourning: Interpersonal and Intrapersonal Dimensions

Because each human being is both a particular individual and a social creature or a member of a community, mourning has two complementary forms or aspects. It is both an outward, public, or *interpersonal* process—the overt, visible, and characteristically shared public efforts to cope with or manage loss and associated grief reactions—and an internal, private, or *intrapersonal* process—an individual's inward struggles to cope with or manage loss and the grief reactions to that loss. Each of these dimensions of mourning deserves recognition and respect. Much of what has already been noted here about mourning applies to its intrapersonal dimensions, but disenfranchisement is also frequently associated with the interpersonal aspects of mourning.

Interpersonal Dimensions of Mourning

Don't keep on talking about how he died. It's not going to make any difference or bring him back. Nobody wants to be around you when you keep going on about it.

What's the point of having a funeral, anyhow? Couldn't they just bury their child privately and leave us out of it? I don't want to get dragged into it.

Many people in contemporary society are unwilling to take part in the public or *interpersonal* rituals of mourning. Some of this has to do with a certain weakness or shallowness in many interpersonal relationships in contemporary society and a loosening of the bonds that formerly bound together families, neighbors, church groups, and other small communities. But it also appears to be linked to a discomfort with public ritual and open expression of strong feelings. Good funeral and memorial rituals are essentially designed to assist human beings in their need to engage in three post-death tasks: 1) to dispose of dead bodies appropriately; 2) to make real the implications of death; and 3) to work toward social reintegration and healthful ongoing living (Corr, Nabe, & Corr, 1994). Without indicating how these tasks will otherwise be met, many act as if society and individuals should do away with all public expressions of mourning. Young people in our society frequently state that when they die no one should be sad and that money that would otherwise be spent for a funeral should only be used for a party. Thoughts like this disenfranchise full appreciation of grief and the needs of individuals to mourn their losses within communities of fellow grievers.

This disenfranchisement of the interpersonal dimensions of mourning is not typical of all individuals in our society and is unacceptable to many ethnic or religious groups. Similarly, it does not apply to rituals following the deaths of public figures (e.g., a president) or very prominent persons (e.g., certain celebrities). In these instances, as well as in the very formal rituals of the armed forces which mandate specific conduct and ceremonial practice in a context of death and bereavement, or the informal but growing practice of members of sports teams wearing black bands on their uniforms or dedicating a game to the memory of someone who has died, the interpersonal needs of a community cry out for expression and guidance in public mourning practices.

In fact, formal or informal rituals—which are a prominent example of the interpersonal dimension of mourning—have been created by human beings as a means of helping to bring order into their lives in times of disorder and social disruption. Thus, Margaret Mead (1973, pp. 89–90) wrote: "I know of no people for whom the fact of death is not critical, and who have no ritual by which to deal with it." Bereavement rituals are intended precisely to give social recognition, legitimation, and support in times of loss and grief. Specific rituals may fall out of favor and no longer serve these purposes for the society as a whole or for some of its members. But to assume that such rituals can simply be abandoned without replacement, that society can satisfactorily conduct its affairs and serve its members without any ritual whatsoever in times of death, is to misconceive the needs of human beings and expose the dangers involved in disenfranchising mourning. As Staples (1994, p. 255) suggested, "The rituals of grief and burial bear the dead away. Cheat those rituals and you risk keeping the dead with you always in forms that you mightn't like. Choose carefully the funerals you miss."

Intrapersonal Dimensions of Mourning

I was proud of her at the funeral. She was so brave and she never cried. But now she's always crying and sometimes she just seems to be preoccupied with her inner feelings. I think she's just chewing on her grief like some kind of undigested food and simply won't let go of it. Last week, I told her that there were times when we all understood it was appropriate to grieve. But she's got to get over it and she just can't keep on gnawing at it when she thinks she's alone.

Why does she keep going back to the cemetery on the anniversary of her husband's death? That's morbid for her to keep on stirring up those feelings over and over again. She doesn't talk much to anyone else about it, but I think she needs to get on with her life without this behavior.

Some authors (e.g., *Oxford English Dictionary,* 1989, Vol. 10, pp. 19–20) seem to restrict the use of the term "mourning" to the expression of sorrow or grief, especially those expressions involving ceremony or ritual. For example, there is a traditional language that uses phrases like "wearing mourning" to refer to dressing in certain ways (e.g., in black or dark-colored garments) as a public expression of one's status as a bereaved person. Despite its historical justification, limiting the term mourning in this way leaves us without a term for the *intrapersonal* processes of coping with loss and grief.

Other authors (e.g., Wolfelt, 1996) maintain and emphasize the distinction between the intrapersonal and interpersonal dimensions of bereavement by using the term "grieving" for the former and reserving the term "mourning" for the latter. Again, there is justification for some linguistic distinction between intrapersonal and interpersonal aspects of coping with loss and grief. But the central point for our purposes is that this last distinction is a linguistic effort to fill out what is involved in both the intrapersonal and interpersonal realms when bereaved persons strive to cope with loss and grief. In this way, linguistic distinctions between intrapersonal and interpersonal aspects of mourning work to expand or enhance what is involved in coping with loss and grief, not to restrict or disenfranchise selected aspects of that coping.

Mourning: Outcomes

It's been almost three weeks and she's still not finished with her grieving. I told her she had to forget him and get on with her new life.

We invited John to come on a blind date with us and Mary's cousin, but he refused. Mary told him that he's got to stop wallowing in tears. He needs to get over his first wife and start looking around for someone new. Six months is long enough to mourn.

A final arena for possible disenfranchisement in bereavement relates to assumptions about the *outcomes* of mourning. This has been touched on above. If mourning is a process of coping with loss and grief, we can rightly ask: What are the results which it strives to achieve? Many would say "recovery," "completion," or "resolution." Each of these terms appears to imply a fixed endpoint for mourning, a final closure after which there is no more grieving and mourning. "Recovery," is perhaps the least satisfactory of the three terms, because it also seems to suggest that grief is a bad situation like a disease or a wound from which one must rescue or reclaim oneself (Osterweis, Solomon, & Green, 1984; Rando, 1993). Recovery is often implied in metaphors of "healing" from grief; talking in this

way may otherwise be quite helpful, but it tends to suggest a time at which one will be done with healing and after which one will apparently be back to one's former self essentially unchanged by the bereavement experience.

It has been argued earlier that it is not desirable to use symptom language to interpret grief and to impose disease models upon healthy experiences in bereavement. To that we can add here that there are no fixed endpoints in mourning. One can never simply go back to a pre-bereavement mode of living after a significant loss. In fact, there is ample evidence, for many at least, that mourning continues in some form for the remainder of one's life. Interpretations to the contrary disenfranchise processes related to loss and grief which take place after the assumed endpoint or completion of mourning. They also disenfranchise the life-changing power of significant losses and the ongoing need to continue to cope with loss, grief, and new challenges in life. The misconception that grief and mourning should be over in a short time or at some predefined point is what leads to the familiar experience of many bereaved persons that over time their grief appears to become disenfranchised (Lundberg, Thornton, & Robertson, 1987).

There are, in fact, different outcomes experienced by different individuals who are bereaved. That is not surprising. Individuals who live their lives in different ways may be expected to cope with loss and grief in different ways, and to come to different results in their coping work. Research by Martinson and her colleagues (McClowry, Davies, May, Kulenkamp, & Martinson, 1987) studied bereaved parents and other family members (mainly siblings) seven to nine years after the death of a child. Results suggested that different individuals and different families dealt with the "empty space" in their lives in different ways. Some worked diligently to "get over it," that is, to put the loss behind them and go on with their lives. Others sought to "fill the space" by turning their focus toward what they perceived as some constructive direction. This type of effort to find some positive meaning in an otherwise horrible event might be illustrated by those bereaved after automobile accidents associated with the use of alcoholic beverages who throw themselves into campaigns to prevent intoxicated drivers from driving motor vehicles or to take such drivers off the road when they have been identified. A third outcome identified in this research was that of "keeping the connection." This appeared in bereaved persons who struggled to maintain a place in their lives for the deceased individual, vividly illustrated by the mother who insists that she has two sons, despite her full awareness that one of them has died (e.g., Wagner, 1994).

The important point in this research is not to argue for one or the other of these three outcomes in mourning, or even to suggest that they are the only possible outcomes. The point is that mourning is a process of acknowledging the reality of a death, experiencing the grief associated with that loss, learning to live without the deceased, and restructuring one's relationship to the deceased in order that that relationship can continue to be honored even while the survivor goes on living in a healthy and productive way (Worden, 1991). This process can be carried out in different ways and it can be expected to have somewhat different results for different individuals. As one astute psychologist observed, it is not the time that one has to use but the use that one makes of the time that one has that makes all the difference in bereavement, grief, and mourning (S. J. Fleming, personal communication, 9/28/95).

Three widows in my own experience acted out their mourning in different ways. One removed her wedding ring after the death of her husband. She said, "I am no longer married to him." Another kept her wedding ring on the third finger of her left hand. She said, "We are still connected." A third removed her husband's wedding ring before his body was buried and had it refashioned along with her own wedding ring into a new ring which she wore on her right hand. She said, "I now have a new relationship with my deceased husband."

These and other possible variations identify alternative courses in bereavement and mourning. In each case, metaphors of healing or resolution are partly correct insofar as the survivor has found a constructive way in which to go forward with his or her life. The intensity of the bereaved person's grief may have abated, but many continue to experience grief and reoccurrences of mourning in some degree, in some forms, and at some times. Grief may no longer consume them as it seemed to do immediately after their loss. They have "gotten through" some difficult times in bereavement, but they are not simply "over" their grief. In fact, many bereaved persons report that their grief and mourning never completely end.

Outsiders must take care not to invalidate or disenfranchise the ongoing grief and mourning of the bereaved, as well as their healthy connectedness to the deceased, by speaking too facilely of closure and completion (Klass, Silverman, & Nickman, 1996; Silverman, Nickman, & Worden, 1992). Such language may speak not primarily about bereavement but about the time at which a helper judges that his or her role as a counselor or therapist is no longer required. Thus, when a bereaved child decides to leave one of the support groups at The Dougy Center in Portland, Oregon (because, as was once said, "he or she now has better things to do with his or her time"), he or she is given a drawstring pouch containing several small stones (Corr and the Staff of The Dougy Center, 1991). Most of the stones in the pouch are polished and thus serve to symbolize what the child has achieved in coping with loss and grief; at least one is left in a rough state to represent the unfinished work that always remains in bereavement.

Conclusion

What have we learned from this reflection on the concept of disenfranchised grief? First, it is a concept with immediate appeal. It resonates with the experiences of many bereaved persons and of many clinicians and scholars who have sought to understand experiences of bereavement or tried to be of assistance to bereaved persons. Second, disenfranchisement involves more than merely overlooking or forgetting to take note of certain types of bereavement and grief. It is more active than that in its nature and more determined in its messages, even if they are often conveyed in subtle and unspoken ways. Whatever is disenfranchised in grief is not free to experience or to express

itself. It is prohibited, tied down, not sanctioned, and not supported by society.

Third, as Doka (1989a) originally pointed out, disenfranchisement can apply to any or all of the key structural elements in bereavement—relationships, losses, and grievers—as well as to certain forms of death. However, as this article has made clear, disenfranchisement can also be associated with the full range of the various reactions to loss (grief) and their expression, the processes of coping with or striving to manage loss, grief, and the new challenges which they entail (mourning), both the intrapersonal and the interpersonal dimensions of those processes, and various ways of living out their implications. In the aftermath of a death, the possible scope of disenfranchisement is not confined merely to the structural elements of bereavement or to grief understood in a kind of global way; it can extend to every aspect or dimension of the experience of bereavement and be applied to all of the dynamics of grief and mourning.

Enhancing our understanding of the concept of disenfranchised grief can contribute to improved appreciation of its breadth and depth. This same effort also provides an added way of drawing out some of the implications of the underlying concepts of bereavement, grief, and mourning. Further, attention to the enhanced concept of disenfranchised grief reminds helpers of the sensitivities they need to keep in mind in order not to devalue or rule out of bounds important aspects of the experiences of bereaved persons.

A caring society ought not incorporate within its death system—either formally or informally—thoughts, attitudes, behaviors, or values that communicate to bereaved persons inappropriate or unjustified messages such as: "Your relationship with the deceased person did not count in our eyes"; "Your loss was not really a significant one"; "You are not a person who should be grieving this loss"; "We do not recognize some aspects of your grief" or "Your grief is not acceptable to us in some ways;" "Your grief is in itself a symptom of psychic disorder or lack of mental health"; "Your mourning has lasted too long"; "You are mourning in ways that are publicly or socially unacceptable"; "You should not continue to mourn inside yourself in these ways"; or "Your mourning should be finished and over with by now."

Rather than the perspectives described in the previous paragraph, a caring society ought to respect the complexities and the individuality of each bereavement experience. While remaining sensitive to the deficits and excesses that define complicated mourning in a relatively small percentage of bereavement experiences (Rando, 1993), a caring society and its members ought to appreciate that healthy grief honors cherished relationships and that constructive mourning is essential for those who are striving to live in productive and meaningful ways in the aftermath of loss. Consider how different our society would be if it listened to and acted on comments such as the following from Frank (1991), who wrote: "Professionals talk too much about adjustment. I want to emphasize mourning as affirmation. . . . To grieve well is to value what you have lost. When you value even the feeling of loss, you value life itself, and you begin to live again" (pp. 40–41).

References

Attig, T. (1991). The importance of conceiving of grief as an active process. *Death Studies, 15,* 385–393.

Attig, T. (1996). *How we grieve: Relearning the world.* New York: Oxford University Press.

Becker, S. M. (1997, 26 June). *Disenfranchised grief and the experience of loss after environmental accidents.* Paper presented at the meeting of the Association for Death Education and Counseling and the 5th International Conference on Grief and Bereavement in Contemporary Society, Washington, DC.

Corr, C. A., and the Staff of The Dougy Center. (1991). Support for grieving children: The Dougy Center and the hospice philosophy. *The American Journal of Hospice and Palliative Care, 8*(4), 23–27.

Corr, C. A., Nabe, C. M., & Corr, D. M. (1994). A task-based approach for understanding and evaluating funeral practices. *Thanatos, 19*(2), 10–15.

Davidowitz, M., & Myrick, R. D. (1984). Responding to the bereaved: An analysis of "helping" statements. *Death Education, 8,* 1–10.

Doka, K. J. (1989a). Disenfranchised grief. In K. J. Doka (Ed.), *Disenfranchised grief: Recognizing hidden sorrow* (pp. 3–11). Lexington, MA: Lexington Books.

Doka, K. J. (Ed.) (1989b). *Disenfranchised grief: Recognizing hidden sorrow.* Lexington, MA: Lexington Books.

Elias, N. (1991). On human beings and their emotions: A process-sociological essay. In M. Featherstone, M. Hepworth, & B. S. Turner (Eds.), *The body: Social process and cultural theory* (pp. 103–125). London: Sage.

Folta, J. R., & Deck, E. S. (1976). Grief, the funeral, and the friend. In V. R. Pine, A. H. Kutscher, D. Peretz, R. C. Slater, R. DeBellis, R. J. Volk, & D. J. Cherico (Eds.), *Acute grief and the funeral* (pp. 231–240). Springfield, IL: Charles C. Thomas.

Frank, A. W. (1991). *At the will of the body: Reflections on illness.* Boston: Houghton Mifflin.

Gyulay, J. E. (1975). The forgotten grievers. *American Journal of Nursing, 75,* 1476–1479.

Hamilton, J. (1978). Grandparents as grievers. In O. J. Z. Sahler (Ed.), *The child and death* (pp. 219–225). St. Louis, MO: C. V. Mosby.

Kaczmarek, M. G., & Backlund, B. A. (1991). Disenfranchised grief: The loss of an adolescent romantic relationship. *Adolescence, 26,* 253–259.

Kamerman, J. (1993). Latent functions of enfranchising the disenfranchised griever. *Death Studies, 17,* 281–287.

Klass, D., Silverman, P. R., & Nickman, S. L. (Eds.) (1996). *Continuing bonds: New understanding of grief.* Washington, DC: Taylor & Francis.

Lazarus, R. S., & Folkman, S. (1984). *Stress, appraisal, and coping.* New York: Springer.

Lindemann, E. (1944). Symptomatology and management of acute grief. *American Journal of Psychiatry, 101,* 141–148.

Lundberg, K. J., Thornton, G., & Robertson, D. U. (1987). Personal and social rejection of the bereaved. In C. A. Corr & R. A. Pacholski (Eds.), *Death: Completion and discovery* (pp. 61–70). Lakewood, OH: Association for Death Education and Counseling.

McClowry, S. G., Davies, E. B., May, K. A., Kulenkamp, E. J., & Martinson, I. M. (1987). The empty space phenomenon: The process of grief in the bereaved family. *Death Studies, 11,* 361–374.

Mead, M. (1973). Ritual and social crisis. In J. D. Shaughnessy (Ed.), *The roots of ritual* (pp. 87–101). Grand Rapids, MI: Eerdmans.

Osterweis, M., Solomon, F., & Green, M. (Eds.) (1984). *Bereavement: Reactions, consequences, and care.* Washington, DC: National Academy Press.

The Oxford English Dictionary (1989). J. A. Simpson & E. S. C. Weiner (Eds.). 2nd ed.; 20 vols; Oxford: Clarendon Press.

Parkes, C. M. (1996). *Bereavement: Studies of grief in adult life* (3rd ed.). New York: Routledge.

Pine, V. R., Margolis, O. S., Doka, K., Kutscher, A. H., Schaefer, D. J., Siegel, M-E., & Cherico, D. J. (Eds.) (1990). *Unrecognized and unsanctioned grief: The nature and counseling of unacknowledged loss.* Springfield, IL: Charles C. Thomas.

Rando, T. A. (1993). *Treatment of complicated mourning.* Champaign, IL: Research Press.

Schwebach, I., & Thornton, G. (1992, 6 March). *Disenfranchised grief in mentally retarded and mentally ill populations.* Paper presented at the meeting of the Association for Death Education and Counseling, Boston.

Silverman, P. R., Nickman, S., & Worden, J. W. (1992). Detachment revisited: The child's reconstruction of a dead parent. *American Journal of Orthopsychiatry, 62,* 494–503.

Staples, B. (1994). *Parallel time: Growing up in black and white.* New York: Pantheon.

Stroebe, M. S., & Schut, H. (1995, June 29). *The dual process model of coping with loss.* Paper presented at the meeting of the International Work Group on Death, Dying, and Bereavement, Oxford, England.

Thornton, G., Robertson, D. U., & Mlecko, M. L. (1991). Disenfranchised grief and evaluations of social support by college students. *Death Studies, 15,* 355–362.

Wagner, S. (1994). *The Andrew poems.* Lubbock, TX: Texas Tech University Press.

Weisman, A. D. (1984). *The coping capacity: On the nature of being mortal.* New York: Human Sciences Press.

Wolfelt, A. D. (1996). *Healing the bereaved child: Grief gardening, growth through grief and other touchstones for caregivers.* Fort Collins, CO: Companion Press.

Worden, J. W. (1991). *Grief counseling and grief therapy: A handbook for the mental health practitioner* (2nd ed.). New York: Springer.

Zupanick, C. E. (1994). Adult children of dysfunctional families: Treatment from a disenfranchised grief perspective. *Death Studies, 18,* 183–195.

From *Omega,* vol. 38, no. 1, 1998/1999, pp. 1–20. Copyright © 1999 by Baywood Publishing Co., Inc. Reprinted by permission.

The Increasing Prevalence of Complicated Mourning
The Onslaught Is Just Beginning

In this article, complicated mourning is operationalized in relation to the six "R" processes of mourning and its seven high-risk factors are identified. The main thesis is that the prevalence of complicated mourning is increasing today due to a number of contemporary sociocultural and technological trends which have influenced 1) today's types of death; 2) the characteristics of personal relationships severed by today's deaths; and 3) the personality and resources of today's mourner. Additionally, specific problems in both the mental health profession and the field of thanatology further escalate complicated mourning by preventing or interfering with requisite treatment. Thus, complicated mourning is on the rise at the precise time when caregivers are unprepared and limited in their abilities to respond. New treatment policies and models are mandated as a consequence.

THERESE A. RANDO, PHD

In the 1990s, the mental health profession (a term herein broadly used to encompass any caregiver whose work places him/her in the position of ministering to the mental health needs of another) and the thanatological community are at a crucial crossroads. Current sociocultural and technological trends in American society are directly increasing the prevalence of complicated mourning at the precise point in time at which the mental health profession is particularly both unprepared and limited in its abilities to respond to the needs created. Thanatology has a pivotal role to play in identifying this crisis, delineating the problems to be addressed, and advocating for the development of new policies, models, approaches, and treatments appropriate to today's grim realities. Failure of either profession to recognize these realities is bound to result not only in inadequate care for those who require it, but to place our society at greater risk for the serious sequelae known to emanate from untreated complicated mourning.[1]

After a brief review of complicated mourning, this article will: 1) identify the high-risk factors for complicated mourning; 2) delineate the sociocultural and technological trends exacerbating these factors, which in turn increase the prevalence of complicated mourning; 3) indicate the problems inherent in the mental health profession that interfere with proper response to complicated mourning and to its escalation; and 4) point out the pitfalls for addressing complicated mourning that reside in the field of thanatology today. The focus on this article is restricted to raising awareness of the problem and discussing its determinants.

Complicated Mourning

Historically, there have been three main difficulties in defining complicated mourning. The first stems from the imprecise and inconsistent terminology employed. The very same grief and mourning phenomena have been described at various times and by various authors as "pathological," "neurotic," "maladaptive," "unresolved," "abnormal," "dysfunctional," or "deviant," just to name some of the designations used. Communication has been hampered by a lack of semantic agreement and consensual validation. This author's preference is for the term "complicated mourning." Such a term suggests that mourning is a series of processes which in some way have become complicated, with the implication being that what has become complicated can be uncomplicated. It avoids the pejorative tone of many of the other terms. Additionally, there is no insinuation of pathology in the mourner. Heretofore, complications typically have been construed to arise from the deficits of the person experiencing the bereavement. The term "complicated" avoids the assumption that the complications necessarily stem from the mourner him or herself. This is quite crucial because it is now well-documented that there are some circumstances of death and some postdeath variables that in and of themselves complicate mourning regardless of the premorbid psychological health of the mourner.

A second difficulty stems from the lack of objective criteria for what constitutes complicated mourning. Unlike the analogous medical situation in which the determination of pathology is more readily discerned and defined (e.g., the diagnosis of a broken bone usually can be easily agreed upon by several physicians following viewing of an x-ray), the phenomena in mourning tend not to be so concrete or unarguable. For instance, a woman hearing her deceased husband's voice in some circumstances is quite appropriate, whereas in others it reflects gross pathology.

The third and related difficulty is found because mourning is so highly idiosyncratic. It is determined by a constellation of thirty-three sets of factors circumscribing the loss and its circumstances, the mourner, and the social support received. No determination of abnormality technically ever can be made without taking into consideration the sets of factors known to influence any response to loss.[2] What may be an appropriate response in one circumstance for an individual mourner may be a highly pathological response for a different mourner in other circumstances. For this reason, it appears most helpful to look at complications in the mourning processes themselves rather than at particular symptomatology.

With this as a premise, complicated mourning can be said to be present when, taking into consideration the amount of time since the death, there is a compromise, distortion, or failure of one or more of the six "R" processes of mourning.[1] The six "R" processes of mourning necessary for healthy accommodation of any loss are:

1. Recognize the loss
   - Acknowledge the death
   - Understand the death
2. React to the separation
   - Experience the pain
   - Feel, identify, accept, and give some form of expression to all the psychological reactions to the loss
   - Identify and mourn secondary losses
3. Recollect and reexperience the deceased and the relationship
   - Review and remember realistically
   - Revive and reexperience the feelings
4. Relinquish the old attachments to the deceased and the old assumptive world
5. Readjust to move adaptively into the new world without forgetting the old
   - Revise the old assumptive world
   - Develop a new relationship with the deceased
   - Adopt new ways of being in the world
   - Form a new identity
6. Reinvest

In all forms of complicated mourning, there are attempts to do two things: 1) to deny, repress, or avoid aspects of the loss, its pain, and the full realization of its implications for the mourner; and 2) to hold onto, and avoid relinquishing, the lost loved one. These attempts, or some variation thereof, are what cause the complications in the "R" processes of mourning.

Complicated mourning may take any one or combination of four forms: symptoms, syndromes, mental or physical disorder, or death.[1]

Complicated mourning symptoms refer to any psychological, behavioral, social, or physical symptom—alone or in combination—which in context reveals some dimension of compromise, distortion, or failure of one or more of the six "R" processes of mourning. They are of insufficient number, intensity, and duration, or of different type, than are required to meet the criteria for any of the other three forms of complicated mourning discussed below.

There are seven complicated mourning syndromes into which a constellation of complicated mourning symptoms may coalesce. They may occur independently or concurrently with one another. Only if the symptoms comprising them meet the criteria for the specific syndrome is there said to be a complicated mourning syndrome present. If only some of the symptoms are present, or there is a combination of symptoms from several of the syndromes but they fail to meet the criteria for a particular complicated mourning syndrome, then they are considered complicated mourning symptoms. The reader should be advised that a syndrome is not necessarily more pathological than a group of symptoms which clusters together but does not fit the description of one of the complicated mourning syndromes. Sometimes just a few complicated mourning symptoms—depending upon which they are—can be far more serious than the complicated mourning syndromes. With the exception of death, severity is not determined by the form of complicated mourning.

The seven syndromes of complicated mourning include three syndromes with problems in expression (i.e., absent mourning, delayed mourning and inhibited mourning); three syndromes with skewed aspects (i.e., distorted mourning of the extremely angry or guilty types, conflicted mourning, and unanticipated mourning); and the syndrome with a problem in ending (i.e., chronic mourning).

The third form that complicated mourning may take is of a diagnosable mental or physical disorder. This would include any DSM-III-R[3] diagnosis of a mental disorder or any recognized physical disorder that results from or is associated with a compromise, distortion, or failure of one or more of the six "R" processes of mourning. Death is the fourth form which complicated mourning may take. The death may be consciously chosen (i.e., suicide) or it may stem from the immediate results of a complicated mourning reaction (e.g., an automobile crash resulting from the complicated mourning symptom of driving at excessive speed) or the long-term results of a complicated mourning reaction (e.g., cirrhosis of the liver secondary to mourning-related alcoholism). The latter two types of death may or may not be subintentioned on the part of the mourner.

Generic High-Risk Factors for Complicated Mourning

Clinical and empirical evidence reveals that there are seven generic high-risk factors which can predispose any individual to have complication in mourning.[1] These can be divided into two categories: factors associated with the specific death and factors associated with antecedent and subsequent variables.

Factors associated with the death which are known especially to complicate mourning include: 1) a sudden and unanticipated death, especially when it is traumatic, violent, mutilating, or random; 2) death from an overly-lengthy illness; 3) loss of a child; and 4) the mourner's perception of preventability. Antecedent and subsequent variables that tend to complicate mourning include: 1) premorbid relationship with the deceased which has been markedly angry or ambivalent or markedly dependent; 2) the mourner's prior or concurrent mental health problems and/or unaccommodated losses and stresses; and 3) the mourner's perceived lack of social support.

To the extent that any bereaved individual is characterized by one or more of these factors, that individual can be said to be at risk for the development of complications in one or more of the six "R" processes of mourning, and hence at risk for complicated mourning.

Sociocultural and Technological Trends Exacerbating the High Risk Factors and Increasing the Prevalence of Complicated Mourning

Social change, medical advances, and shifting political realities have spawned the recent trends that have complicated healthy grief and mourning.

Social change, occurring at an increasingly rapid rate, encompasses such processes as urbanization; industrialization; increasing technicalization; secularization and deritualization (particularly the trend to omit funeral or memorial services and not to view the body); greater social mobility; social reorganization (specifically a decline in—if not a breakdown of—the nuclear family, increases in single parent and blended families, and the relative exclusion of the aged and dying); rising societal, interpersonal, and institutional violence (physical, sexual, and psychological); and unemployment, poverty, and economic problems. Consequences include social alienation; senses of personal helplessness and hopelessness; parental absence and neglect of children; larger societal discrepancies between the "haves" and the "have nots"; epidemic drug and alcohol abuse; physical and sexual abuse of children and those without power (e.g., women and the elderly); and availability of guns. All of these sequelae have tended to increase violence even more, to sever or severely damage the links between children and adults, and to expose individuals to more traumatic and unnatural deaths.

Medical advances have culminated in lengthier chronic illnesses, and increased age spans, altered mortality rates, and intensified bioethical dilemmas. These trends, plus those involving social change, accompany contemporary political realities of increasing incidence of terrorism, assassination, political torture, and genocide, which get played out against the ever-present possibility of ecological disaster, nuclear holocaust, and megadeath to impact dramatically and undeniably on today's mourner.[4–6]

Violence: A Particularly Malignant Trend

Any commentary on present-day trends would be negligent if it did not elaborate somewhat upon the phenomenon of violence in today's society. Violence contributes significantly to the increasing prevalence of complicated mourning, and is associated with most of its generic high-risk factors. One crime index offense occurs every two seconds in the United States, with one violent crime occurring every nineteen seconds.[7] Violent crime has risen to the extent that in April 1991 Attorney General Richard Thornburgh issued the statement that "a citizen of this country is today more likely to be the victim of a violent crime than of an automobile accident."[8] The U.S. Department of Justice estimates that five out of six of today's twelve-year-olds will become victims of violent crime during their lifetimes,[9] with estimates for the lifetime chance of becoming a victim of homicide in the United States ranging from one out of 133 to one out of 153 depending upon the source of the statistics.[10] One category of homicide—murder by juvenile—is increasing so rapidly that it is now being termed "epidemic" by psychologist and attorney Charles Ewing,[11] an authority on child perpetrators of homicide.

Other types of crime and victimization are on the rise in the United States. The National Victim Center Overview of Crime and Victimization in America[12] provides some of the horrifying statistics:

- Wife-beating results in more injuries that require medical treatment than rape, auto accidents, and muggings combined.
- More than one out of every 200 senior citizens are the victim of a violent crime each year, making a total of 155,000 elderly Americans who are attacked, robbed, assaulted, and murdered every year—435 each day.
- New York City has reported an eighty percent increase in hate-motivated crimes since 1986, with seventy percent of them perpetrated by those under age nineteen.
- One in three women will be sexually assaulted during her lifetime.
- Every forty-seven seconds a child is abused or neglected.

Certainly, society not only condones, but escalates, violence. Books, movies, music videos, and songs perpetuate the belief that violence is not merely acceptable, but exciting. Books focusing on real-life serial killers; escalating movie violence associated with anatomically precise and sexually explicit images; and music portraying hostility against women, murder, and necrophilia are routine. According to Thomas Radecki, Research Director for the National Coalition on Television Violence, by the age of 18 the average American child will have seen 200,000 violent acts on television, including 40,000 murders.[13] Children's programming now averages twenty-five violent acts per hour, which is up fifty percent from that in the early 1980s.[14]

The recently popular children's movie, *Teenage Mutant Ninja Turtles,* had a total of 194 acts of violence primarily committed by the "heroes" of the film, which was the most violent film ever to be given a "PG" rating.[15] In the week of March 11, 1990, *America's Funniest Home Videos* became the highest-rated series on television. Some of the stories on that program that viewers found particularly amusing included a child getting hit in the face with a shovel, seven women falling off a bench, a man getting hit by a glider, and a child bicycling into a tree.[15] All of this provides serious concerns given the twenty-year research of Leonard Eron and L. Rowell Huesmann, who found that children who watch significant amounts of TV violence at the age of eight were consistently more likely to commit violent crimes or engage in spouse abuse at age thirty.[13] These researchers determined that heavy exposure to media violence is one of the major causes of aggressive behavior, crime, and violence in society.

Other forms of violence are increasing as well. Reports of abused and neglected children continue to rise. They reached 2.5 million in 1990, an increase of 30.7 percent since 1986, and 117 percent in the past decade.[16] One out of three girls, and one out of seven boys, are sexually abused by the time they reach eighteen.[17] In the United States, when random studies are conducted without the inclusion of high-risk groups, one in eight husbands has been physically aggressive with his wife in the preceding twelve months.[18] At least 2,000,000 women are severely and aggressively assaulted by their partners in any twelve-month period.[18] It is a myth that what has been termed "intimate violence" is confined to mentally disturbed individuals. While ten percent of offenders do sustain some form of psychopathology, ninety percent of offenders do not look any different than the "normal" individual.[19]

Sequelae of the Trends Predisposing to Complicated Mourning

As a result of all the aforementioned sociocultural and technological trends, there have been changes in three main areas which have significantly increased the prevalence of complicated mourning:

1. the types of death occurring today
2. the characteristics of personal relationships that are severed by today's deaths
3. the personality and resources of today's mourner.

Each of these adversely impacts in one or more ways upon one or more of the high-risk factors for complicated mourning, thereby increasing its prevalence.

Types of Death Occurring Today

Contemporary American society is witnessing the increase in three types of death known to be at high risk for complicated mourning: 1) sudden and unanticipated deaths, especially if they are traumatic (i.e., characterized not only by suddenness

and lack of anticipation, but violence, mutilation, and destruction; preventability and/or randomness; multiple death; or the mourner's personal encounter with death;[20] 2) deaths that result from excessively lengthy chronic illnesses; and 3) deaths of children. Each of these deaths presents the survivors with issues known to compromise the "R" processes of mourning, hence each circumstance is a high-risk factor for complicated mourning.

Sudden and Unanticipated Traumatic Deaths

Sudden and unanticipated traumatic deaths stem primarily from four main causes: 1) accidents; 2) technological advances; 3) increasing rates of homicide and the escalating violence and pathology of perpetrators; and 4) higher suicide rates. Although mortality rates for children and youth in the United States have decreased since 1900, the large proportion of deaths from external causes—injuries, homicide, and suicide—distinguishes mortality at ages one to nineteen from that at other ages; with external causes of death accounting for about ten percent of the deaths of children and youth in 1900 and rising to 64 percent in 1985.[21]

Current trends reveal that "accidents"—a term covering most deaths from motor vehicle crashes, falls, poisoning, drowning, fire, suffocation, and firearms—are the leading cause of death among all persons aged one to thirty-seven and represent the fourth leading cause of death among persons of all ages.[22] On the average, there are eleven accidental deaths and approximately 1,030 disabling injuries every hour during the year.[22] Accidents are the single most common type of horrendous death for persons of any age, bringing deaths which are "premature, torturous, and without redeeming value".[23]

Technological advances simultaneously have both decreased the proportion of natural deaths that occur and increased the proportion of sudden and unanticipated traumatic deaths. For instance, substantial improvements in biomedical technology have culminated in higher survival rates from illnesses which previously would have been fatal. This leaves individuals alive longer to be susceptible to unnatural death. Additionally, the increase in unnatural death is due to greater current exposure to technology, machinery, motor vehicles, airplanes, chemicals, firearms, weapon systems, and so forth that put human beings at greater risk for unnatural death. For example, prior to the advent of the airplane, a crash of a horse and buggy could claim far fewer lives and be less mutilating to the bodies than the crash of a DC-10.

The third reason for the increase in sudden and unanticipated traumatic deaths stems from the increasing rates of homicide and the escalating violence and pathology of those who perpetrate these crimes upon others. The increase in actual homicide incidence; the rising percentage of serial killers; and the types of violence perpetrated before, during, and after the final homicidal act suggest that there are sicker individuals doing sicker things. More than ever before, homicide may be marked by cult or ritual killing, thrill killing, random killing, drive-by shootings, and accompanied by predeath torture and postdeath defilement. The increasing pathology of those who commit violent crimes may be seen as the result of the previously mentioned sociocultural trends, especially but not exclusively the individual's decreasing social connections and sense of power; fewer social prohibitions, and increasing societal violence. It reflects the increasing number of individuals with impaired psychological development, characterized often by an absent conscience, low frustration tolerance, poor impulse control, inability to delay gratification or modulate aggression, a sense of deprivation and entitlement, and notably poor attachment bonds and pathological patterns of relationships.

The fourth reason for the increase in sudden and unanticipated traumatic deaths follows from the higher suicide rates currently found in Western society. As above, these types of death appear to derive from all of the aforementioned trends contributing to complicated mourning in general.

The reader will note that most of the sudden and unanticipated traumatic deaths in this category also are preventable. Given that the perception of preventability is a high-risk factor predisposing to complicated mourning, to the extent that a mourner maintains this perception as an element in his or her mourning of the death, that individual sustains a greater chance for experiencing complications in the process.

Long-Term Chronic Illness Death

This type of death is increasing in frequency because of biomedical and technological advances that can combat disease and forestall cessation of life. Consequently, today's illnesses are longer in duration than ever before. However, it has been well-documented that there are significant problems for survivors when a loved one's terminal illness persists for too long.[24] These illnesses often present loved ones with inherent difficulties that eventually complicate their postdeath bereavement and expose them to situations and dilemmas previously unheard of when patients died sooner and/or without becoming the focus for bioethical debates around the use of machinery and the prolongation of life without quality. With the increase in the Human Immunodeficiency Virus (HIV) and Acquired Immunodeficiency Syndrome (AIDS), significant multidimensional stresses arise which engender those known to complicate mourning in anyone (e.g., anger, ambivalence, guilt, stigmatization, social disenfranchisement, problems obtaining required health care, and so forth). The fact that an individual may be positive for the HIV virus for an exceptionally long period of time prior to developing the often long-term, multiproblemic, and idiosyncratic course of their particular version of AIDS, with all of its vicissitudes, gives new meaning these days to the stresses of long-term chronic illness.

Parental Loss of a Child

In earlier years, by the time an adult child died, his or her parents would have been long deceased. Today, with increases in lifespan and advances in medical technology, parents are permitted to survive long enough to witness the deaths of the adult children they used to predecease. Clinically and empirically, it is well-known that significant problematic issues are associated with the parental loss of a child—issues which when compared to those generated by other losses appear to make this loss the

most difficult with which to cope.[25] These problematic issues and complicated mourning are now visited upon older parents who remain alive to experience the death of their adult child. There is even some suggestion that additional stresses are added to the normal burdens of parental bereavement when the child is an adult in his or her own right.[26] It is a uniquely contemporary trend, therefore, that associated with all of today's deaths are a greater percentage of parents who, because of medical advancements, are alive to be placed in the high-risk situation for complicated mourning upon the death of their adult child. This is a population that can be expected to increase, and consequently swell the numbers of complicated mourners as well.

Characteristics of Personal Relationships Severed by Today's Deaths

As a consequence of societal trends, there has been an increase in conflicted and dependent relationships in our society. Both types are high-risk factors when they characterize the mourner's premorbid relationship with the deceased.[1] With more of these types of relationships than ever before, there is a relative increase in the prevalence of complicated mourning, which is predisposed to develop after the death of one with whom the mourner has had this type of bond.

In 1957, Edmond Volkart offered a classic discussion of why death in the American family tends to cause greater psychological impact than in other cultures, specifically causing the family to be uniquely vulnerable to bereavement.[6] The reasons he delineated are even more salient today, and are part of the trends already cited above. Among other trends, he noted that the limited range of interaction in the American family fosters unusually intense emotional involvement as compared to other societies, and that there is an exclusivity of relationships in the American family. Both trends breed overidentification and overdependence among family members, which in turn engender ambivalence, repressed hostility, and guilt that create greater potential for complications after the death. Adding fuel to this fire is the societal expectation that grief expression concentrates on feelings and expression of loss. There is a failure both to recognize and to provide channels for hostility, guilt, and ambivalence.

Problematic relationships are on the rise in our society for other reasons as well. Quite importantly, there is an overall increase in sexual and physical abuse of children, as well as other adults. Research repeatedly documents the malignant intrapsychic and interpersonal sequelae of abuse and victimization.[27,28] This leaves the victim susceptible to complications in mourning not only because of the myriad symptomatology and biopsychosocial issues they caused, but typically with significant amounts of the anger, ambivalence, and/or dependence known to complicate any individual's mourning. In addition, the victimization may interfere with the mourner permitting him or herself to mourn the death of the perpetrator—an often necessary task that many victims resist because of inaccurate beliefs about mourning in general and/or misconstruals of what their specifically mourning the perpetrator's death may mean.[1] This only further victimizes the person through the consequences of incomplete mourning.

These forms of victimization are not the only experiences which give rise to the conflicted and dependent relationships identified as predisposing to complicated mourning. Individuals raised in families with one or more alcoholic parents or a parent who is an adult child of an alcoholic (ACOA), or with one or more parents who are psychologically impaired, rigid in beliefs, compulsive in behaviors, codependent, absent, neglectful, or chronically ill are vulnerable too. As sociocultural trends escalate these scenarios, relationships characterized by anger, ambivalence, and dependency will become prevalent, and complicated mourning will, in turn, become more frequent.

The Personality and Resources of Today's Mourner

Current trends suggest that the personality and resources of today's mourner leave that individual compromised in mourning for three reasons. First, given the trends previously discussed, the personalities and mental health of today's mourners are often more impaired. These impaired persons—who themselves frequently sustain poor attachment bonds with their own parents because of these trends—typically effect intergenerational transmission of these deficits via the inadequate parenting provided to their own children and the unhealthy experiences those children undergo. Clinically, one sees more often these days impaired superego development, lower level personality organization, narcissistic behavior, character disorder, and poor impulse control. Given that one's personality and previous and current states of mental health are critical factors influencing any mourner's ability to address mourning successfully, a trend toward relatively more impairment in this area has implications for greater numbers of people being added to the rolls of complicated mourners.

Another liability for a mourner is the existence of unaccommodated prior or concurrent losses or stresses. In this regard, a second reason for the increased prevalence of complicated mourning comes from the presence of more loss and stress in the life of today's mourner as compared to times in the past. To the extent that contemporary sociocultural trends bring relatively more losses and stresses for a person, both prior to a given death (e.g., parents' divorce) and concomitant with it (e.g., unemployment), today's mourner is relatively more disadvantaged given his or her increased exposure to these high-risk factors.

The third reason for increased complications in mourning arises from the compromise of the mourner's resources. Disenfranchised mourning[29] is on the rise, and the consequent perceived lack of social support it stimulates is a high-risk factor for complicated mourning. It is quite evident that conditions in contemporary American society promote all three of the main reasons for social disenfranchisement during mourning, i.e., invalidation of the loss, the lost relationship, or the mourner.[29] Examples of unrecognized losses that are increasing in today's

society include abortions, adoptions, the deaths of pets, and the inherent losses of those with Alzheimer's disease. Cases of the second type of disenfranchised loss that are on the increase include relationships that are not based on kin ties, or are not socially sanctioned (e.g., gay or lesbian relationships, extramarital affairs), or those that existed primarily in the past (e.g., former spouses or in-laws). Increasingly prevalent situations where the mourner is unrecognized can be found when the mourner is elderly, mentally handicapped, or a child. The more society creates, maintains, or permits individuals to be disenfranchised in their mourning, the more those individuals are at risk for complicated mourning given that disenfranchisement is so intimately linked with the high-risk factor of the mourner's perception of lack of social support.

Problems Inherent in the Mental Health Profession which Interfere with Proper Response to Complicated Mourning and to Its Escalation

There are three serious problems inherent in mental health today that interfere with the profession's response to complicated mourning and its escalation. Each one contributes to increasing the prevalence of complicated mourning either by facilitating misdiagnosis and/or hampering requisite treatment. The three problems are: 1) lack of an appropriate diagnostic category in the DSM-III-R; 2) insufficient knowledge about grief, mourning, and bereavement in general; and 3) decreased funds for and increased restrictions upon contemporary mental health services.

In the DSM-III-R, there is the lack of a diagnostic category for anything but the most basic uncomplicated grief, with the criteria even for this being significantly unrealistic for duration and symptomatology in light of today's data on uncomplicated grief and mourning. If they want to treat a mourning individual, mental health clinicians are often forced to utilize other diagnoses, many of which have clinical implications that are unacceptable. Other diagnoses that clinicians employ to justify treatment and to incorporate more fully the symptomatology of the bereaved individual frequently include one of the depressive, anxiety, or adjustment disorders; brief reactive psychosis; or one of the V code diagnoses.

The second area of problems in the mental health profession is the shocking insufficiency of knowledge about grief and bereavement in general. Mental health professionals tend, as does the general public, to have inappropriate expectations and unrealistic attitudes about grief and mourning, and to believe in and promote the myths and stereotypes known to pervade society at large. These not only do not help, but actually harm bereaved individuals given that they are used to (a) set the standards against which the bereaved individual is evaluated, (b) determine the assistance and support provided and/or judged to be needed, and (c) support unwarranted diagnoses of failure and pathology.[30] Yet, the problem is not all in *mis*information. Too many clinicians actually do not even know that they lack the requisite information they must possess if they want to treat a bereaved person successfully. Without a doubt, the majority of clinicians know an insufficient amount about uncomplicated grief and mourning; and of those who do know an adequate amount, only a fraction of them know enough about complicated mourning. Clinician lack of information and misinformation is the major cause of iatrogenesis in the treatment of grief and mourning.

An overall decrease in funds permitted and an increase in third-party payer insurance restrictions mark contemporary mental health services and constitute the third problem in the field adding to the prevalence of complicated mourning. These changes occur at a time when it not only is becoming more clearly documented that uncomplicated grief and mourning is more associated with psychiatric distress than previously recognized[31] and that it persists for longer duration,[32] but precisely when the incidence of complicated mourning is increasing and demanding more extensive treatment for higher proportions of the bereaved. Consequently, at the exact point in time that the mental health community will have more bereaved individuals with greater complicated mourning requiring treatment for longer periods of time, mental health services will be increasingly subjected to limitations, preapprovals, third-party reviews by persons ignorant of the area, short-term models, and forced usage of inappropriate diagnostic classification. This scenario demands that the mental health professional working with the bereaved find new policies, models, approaches, and treatments which are appropriate to these serious realities. Failing to do so, the future is frightening as the current system simply is not equipped to respond to the coming onslaught of complicated mourners.

The Pitfalls for Addressing Complicated Mourning Residing in the Field of Thanatology Today

It is unfortunate, but true: Thanatologists are contributing to the rising prevalence of complicated mourning as are contemporary sociocultural and technological trends and the mental health profession. While it is not in the purview of this article to discuss at length the myriad problems inherent in our own field of thanatology that contribute to complicated mourning, it must be noted:

- A significant amount of caregivers lack adequate clinical information about uncomplicated grief and mourning, e.g., the "normal" psychiatric complications of uncomplicated grief and mourning.
- Many thanatologists, in their effort to promote the naturalness of grief and mourning and to depathologize the way they construe it to have been medicalized, maintain an insufficient understanding of complicated grief and mourning.

- There is nonexistent, or at the very least woefully insufficient, assessment conducted by caregivers who assume that the grief and mourning they observe must be related exclusively to the particular death closest in time and who do not place the individual's responses within the context of his or her entire life prior to evaluating them.
- The phenomenon of "throwing the baby out with the bathwater" has occurred regarding medication in bereavement. Out of a concern that a mourner not be inappropriately medicated as had been done so often in the past, caregivers today often fail to send mourners for medication evaluations that are desperately needed, e.g., antianxiety medication following traumatic deaths.
- The research in the field has not been sufficiently longitudinal and has overfocused on certain populations (e.g., widows), leaving findings that are not generalizable over time for many types of mourners, especially complicated mourners.
- Caregivers do not always recognize that any work as a grief or mourning counselor or therapist must overlay a basic foundation of training in mental health intervention in general. While education in thanatology, good intentions, and/or previous experience with loss may be appropriate credentials for the individual facilitating uncomplicated grief and mourning (e.g., a facilitator of a mutual help group for the bereaved), this is not sufficient for that person offering counseling or therapy.
- Given that thanatology itself is a "specialty area," thanatologists often fail to recognize that the field encompasses a number of "subspecialty areas," each of which has its own data base and treatment requirements, i.e., all mourners are not alike and caregivers must recognize and respond to the differences inherent in different loss situations (e.g., loss of a child versus loss of a spouse or sudden and unanticipated death versus an expected chronic illness death).
- Clinicians working with the dying and the bereaved are subject to countertransference phenomena, stress reactions, codependency, "vicarious traumatization",[33] and burnout.

This constitutes a brief, and by no means exhaustive, listing of the types of pitfalls into which a thanatologist may fall. Each "fall" has the potential for compromising the mourning of the bereaved individual and in that regard has the potential for increasing the prevalence of complicated mourning today.

Conclusion

This article has discussed the causes and forms of complicated mourning, and has delineated the seven high-risk factors known to predispose to it. The purpose has been to illustrate how current sociocultural and technological trends are exacerbating these factors, thereby significantly increasing the prevalence of complicated mourning today. Problems both in the mental health profession and in the field of thanatology further contribute by preventing or interfering with requisite intervention. It is imperative that these grim realities be recognized in order that appropriate policies, models, approaches, and treatments be developed to respond to the individual and societal needs created by complicated mourning and its sequelae.

Notes

1. T. Rando, *Treatment of Complicated Mourning,* Research Press, Champaign, Illinois, 1993.
2. T. Rando, *Grief, Dying, and Death: Clinical Interventions for Caregivers,* Research Press, Champaign, Illinois, 1984.
3. American Psychiatric Association, *Diagnostic and Statistical Manual of Mental Disorders* (3rd ed. rev.), Washington, D.C., 1987.
4. H. Feifel, The Meaning of Death in American Society: Implications for Education, in *Death Education: Preparation for Living,* B. Green and D. Irish (eds.), Schenkman, Cambridge, Massachusetts, 1971.
5. R. Lifton, *Death in Life: Survivors of Hiroshima,* Random House, New York, 1968.
6. E. Volkart (with collaboration of S. Michael), Bereavement and Mental Health, in *Explorations in Social Psychiatry,* A. Leighton, J. Clausen, and R. Wilson (eds.), Basic Books, New York, 1957.
7. Federal Bureau of Investigation, U.S. Department of Justice, *Uniform Crime Reports for the United States,* U.S. Government Printing Office, Washington, D.C., 1990.
8. Violent Crimes up 10%, *Providence Journal,* pp. A1 and A6, April 29, 1991.
9. National Victim Center, *America Speaks Out: Citizens' Attitudes about Victims' Rights and Violence* (Executive Summary), Fort Worth, Texas, 1991.
10. Bureau of Justice Statistics Special Report, *The Risk of Violent Crime* (NCJ-97119), U.S. Department of Justice, Washington, D.C., May 1985.
11. Killing by Kids "Epidemic" Forecast, *APA Monitor,* pp. 1 and 31, April, 1991.
12. National Victim Center, *National Victim Center Overview of Crime and Victimization in America,* Fort Worth, Texas, 1991.
13. Violence in Our Culture, *Newsweek,* pp. 46–52, April 1, 1991.
14. J. Patterson and P. Kim, *The Day America Told the Truth,* Prentice Hall Press, New York, 1991.
15. National Victim Center, *Crime, Safety and You!,* 1:3, 1990.
16. Children's Defense Fund Memo on the Family Preservation Act, Washington, D.C., July 2, 1991.
17. E. Bass and L. Davis, *The Courage to Heal: A Guide for Women Survivors of Child Sexual Abuse,* Harper and Row Publishers, New York, 1988.
18. A. Brown, *"Women's Roles" and Responses to Violence by Intimates: Hard Choices for Women Living in a Violent Society,* paper presented at the conference on "Trauma and Victimization: Understanding and Healing Survivors" sponsored by the University of Connecticut Center for Professional Development, Vernon, Connecticut, September 27–28, 1991.
19. R. Gelles, *The Roots, Context, and Causes of Family Violence,* paper presented at the conference on "Trauma and Victimization: Understanding and Healing Survivors" sponsored by the University of Connecticut Center for Professional Development, Vernon, Connecticut, September 27–28, 1991.
20. T. Rando, Complications in Mourning Traumatic Death, in *Death, Dying and Bereavement,* I. Corless, B. Germino, and M. Pittman-Lindeman (eds.), Jones and Bartlett Publishers, Inc., Boston (in press).
21. L. Fingerhut and J. Kleinman, Mortality Among Children and Youth, *American Journal of Public Health, 79,* pp. 899–901, 1989.
22. National Safety Council, *Accident Facts, 1991 Edition,* Chicago, 1991.
23. M. Dixon and H. Clearwater, Accidents, in *Horrendous Death, Health, and Well-Being,* D. Leviton (ed.), Hemisphere Publishing Corporation, New York, 1991.
24. T. Rando (ed.), *Loss and Anticipatory Grief,* Lexington Books, Lexington, Massachusetts, 1986.
25. T. Rando (ed.), *Parental Loss of a Child,* Research Press, Champaign, Illinois, 1986.
26. T. Rando, Death of an Adult Child, in *Parental Loss of a Child,* T. Rando (ed.), Research Press, Champaign, Illinois, 1986.
27. C. Courtois, *Healing the Incest Wound: Adult Survivors in Therapy,* Norton, New York, 1988.
28. F. Ochberg (ed.), *Post-Traumatic Therapy and Victims of Violence,* Brunner/Mazel, New York, 1988.
29. K. Doka (ed.), *Disenfranchised Grief: Recognizing Hidden Sorrow,* Lexington Books, Lexington, Massachusetts, 1989.
30. T. Rando, *Grieving: How To Go On Living When Someone You Love Dies,* Lexington Books, Lexington, Massachusetts, 1988.
31. S. Jacobs and K. Kim, Psychiatric Complications of Bereavement, *Psychiatric Annals, 20,* pp. 314–317, 1990.
32. S. Zisook and S. Shuchter, Time Course of Spousal Bereavement, *General Hospital Psychiatry, 7,* pp. 95–100, 1985.
33. I. McCann and L. Pearlman, Vicarious Traumatization: A Framework for Understanding the Psychological Effects of Working with Victims, *Journal of Traumatic Stress, 3,* pp. 131–149, 1990.

This article is adapted from a keynote address of the same name presented at the 13th Annual Conference of the Association for Death Education and Counseling, Duluth, Minnesota, April 26–28, 1991, and from the author's book, *Treatment of Complicated Mourning,* Research Press, Champaign, Illinois, 1993.

Counseling with Children in Contemporary Society

This article examines elements related to children's developmental understandings of death, ways to talk to children about death, a broad understanding of the nature of children's grief and bereavement, recognition of the common characteristics of grieving children, and useful interventions for the bereaved child by mental health counselors.

LINDA GOLDMAN

This article examines elements related to children's developmental understandings of death, ways to talk to children about death, a broad understanding of the nature of children's grief and bereavement, recognition of the common characteristics of grieving children, and useful interventions. The research related to the child grief process and the intrinsic value of therapeutic and educational supports in working with grieving children are discussed through case studies, the professional literature, and practical interventions that support the process of grief therapy for mental health counselors and the bereaved child.

Grief counseling with children in contemporary society is a complex enterprise for mental health counselors (MHCs). Today's children are bombarded with loss in a way that many adults did not experience growing up. Common childhood losses are amplified by a world filled with terrorism, war, bullying, drugs, violence, sexuality, gender issues, and fear of nuclear or biological annihilation. Grief counseling with children benefits from the creation of a community grief team, whereby the parent or guardian, the school system, and the mental health counselor are part of an integral group that nurtures and supports the grieving child in an often confusing and unpredictable world. The purpose of this article is to address children's grief, focusing on their developmental understandings of death, ways to talk to children about death, the nature of children's bereavement, and the implications for mental health counselors. The research related to the child's grief process and the intrinsic value of supports through counseling and education in working with bereaved children is woven into this material. This infor-ation is presented through case studies, research, and intellec- understandings to support the process of grief therapy for health professionals and their clients.

Bereaved Children

It is essential when working with children who have experienced the death of someone close to them to be aware of the many childhood losses incurred. Often there are secondary losses for bereaved children. The death of a loved one can be the catalyst creating many secondary losses including loss of friends, home, schools, neighborhoods, self-esteem, and routines. Angela was a 7-year-old in a single parent home. She rarely saw her dad after her parent's divorce. Mom had died in a plane crash. Within a week she moved to another state to live with her dad and a stepmother and stepbrother she barely knew. Angela began to do poorly in school and said she "couldn't concentrate." She told her dad that she had no energy to play soccer anymore. She felt different now that her mom had died, and she "didn't want to talk about it with anyone." Within a short time she had lost her mom, her home, her school, her friends, her neighborhood, her ability to learn, and her day-to-day life as she knew it. These are multiple childhood losses that can occur due to the death of a parent.

MHCs' awareness of the following common losses experienced by children (Goldman, 2000b) can give insight into the complexities of children's grieving process. In addition to the types of losses that come easily to mind, like the loss of a family member or friend, children experience more subtle or less obvious losses. Other relationship losses include the absence of teacher or a parent being unavailable due to substance abuse, imprisonment, or divorce. Children experience loss of external objects through robbery or favorite toys or objects being misplaced. Self-related losses include loss of a physical part of the body or loss of self-esteem perhaps through physical, sexual, emotional, or derivational abuse. Many children live with loss in their environment including fire, floods, hurricanes, and other natural disasters. A primary death can often create the secondary loss of a move, change of school, change in the family structure, or family separation. Other childhood losses are loss of routines and habits and loss of skills and abilities after the death of a close loved one. Lastly, the loss of a future and the protection of the adult world are common experiences for the grieving child, causing them sometimes to exhibit a lack of motivation and an inclination to choose violence as a way of solving problems.

Children's Developmental Understanding of Death

A child's understanding of death changes as he or she develops, as explained by Piaget's (Ginsberg & Opper, 1969) cognitive stages of development. Gaining insight into children's developmental stages allows the MHC to predict and understand age-appropriate responses. During the pre-operational stage, usually ages 2–7, magical thinking, egocentricity, reversibility, and causality characterize children's thinking. Young children developmentally live in an egocentric world, filled with the notion that their words and thoughts can magically cause a person to die. Children often feel they have caused and are responsible for everything (Ginsberg & Opper). For instance, 5-year-old Sam screamed at his older brother, "I hate you, and I wish you were dead!" He was haunted with the idea that his words created his brother's murder the following day. Due to Sam's age-appropriate egocentrism and magical perception, he saw himself as the center of the universe, capable of creating and destroying at will the world around him. Reversibility also characterizes children's grieving. For example, Jack, a 5-year-old first grader, was very sad after his dad died in a plane crash. Age-appropriately, he perceived death as reversible and told his friends and family that his dad was coming back. Jack even wrote his dad a letter and waited and waited for the mailman to bring back a response. Alice, age 7 years, who told me that she killed her mother, exemplifies the common childhood notion of causality in the following story. She was 4 years old when her mom died. When I asked how she killed her, she responded, "My mom picked me up on the night she had her heart attack. If she hadn't picked me up, she wouldn't have died; so I killed her."

Piaget's next stage of development, concrete operations, usually includes ages 7–12 years (Ginsberg & Opper, 1969). During this stage the child, in relation to death, is very curious and realistic and seeks information. Mary, at age 10, wanted to know everything about her mother's death. She stated that she had heard so many stories about her mom's fatal car crash that she wanted to look up the story in the newspaper to find out the facts. Jason, age 11, wondered about his friend who was killed in a sudden plane crash. "What was he thinking before the crash, was he scared, and did he suffer?" Tom age-appropriately wondered at age 9 if there was an after-life and exactly where his dad was after his sudden fatal heart attack. These examples illustrate that, at this stage of development, children commonly express logical thoughts and fears about death, can conceptualize that all body functions stop, and begin to internalize the universality and permanence of death. They may ponder the facts

about how the terrorists got the plane to crash, wanting to know every detail. When working with this age group, it is important to ask, "What are the facts that you would like to know?" and to assist children in finding answers through family, friends, media, and experts.

Adolescents' (age 13 and up) concept of death is often characterized in accord with Piaget's prepositional operations, implications, and logic stage of development (Ginsberg & Opper, 1969). Many teenagers, being self-absorbed at this age, see mortality and death as a natural process that is very remote from their day-to-day life and something they cannot control.

Teenagers are often preoccupied with shaping their own life and deny the possibility of their own death. Malcolm, 16 years old, expressed age-appropriate thoughts when he proclaimed, "I won't let those terrorists control my life. I'll visit the mall in Washington whenever I want. They can't hurt me!"

Children can misinterpret language at different developmental stages. The young child can misunderstand clichés associated with grieving, and these clichés can actually block the grieving process. Sammy, at age 6, began having nightmares and exhibited a fear of going to sleep after he was told that his dog Elmo died because "the vet put him to sleep." Alice was told it was "God's will" that her grandmother died because "God loved her so much." Alice questioned, "Why would God take Grandma away from me, doesn't God love me, and will God take me too?" Tom, age 9 years, continually heard the message that dad was watching over him. One day he asked the mental health clinician, "Do you really think my dad is watching over me all of the time? That would be very embarrassing."

Talking to Children about Death

Sudden or traumatic deaths, divorce and abandonment, the death of a grandparent, and the loss of a pet are a few of the many grief issues that children face (Goldman 2000b). These losses shatter the emotional and physical equilibrium and stability a child may have had. The terror, isolation, and loneliness experienced by too many of today's children after a death leave them living in a world without a future, without protection, and without role models. Children normally and naturally assume the adult world will care for them, support them, and nurture them. When Grandpa has a sudden fatal heart attack, Dad dies in a car crash, Mom dies of suicide, or sister Mary overdoses on drugs, a child's world is shattered. "How could this have happened to me?" is the first question.

Children need to know the age-appropriate truth about a death (Goldman, 2000b). They often have a conscious or unconscious knowing of when they are being lied to, and this knowing can create a secondary loss of the trust of their emotional environment. In talking with children, mental health counselors, parents, and teachers can define death as "when the body stops working." In today's world we need to provide specific definitions for children for different kinds of death. Suicide is when "someone chooses to make his or her body stop working," and homicide is "when someone chooses to make someone else's body stop working." MHCs can say, "Sometimes people die when they are very, very, very old or very, very, very sick; or they are so, so, so injured that the doctors and nurses can't make their bodies work any more." It is important to know that children ask questions such as "Will I die too?" The common questions that children ask about death and grieving give the MHC an insight into their process. The questions serve as a mirror to reflect the child's inner thoughts and feelings that might be otherwise hidden. By responding to questions like the following, the mental health professional or other adult can create an openness to grieve: (a) Who will take care of me if you die too?, (b) Will you and daddy die too?, (c) What is heaven?, (d) Can I die if I go to sleep?, (e) Where did grandpa go?, (f) Will it ever stop hurting?, (g) Why did God kill my mom?, (h) Will Grandpa come back?, (i) Will I forget my person?, (j) Did my person suffer?, and (k) Was it my fault?

Understanding the Nature of Children's Bereavement

Fox (1988) explained that one useful way to help bereaved children and monitor their ongoing emotional needs is to "conceptualize what they must do in order to stay psychologically healthy" (p. 8). Fox emphasized that, in order to assure children's grief will be good grief, they must accomplish four tasks: understanding, grieving, commemorating, and going on. Each child's unique nature and age-appropriate level of experience can influence how he or she works through these tasks. The specific cause of death can also influence the way a child accomplishes these tasks. A dad's death by suicide may create significantly different issues than an anticipated grandfather's death from pneumonia.

Bereaved children may not process grief in a linear way (Goldman 2000b). The tasks may surface and resurface in varying order, intensity, and duration. Grief work can be "messy," with waves of feelings and thoughts flowing through children when they least expect it to come. Children can be unsuspectingly hit with these "grief bullets" in the car, listening to a song or the news, seeing or hearing an airplane overhead, reading a story in school, or watching the news about a terrorist attack. A fireman's siren, a jet fighter, a soldier in uniform, a postal letter, or a balloon bursting can trigger sudden and intense feelings without any warning, and often without any conscious connection to their grief and loss issue.

Common characteristics of grieving children. Children in the 21st century experience grief-related issues involving safety and protection that many adults may not have had as children. Whether children ever really enjoyed the protection of the adults in their lives is a debatable question, but the perception of that safety seems to have existed in previous generations. Although grief-related issues have always existed through time, today's children are exposed to an extraordinary visual and auditory barrage of input. The news, the World Wide Web, music, and videos are constantly bombarding children with sounds and images of school shootings, killings, violence, and abuse. Children are left with feelings of vulnerability and defenselessness. Either by real circumstances or vicariously through media reports, young people are inundated with issues such as murder, suicide, AIDS, abuse, violence, terrorism, and bullying that often hinder their natural grief processes. This disruption is an overlay for other interactive components that may affect a child's grief process.

Three categories of interactive components can be examined in assessing the grieving child (Webb, 2002):

- Individual factors
- Death-related factors
- Support system factors

The flowing and overlapping of these components create a complex world for the grieving child. Individual factors include cognitive and developmental age; personality components; past coping mechanisms in the home, school, and community environments; medical history; and past experience with death. Death-related factors involve the type of death, contact with the deceased such as being present at death, viewing the dead body, attending funerals and gravesite, expressions of "goodbye," and grief reactions. The third group of variables concerns the child's support system including grief reactions of the nuclear family and extended family; school, peer, and religious recognition and support of the grief process; and cultural affiliation including typical beliefs about death and the extent of a child's inclusion. Other factors related to a death that may increase complications for the grief process include suddenness and lack of anticipation, violence, mutilation, and destruction, preventability and/or randomness, multiple death, and personal encounter of the mourner such as a threat or shocking confrontation.

As noted by Webb (2002), "although virtually any death may be perceived by the mourner as personally traumatic because of the internal subjective feeling involved . . . circumstances that are objectively traumatic are associated with five factors known to increase complications for mourners" (p. 368). Learning to recognize the signs of grieving and traumatized children is essential to normalizing their experience of grief and trauma. A mental health counselor needs to be educated in these common signs in order to reinforce for bereaved children, families, and educators that these thoughts, feelings, and actions are natural consequences in the child's grief process. This reassurance helps to reduce anxiety and fear.

Children may experience the following physical, emotional, cognitive, and behavioral symptoms common in the grieving process: The child (a) continually re-tells events about his or her loved one and their death; (b) feels the loved one is present in some way and speaks of him or her in the present tense; (c) dreams about the loved one and longs to be with him or her; (d) experiences nightmares and sleeplessness; (e) cannot concentrate on schoolwork, becomes disorganized, and/or cannot complete homework; (f) finds it difficult to follow directions or becomes overly talkative; (g) appears at times to feel nothing; (h) is pre-occupied with death and worries excessively about health issues; (i) is afraid to be left alone; (j) often cries at unexpected times; (k) wets the bed or loses his or her appetite; (l) shows regressive behaviors (e.g., is clingy or babyish); (m) idealizes or imitates the loved one and assumes his or her mannerisms; (n) creates his or her own spiritual belief system; (o) becomes a class bully or a class clown; (p) shows reckless physical action; (q) has headaches and stomach aches; and (r) rejects old friends, withdraws, or acts out.

Complications in children's grief. In addition, children's grief can be complicated, and common signs include withdrawal, sleep disorders, anxiety, difficulty in concentration, and regression. The common signs associated with children's bereavement may become heightened by their intensity, frequency, and duration. The term disenfranchised grief is used by Doka (1989) to refer to losses that cannot be openly acknowledged, socially sanctioned, or publicly mourned. Five categories of situations may create complications for the bereaved child (adapted with permission from Goldman, 2001). These categories are:

- Sudden or traumatic death
- Social stigma and shame
- Multiple losses
- Past relationship with the deceased
- The grief process of the surviving parent or caretaker

They explain circumstances that can create complications leading to obstructions in the child's grief process. Awareness of the commonality of feelings and thoughts surrounding these situations can aid the mental health counselor in normalizing what may seem so unfamiliar for the children.

Sudden or traumatic death can include murder, suicide, a fatal accident, or sudden fatal illness. With a sudden or traumatic death, an unstable environment is immediately created in the child's home. Children feel confusion over these kinds of death. A desire for revenge often is experienced after a murder or fatal accident. Rage or guilt, or both, emerge against the person who has committed suicide. A terror of violence and death unfolds, and the child feels shock and disbelief that suddenly this death has occurred.

Social stigma and shame frequently accompany deaths related to AIDS, suicide, homicide, terrorist attacks, or school shootings. Children as well as adults often feel too embarrassed to speak of these issues. They remain silent out of fear of being ridiculed or ostracized. These suppressed feelings get projected outward in the form of rage or inward in the form of self-hatred. Often times these children feel lonely and isolated. They cannot grieve normally because they have not separated the loss of the deceased from the way the deceased died.

Multiple losses can produce a deep fear of abandonment and self-doubt in children. The death of a single parent without a partner is a good example of a multiple loss. When the only parent of a child dies, the child can be forced to move from his or her home, the rest of his or her family and friends, the school, and the community. The child is shocked at this sudden and complete change of lifestyle and surroundings, and may withdraw or become terrified of future abandonment. Nightmares and/or bed-wetting could appear.

The past relationship to the deceased can greatly impact the grieving child. When a child has been abused, neglected, or abandoned by a loved one, there are often ambivalent feelings when the loved one's death occurs. A 5-year-old girl whose alcoholic father sexually abused her may feel great conflict when that parent dies. Part of her may feel relieved, even glad, to be rid of the abuse yet ashamed to say those feelings out loud. She may carry the secret of the abuse and become locked into that memory and be unable to grieve. Children often feel guilt,

fear, abandoned, or depressed if grief for a loved one is complicated by an unresolved past relationship.

The grief process of the surviving parent or caretaker greatly affects children. If the surviving parent is not able to mourn, there is no role model for the child. A closed environment stops the grief process. Many times the surviving parent finds it too difficult to watch his or her child grieve. The parent may be unable to grieve him or herself or may be unwilling to recognize the child's pain. Feelings become denied and the expression of these feelings is withheld. The surviving parent may well become an absentee parent because of his or her own overwhelming grief, producing more feelings of abandonment and isolation in the child. Children often fear something will happen to this parent or to himself or herself and, as a result, become overprotective of the parent and other loved ones (Goldman, 2001).

Implications for Mental Health Counselors

There are important general purposes for the MHC when working with grieving children. A major purpose is allowing children freedom to express emotion. This expression of emotion is an integral component of counseling and includes interventions with writing, drawing, poetry, projective techniques, and dream work. Support groups for children enhance the expression of emotions with peers who are working through similar situations. Allowing children to connect to and maintain memories serves as another important purpose for the MHC professional. Through remembering and sharing with others, the bereaved child can maintain a continuing bond with the person who died. Educating grieving children and the adults around them underscores another purpose for the mental health counselor: To create common thoughts and practices that harmoniously integrate the network of support surrounding the bereaved child.

Identifying At-Risk Children

Grieving children wonder if the pain will ever stop hurting. As Celotta, Jacobs and Keys (1987) identified, two questions that at-risk children respond to 100% of the time are: "Do you feel hopeless?" and "Do you feel sad?" These responses were part of a checklist given to elementary school children to identify depression. Mental health counselors can create simple tools to help target children who are traumatized and may be at-risk. Asking them to write or draw in response to questions such as "What makes you the most sad?," "What makes you the angriest?," or "What makes you feel the loneliest?" can provide useful information. Jim, a 10-year-old student from China, explained his picture showing a boy with his soul next to him. His older brother had recently died of suicide. Jim explained, "This is me, and this is my soul. Sometimes I feel like killing myself so I won't feel all of the pain. Sometimes I wish I would just disappear." This simple intervention created the identification of an at-risk child and pointed out the need for further exploration and evaluation.

Interventions for Individual Counseling

"The goal of helping children of all ages to cope with death is to promote their competence, facilitate their ability to cope, and recognize that children are active participants in their lives" (Silverman, 2000, p. 42). Mental health counselors need to be prepared to respond to children's questions. Grieving children are becoming a larger and larger, growing segment of our youth; and their grief issues arise at younger and younger ages. Not that long ago, parents were advised to exclude their children from memorials and not talk to them about death or about feelings about their loved one. Today, mental health professionals can emphasize the importance of seeing children as recognized mourners and as an integral part of the family system's bereavement process. Mental health counselors can speak, share, and create a space for young people to freely participate in the family's mourning. The MHC's goal is to allow safe expression of children's grief responses in a respectful environment. Grief-resolution techniques are important to create and stimulate discussion and exploration of thoughts and feelings, because bereaved children cannot always integrate their emotions and their intellect. While the MHC is building a relationship of trust, children also experience support and affirmation in an atmosphere that honors and respects them. The following techniques allow them to spontaneously and safely work through difficult spaces at their own comfort level. Healing is promoted when children put their feelings outside of themselves (Goldman, 1998a).

Expression of feelings. There are several interventions that are useful for helping children to express themselves. Worry lists, letter writing, reality checks, worry and safe boxes, drawing, and poetry are all valuable interventions with children. Projective techniques and dream work are interventions that allow release of thoughts and feelings in verbal and nonverbal ways.

One of the common signs of grieving children is that they worry excessively about their health and the health of the surviving parent or guardian. Roxanne, 10 years old, had multiple deaths in her family and worked in grief therapy for many months. In one counseling session, she seemed worried and agitated. When asked to list her five greatest worries, her first was a concern she had never mentioned until that moment: "I'm so scared my dad will die too! He smokes and I want him to stop." She burst into tears. Roxanne decided to write her dad a letter to express her feelings; and after being given the choice to send it or not, she decided to give it to him. Her anger and frustration are obvious in the letter:

> Dear Dad, You know how I feel about you smoking right now. You know how many losses I've had already . . . I don't want you to go next. I really worry about you; so please stop smoking. I feel like ripping your head off to make you stop. Think before you buy so many cigarettes. Love, Roxanne P.S. Write me back. (Goldman, 2000b, p. 69)

Seven-year-old Brian's dad died in a sudden car crash. He confided during one session, "I'm worried my mom will die too. I think about it at school and before I go to bed." An intervention Brian found comforting was a reality check at mom's doctor.

She had a complete check up and asked the doctor to write a note to Brian to reassure him that mom seemed healthy. This note provided a concrete and tangible linking object that comforted his worry about his mom's health. The letter read, "Dear Brian, I wanted to let you know that your mom had a complete physical exam and she seems to be very healthy. Dr. Jones."

Margie's dad was killed in the Pentagon attack. She began having nightmares and had great difficulty sleeping. She decided to create a safe box, with objects inside that made her feel safe and peaceful. She decorated her box in grief therapy, using magazines and stickers, to create images that were calming to her. Inside her box, she put a favorite stuffed animal; her dad's medal from the military; a picture of her dog, Snuffy; and a bracelet her best friend Tanya had given her. Margie put her safe box on her dresser in her bedroom where it made her feel better whenever she went to it.

Adam, a 13 year old, witnessed his brother being killed in a ride-by shooting. He was bombarded with stimuli that re-triggered his panic about the violent way his brother died. Loud noises, sirens, and even the burst of a balloon could immediately begin difficult feelings of panic and anxiety for him. One intervention that he found soothing was the creation of a worry or fear box in which he could place his fears. Adam drew pictures and found slogans that illustrated things that made him scared. Drugs, guns, and terrorists were a major theme. He cut a hole in the top of his box and began placing little notes, his own private fears, inside. Sometimes he shared them, but other times he did not. Writing down his fears was a first step for Adam to begin to identify and cope with them.

Writing, drawing, and poetry are useful interventions for expression of feelings for the bereaved child. They serve to allow safe release of often hidden feelings. Writing was useful for 8-year-old Julia whose best friend, Zoe, and Zoe's family died in the terrorist attack. The following is a part of a poem she created as a tribute to her friend in her memory book. "Julia. Remembers by memories and hearing her name. Who wishes for peace and unity. Strong" (Goldman, 2003, p.146). Tyler's best friend Juan was killed in a car crash. He drew a picture of one of his favorite memories with his friend Juan. They were playing soccer at the park and fell, and they both burst into laughter. Tyler said that, when he looked at his picture, he felt happy. Andrew was 16 years old when his grandfather and his favorite aunt died. His grief was coupled with his sadness as he watched family members grieve too. He expressed his grief through poetry in the following way: "Tears flow—As time passes—The relatives grieve—In love for the deceased" (Andrew Burt, personal communication, December 11, 2001).

Middle and high school students may successfully respond to writing in locked diaries. Melissa was a teenager who came to counseling after the suicide of her older brother Joey. The shame she felt about the way her brother Joey died made it difficult to discuss complex feelings openly. She mentioned in session that she loved her diary, and kept it under her bed locked, safe, and private. She wrote her "sacred" thoughts and feelings in her diary. She used her diary not only as a safe receptacle for feelings, but also as an avenue for expression she could choose to use according to her readiness.

Projective play and dream work are grief interventions that allow children to use their unconscious mind and their imagination to safely express thoughts and feelings (Goldman, 2001). Young children learn through play, and they also grieve through play. Role-playing, puppets, artwork, clay, and sand table work are a few of the many ways that they can imagine, pretend, and engage in meaningful activities that allow them to act out or project their grief feelings without having to directly verbalize them. Play therapy is especially useful with bereaved children. Children have a limited verbal ability for describing their feelings and a limited emotional capacity to tolerate the pain of loss, and they communicate their feelings, wishes, fears, and attempted resolutions to their problems through play (Webb, 2002). Projective play allows many young children to work through difficult times. Having props such as helping figures, puppets, costumes, and building blocks allows children to recreate their experience and role-play what happened and ways to work with what happened. Bereaved children feel empowered when they can imagine alternatives and possible solutions, release feelings, and create dialogue through projective play.

Sometimes, what may appear as a frivolous play activity can be an extremely meaningful outlet for children to recreate an event and safely express conflicting ideas. For example, 6-year-old Jared was very sad in a beginning grief therapy session. He missed his dad, who was killed in a car accident. He walked around the office, talking about how much he missed Dad and that he wished he could talk to him. Jared picked up a toy telephone and followed the mental health professional's suggestion that he call and tell him how he feels. Jared sat down on the floor, dialed the number, and began an ongoing, very present conversation with his dad including "Hi Dad. I love you and miss you so much. Are you ok? Do you miss me? I hope heaven is fun and you can play baseball there. Let me tell you about my day." Children may commonly reach out to initiate a connection to their deceased parent. Through projective play, Jared was able to feel he could communicate in a satisfying way with his father. Alex, who was bereaved in the Sept. 11th terrorist attack, spontaneously built towers of blocks to represent the Twin Towers, and then knocked them down with an airplane. When replaying the attack and the falling of the towers, Alex explained, "Airplanes make buildings go BOOM!" Allyson, a kindergartner, suffered the tragic death of her mom at the Pentagon. She created a cemetery out of blocks and explained what was bothering her through the use of toy figures. She reported, "When me and Daddy visit the cemetery I wonder about Mommy. There was no coffin or body at the cemetery. I wonder where my Mommy's body is now." Play allowed the expression of deep concern about her mom's body and opened communication about this in the therapeutic environment. Allyson agreed to share her block cemetery and questions about mom with dad, as a way to begin to answer them. Michael, age 5 years, recreated the disaster setting of his dad's death. Dad was inside his office when a tragic fire took his life. Using toy doctors, nurses, fireman, and policeman as props, he pretended to be a rescue worker and saved his dad. Then he put on a fire hat and gloves and shouted, "Don't worry I'll save you. Run for your life."

Puppets and stuffed animals are also a safe way for children to speak of the trauma through projecting thoughts and feelings onto props, and dream work is another tool allowing children to process difficult feelings. For example, the MHC might inquire of a bereaved child, "I wonder what Bart (the dog puppet) would say about the trauma. Let's allow Bart to tell us about his story." In addition, children often feel survivor guilt after a sudden death (Worden, 1991). In dreams, sadness and depressing thoughts and feelings surface, accompanied by guilt that the child has survived, another person has died, and the child did not or could not help the deceased. Justin, a 10-year-old, explained a common theme in his dream. Justin continually revisited a nightmare after Uncle Max suddenly died during his military deployment. He shared his dream with his mental health professional and drew a picture showing his uncle calling out for help and Justin being unable to reach him.

Connecting to and maintaining memories. Silverman, Nickman, & Worden (1992) found that it was normal for children "to maintain a presence and connection with the deceased and that this presence is not static" (p. 495). The bereaved child constructs the deceased through an ongoing cognitive process of establishing memories, feelings, and actions connected to the child's development level. This inner representation leads to a continuing bond to the deceased, creating a relationship that changes as the child matures and his or her grief lessens. There are five strategies of connection to a deceased parent: (a) making an effort to locate the deceased, (b) actually experiencing the deceased in some way, (c) reaching out to initiate a connection, (d) remembering, and (e) keeping something that belonged to the deceased.

Those MHCs who work with bereaved children "may need to focus on how to transform connections and place the relationship in a new perspective, rather than on how to separate from the deceased" (Silverman et al., 1992, p. 503). In locating the deceased, many children may place their loved one in a place called "heaven" (p. 497). Michelle was 7 years old when she began in counseling. Her mom had died in a sudden car crash. One day Michelle asked in session, "What do you think heaven is?" Reflecting Michelle's question, the mental health professional asked, "What do you think it is?" Both began to draw a picture of their image of heaven. This intervention helped Michelle reflect on her own question, and she was able to remember her mother by sharing the place where she thought Mom was. It was also a way to honor Mom, express things about Mom, and symbolically again tell Mom how much she loved her. In addition, Michelle wrote the following story about heaven:

> What is heaven? This is what heaven is to me. It's a beautiful place. Everyone is waiting for a new person, so they can be friends. They are also waiting for their family. They are still having fun. They get to meet all the people they always wanted to meet (like Elvis). There are lots of castle where only the great live, like my Mom. There's all the food you want and all the stuff to do—There's also dancing places, disco. My mom loved to dance. I think she's dancing in heaven. Animals are always welcome. (My Mom loved animals.) Ask her how Trixie is. That's her dog that died. Tell her I love her. (Goldman, 2000b, pp. 79–80).

Memory books, memories boxes, and memory picture albums can all be used to address bereaved children's questions of "Will I forget my person?" Memory work is an important part of the therapeutic process. Children often fear they will forget their person who died, and memory work can provide a helpful tool to safely process the events of their grief and trauma. Memory books store pictures and writings about loved ones; memory boxes hold cherished objects belonging to a special person; and memory picture albums hold favorite photographs. Mental health counselors can ask children the following questions as a foundation for discussion and processing memories after a death: (a) Where were you when your person died?, (b) What was your first thought?, (c) What are the facts about how your person died?, (d) What makes you sad, happy, angry, frustrated?, (e) What sticks with you now?, (f) Did you do anything wrong?, (g) What is it you still want to know?, (h) What scares you the most?, (i) What makes you feel peaceful?, and (j) What can you do to feel better?

Memory books are extremely useful tools to allow children to express feelings and complete unfinished business, including feelings and thoughts that boys and girls were unable to communicate at the time of their person's death. Inside a memory book, grieving children can use stars, stickers, photographs, and other decorations to expand their own writings and drawings about their person. These are a few suggestions about various themes for memory book work: (a) The most important thing I learned from my person is . . . , (b) What was life like before your person died?, (c) What is life like now?, (d) My funniest memory is . . . , (e) My most special memory is . . . , (f) If I could tell my loved one just one more thing, I would say . . . , and (g) If I could say one thing I was sorry for it would be . . . (Goldman, 2000b). For example, Alfred, age 10, made a memory book page illustrating the events of September 11, 2001. It was his attempt to make sense of his world after the disaster. His memory page was a picture that helped him release feelings, tell stories, and express worries and concerns. The picture he drew showed where he was and what was happening at his New York school situated so close to ground zero. His only message was "Run for your life." With this memory book page, Alfred was able to begin to release some of the terror he felt that day at being so close to the Twin Towers as he also told his story.

Memory boxes are an excellent craft project for grieving children. They can be used to hold special articles, linking objects that are comforting because of belonging to or being reminders of the person who died. These objects can be put in a shoebox and decorated by the child as a valuable treasure of memories, which is also a tool for stimulating conversation. Memory boxes serve as a linking object by holding something that belonged to the deceased. These linking objects help the child maintain his or her connection or link to his or her loved one (Silverman et al., 1992). For instance, Tanya, an 8-year-old, made a memory box with pictures and special objects that reminded her of her friend Angie who died in a sudden plane crash. Tanya included pictures, stuffed animals, a list of her top favorite memories, and a bracelet her friend had given her. She explained that it made her "feel good" whenever she held it and she loved to share it with her friends and family. The memory box created a place where Tanya could "be with her friend Angie."

Creating memory picture albums with children titled "My Life" is often an extremely useful tool in creating dialogue and sharing feelings. Henry's dad died of cancer when he was 11. Henry created his memory album by choosing pictures he loved to make an album about his life before and after dad died. He placed each picture in his book and wrote a sentence telling about it.

Children love to express memories through artwork. Memory murals and memory collages are examples of memory projects that are helpful therapeutic interventions for grieving children. Children can creatively express feelings and thoughts about their loved ones. Fifteen-year-old Megan prepared a collage of magazine pictures that reminded her of her best friend, Ashley, who had recently died of cancer. She included Ashley's favorite foods, favorite clothes, favorite music, and favorite movie stars. Zack, age 9 years, was a best friend to Andrew, who had died when he was 6. Zack drew a picture for the cover of Andrew's third memorial booklet, "On the Occasion of Andrew's Third Anniversary." He explained that his drawing showed Andrew "shooting hoops in heaven." He felt in the few years since Andrew's death, he had been playing basketball, and assumed Andrew was doing the same in heaven. By participating in the memorial booklet, and being given a voice to explain his work, Zack was able to continue to actively remember his friend and participate in ongoing involvement with memory work.

Memory e-mails are a creative example of memory work and computer use. After 14-year-old Donald's classmate Ethan got killed in a car crash, Donald and his classmates decided to create a chat room only for e-mail memories about Ethan. They also created a memory video of Ethan, using a popular rock group as a background for a montage of pictures of Ethan from birth until he died, including friends, pets, and family.

Using children's grief and loss resources is an excellent technique to allow discussion and expression of sometimes hidden feelings. It's often reassuring to bereaved children to read words that speak of the loss they have experienced and the many new feelings they have associated with grief. Children's resources can become a helpful tool for parents. These books create meaningful discussion and often allow adults to dialogue about their common loss issues (Goldman, 2000b). A few examples of useful books for children on grief are: *When Dinosaurs Die* (Brown & Brown, 1996), *When Someone Very Special Dies* (Heegaard, 1988), *Bart Speaks Out: Breaking the Silence on Suicide* (Goldman, 1998a), *Honoring Our Loved Ones: Going to a Funeral* (Carney, 1999), and *After a Murder: A Workbook for Kids* (The Dougy Center, 2002). Suggestions for useful books for grieving teens include: *Death Is Hard to Live With* (Bode, 1993), *When a Friend Dies* (Gootman, 1994), *Facing Change* (O'Toole, 1995), and *Fire in My Heart, Ice in My Veins* (Traisman, 1992). Readers can contact the author for a more complete list.

Support Groups

Many bereaved children feel alone and find peers and family members so often want them to move on and stop talking or even thinking about their person (Goldman, 2000b). They wonder who they can really talk with about their mom or dad or sister who has died. Often they feel different and choose not to share. Grief support groups can provide a safe haven for them to explore their overwhelming and often confusing feelings with others that understand because they are going through a grief process also. Becoming a member of an age-appropriate grief support group allows children and teens a safe place to share with others and create friendships.

Education

If mental health counselors can join together with parents, educators, therapists, and other caring professionals to create a cohesive unit, sharing similar thought forms, supports, resources, and information, a child's grieving experience becomes more congruent. Usually when children grieve, their world feels fragmented. The more consistency MHCs can create within children's lives, the more solid and secure their world will become. The role of mental health counselors as liaisons to parents, educators, and community members is an important aspect of children's grief therapy. Educating caring adults provides a united multiple support system for the grieving child.

Mental health professionals can educate surviving parents and guardians on common signs of grieving children and coach the adults on how to reduce the children's fear and anxiety about new thoughts and feelings. This education helps adults reduce their own anxieties that can unconsciously be projected onto their children. MHCs can provide age-appropriate words to help family members create open dialogue and identify their own unresolved grief and the impact of their grieving process on their children. For example, 15-year-old Mark lived with his grandmother after his mom's death. Grandma often told the mental health professional that she was concerned because Mark "doesn't seem to be grieving." One day in a seemingly unrelated conversation, she mentioned that Mark takes a nap every day on his mother's bed. Grandma was unaware that grieving teens commonly reach out to initiate a connection with their person who died (Silverman et al., 1992). That connection may well be taking a daily nap on mom's bed.

The MHC can also be an advocate for the grieving child in the school system. This advocacy can offer suggestions to educators, who are working with bereaved children, as a support after their person's death. Because children are sometimes flooded with feelings and are not immediately able to verbalize them, MHCs can work with educators in developing strategies for children to follow when they feel upset. In doing so, MHCs can emphasize the importance of the child being part of the decision-making process in choosing appropriate people or places they are comfortable with to be used to implement these strategies. These ideas can be implemented throughout the school year and continued for the next year if necessary. Suggestions include any or all of the following (Goldman, 1998b). The child (a) has permission to leave the room, if needed, without explanation, (b) can choose a designated adult or location within the school as a safe space, or (c) can call home if needed. Amy, who worried about Mom after Dad died, provides an example of how this might occur. She thought about her Mom a lot in the mornings and chose to call home at that time to make sure she was all right. Other strategies include the child's having (a) permission to visit the school nurse if needing a reality check, (b) a class helper, (c) private teacher time, (d) some

modified work assignments, and (e) school personnel inform faculty, PTA, parents, and children of the loss. In addition, it may be useful to give the child more academic progress reports such as was done for Henry who had a hard time concentrating after his brother Sam died (Goldman, 2000a). Henry could not remember as well and found his test scores declined. Having frequent progress reports helped him keep his studies on track.

The MHC serves as a liaison to the school system to inform those involved that there is a grieving child in the school. Presenting a loss inventory (Goldman, 2000a) that can be shared with educators is a helpful tool for communication within the school. All too often school systems do not communicate to their entire staff that a child has experienced the death of a close loved one. This lack of knowledge can create trauma and an added layer of sadness for students. Liam was a fifth grader who was star athlete for the soccer game. Many parents and friends had gathered to watch the team in their tournament finals. Coach McGuire approached Liam before the game and asked, "Is your dad here today?" "No," Liam grumbled. "He had to work." Liam played his worst game. Coach McGuire was unaware that Liam's dad had died recently; there was no written record to communicate this within the school. If this school system had an established practice of using a loss inventory, this lapse in communication and its devastating impact on Liam may not have occurred.

A grief therapy homework assignment, which can be used even in educational or advocacy situations, can help children and teens identify their individual support systems. Children can be asked to create a "circle of trust," placing a picture of themselves in the center and three trusted people with their phone numbers that they can call for support. They can create a second circle for people they would call next. They may even create a third circle for people they know they cannot trust. Their circle of trust can stimulate dialogue in therapy as well as serve as a tool for recognition of those they can and cannot count on for support during their present loss (Goldman & Rosenthal, 2001).

Childhood Commemoration

Children become recognized mourners when adults create ways for bereaved children to ask questions and share thoughts and feelings about death. Adults can also prepare and invite children to participate in funerals, memorials, and other rituals. When children can attend a memorial service they gain a great gift, the gift of inner strength (Goldman, 1996). It assists their grief process to be included in the funeral and other rituals associated with the death of a loved one (Rando, 1991). Knowing they could participate and be present with adults in a community remembrance of a friend or family member gives them awareness of how people honor a life, come together for each other as a community, and say good-bye. Honoring a life gives children a way to value and respect their own lives. They become identified mourners and an ever present and integral part of the grief process. Research indicates that children who were allowed to attend the funeral of a loved one later expressed positive feelings about going and about the meaning they attached to their attendance (Silverman & Worden, 1992). Children in the study felt "it was important to them that they had attended. Attendance helped them to acknowledge the death, provided an occasion for honoring their deceased parent, and made it possible for them to receive support and comfort" (p. 319). This nurturing environment supports their emotional and spiritual growth as human beings. So often caring adults are too uncomfortable talking to children about death. They may not have the words to use, may feel powerless when children are sad or cry, and ultimately may inhibit tears and stop the grief process.

Bereaved children can actively commemorate their loss by participating in safe and comfortable processes that allow for the expression of grief (Goldman, 1996). The following are age-appropriate ways children and teens can give meaning to their many thoughts and feelings. They can plant a flower or tree, send a balloon, blow bubbles, or say a prayer. Bereaved children might light a candle or write a poem, story, or song about their loved one and share it. Some boys and girls find talking into a tape recorder or creating a video of memories is helpful. Others enjoy (a) making cookies or cakes and bringing them to the family of the person who has died, (b) creating a mural or collage about the life of the person who has died, or (c) drawing a picture or making a memory book. Christina and Christy were two young children who were prepared, invited, and given choices about joining in a memorial service for their friend, Andrew. They were an active part of the service, sitting with family members, blowing bubbles, sharing, listening, and drawing pictures for their friend.

Conclusion and Recommendations

Research suggests that certain mental health outcomes may emerge for grieving children (Lutzke, Ayers, Sandier, & Barr, 1997). Bereaved children may show (a) more depression, withdrawal, and anxiety; (b) lower self-esteem; and (c) less hope for the future than non-bereaved children. Adults who were bereaved children tend to exhibit higher degrees of suicide ideation and depression and are more at risk for panic disorders and anxiety. Support for bereaved children is essential in helping to reduce negative outcomes related to unresolved or unexplored grief during childhood. The findings suggest that, although trauma associated with death-related situations could not always predict later symptom formation, therapeutic intervention at the time of the death may help to reduce or extinguish future anxiety that could escalate without intervention.

A key debilitating factor creating ongoing trauma for grieving children is often a sense of loss of control in their lives. Early interventions through counseling and grief support groups can help boys and girls regain their sense of control and reduce the stress associated with the death of a friend or family member. Early interventions may also support children in their grief by providing a meaningful relationship with at least one caring adult (e.g., the MHC). Mishara (1999) reported that children with strong social supports have a reduced presence of suicide ideation. Another study (U.S. Secret Service, 2002) clearly indicates "the importance of giving attention to students who

are having a difficult coping with major losses . . . particularly when feelings of desperation and hopelessness are involved" (p. 14). The report suggests that an important aspect in prevention may be to allow young people the opportunity to talk and connect with caring adults.

The MHC needs to view him or herself not only as a therapist, but also as an advocate for bereaved children. MHCs' role as an ally and friend creates a link to the child's larger community that extends to parents, clergy, educators, physicians, and other health care professionals. Educating members of these supportive networking systems in the common signs of bereaved children and suggesting age-appropriate interventions can extend the boundaries of mental health services into the child's home, school, and community. MHCs are trained to see the child in the present and to view changes in behaviors as a cry for help. Using therapeutic interventions such as projective techniques, sharing, and listening allows children to work through their grief. Active involvement in commemoration, rituals, and support groups facilitates the healing process of the bereaved child. Giving boys and girls the opportunity to release their emotions within a safe haven is the underlying thread inherent in counseling grieving children.

References

Bode, J. (1993). *Death is hard to live with.* New York: Dell.

Brown, L., & Brown, M. (1996). *When dinosaurs die.* New York: Little, Brown.

Carney, K. L. (1999). *Honoring our loved ones: Going to a funeral.* Wethersfield, CT: Dragonfly.

Celotta, B., Jacobs, O., & Keys, S. (1987). Searching for suicidal precursors in the elementary school child. *American Mental Health Counselors Association Journal, 9,* 38–48.

Doka, K. J. (Ed.). (1989). *Disenfranchised grief: Recognizing hidden sorrow.* New York: Lexington Books.

Dougy Center. (2002). *After a murder: A workbook for kids.* Portland, OR: Author.

Fox, S. S. (1988). *Good grief: Helping groups of children when a friend dies.* Boston, MA: The New England Association for the Education of Young Children.

Ginsberg, H., & Opper, S. (1969). *Piaget's theory of intellectual development.* Englewood, NJ: Prentice Hall.

Goldman, L. E. (1996). We can help children grieve: A child-oriented model for memorializing. *Young Children: The National Association for the Education of Young Children, 51,* 69–73.

Goldman, L. E. (1998a). *Bart speaks out: Breaking the silence on suicide.* Los Angeles, CA: Western Psychological Services.

Goldman, L. E. (1998b). Helping the grieving child in the school. *Healing Magazine, 3,* 15–24.

Goldman, L. E. (2000a). *Helping the grieving child in the school.* Bloomington, IN: Phi Delta Kappa International.

Goldman, L. E. (2000b). *Life and loss: A guide to help grieving children* (2nd ed.). New York: Taylor & Francis.

Goldman, L. E. (2001). *Breaking the silence: A guide to help children with complicated grief suicide, homicide, AIDS, violence and abuse* (2nd ed.). New York: Taylor & Francis.

Goldman, L. E. (2003). Talking to children about terrorism. In M. E. Eicht & K. J. Doka (Eds.), *Living with grief, coping with public tragedy* (pp. 139–149). Washington, D.C. Hospice Foundation of America.

Goldman, L. E. (2001). Circle of trust: Support for grief. In H. G. Rosenthal (Ed.), *Favorite counseling and therapy homework assignments* (pp. 108–110). New York: Taylor & Francis.

Gootman, M. (1994). *When a friend dies*. Minneapolis, MN: Free Spirit.

Heegaard, M. (1988). *When someone very special dies*. Minneapolis, MN: Woodland.

Lutzke, J. R., Ayers, T. S., Sandler, N. S., & Barr, A. (1997). Risk and interventions for the parentally bereaved child. In N. Sandier. & S. Wolchik (Eds.), *Handbook of children's coping: Linking theory and intervention* (pp. 215–242). New York: Plenum.

Mishara, B. (1999). Conceptions of death and suicide in children ages 6–12 and their implications for suicide prevention. *Suicide and Life-Threatening Behavior, 29,* 105–118.

O'Toole, D. (1995). *Facing change*. Burnsville, NC: Compassion Books.

Rando, T. (1991). *How to go on living when someone you love dies*. New York: Bantam.

Silverman, P. (2000). *Never to young to know: Death in children's lives*. NY: Oxford University.

Silverman, P., Nickman, S., & Worden, J. W. (1992). Detachment revisited: The child's reconstruction of a dead parent. *American Journal of Orthopsychiatry, 62,* 494–503.

Silverman, P., & Worden, J. W. (1992). *Children's understanding of funeral ritual*. Omega, 25, 319–331.

Traisman, P. S. (1992). *Fire in my heart: Ice in my veins*. Omaha, NE: Centering.

U.S. Secret Service. (2002). Preventing school shootings: A summary of U. S. Secret Service Safety school initiative. *National Institute of Justice Journal, 248,* 10–15.

Webb, N. B. (Ed.). (2002). *Helping bereaved children: A handbook for practitioners* (2nd ed.). New York: Guilford.

Worden, J. W. (1991). *Grief counseling and grief therapy: A handbook for the mental health practitioner*. New York: Springer.

LINDA GOLDMAN, CLPC, CT, is a grief therapist, author, and adjunct faculty at John Hopkins University, Baltimore, MD. E-mail: lgold@erols.com.

A Grim Fight for 'Proper Burial'

A grieving mother still argues for victims' remains to be moved.

Nikki Schwab

Diane Horning looks tearfully through a collage of photographs to the gaping hole that is ground zero, 20 stories below. Out the window she finds the usual scene: commuters hurrying to the subway, clusters of tourists peering into the infamous pit. Exclusively for the families of 9/11 victims, this flower-filled room is where Horning comes to mourn her son Matthew, a 26-year-old information technologist who worked on the 95th floor of the World Trade Center. It is here, too, that Horning takes fresh inspiration to press on with a grim legal dispute.

A total of 2,750 people lost their lives at the World Trade Center on Sept. 11, 2001, but only 292 intact bodies were recovered. Much of the debris was carted off to a Staten Island landfill, where it was sifted. The process recovered 2,335 remains, but Horning contends there are far more. The organization she heads, World Trade Center Families for Proper Burial, is demanding that the city continue the search and move the whole pile of material to another place. "There is no amount of money you could give any mother to leave her child in the garbage for all eternity," says Horning.

The group, which filed the suit in 2005, originally asked for the removal only of cremated ash—so-called finds containing human DNA that are small enough to pass through a quarter-inch screen. But workers who did the sifting have since testified that the initial work was rushed, and they believe other body parts remain.

How much is enough? City attorney Peter Wies argues that the city went to extraordinary lengths to screen the material. At the height of the operation, a crew of about 1,500—including police detectives and FBI agents—painstakingly separated garbage from potential body fragments. "Having lost so many of their colleagues . . . [the workers] had a very personal stake in the effectiveness of the search," said New York City police inspector James Luongo.

Further, attorneys argue that New York was not obligated to sift any of the material in the first place. "The possibility that the remains of some victims may not have been found," city attorneys said in court filings, ". . . does not empower this court to order the city of New York to commit tens of millions of taxpayers' dollars to resift and relocate the material."

Yet Horning is unrelenting. A former high school English teacher from Scotch Plains, N.J., she carries a purse adorned with her son's picture and scolds ground zero vendors for selling photos of the burning trade center. No one has named a specific price for the work that Horning is asking the city to do, but when asked how the city could justify any further expense, she asks another question. "How does Mayor Bloomberg get permission to spend how many millions of taxpayer dollars to fight us?"

Bereavement expert Charles A. Guarnaccia, an associate professor of psychology at the University of North Texas, said that because of the horrific circumstances, the families of 9/11 victims would have particular difficulty recovering and a need for the closure of burial. As to whether New York should comply with the families' request, Guarnaccia said, "It depends on how much you want to pay attention to people's psychological needs. It's a judgment call. I know I would find [the decision] personally difficult."

Parents and the Death of a Child

SANGEETA SINGG

Experiencing intense emotional distress following the death of a loved one is a normal human reaction. When a child dies, however, the unique dynamics of parent-child relationship further intensify bereavement reactions of parents. In the modern Western world, children are expected to outlive their parents. Parents not only expect to see their children grown and settled, they even expect to see their grandchildren growing and settling. A child's death disrupts the normal life cycle expectations of parents, and the loss creates the havoc of emotional and familial crises. Because children provide parents a sense of purpose and hope for the future, parents envision their immortality and life continuation through their children's lives. This sense of self-continuity through progeny leads to parents' denial of their own death (Rando 1986d). Consequently, when a child dies, it leads to an overwhelming and enduring loss that may drastically affect the well-being of parents. Some researchers suggest that the trauma of experiencing a child's death may lead to posttraumatic stress symptoms and a complicated mourning (Wheeler 2001). And if the death occurs suddenly, violently, or due to genetic factors, some additional issues of unpreparedness, preventability, and helplessness compound the grief process.

Compared with other losses, the death of a child is a more devastating experience for most people because they are confronted with many secondary losses as well (Rando 1986d). Beverly Raphael (1994) enumerates the many losses parents experience when a child dies:

> A child is many things: a part of the self and of the loved partner; a representation of generations past; the genes of the forebears; the hope of the future; a source of love, pleasure, even narcissistic delight; a tie or burden; and sometimes a symbol of the worst part of the self and others. (P. 229)

A child's death changes the family forever. In addition to the loss of dreams and future expectations of life with the child, a sense of failure as parents and survival guilt compound the grief process, making it a "bereavement overload" (Rando 1986c:51). Parental grief often escalates to a pathological level, turning into some form of unresolved grief, which is often considered abnormal in other types of bereavements. The tradicial symptoms of unresolved grief seem normal components of parental bereavement, however (Rando 1986b). Diseases, accidents, suicide, and homicide victimize many lives, leaving many bereaved parents of all ages. In Western society, with increasing life expectancy, the number of elderly people who experience the death of a middle-aged child has also increased (Osterweis, Solomon, and Green 1984).

Reactions to losing a child are perhaps as varied as the number of parents. However, researchers have found some dynamics and reactions that are common among bereaved parents. A variety of bereavement reactions emerge at different grief stages. Therese A. Rando (1986d) describes various grief reactions occurring in three phases: avoidance, confrontation, and reestablishment (accommodation). The *avoidance phase* is the first stage of parental grief. This phase begins with the event of the child's death, leaving parents in shock and denial. Feelings of bewilderment and numbness are initial reactions along with the disbelief about the news of the child's death. At this stage, parents may be perceived by some people as strong or pretentious. What they may not know, however, is that these early reactions of shock, denial, and numbness act as buffers against grief until parents can collect their resources to face reality. According to Bernstein (1997:10), these brief periods of denial act as "shock absorbers" with a protective effect. Confusion and disorganization are also common reactions during the first phase.

The second phase described by Rando is the *confrontation phase,* which begins with the recognition of the loss and progresses to the most intense suffering and pain. It is also called the period of "angry sadness" (Rando 1986d:14). Extreme emotions such as fear, anxiety, anger, guilt, longing, despair, depression, obsession, and search for meaning are common reactions during this stage. Some individuals may have difficulty sharing their feelings, whereas others may cry and talk incessantly. Bereaved parents may even experience "grief attacks" involving waves of painful emotional and physical symptoms. These grief attacks can cause accidents if parents do not stop their activities and deal with their disabling feelings until they subside. Some of the common physiological reactions are gastrointestinal disturbances, weight loss, insomnia, physical exhaustion, heart palpitations, shortness of breath, weakness, and sighing. These symptoms tend to persist during the early stages. However, 5 years past the death, these physical symptoms may not persist, with the exception of insomnia (Bernstein 1997:14).

The final phase is the *reestablishment phase* in which finality of the child's death sets in and the grief gradually declines. The parent resumes the normal routine of daily activities and learns to live with the loss. The emotional energy is reinvested in other relationships and pursuits. This phase often overlaps with the confrontation phase, taking the parent gradually to the final stage of grief. Because the parent begins living again, guilt is often experienced in the initial stages of this phase. As time passes, however, intensely painful days begin to be less frequent. Although the anniversary of the child's death, child's birthday, holidays, and other special days bring back memories and intense pain, crossing each milestone takes the parent closer to accommodation or adaptation. These terms are preferred to *recovery* in reference to parental bereavement, because recovery means returning to normal, and bereaved parents never completely return to normal; they mourn, integrate, and adapt (Bernstein 1997:xvi).

According to Rando (1986c), traditional grief models are inadequate to explain parental bereavement. An example is the popular model developed by Worden (2002) that consists of four tasks of mourning. Unlike other types of mourners, bereaved parents have trouble meeting all four tasks: (a) accepting the reality of the loss, (b) experiencing the pain of grief, (c) adjusting to the environment in which the deceased is missing, and (d) emotionally relocating the deceased and moving on with life. The failure to meet these four tasks has to do with the unique nature of the parent-child relationship, characterizing the loss to be multifaceted and enduring. Therefore, what is a normal process in parental bereavement is considered pathological in other types of bereavement. Four types of unresolved grief that may constitute normal facets of parental grief are (a) *inhibited, suppressed, or absent grief* when a parent does not accept the loss, (b) *distorted/conflicted grief,* consisting of feelings of extreme guilt and anger; (c) *chronic grief,* involving the grief process that continues; and (d) *unanticipated grief syndrome,* characterized by complicated "recovery."

Feelings of being robbed, incomplete, inadequate, unsuccessful, and guilty are common feelings of bereaved parents reported in the literature. Most devastating, and a prominent feature of parental bereavement, are feelings of extreme guilt, especially in the early stages. Margaret Shandor Miles and Alice Sterner Demi (1986) identify six possible sources of parental guilt:

1. *Death causation guilt* results from parents' perception that they may have contributed to the child's death or that they failed to protect the child from the death.
2. *Illness-related guilt* involves their belief that they did not behave in optimal ways in relation to the sick or dead child.
3. *Parental role guilt,* originally labeled as cultural role guilt, is related to the parent-child relationship before and at the time of child's death. Parents believe that they failed to fulfill the socially prescribed overall parental role, and now they have no opportunity to rectify their mistakes because the child is dead.
4. *Moral guilt* stems from having an overly strict conscience or religious belief system that stresses guilt and punishment. The child's death is perceived as the punishment for parents' wrong deeds.
5. *Survival guilt* may result because a child's death does not fit in the expected normal life cycle events.
6. *Grief guilt* relates to parents' perception of their actions at or after the time of child's death. This guilt may progress through three phases: (a) in relation to parents' emotional reactions at the time of death, (b) in relation to grief reactions during bereavement, and (c) in relation to the "recovery phase" when the grief intensity begins to decline.

Different parents may experience grief differently. There is no set sequence of stages of grief and no really predictable pattern for all bereaved parents (Bernstein 1997). A bereaved mother and a health professional, Pamela Elder (1998) states, "I did not experience emotions in serial stages. . . . I dipped in and out of grief, sometimes coping, sometimes not. I did not feel that I 'worked' through my grief, rather that 'it' worked through me" (p. 121).

The nature and intensity of grief that a parent experiences are influenced by many factors, such as the nature of the death, ambivalence in parent-child relationship, age of the deceased child, sex of parents, marriage of parents, search for meaning, duration of grief, and social support. Some of these factors have been identified as risk factors for adverse outcomes for parents, whereas the others may be growth producing.

Nature of Death

People die either suddenly or with forewarning due to some terminal illness. The sudden death of a child is a tragedy that prompts intense emotional reactions in parents. Accidents, acute diseases, suicide, and homicide are often the causes of sudden death. Although suddenness of death is defined differently by experts, a common criterion in all definitions is the death without warning that catches survivors unprepared (Osterweis et al. 1984). Also, sudden deaths are more likely to result in more intense bereavement of longer duration (Raphael 1994).

In a study of 134 Caucasian married parents experiencing death of one child, Cole and Singg (1998) examined the bereavement reactions (despair, panic behavior, blame and anger, detachment, disorganization, and personal growth measured by the Hogan Grief Reaction Checklist) in relation to duration of grief and several psychosocial variables. The results show that regardless of the length of time since death, the parents whose children died suddenly experienced more panic and disorganization than those whose children's deaths were anticipated. With sudden death, there is no time to collect one's resources to cope with the loss. Parents feel an overwhelming need to search for answers. Feelings of lack of control over events create panic in the newly and suddenly bereaved parent (Bernstein 1997). According to Knapp (1986), "Parents who suffer the shock of sudden death pay their dues all at once rather than a little at a time!" (p. 79). These parents have a hard time returning to the level of functioning prior to death. Ronald J. Knapp (1986) calls this state the "shadow grief" marked by a dull "ache" that always lingers on (p. 67). On the other hand, parents who experience an anticipated death of a child move through the grief process more quickly and arrive at a level of functioning that is sometimes higher than before the tragedy.

Two major predictors of the intensity and duration of grief reported in the previous research are quality of the relationship and the mourner's perception of preventability of the death, the latter being the most crucial factor (Bugen 1977). A child's death presents both factors. Because deaths of children and young adults are more likely to be sudden and accidental, they are often perceived as "preventable" by bereaved parents, resulting in extreme guilt. Inability to prevent the death often creates a sense of failure in the parent. Even when a child dies as a result of genetic factors unknown to parents before the child's diagnosis, they feel responsible for the child's condition. If the cause of death was a disease, parents wonder if they had taken the child to the doctor sooner or noticed the symptoms sooner, the death could have been prevented (Rando 1986c). This kind of thinking refers more to what "should have been," than to actual preventability of death (Bugen 1977:202). Pamela Elder (1998) aptly depicts the pattern of feelings that emerges with a child's death that the parent feels could have been prevented:

> At times, I was suspended with shock, then raging with anger, at the injustice of it all, followed by periods of great calm. There were days when I felt perfectly normal, as if nothing had really changed, but then I worried about whether I was a cold, uncaring mother. Kate had been so vital, so filled with joy and confidence in living. Yet she was dead, and I had had no power to save her. And so began the everyday business of living with grief. (P. 120)

Although not less painful, the death after prolonged illness, frequent hospitalizations, and expensive unsuccessful treatments may be a gradual and quieter experience as opposed to the experience of utter devastation with a sudden death. The parents whose children are diagnosed with a terminal illness have some time to prepare, a state called "anticipatory grief." They begin the grief work at the time of diagnosis. Their journey after death is shorter and less volatile than for the parents with sudden loss (Bernstein 1997). Also, when a death is anticipated, the parents may nurture the child with more affection and help the child fulfill his or her wishes. As a result, they may have fewer regrets.

Ambivalence in the Parent-Child Relationship

Another factor involved in the intensity of parental grief is the degree of ambivalence in the parent-child relationship. This may result from unrealistic expectations of roles of parent and child in our society. Parents are expected to be all sacrificing and loving, and children are expected to be obedient, respectful, and lovable (Raphael 1994). Such idealistic expectations create ambivalence in the parent-child relationship. Although all relationships are subject to some degree of ambivalence, difficult reactions result when strong conflicting feelings are experienced by some parents toward their children. They love their children, but at times they feel angry or burdened when children behave in a rebellious manner or become terminally ill. A terminally ill child may require expensive treatments and may be noncompliant, and parents may feel angry and wish at times for the child to die (Miles and Demi 1986). These feelings lead to extreme guilt after a child's death. Also, rebellious behaviors of children may cause embarrassment, undue financial expense, or significant distress to parents. Some parents may at times wish they did not have such a difficult or demanding child. Self-blame and feeling guilty are common reactions when a high degree of ambivalence exists in a parent-child relationship. A sense of relief may be experienced by some parents when a child dies after a prolonged illness or a problematic life. This may further compound the guilt reaction of a parent (Rando 1986d).

Age of the Deceased Child

Although many similar feelings and issues are experienced by all bereaved parents, different grief patterns emerge because of different developmental stages at the time of loss. Because of the nature of parent-child relationship, the tasks of mourning for an infant or an adult take different courses (Rando 1993). As a result, researchers have examined death of children ranging from the fetal stage to middle age.

Fetal and Infant Deaths

Fetal deaths are known as miscarriages and stillbirths, which occur either during gestation or birth. In the United States, the fetal (20 weeks or more gestation) mortality rate reported for 1998 was 6.7 per 1,000 registered live births plus fetal deaths (National Center for Health Statistics 2002). These deaths are differentiated from elected abortions. Miscarriage, also called spontaneous abortion, refers to a pregnancy loss that occurs before the 20th week. Different statistical estimates are available for miscarriages since classification is fraught with uncertainty. A conservative estimate is that 1 in 6 pregnancies ends in miscarriage (Daiter 1998). Miscarriages leave grieving parents with shattered dreams and hopes, especially the mother. A predominant feeling of sadness prevails. The attachment of a mother to the unborn child may form very early during the pregnancy. She may feel like a failure for not being able to deliver a live, healthy baby. Also, previous feelings of ambivalence about the pregnancy may compound feelings of guilt and anger. Fathers also attach to the unborn child by fantasizing what it will be like and how they will do various fatherly things with the child, but their sadness is often less intense (Raphael 1994).

A child under 1 year of age is called an infant. The infant mortality rate reported for 1999 was 7.1 per 1,000 registered live births excluding fetal deaths (National Center for Health Statistics 2002). Contrary to common belief, Cole and Singg (1998) found that the parents of infants tend to experience more despair than the parents of older children, regardless of the time since death. Parents experiencing the death of an infant are more likely to be younger and may not have any previous experience of losing a loved one. Although losing a child is the worst kind of loss, successful coping with the previous losses has beneficial effect on the bereavement process (Bernstein 1997). Also, the great dependency of an infant on parents, especially mothers, creates a strong bond that may leave them in greater despair. I will examine infant deaths in the following three categories: stillbirths, neonatal deaths, and sudden infant deaths.

Stillbirths

One in every 80 deliveries results in a stillbirth. In most cases, the baby dies just before or during delivery. In some cases, however, mothers have a forewarning prior to the delivery about the death of the fetus in utero (Osterweis et al. 1984:76). Emotional reactions to both an anticipated and a sudden stillbirth are reported to be similar, because bonding with the baby, especially by mothers, has already been established by the time stillbirth occurs. The modern technology of ultrasound often creates this bonding for parents very early when they observe the fetus on the monitor in a doctor's office and obtain an image of their child. Fathers' feelings are often ignored at these times, because they are expected to take on the role of protector. Mothers often feel anger, loneliness, and shame for not being able to bear a healthy baby, and these feelings can become exacerbated if there is insufficient support or "conspiracy of silence" (Osterweis et al. 1984:77). Often, the lack of social support when a woman goes home empty-handed complicates her mourning. In the past, parents were spared the sight of their stillborn babies due to a mistaken belief that not seeing the baby would be less traumatic. But now it is believed that seeing and even holding the dead infant may be therapeutic. Parents in hospitals are allowed to name the infant and collect mementos such as locks of hair and a picture of the baby (Osterweis et al. 1984; Raphael 1994).

Neonatal Death

The neonatal (under 28 days) mortality rate reported for 1999 was 4.7 per 1,000 registered live births excluding fetal deaths (National Center for Health Statistics 2002). Modern medicine has dramatically changed the survival rate of premature babies and babies with birth defects. However, sometimes in spite of the modern medical interventions, some babies survive for only a short period of time. In these situations, parents have some opportunity to bond with the baby, and they hope for a cure or miracle. When the infant dies, mothers often blame themselves more than fathers do and feel responsible for causing the death. Their behaviors such as smoking, drinking, and not taking better care of themselves are considered possible reasons for death. Anxiety and anger for the child's not having had a chance compound the feelings of guilt in these mothers. Nevertheless, more emotional support is available to parents of these babies compared with parents of stillborn babies (Osterweis et al. 1984; Raphael 1994).

Sudden Infant Death

In 1999, a total of 2,648 infant deaths were attributed to sudden infant death syndrome, or SIDS. This total is equivalent to about 1 in 10 infant deaths for this particular year (National Center for Health Statistics 2002). SIDS is the leading cause of deaths in infants 1 to 12 months of age, an occurrence that usually happens during the first 2 to 4 months. For an infant's sudden death to be diagnosed as SIDS, the infant has to be less than 1 year of age, with death investigation resulting in no causal explanation. Besides strong feelings of guilt and anger, overprotection of surviving children and fear of losing future children are common reactions of parents. Also, because a SIDS death often remains unexplained, the parental grief may become complicated with additional factors. For example, involvement of law enforcement officers may pose additional stress for parents who might be suspected of child abuse. Efforts have been made to educate homicide officers about SIDS so that innocent parents are spared the undue stress. Nonetheless, extreme guilt is often experienced by the parents due to the unexplainable nature of the child's death, which leads to their relentless searching for the cause (Osterweis et al. 1984; Raphael 1994).

Death of an Older Child

Fewer older children die than infants. In 1999 in the United States, 12,844 children between 1 and 14 years of age died compared with 27,337 infants less than 1 year of age (National Center for Health Statistics 2002). Accidents are the major cause of death (45% of the deaths), especially in adolescence. Other major causes at this age are leukemia and other types of cancers. As in the case of the death of an infant, anger is a common emotion, accompanied by despair experienced by bereaved parents of an older child. Death of an adolescent is often more traumatic because parent-child relationship ambivalence is very high during this stage, possibly due to the child's rebellion. Parents who can understand the cause of their child's death and those who provide home care instead of hospital care, however, tend to have better bereavement outcomes (Osterweis et al. 1984; Raphael 1994).

Death of an Adult Child

When a younger adult child dies, grief reactions and family dynamics are similar to those that emerge when an adolescent child dies. When a middle-aged child dies, however, the parental bereavement takes on a little different form, with different grief dynamics for the elderly parent. It is estimated that at age 60, 10% of parents deal with death of an adult child. The untimeliness of the death of a child seems even more pronounced to elderly parents because of their age and expectation to die first. In some cases, the loss becomes more devastating because the child was the primary caregiver of the elderly parents. Also, because they suffer from many "normative-age graded losses," such as their health, spouse, home, income, identity, and status, the multiplicity of losses complicates depression, a common problem among the elderly (Moss, Lesher, and Moss 1986–87).

According to Rando (1986a), the death of an adult child poses five special bereavement problems in parents:

1. Successful accommodation of the loss is compromised. They have extreme difficulty in meeting the four tasks of grief work prescribed by Worden (2002), especially the first task of accepting the reality of the loss.

2. They are excluded from the concern of others. Attention is usually given to the adult child's spouse and children, and elderly parents are often overlooked. This leaves them feeling invalidated and without much social support.
3. Their grief and mourning are complicated with multiple factors, such as bereavement overload from other losses and health problems.
4. As children become adults, parents have less control and involvement in their lives. This further complicates the bereavement process. For example, parents may have no say about the funeral or funerary rituals.
5. Their grief is further complicated with additional secondary losses, such as losing contact with the grandchildren because of the family's moving away or losing financial and other support provided by the adult child.

Because of these problems, older parents seem less resilient, and the death of their adult child remains one of the most dominant issues of their later life. There is a sharp beginning of the tasks of grief work "but literally no end as long as life is lived and experienced" (Rubin and Malkinson 2001:232).

Sex of Parents

Another factor involved in dynamics of bereavement is the sex of parents. Generally, mothers experience more intense and more prolonged grief reactions than fathers. They also show different grieving patterns. For example, Cole and Singg (1998) found that bereaved mothers experience more intense symptoms of despair, panic, and disorganization than fathers do, regardless of the length of time since death. Fathers on the other hand experience higher levels of anger and loss of control (Osterweis et al. 1984). After some years, however, they function more like nonbereaved fathers, whereas mothers continue to resemble the recently bereaved mothers, showing greater affective, somatic, social, and psychological distress (Bernstein 1997).

Mothers of younger children exhibit more intense symptoms of grief than fathers do. This may be because mothers are more involved in the day-to-day tasks associated with child care, especially if they do not work outside the home (Rando 1986d). Many daily reminders become part of the mother-child interaction because of the more involved relationship. When a child dies, every environmental and sensory cue associated with the child elicits memories and adds to mothers' grief. It will be interesting to see, however, if the styles of grieving will change for mothers and fathers in the future because more fathers are now sharing the parenting role in our society (Bernstein 1997).

Sex role socialization also contributes to sex differences in parental grief. Whereas women are socialized to accept help and express their emotions, men are expected to be self-sufficient and show emotional control (Rando 1986d). As a result, mothers tend to openly express their grief, whereas fathers deal with it more privately. Mothers may perceive fathers' emotional restraint as a lack of love for the child, whereas mothers' open expression of grief may leave fathers feeling helpless because they cannot control the situation. Each experiences a very solitary grief as noted by Knapp (1986), "I talk about 'parents' suffering, but it should be noted that this was an individual hell, containing only *one* person. Even one's spouse became 'out of reach' during this stage" (p. 145). Because of this lack of emotional connection, the marriage often provides little support for the couple.

Fathers often immerse themselves in work after the child's death. This leaves the mother feeling even more alone. The cultural conditioning further adds to this dilemma. Fathers normally assume the role of a family protector and provider who is in control. When a child dies, however, the father is presented with a situation he cannot control. Feelings of failure coupled with the social image of strong man exacerbate his grief. Nevertheless, work may provide social support and good distraction for some parents (often fathers); therefore, returning to work may be beneficial. A grieving parent may feel useful and valuable at work. The death of a child often lowers the self-esteem of parents, reminding them that they have failed to prevent the tragedy; work may provide opportunities for them to feel productive and useful, which may improve their feelings of self-worth (Bernstein 1997; Rando 1986d).

Marriage of Parents

Losing a child can place enormous stress on a marriage. Some marriages may deteriorate or dissolve after dealing with a child's illness and death, whereas other marriages may be strengthened depending on the quality of interpersonal communication the couple had before the tragedy. One reason for marital discord may have to do with different styles of grieving for fathers and mothers (Osterweis et al. 1984). This lack of synchrony may result in communication problems and feelings of lack of support (Rando 1993). Also, because fathers adjust to the loss more quickly than mothers, mothers may perceive this reaction as a lack of love for the child or themselves.

Another area of marital stress after a child's death is the sexual relationship. A frequent problem in this area is the lack of desire in one or both parents. The incongruency of needs for sexual intimacy of the couple can cause misunderstandings and a major secondary loss for some couples. However, grief can suppress the sexual desire for 2 or more years (a common symptom) after a child's death (Rando 1986d:29). In a study by Hagemeister and Rosenblatt (1997) of the sexual relationship of bereaved parents, 67% of the couples reported a break or decline in sexual intercourse after their child's death. Problems in this area of marriage were related to meanings they attached to the continuation or resumption of the intercourse. Meanings most often associated to sexual intercourse had to do with how the child was made, pleasure, and making another baby that one or both partners may not want.

All these dynamics add to the overwhelming grief experience of parents. Until recently, an erroneous belief has prevailed among many professionals and laypeople who assume that a high divorce rate exists among bereaved parents. Rando

(1986d) argues that early research with methodological problems fostered this belief. Recently, the Compassionate Friends commissioned NFO Research (2002) to assess the impact of a child's death on the American family. The survey results showed that of those parents who were married at the time of their child's death, only 12% divorced. Furthermore, of that 12%, only 25% reported that the death of their child contributed to their divorce. In a recently conducted literature review to determine the incidence of divorce among bereaved parents, Schwab (1998) concluded that "the often-heard claim that there is an unusually high rate of divorce among bereaved parents is a myth" (p. 465). Instead, most marriages survive the stress presented by a child's death.

Duration of Grief

A general consensus is that an average period of time for grief lasts approximately 12 to 18 months. However, duration of grief is much longer when a child dies (Rosen 1988–89). Some symptoms may take 3 or more years to be resolved, whereas the more intense symptoms may subside within 6 to 12 months.

The bereavement process does not follow a prescribed pattern; rather, it has many ups and downs. Symptoms may subside, then return with full force long after the child's death. Brief upsurges may also occur during certain special times of the year, such as anniversaries and birthdays (Rando 1986b). A dull ache always lurks in the background; triggered by the appropriate stimulus, the pain comes bubbling to the surface (Knapp 1986). The pain may lessen and change, but there are some aspects of the loss that stay with parents as long as they live (Rando 1986b).

Bereaved parents often expect grief to be much improved after 1 year, but then they realize that life will never be the same again (Bernstein 1997). After several years of experiencing intense grief, the pain may lessen and personal growth may follow. As the finality of the child's death becomes a reality for parents, accommodation occurs. Parents begin to take a more active part in their own lives, which begin to have meaning once again. The pain of their child's death becomes less intense but is not forgotten. In time, however, the impact of loss of a child reaches a relatively steady state, but the meaning of the loss stays in constant flux throughout one's life (Rubin and Malkinson 2001). Elder (1998) summarizes it well:

> Kate died on 15 June 1988. Over the intervening nine years this subjective view of her death, always uncertain, has shifted and changed. There has been a continuing process of reassessment and reconstruction of the experience in order to enlarge the understanding of it. We have, as a family, reached the point when the concentration on the past, on Kate's death, has moved so that we all feel able to live in the present and invest in the future. The intensity of feelings has lessened. Tears are no longer so upsetting. However, the past is always there and we are always working with it, but it no longer dominates every waking moment. A part of our life has gone, a part that won't ever come back. . . . We have reached

an accommodation with it, by accepting that we won't "recover" from it. For this implies we can go back to being the family we were before Kate's death. Losing her changed everything. (Pp. 122–23)

Search for Meaning

A child is an extension of parents' hopes, dreams, needs, and wishes for immortality and holds multiple meanings for parents. Therefore, a child's death shatters the meaning and purpose of parents' lives, leaving behind painful confusion (Rando 1986b). According to Wheeler (2001), the death of a child becomes a crisis of meaning for parents. This process involves both seeking understanding (cognitive mastery) and finding reasons to continue living (finding purpose in life). Because the death of a child violates previous assumptions and meanings, bereaved parents tend to lose both cognitive mastery and previously held goals and purpose. In a study of 176 bereaved parents, Wheeler asked open-ended questions about the experience of child's death and the meaning of parents' lives since the death to assess the crisis of meaning in parental bereavement. Responses of most parents suggested that the search for meaning was a major factor in their journey to gain cognitive mastery of the traumatic event. Finding the meaning of the death leads to a renewed purpose of their lives. The renewed meaning and cognitive understanding come from involvement with people and activities and their memory of the child. Wheeler considered the search for meaning to be the most important factor in the read-justment process after losing a child. Findings from another study by Hogan, Greenfield, and Schmidt (2001) support this contention. The parents who had lost their children 3 years ago had significantly lower scores on the Personal Growth subscale of the Hogan Grief Reaction Checklist than those who had grieved longer than 3 years. Rather than returning to an earlier level of functioning, parents had become different than they had been before the death. They viewed themselves as more tolerant, forgiving, compassionate, resilient, and loving after dealing with the child's death.

Cole and Singg (1998) also used the Hogan Grief Reaction Checklist and found that recently bereaved mothers and fathers experience more detachment and less growth than parents bereaved for 2 or more years. These findings make sense because withdrawal from others is a normal bereavement symptom during the early grief stages. It is also logical that growth would have an inverse relationship with time since death.

To elicit more spontaneous responses, Cole and Singg (1998) asked the following questions in their study: "Have your views about life changed since the death of your child? If so, what are some of these changes?" Bereaved parents provided a multitude of meaningful information. Of the 134 bereaved parents, 79% showed increased altruism by reaching out to others in memory of the deceased child—for example, setting up scholarships or memorials, planting trees, revamping parks, writing books, collecting food for the poor, establishing program to facilitate the writing of caring/sharing/supporting notes to other parents who have lost children in a hospital, and getting involved in awareness programs such as those for drinking and driving. Parents attempted to give meaning and purpose to the child's life and death (the main reason stated) by these endeavors. Altruism helps mitigate guilt, which is a common and pervasive emotional response by bereaved parents (Miles and Demi 1986).

After the tragedy, bereaved parents often feel that they had spent too much time doing things for the family rather than with the family (Knapp 1986). This was supported by Cole and Singg (1998). Of the parents in their study, 38% reported having a deeper appreciation for family and friends after dealing with the child's death. Furthermore, an increased awareness of the fragility and preciousness of life was expressed by 31% of the parents, and 21% reported being more compassionate and caring toward others after experiencing their loss.

Several writers contend that suffering is a prerequisite to growth. For example, Frankl (1959) considered the suffering following a loss as the motivating force that gives one a chance to actualize to the highest value. Although suffering promotes change, this process does not always result in growth. Depending on several factors, but mainly on their attitude, some bereaved parents never recover their trust and remain chronically angry without finding any meaning in their child's death (Rando 1986d). Of the parents in Cole and Singg's (1998) study, 10% reported an increased feeling that life is meaningless, Knapp (1986) summarizes it best by saying that bereaved parents have two choices:

> (1) They can die themselves, emotionally or physically— virtually following their child to the grave. In reality this isn't a choice at all, although some parents do have a strong desire to do just that. Or (2), after floundering about aimlessly for a time, they can begin the long, hard struggle forward. . . . These are not easy choices but they are all that is available! (P. 19)

Social Support

Bereaved parents often lack social support compared with other types of mourners. They are avoided by other parents because of the "anxiety-provoking nature of the loss" (Rando 1986c:53). When an infant or an older adult child dies, a lack of social validation of loss is experienced by bereaved parents. In cases of murder or suicide, parents feel additional isolation because of the sensitive nature of the death. Some parents feel judged because they are taking too long to get over the tragedy. Also, other people do not know what to say and they "hide behind the canned phrases" (Bernstein 1997:170). To adapt, however, parents need social support during the entire grief process. Social support may come from many sources, such as family, friends, neighbors, coworkers, and support groups (Rando 1986b).

Cole and Singg (1998) found that parents who share their grief with others tend to have less anger and despair than parents who do not share. Asynchronicity of grieving styles between couples, discussed earlier, is often perceived as an impediment for spousal support. In the national survey by NFO Research (1999), however, most bereaved parents found support through their family and community. They reported family members and clergy to be the most helpful sources and friends, coworkers, and funeral homes to be the least helpful sources.

According to Bernstein (1997), although friends and other caring persons want to help, they often feel frustrated and inadequate when bereaved parents do not respond quickly. They feel anxious about saying the wrong thing, and they often do just that because of tension they feel during face-to-face interactions with bereaved parents. Often, bereaved parents hear clichés such as "time heals," "he's in a better place," or "you still have two other children," which add to their grief and may send the message that they are not grieving correctly. Honest comments such as, "I can't imagine what it must be like for you," are more helpful because it shows one's willingness to listen. Silence and a comforting gesture or posture are also helpful. All that is needed is the validation of parents' feelings about the child's death as an unfair and dreadful tragedy.

Many parents consult mental health professionals or join support groups, because they believe they cannot cope with their grief without some additional support. Although many of these parents benefit from counselors, many feel worse, "additionally criticized and isolated" (Bernstein 1997: 171). Those who are helped through professional counseling have usually moved out of the initial grief stages. From the beginning of the bereavement process, however, support groups can be very helpful. They allow bereaved parents to associate with other bereaved parents who can empathize with their pain. While emphasizing the value of support groups, Stearns (1988) states, "It has been my experience in more than twenty years of helping people that support groups offer a healing balm which often is more curative than any other type of support, including professional counseling" (p. 151).

Joining a support group can be very therapeutic, especially for those who lack support from families or friends. Through mutual sharing and support of group members, bereaved parents learn that their reactions are normal (Rando 1986b). Many local churches and hospitals have lists of such groups. One well-known group is The Compassionate Friends. There are other groups devoted to specific causes of bereaved parents, such as Mothers Against Drunk Driving, National Sudden Infant Death Syndrome Foundation, Parents of Murdered Children, Survivors of Suicide, and SHARE Pregnancy and Infant Loss. Many websites are now available that provide information, support, and opportunities for bereaved parents to talk to other bereaved parents.

However, although support groups are usually very therapeutic, Bernstein (1997) elaborates on another aspect. A support group is as helpful as its members make it at any given moment. Because these groups are open groups, continual entry of new members can be disruptive, and the functioning of the group may remain superficial. Leaders are self-selected and usually have no formal training in group work; they may also not be able to provide adequate safety for members. In addition, for some bereaved parents, a group may become a place to hide and hold on to the past.

Concluding Remarks

Although we all cope with grief in our own unique ways, an understanding of some common denominators helps and acts as a road map. Knowing how most parents feel and cope when a child dies gives a newly bereaved parent hope that there may be an end to torture and hopelessness and that there is a life after the child's death. A parent never completely gets over the child's death, but in time and with adequate support, the parent learns to live with the pain. Some important issues a professional or a caregiver needs to be aware of are reiterated below.

Because of the severity and lengthy duration of parental grief, bereaved parents may be at a greater risk for physical health problems, the excessive use of pain avoidance techniques (e.g., radical changes in lifestyle, overinvolvement with work, chemical abuse, etc.), and marital problems. Also, because fathers in our society are less expressive of their grief and they maintain a strong front, they may need more help by professionals. Professionals should be especially cognizant of the alternative practices for dealing with grief by persons from ethnic minority groups. Sometimes being a member of an ethnic minority group, especially with social marginality and low income, can intensify feelings of social alienation, helplessness, and hopelessness when adequate support and understanding are lacking during bereavement (Osterweis et al. 1984; Rando 1993).

Because of the solitary nature of grief and high intensity of pain involved, communication problems may arise within the family. Parents may be too self-engrossed in their own pain and suffering to adequately support the other family members, especially the remaining children. Therefore, other sources of support, such as extended family, friends, clergy, and support groups, can be very helpful for both parents and siblings.

In the past, many professionals and laypersons did not realize the intensity of pain felt by parents who miscarried or lost an infant. This may be due to the belief that parents experience less pain when the child is not born or the child lives only for a brief period. Also, young parents may need help from many sources. Lack of grieving experience with past losses, limited financial resources, lack of social support, and limited time because of work and family demands may exacerbate the trauma experienced by young bereaved parents.

Some parents may take extreme measures to compensate and ameliorate the loss due to the death of a child. They may get pregnant right away or decide never to have another child. Having another child soon after the death of one child may interrupt grieving. This may have negative effects on both the replacement child and the grieving parent who may actually be extending the denial stage of grief. On the other hand, as also pointed out by Osterweis et al. (1984), waiting to get pregnant until the bereavement process completes may not be realistic, because grieving for a lost child never ends.

References

Bernstein, Judith R. 1997. *When the Bough Breaks: Forever After the Death of a Son or Daughter.* Kansas City, MO: Andrews & McMeel.

Bugen, Larry A. 1977. "Human Grief: A Model for Prediction and Intervention." *American Journal of Orthopsychiatry* 47: 96–206.

Cole, Betty C. and Sangeeta Singg. 1998. "Relationship Between Parental Bereavement Reactions and Selected Psychosocial Variables." Paper presented at the Annual Convention of American Psychological Society, May, Washington, DC.

Daiter, Eric. 1998. *Recurrent Miscarriage (Pregnancy Loss).* Retrieved June 3, 2003 (www.drdaiter.com/pregtable.html).

Elder, Pamela. 1998. "Portrait of Family Grief." In *Loss and Bereavement: Managing Change,* edited by Ros Weston, Terry Martin, and Yvonne Anderson. Oxford, UK: Blackwell Science.

Frankl, Victor E. 1959. *Man's Search for Meaning.* Boston: Beacon Press.

Hagemeister, Annelies K. and Paul C. Rosenblatt. 1997. "Grief and the Sexual Relationship of Couples Who Have Experienced a Child's Death." *Death Studies* 21:231–52.

Hogan, Nancy S., Daryl B. Greenfield, and Lee A. Schmidt. 2001. "Development and Validation of the Hogan Grief Reaction Checklist." *Death Studies* 25:1–32.

Knapp, Ronald J. 1986. *Beyond Endurance: When a Child Dies.* New York; Schocken Books.

Miles, Margaret Shandor and Alice Sterner Demi. 1986. "Guilt in Bereaved Parents." In *Parental Loss of a Child,* edited by Therese A. Rando. Champaign, IL: Research Press.

Moss, Miriam S., Emerson L. Lesher, and Sidney Z. Moss. 1986–87. "Impact of the Death of an Adult Child on Elderly Parents: Some Observations." *Omega* 17: 209–18.

National Center for Health Statistics. 2002. "Table 2: Number of Deaths and Death Rates by Age, Race, and Sex: United States, 1999." *National Vital Statistics Report* 49(8): 18.

NFO Research. 1999. *When a Child Dies: A Survey of Bereaved Parents,* June 1999. Retrieved February 18, 2001 (www.compassionatefriends.org/survey.shtml).

Osterweis, Marian, Fredric Solomon, and Morris Green, eds. 1984. *Bereavement Reactions, Consequences, and Care.* Washington, DC: National Academy Press.

Rando, Therese A. 1986a. "Death of the Adult Child." In *Parental Loss of a Child,* edited by Therese A. Rando. Champaign, IL: Research Press.

———. 1986b. "Individual and Couples Treatment Following, the Death of a Child." In *Parental Loss of a Child,* edited by Therese A. Rando. Champaign, IL: Research Press.

———. 1986c. "Parental Bereavement: An Exception to the General Conceptualizations of Mourning." In *Parental Loss of a Child,* edited by Therese A. Rando. Champaign, IL: Research Press.

———. 1986d. "The Unique Issues and Impact of the Death of a Child." In *Parental Loss of a Child,* edited by Therese A. Rando. Champaign, IL: Research Press.

———. 1993. *Treatment of Complicated Mourning.* Champaign, IL: Research Press.

Raphael, Beverly. 1994. *The Anatomy of Bereavement.* Northvale, NJ: Jason Aronson.

Rosen, Elliott J. 1988–89. "Family Therapy in Cases of Interminable Grief for the Loss of a Child." *Omega* 19:187–202.

Rubin, Simon Shimshon and Ruth Malkinson. 2001. "Parental Response to Child Loss Across the Life Cycle: Clinical and Research Perspectives." In *Handbook of Bereavement Research: Consequences, Coping, and Care,* edited by Margaret S.

Stroebe, Robert O. Hansson, Wolfgang Stroebe, and Henk Schut. Washington, DC: American Psychological Association.

Schwab, Reiko. 1998. "A Child's Death and Divorce: Dispelling the Myth." *Death Studies* 22:445–68.

Stearns, Ann Kaiser. 1988. *Coming Back: Rebuilding Lives After Crisis and Loss.* New York: Ballantine Books.

Wheeler, Inese. 2001. "Parental Bereavement: The Crisis of Meaning." *Death Studies* 25:51–66.

Worden, J. William. 2002. *Grief Counseling and Grief Therapy: A Handbook for the Mental Health Practitioners.* 3d ed. New York: Springer.

Author note—Please address correspondence to Sangeeta Singg, Professor of Psychology, Department of Psychology and Sociology, Angelo State University, P.O. Box 10907, San Angelo, TX 76909; e-mail: Sangeeta.Singg@angelo.edu.

Coping with the Loss of Loved Ones

MAURIZIO POMPILI

To be involved in close relationships inevitably means that one will eventually experience the loss of a loved one. Those who experience such loss are usually surrounded by people in mourning, which is a powerful and stressful emotional state that is rooted in the unconscious psychological reactions to a loss. Grief, although not considered an illness, may nevertheless be so severe as to jeopardize the individual's life. There is no time frame for grief and, in some cases, it involves subtle factors that can result in self-destructive behavior in the grieving person. Such self-destructive behavior may involve alcohol or drug abuse, malnutrition, disorders related to the neglect of oneself, including the disregard of a prescribed medical regimen or commonsense precautions, and even a seemingly unconscious boredom with life. Successful coping with the loss of a loved one is critical to maintaining the course of social activity.

There are different reactions to the death of a loved one, depending on the age, marital status, social class, ethnicity, and the circumstances of those left behind. The death of a child is a devastating experience for parents. The death of a spouse or a partner involves the loss of a chosen relationship, companion, lover, parent of one's children, friend, and soulmate. Such loss can result in feelings of disorientation, uncertainty, and confusion as one may need to take on roles and tasks previously carried out by the deceased.

Premature Death

Premature death may be incurred in various ways—deliberately by human hands (such as in homicide, suicide, war, and death sentences meted out by the State), as a result of nonhuman creatures (e.g., bacteria and animals), or as a result of accidents. Loved ones who have lost a significant other as a result of suicide are generally called "survivors." Among people who have lost a loved one, survivors of suicide represent the largest group of mental health casualties. The loss of a loved one by suicide is often shocking, painful, and unexpected, and the grief that ensues can be intense, complex, and long term.

In the case of the sudden death of a loved one due to unexpected events, such as natural disasters including earthquakes, large-scale explosions, or disasters in general, there are unique reactions to the event. The "disaster syndrome" consists of a combination of emotional dullness, unresponsiveness to outer stimulation, and inhibition of activity. Individuals who have just experienced a disaster are apt to suffer from at least a transitory sense of worthlessness, and their usual capacity for self-love becomes impaired. In other cases, psychic shock is a common reaction followed by motor retardation, flattening of affect, somnolence, amnesia, and suggestibility. Moreover, a process of "psychic closing off" has been reported in loved ones who lost a dear person in a catastrophic event; this closing off can last from days to even months or can become a more lasting psychic numbing.

Although most people adjust to the trauma surrounding the death of a loved one, and are able to successfully move on to live full and satisfying lives, there are circumstances when adjustment to such loss is difficult. In these cases, acute grief does not resolve (thoughts and memories of the deceased remain accessible but are no longer preoccupying)—the permanence of the loss and the thoughts related to it are neither comprehended nor integrated into attachment-related long-term memory.

Adjustment to the death of a loved one can be complicated by maladaptive attitudes and behaviors. Blame of self or others, fear of the intensity of grief, the prospect of living without the deceased, and a disinclination to engage in activities that were shared with the deceased may impede the resolution of grief. Over the past decade, some investigators studying persons who have persistent symptoms and impairment following bereavement have concluded that there is a syndrome of chronic abnormal grief, also called complicated grief, and recently renamed prolonged grief disorder, a disorder occurring after a loss that causes significant impairments in functioning for at least 6 months. Characterized by either separation distress or cognitive, emotional, and behavioral symptoms such as feelings of confusion or emptiness, it is as if a part of the self has died. There is trouble accepting the loss as real, an inability to trust others, extreme bitterness or anger related to the loss, and avoidance of reminders of the loss. Other features include numbness or absence of emotion; a feeling that life is unfulfilling, empty, and meaningless; and a feeling of being stunned, dazed, or shocked by the loss.

Scholars demonstrate that the symptoms of disordered grief form a syndrome that is distinct from those of depression and anxiety. Characteristic features of such a state include persistent preoccupation with thoughts about the lost person, along with yearning, longing, and an inability to accept the death, distressing intrusive thoughts about the death, and avoidance of reminders of the loss. A major issue is the timely recognition of the transition from normal to abnormal grief as well as what risk factors lead to the emergence of complicated grief or lead to the development of comorbid disorders such as major depression, anxiety disorders, or somatoform disorders. Recent studies confirm the hypothesis that post-traumatic stress disorder can occur following a natural death. Violent events are time-limited, threaten one's sense of safety, incite fear, and produce hypervigilance to danger.

The loss of a loved one is a permanent ongoing reality that engenders sadness and longing, and produces hypervigilance for the lost person. Images, thoughts, and memories of the deceased, even when intrusive, evoke a bittersweet mix of sadness and yearning. Failure to integrate the information about a violent event may result in post-traumatic stress disorder, while failure to integrate the permanent loss of a loved one may produce complicated grief.

How Children Cope

Children experience grief after the loss of a parent or someone close. Their grief is different from adult grief, as children do not have the same understanding of death. They need to be informed in simple language, with information appropriate for a given age. They should be involved but never obligated to take part in funerals or to observe dead parents or relatives. Children need reassurance and their usual activities and routines should be maintained. Children's knowledge of death varies with age. Under 9 years of age, death is not completely understood as the end of life, but rather it is equated with fear of abandonment or related to magical thinking.

Postvention

Postvention consists of activities that reduce the aftereffects of a traumatic event in the lives of those left behind. Its purpose is to help survivors live longer, more productively, and with less stress. Postventive efforts are not limited to the initial stage of the shock, but rather should be on a day-to-day basis spanning up to a year following the first shock.

Postvention incorporates many tools of psychotherapy, including talk, abreaction, interpretation, reassurance, directions, and even gentle confrontation. The therapist should avoid banal platitudes or the common mistakes often encountered in psychotherapy such as misapplication of the mental examination, for most people who experience grief are not clinically depressed. Common errors that occur are often based on countertransference or a failure to utilize support from within the community. Suicide assessment should always be performed when exploring grief, for there might be fantasies of reunion that fuel suicide wishes. The counselor should play the role of reality tester. Support groups so useful in the healing process can be a helpful source of guidance and understanding as well.

References

Maercker, A. (2007). When grief becomes a disorder. *European Archives of Psychiatry and Clinical Neuroscience, 257,* 435–436.

Shneidman, E. S. (1973). *Deaths of man.* New York: Quadrangle/The New York Times Book Co.

Shneidman, E. S. (1980). *Death: Current perspectives.* Palo Alto, CA: Mayfield.

Shneidman, E. S. (2008). *A commonsense book of death: Reflections at ninety.* New York: Rowman & Littlefield.

Test-Your-Knowledge Form

We encourage you to photocopy and use this page as a tool to assess how the articles in *Annual Editions* expand on the information in your textbook. By reflecting on the articles you will gain enhanced text information. You can also access this useful form on a product's book support website at www.mhhe.com/cls

NAME: DATE:

_____

TITLE AND NUMBER OF ARTICLE:

_____

BRIEFLY STATE THE MAIN IDEA OF THIS ARTICLE:

_____

LIST THREE IMPORTANT FACTS THAT THE AUTHOR USES TO SUPPORT THE MAIN IDEA:

_____

WHAT INFORMATION OR IDEAS DISCUSSED IN THIS ARTICLE ARE ALSO DISCUSSED IN YOUR TEXTBOOK OR OTHER READINGS THAT YOU HAVE DONE? LIST THE TEXTBOOK CHAPTERS AND PAGE NUMBERS:

_____

LIST ANY EXAMPLES OF BIAS OR FAULTY REASONING THAT YOU FOUND IN THE ARTICLE:

_____

LIST ANY NEW TERMS/CONCEPTS THAT WERE DISCUSSED IN THE ARTICLE, AND WRITE A SHORT DEFINITION:

We Want Your Advice

ANNUAL EDITIONS revisions depend on two major opinion sources: one is our Advisory Board, listed in the front of this volume, which works with us in scanning the thousands of articles published in the public press each year; the other is you—the person actually using the book. Please help us and the users of the next edition by completing the prepaid article rating form on this page and returning it to us. Thank you for your help!

ANNUAL EDITIONS: Dying, Death, and Bereavement 11/12

ARTICLE RATING FORM

Here is an opportunity for you to have direct input into the next revision of this volume.
We would like you to rate each of the articles listed below, using the following scale:

1. **Excellent: should definitely be retained**
2. **Above average: should probably be retained**
3. **Below average: should probably be deleted**
4. **Poor: should definitely be deleted**

Your ratings will play a vital part in the next revision.
Please mail this prepaid form to us as soon as possible.
Thanks for your help!

RATING	ARTICLE	RATING	ARTICLE
	1. Grief in the Age of Facebook		20. Gender and Suicide Risk: The Role of Wound Site
	2. Death, Dying, and the Dead in Popular Culture		21. Treat People Like Dogs
	3. How Much Is More Life Worth?		22. When a Cherished Pet Dies
	4. Brain Death Guidelines Vary at Top US Neurological Hospitals		23. Book Profiles Furry Angel of Death: Oscar the Cat
	5. Criteria for a Good Death		24. Veterinary Hospice: Ways to Nurture Our Pets at the End of Life
	6. Death in Disney Films: Implications for Children's Understanding of Death		25. What Living Wills Won't Do: The Limits of Autonomy
	7. Saying Goodbye		26. The Comfort Connection
	8. Helping Military Kids Cope with Traumatic Death		27. Ethics and Life's Ending: An Exchange
	9. Needs of Elderly Patients in Palliative Care		28. When Students Kill Themselves, Colleges May Get the Blame
	10. Altered States: What I've Learned about Death & Disability		29. The Contemporary American Funeral
	11. Dying on the Streets: Homeless Persons' Concerns and Desires about End-of-Life Care		30. How Different Religions Pay Their Final Respects
	12. End-of-Life Care around the World: Achievements to Date and Challenges Remaining		31. Green Graveyards—A Natural Way to Go
	13. Are They Hallucinations or Are They Real? The Spirituality of Deathbed and Near-Death Visions		32. Social Workers' Final Act of Service: Respectful Burial Arrangements for Indigent, Unclaimed, and Unidentified People
	14. A Spreading Appreciation for the Benefits of Hospice Care		33. The Grieving Process
	15. When Death Strikes without Warning		34. Disenfranchised Grief
	16. Suicide Rates in the World: 1950–2004		35. Enhancing the Concept of Disenfranchised Grief
	17. On "Intention" in the Definition of Suicide		36. The Increasing Prevalence of Complicated Mourning: The Onslaught Is Just Beginning
	18. Ethical, Legal, and Practical Issues in the Control and Regulation of Suicide Promotion and Assistance over the Internet		37. Counseling with Children in Contemporary Society
	19. A Search for Death: How the Internet Is Used as a Suicide Cookbook		38. A Grim Fight for 'Proper Burial'
			39. Parents and the Death of a Child
			40. Coping with the Loss of Loved Ones

ABOUT YOU

Name   Date
_____

Are you a teacher? ☐ A student? ☐
Your school's name
_____

Department
_____

Address   City   State   Zip
_____

School telephone #
_____

YOUR COMMENTS ARE IMPORTANT TO US!

Please fill in the following information:
For which course did you use this book?
_____

Did you use a text with this ANNUAL EDITION? ☐ yes ☐ no
What was the title of the text?
_____

What are your general reactions to the Annual Editions concept?
_____

Have you read any pertinent articles recently that you think should be included in the next edition? Explain.
_____

Are there any articles that you feel should be replaced in the next edition? Why?
_____

Are there any World Wide Websites that you feel should be included in the next edition? Please annotate.
_____

May we contact you for editorial input? ☐ yes ☐ no
May we quote your comments? ☐ yes ☐ no

NOTES

NOTES

NOTES

NOTES